MW00812763

Ordinary Meaning

Ordinary Meaning

A Theory of the Most Fundamental Principle of Legal Interpretation

BRIAN G. SLOCUM

THE UNIVERSITY OF CHICAGO PRESS   CHICAGO AND LONDON

BRIAN G. SLOCUM is a professor of law at the University of the Pacific, McGeorge School of Law in Sacramento, California.

The University of Chicago Press, Chicago 60637
The University of Chicago Press, Ltd., London
© 2015 by The University of Chicago
All rights reserved. Published 2015.
Printed in the United States of America

24 23 22 21 20 19 18 17 16 15   1 2 3 4 5

ISBN-13: 978-0-226-30485-4 (cloth)
ISBN-13: 978-0-226-30499-1 (e-book)
DOI: 10.7208/chicago/9780226304991.001.0001

Library of Congress Cataloging-in-Publication Data
Slocum, Brian G., author.
    Ordinary meaning : a theory of the most fundamental principle of legal interpretation / Brian G. Slocum.
       pages ; cm
    Includes bibliographical references and index.
    ISBN 978-0-226-30485-4 (cloth : alk. paper) — ISBN 978-0-226-30499-1 (ebook) 1. Law—Language. 2. Communication in law. 3. Law—Terminology. 4. Law—Interpretation and construction. 5. Law—United States—Terminology. I. Title.
    K487.L36S56 2015
    340'.14—dc23

                                                                              2015014456

♾ This paper meets the requirements of ANSI/NISO Z39.48-1992 (Permanence of Paper).

FOR JENNIFER

Contents

Acknowledgments

This book has taken me quite some time to write, and I consequently owe debts of gratitude to the many people who have helped me along the way. The book was largely conceived during my research at the University of California, Davis. I would like to thank my mentors, Raúl Aranovich, Patrick Farrell, Almerindo Ojeda, Adam Sennet, and Lawrence Solan. Raúl Aranovich has been particularly helpful and encouraging, as well as insightful and rigorous. Others at Davis have similarly been invaluable in helping me develop the ideas in this book, including Robert May and Michael Glanzberg.

I have also benefited from presenting portions of the book at various universities and conferences. Among them are the "Legal Rules" conference organized by the Department of Legal Theory at Jagiellonian University in Krakow, Poland, "The Pragmatic Turn" conference at the University of British Columbia, and the Eleventh Biennial Conference on Forensic Linguistics/Language and Law held at the Universidad Nacional Autónoma de México, Mexico City. In addition, the annual West Coast Roundtable on Language and Law has given me multiple opportunities to present my ideas to an impressive collection of experts on language and the law.

I am also grateful for the tremendous support I have received from McGeorge School of Law, University of the Pacific. McGeorge has supported me through generous writing grants, and in many other ways. In particular, Ruth Jones and Anne Bloom have been extremely supportive of my scholarship. Aimee Martin's research assistance was first rate and will be sorely missed.

Finally, I would like to thank the editors at the University of Chicago Press for their fantastic assistance, and especially Christopher Rhodes for his helpful advice and guidance. As well, I benefited greatly from the generous comments and criticisms made by the anonymous referees organized by the University of Chicago Press.

In addition to the professional support, advice, and criticism outlined above, I have been blessed with incredible support, and advice (and sometimes criticism) in my personal life. At the risk of failing to acknowledge the many individuals who have helped me, I will highlight the tremendous support of my wife, Jennifer. Without her help, none of this would be possible.

The Ordinary Meaning Doctrine

1.1: The Ordinary Meaning Doctrine and Its Justification

By what standard should legal texts be interpreted? The cases requiring a precise answer to this question are seemingly endless. Consider a criminal sentencing provision that provides for an enhanced punishment if the defendant "uses" a firearm "during and in relation to . . . [a] drug trafficking crime." Has the defendant violated the provision if he trades a gun for drugs, or drugs for a gun, during a drug trafficking crime?[1] Alternatively, consider a statute that authorizes the Secretary of the Interior to take land and hold it in trust "for the purpose of providing land for Indians," where the term "Indian" is defined as "all persons of Indian descent who are members of any recognized Indian tribe *now* under Federal jurisdiction" (emphasis added). If, decades after the enactment of the statute, the secretary takes land in trust for a recognized Indian tribe that was not yet recognized at the time of the enactment of the statute, does the statute nonetheless authorize the secretary's action?[2] Consider a different case involving a statute protecting the federal government from liability. Do federal prison officials fall under the phrase "any officer of customs or excise or *any* other law enforcement officer" (emphasis added)?[3] To take an extremely accessible example, consider a statute providing for tariffs that distinguishes between vegetables and fruit. Should a tomato, designated by botanists as a fruit, nonetheless be considered a vegetable?[4] Speaking of food and meaning, in a contract that makes the term "sandwich" legally decisive, should a burrito be considered a sandwich, or is it something different?[5]

In each of the above examples, the court considered the answer to the interpretive question to be one determined by general principles of language usage that apply equally outside the law. Such cases are not exceptional but rather are illustrative of the judicial commitment to interpreting language in legal texts according to its "ordinary meaning." For instance, in its (in)famous decision, *District of Columbia v. Heller*,[6] which determined whether the Second Amendment to the United States Constitution confers an individual right to keep and bear arms, the US Supreme Court stated that

> In interpreting this text, we are guided by the principle that "the Constitution was written to be understood by the voters; its words and phrases were used in their normal and ordinary as distinguished from technical meaning." Normal meaning may of course include an idiomatic meaning, but it excludes secret or technical meanings that would not have been known to ordinary citizens in the founding generation.[7]

Similarly, in a recent but less politically contentious case, *Taniguchi v. Kan Pacific Saipan, Ltd.*,[8] the Supreme Court had to determine whether a statute providing for the "compensation of interpreters" included within its scope the cost of translating from Japanese to English certain documents that the defendant had used in its defense of a personal injury lawsuit.[9] Indicating that a legislatively undefined term should be given "its ordinary meaning," the Court viewed a meaning of "interpreter" that would include document translation as unordinary, but perhaps occasionally used and "acceptable."[10] The Court, determining on the basis of a "survey" of multiple dictionary definitions that "interpreter" can, but does not ordinarily, include one who translates written documents, reasoned that just because a "dictionary definition is broad enough to encompass one sense of a word does not establish that the word is *ordinarily* understood in that sense" (emphasis in original).[11]

As the above cases illustrate, courts have agreed that words in legal texts should be interpreted in light of accepted and typical standards of communication (Jackson 1995; Phillips 2003). In fact, Dickerson (1975, 10) argues that the constitutional presumption is that a "statute is subject to the accepted standards of communication in effect in the given environment." The constituent question of what makes some meaning the ordinary one and the evidential question of how the determinants of the ordinary meaning of legal texts are identified are thus of crucial importance to the interpretation of legal texts. Yet, beyond very general characterizations or assumptions that the answers are self-evident, or examinations of relatively narrow questions regarding ordinary meaning, neither the constituent nor the evidential question has been comprehensively examined by courts or commentators. For instance, Justice Scalia, a supporter of the ordinary meaning doctrine, wondered in a dissenting opinion whether

> the acid test of whether a word can reasonably bear a particular meaning is whether you could use the word in that sense at a cocktail party without having people look at you funny. The Court's assigned meaning would surely fail that test, even late in the evening.[12]

Not surprisingly, the Court in its majority opinion indicated that it did not "consider usage at a cocktail party a very sound general criterion of statutory meaning."[13] Elsewhere, in a concurring opinion that argued for a restricted meaning for "tangible object" in the statutory phrase "any record, document, or tangible object," Justice Alito wondered, "who wouldn't raise an eyebrow if a neighbor, when asked to identify something similar to a 'record' or 'document,' said 'crocodile'?"[14] Despite the seemingly idiosyncratic standards for meaning described by Justices Scalia and Alito, this book will explain how dictionary definitions, frequently considered by courts to be an authoritative source of ordinary meaning, are often used in ways that make them less legitimate than a "cocktail party" or "neighbor" standard.

Notwithstanding the lack of development of the ordinary meaning doctrine, it should not be surprising that courts typically seek to determine the ordinary meaning of legal texts when deciding cases. A characteristic feature of legal texts is that they employ natural language in order to accomplish their purposes (Mattila 2002). Further, legal texts are widely viewed as a form of communication (McCubbins and Rodriguez 2011; Van Schooten 2007). If one assumes that successful communication is the goal in most cases, then these texts should be understood by different people in the same way. One aspect of this broad requirement is that legal texts should be understandable to the general public, as well as to judges and sophisticated practitioners. As Cappelen (2007, 19) explains, "[w]hen we articulate rules, directives, laws and other action-guiding instructions, we assume that people, variously situated, can grasp that content in the same way." Such a goal requires that absent some reason for deviation, such as words with technical or special legal meanings, the language used in legal texts should be viewed as corresponding with that used in nonlegal communications (Mellinkoff 1963).

An assumption that language in legal texts can have an ordinary meaning does not entail, as some commentators have claimed, the false proposition that all readers of the language will always understand the words to mean what the author intended or will all agree on a single meaning. Readers may, of course, disagree about the meaning of a text regardless of the applicable standard of meaning. Instead of such an unrealistic expectation, the ordinary meaning doctrine stands for the proposition that the standard for determining the meaning of a legal text will be an objective one that is external to the author's intentions (although it may often correspond with those intentions).[15] As the famous Supreme Court Justice Oliver Wendell Holmes (1899, 417–18) explained, the interpreter's role is not to ask what the author meant to convey but instead determine "what those words would mean in the mouth of a normal speaker of English, using them in the circumstances in which they were used." As an objective standard, the ordinary meaning doctrine is similar to other legal principles. For instance, Justice Holmes (1899, 418) viewed the normal speaker of English as a variety of the "prudent man" (another legal construction) and explained that reference to this speaker is "simply another instance of the externality of law."

Consistent with Holmes's views, that language in legal texts should be interpreted in accordance with its ordinary meaning is a uniformly accepted presumption among judges. In fact, it is perhaps the most widely cited axiom of legal interpretation. Scalia and Garner (2012, 6) refer to the ordinary meaning doctrine as "the most fundamental semantic rule of interpretation." Its use is both long-standing and widespread.[16] According to some, the Supreme Court has in recent years placed an increased emphasis on the meaning of the text in both statutory and constitutional cases, thereby increasing the doctrinal significance of the ordinary meaning doctrine (Scalia and Manning 2012). The ordinary meaning doctrine's influence is not limited to statutory and constitutional cases, but rather is applied by judges when interpreting virtually every type of legal text, including contracts, trusts, wills, and even jury instructions.[17] The typical sequential process of statutory interpretation illustrates its importance as the presumptive meaning of the relevant text. Courts first apply "general principles of statutory construction to the language of the statute in order to construe any ambiguous language to accurately reflect the intent of the legislature."[18] If the language is not ambiguous, however, "there is no room for further construction" and, with some exceptions, is given its "ordinary and obvious meaning."[19] The sequence is standard, if not always followed. In a recent case, for instance, the Supreme Court indicated that it was "depart[ing] from a normal order of discussion, namely an order that first considers [the party's] statutory language argument[,]" in order to first consider the purpose and legislative history of the statute at issue.[20]

1.2: Doubting the Decisiveness of the Ordinary Meaning Doctrine

Before significant time is spent conceptualizing the ordinary meaning doctrine, it is appropriate to consider arguments that the doctrine is not, and should not be, influential. As discussed below, notwithstanding the frequent judicial invocations of ordinary meaning, given the nature of judicial decision making and the importance of nonlanguage legal concerns in any given case, as well as the difficult and specialized language and structure of legal texts, it may seem odd that the ordinary meaning doctrine should (at least ostensibly) be so influential. Some scholars have argued that even if legal texts are a form of communication, it does not follow that the communicative content of a legal text (i.e., the linguistic meaning communicated by the text considering all the sources of meaning relevant to the message the author was trying to convey) represents its legal meaning, which is the authoritative meaning given to the text by a judge.[21] As explained in more detail in chapter 3, the communicative meaning of a legal text is sometimes different than the ordinary meaning of the language in the text. At this point, a sufficient understanding of the distinction is that the ordinary meaning of the language must be based on a narrower consideration of context (and thus fewer determinants of meaning) than the communicative meaning of the text. If the communicative meaning of the text is not decisive, the ordinary meaning will similarly not be decisive.[22]

Greenberg (2011, 2010) rejects what he terms the communicative content theory of law, which maintains that as a linguistic text the content of a legal text is an instance of linguistic meaning generally, and interpretation should thus focus on valid theories of language and communication. Specifically, Greenberg argues that viewing legislation on a communicative content model is misguided because legislation and legislative systems have purposes that have no parallel in general, nonlegal communication. In his view, a statute's contribution to the content of the law should not necessarily be constituted by what is communicated by the legislature. Flanagan (2010) similarly argues that literal meaning (by which he means something analogous to ordinary meaning) cannot be decisive of what is a legally correct outcome and that it follows that an enactment's literal meaning does not weigh in the determination of correct legal outcomes.[23]

As noted above, Greenberg and Flanagan, as well as other scholars, offer arguments as to why the communicative content of a legal text is not necessarily its legal content. The judiciary, though, through the ordinary meaning concept and otherwise, sometimes makes statements that suggest that the contrary is true. For instance, Justice Frankfurter (1947, 538) once said, "Only a day or two ago—when counsel talked of the intention of a legislature, I was indiscreet enough to say I don't care what their intention was. I only want to know what the words mean." As well, the Supreme Court consistently proclaims—as do lower federal courts and most, if not all, state courts—that it will it "enforce plain and unambiguous statutory language according to its terms."[24] These quotes, as well as other statements that have been made regarding ordinary meaning, do not, however, offer a complete picture of judicial decision making because they misleadingly imply that textual meaning, if clear, is always determinative of legal meaning.

In many circumstances, the communicative content of a text cannot represent its legal meaning. As the Supreme Court quote above indicated, courts purport to enforce *plain and unambiguous* statutory language according to its terms. Much statutory language (as well as language in other legal texts), however, is not plain and unambiguous. Instead, it may be ambiguous, vague, or otherwise underdetermined. Sometimes the distinction between ambiguity and vagueness is important in legal interpretation, even though courts typically do not properly distinguish between the two concepts. If a statute is ambiguous, a court may resolve the ambiguity through some judicially created interpretive principle. For example, the rule of lenity provides that ambiguities in criminal statutes should be construed in favor of the defendant (Price 2004). If a statute is vague, a court may attempt to precisify (i.e., make more determinate) the text in some manner or, if the statute is a criminal one, it may (but only rarely) strike down the relevant provision on void-for-vagueness grounds (Goldsmith 2003). In these situations, the communicative meaning of the text will differ from its legal meaning.

Even in situations not involving ambiguity or vagueness, the communicative meaning of a text may differ from its legal meaning. One view is that a particular case will always contain some circumstance not covered by the enactment, where that omission alone cannot determine the circumstance's relevance to whether the relevant interest should prevail (Flanagan 2010). The text alone is never decisive because the circumstance, not contemplated by the enactment's ordinary meaning, may be controlling. Even when putting aside a judge's ideological motivations, which may cause the court to distort or ignore a text's communicative content in favor of the judge's preferred interpretation, circumstances outside the communicative meaning of a text may therefore always control the outcome of a case. For instance, most, if not all, judges agree that if applying the communicative meaning of a text would cause absurd results, some other meaning should control.[25] Also, some judges believe that if the purpose of the enactment is at odds with its ordinary or communicative meaning, a meaning consistent with the purpose should control.[26] Many other principles inconsistent with the decisiveness of a text's communicative meaning are also applied by judges. So-called clear statement rules of interpretation are one prominent example. Clear statement rules often create "implied limitation[s] on otherwise unambiguous general terms of the statute."[27] Thus, for example, pursuant to the presumption against retroactivity, a statute that is full of broad terms but is silent with respect to retroactive application is construed to be unambiguously prospective in effect (Slocum 2010).

As the above discussion illustrates, a provision's legal meaning will often deviate from its ordinary meaning. In fact, it is well accepted amongst scholars that the legal meaning of a text may depend on interpretive principles and judgments that are based on legal rather than linguistic concerns. Some scholars have developed ontologies to explicate the distinctions typically involved when a court makes use of a legal text. Tiersma (1995) argues that the circumstances explained in the preceding paragraph require that a distinction be made between "interpretation," which represents the linguistic or philosophical understanding of the provision at issue, and "construction," which represents instances where judges choose meanings that transcend interpretations. In addition, scholars like Marmor (2005) make other terminological distinctions, such as distinguishing between "meaning," which refers to the rules of the pertinent language, and "interpretation," which is usually required because the interpretive issue is not determined by rules or conventions. While the careful distinctions described above are useful for some purposes, this book will focus on other terms that better explicate the concepts being compared and contrasted. Thus, "interpretation" will be used broadly to cover all situations where a court gives an authoritative meaning to a text (Soames 2011). As explicated later, distinctions will instead be made between the *ordinary linguistic meaning* of a text and other concepts, such as *unordinary meaning, communicative meaning, legal meaning*, and *ordinary legal meaning*.

It may be that the communicative meaning of a text is never by itself decisive of legal meaning, but such a reality does not undermine the significance of the ordinary meaning doctrine. In determining the legal content of a text it must still be acknowledged that the communicative meaning (and thus ordinary meaning) is influential in that determination. Even critics who question the decisiveness of ordinary meaning concede the doctrine's influence. Flanagan (2010, 258), for example, "offer[s] no objection to the idea that enactments' literal meaning is of great assistance in determining their legal meaning." Similarly, Greenberg (2010, 221) emphasizes that "on any plausible view, the meaning of a statutory text is highly relevant to the statute's contribution" to the legal meaning of the text.

1.3: Why the Ordinary Meaning Doctrine is Influential

It is not surprising that even critics concede the relevance of the communicative meaning (and ordinary meaning) of a text to its legal meaning. Chapter 3 outlines justifications for the ordinary meaning doctrine and explains why it is necessary to distinguish between communicative meaning and ordinary meaning. An abridged discussion of the necessity of the ordinary meaning doctrine, which is given here, should focus on rule of law and notice rationales. While various, related reasons for the influence of the ordinary meaning doctrine have been offered, some of these reasons are flawed. Nevertheless, they collectively demonstrate the prominence and necessity of the doctrine.

One reason that has been consistently given by courts and commentators is that the ordinary meaning of the language in a statutory text offers the best indication of legislative intent. According to the Supreme Court, "[c]ourts assume that the ordinary meaning of statutory language accurately expresses the legislative purpose."[28] This assertion, though, is at best a generalization and fails to acknowledge that many legislators do not read the language of the bills on which they vote, or may not have seriously considered the language in any case.[29] Another justification has to do with the rule of law and democratic principles. According to the Supreme Court, applying the ordinary meaning doctrine is deferential to the supremacy of the legislature and recognizes that congressmen vote on the language of a bill, not on some nontextual purpose.[30] The text is the content that legislators vote on in the final passage of the bill, not some other content such as the intentions and motives that the enacting legislators might possess. As such, it is the text that is the law. Another rationale is that fair notice requires that the ordinary meaning of criminal statutes be decisive. Such a principle is reflected in the rule of lenity, which requires that ambiguities in criminal statutes be interpreted in favor of the defendant.[31] Other reasons have also been suggested. Strauss (1997, 1566), for example, reasons that the ordinary meaning doctrine is justified as a kind of default rule that is applicable in circumstances in which disagreement is costly. On this view, ordinary meaning provides a convenient, "easy" way to get matters settled.

Undoubtedly, as the reasons given above suggest, the ordinary meaning doctrine is influential because it is difficult to conceive of a realistic methodology of interpretation in which it would *not* be influential. Even those who advocate in favor of methodologies that find facts other than textual meaning decisive typically allow for considerations of ordinary meaning. For example, consider the once-influential legal process approach of Professors Henry Melvin Hart Jr. and Albert M. Sacks, which advocated a purposivist approach to interpretation where courts should assume that legislatures are "made of reasonable persons pursuing reasonable purposes reasonably" (Eskridge and Frickey 1995, 1378). Even Hart and Sacks (1994, 1374), though, maintained that in interpreting the words of the statute so as to carry out the purpose a court should not give the words "a meaning they will not bear."[32] Similarly, intentionalists, who advocate that the intentions of the legislature should constitute the meaning of the text, must also rely on the ordinary meaning doctrine (or something equivalent), as chapter 2 discusses in greater depth.

Although no one can plausibly argue that the ordinary meaning of a text should always prove decisive of its legal meaning, objections to the relevance of ordinary meaning are typically unpersuasive. If one concedes that the ordinary meaning may not be decisive of the legal meaning, continued criticisms must offer alternative ways to determine textual meaning (or reject its relevance altogether). Suggested alternatives are not, however, persuasive. One such claim is that the ordinary meaning doctrine adds unnecessary costs to the legislative drafting process. Greene (2006, 1917) argues that using ordinary meaning as the default meaning is costly because it forces "the legislature to further specify a term's meaning if it doesn't want the most likely meaning." According to Greene, this result is objectionable because it might force the legislature "to conduct a linguistic analysis of every word in every statute, determine the most likely meaning of each, and then write elaborate subsections and definition sections each time it wants to define a term differently" (1917).

Greene's arguments might highlight the challenging nature of natural language, with its inherent polysemy, which makes drafting texts to cover future circumstances a difficult proposition. These realities do not, however, undermine the ordinary meaning doctrine. To the contrary, they offer support for the doctrine. If the ordinary meaning is not the default meaning of an undefined word, it is difficult to imagine an alternative except for something like "possible meaning" (or, even worse, "any meaning"). Considering the dynamic nature of language, and the lack of language-based constraints on the possible meanings a word may have, a "possible meaning" approach would result in broad statutory meanings that the legislature likely would not have contemplated. Furthermore, regardless of a court's method of giving meaning to statutory words, the legislature, if it is being at all careful, will have considered to some degree the meanings that courts could give to the statutory language. How could it not? Importantly, with an ordinary meaning approach, as compared to a possible meaning approach, the legislature will be in a much better position to make predictions about meaning. Far from increasing the costs of drafting, the ordinary meaning doctrine reduces the costs of drafting compared to a possible meaning approach. With an ordinary meaning approach, elaborate subsections and definition sections are only required if some specific meaning (which may be an unordinary meaning) is intended. In contrast, with a possible meaning approach, the legislature would be more inclined to draft elaborate subsections and definitions sections in order to ensure that the statute's scope did not exceed reasonable expectations. Of course, other considerations also support an ordinary meaning, as opposed to a possible meaning, approach. One is that an ordinary meaning approach is more consistent with the judiciary's other tools of interpretation, which, as discussed throughout this book, typically counsel in favor of narrow interpretations.

1.4: Difficulties Stemming from the Language of Legal Texts

As the above discussion shows, that the ordinary meaning of the relevant textual language is not always decisive does not eliminate the relevance of the doctrine, and persuasive substitutes are difficult to imagine. Nevertheless, for various reasons, some have questioned the very existence of ordinary meaning. Waismann (1951, 122), for instance, argues that "to speak of *the* ordinary use of language is already questionable, implying as it does, that *there is* such a thing, and a unique one, and that one can find out what it is." One problem for the concept of ordinary meaning, which is addressed throughout this book, is the contribution that context makes to meaning. Another problem, discussed here, concerns the proposition that a term other than "ordinary meaning" should be used to describe a meaning that purports to be based on the text of a legal document. Some scholars have suggested that there is nothing ordinary about the language in legal texts and that the meanings given to words in such texts necessarily differ from the meanings given to words in a nonlegal context. Mattila (2002, 3), for instance, suggests that "legal language may be incomprehensible from the standpoint of the general public."

Certainly, the language of legal texts, which commonly contain technical and unusual language and difficult syntax and structure, may make it seem odd that the ordinary meaning doctrine should be so influential with the judiciary. Technical vocabulary is used in courtroom interactions and conversations between lawyers and clients, but these interactions do not often contain an abundance of legalese (Tiersma 2012). Legal texts are different, however, with the most authoritative texts such as statutes and wills having the highest percentage of legalese (Tiersma 2012). Various syntactic and semantic characteristics of legal texts make them complex, often unnecessarily so, and unlike language found in other contexts (Tiersma 2005a). In one well-known work, Mellinkoff (1963) focused on word usage in legal texts and observed that the texts frequently used common words with uncommon meanings (such as "consideration" and "party"), Old French and Anglo-Norman words which had not been taken into the general vocabulary (such as "quash" and "voire dire"), Latin words and phrases (such as "prima facie" and "habeas corpus"), terms of art (such as "agency" and "appeal"), and stilted and formal words. Jackson (1995) has similarly described the tendency of legal texts to use unusual words and to use "usual" words in an unusual sense from the standpoint of the ordinary nonlegal speaker. In addition to the above usages, Mellinkoff (1963) further observed that legal language has both deliberate uses of words and expressions with flexible meanings (such as "clearly erroneous" and "adequate consideration") and attempts at extreme precision (such as "last clear chance").

Besides having challenging word usage, legal texts are often structurally difficult. Tiersma (1999, 2005a, 2005b) has observed that legal texts

tend to have very long sentences with redundancy and more conjoined
and embedded clauses than are found in most journalistic, literary, or
scientific texts. Also, the sentence structure can be unusual. For example,
Tiersma (1999) observes that the sentence structure is often a verb (V)
followed by a prepositional phrase (PP) followed by a noun phrase (NP),
V-PP-NP, instead of the more typical word order in modern English,
V-NP-PP, where a V is followed by an NP and then a PP. Thus, to use an
example from Tiersma (1999, 65), an insurance contract might contain the
phrase, "a proposal to effect with the Society an assurance," instead of
the more common, "a proposal to effect an assurance with the Society."
Tiersma (2005a, 2012) also notes that legal texts often feature impersonal
constructions (i.e., avoidance of the first and second person pronouns "I"
and "you"), passive constructions, multiple negation, and nominalizations
(e.g., "the injury occurred . . .").

The unique language and structure of legal texts underscore that they
are, at least de facto and sometimes de jure, written for specialists rather
than for the general public. The ordinary meaning doctrine would be misplaced if this meant that, putting aside the technical or legal words exceptions to the doctrine, the meanings given to words in a legal context
should differ from the meanings given to those words in a nonlegal context. If true, the ordinary meaning doctrine should be replaced by some
sort of "ordinary specialized meaning" doctrine. Many legal scholars have
made arguments to this effect, rejecting the relevance of ordinary linguistic meaning in a legal context.

Solum (2013) observes that a text can have variant meanings that depend on context, with a text having one meaning as a legal text and another if it were in a technical manual or novel. Solum reasons that the
meaning of a legal text should be framed as what would be understood
by competent speakers of the natural language in which the text was written, who are within the intended readership of the text and who understand that the text is a legal text of a certain type. Popkin (1999, 181) similarly argues that the "[t]he proper question to ask, if we are to insist on
a link to ordinary language usage, is *not* what do words ordinarily mean,
but how would ordinary people want language to be interpreted in specialized settings." Further, Strauss (1997) and Schauer (1990) argue that
the "ordinary meaning" concept is a misnomer and that it should really be
described as the "ordinary legal meaning" concept. Strauss (1997, 1568)
observes that "[t]erms like 'witness,' 'zoning,' and even 'speed limit,' when
used in a legal context, can mean something quite different from what

they might mean when used in other contexts." Making a slightly different claim, McGreal (2004) argues that "ordinary conversation" is a poor model for understanding legal texts.

It is true that the objective, reasonable person that courts use to judge the ordinary meaning of texts is more sophisticated, as well as more knowledgeable about law, than is an ordinary person. Furthermore, it is undoubtedly true that courts consider legal consequences even when determining the ordinary meaning of legal texts. Later chapters address these issues in greater depth. Nevertheless, the problem with the above critiques is that emphasizing the unique features of legal texts as problematizing the application of the ordinary meaning concept overemphasizes the contribution of uniqueness to the difficulties inherent in legal interpretation. Literary language is similar to legal language in the sense that it is often more complex and contains challenging word usage, along with characteristically difficult "literary" meanings. Yet, Fabb (2010) explains that the "Development Hypothesis" holds that literary language is formed and regulated by developing only the elements, rules, and constraints of ordinary language, and which refer only to representations that are present (at some stage in a derivation) in ordinary language. Fabb (2010, 1228) reasons that "[i]t seems quite unlikely that literary texts are interpreted in a different way" from ordinary texts. It seems similarly correct that legal texts are formed by developing only the elements, rules and constraints of ordinary language, and are interpreted in similar ways as ordinary texts, even if legal texts are more complex in various ways. In fact, Azuelos-Atias (2011) argues that legal language is ordinary language used, in an ordinary way, in the special context of legal discourse.

In addition, it is undoubtedly correct that legal texts are typically not drafted with the layperson in mind, but this does not establish the inappropriateness of the ordinary meaning doctrine. The claims that ordinary meaning should more accurately be deemed "ordinary legal meaning" conflates the legal content of a text with the meanings of its words and phrases. While a legal text *as a whole* must of course be given some legal meaning that reflects, in most cases, changes to legal rights and obligations, it does not follow that every word and phrase (or even sentences) must be given some specialized legal meaning (or even that they could be given some specialized meaning). Often, legal disputes involve the meaning of some particular word in a legal text that is perfectly comprehensible outside of a legal context and does not obviously have some particular legal meaning. The Supreme Court has had to define words such as "use,"[33] "tomato,"[34] "age,"[35] "vehicle,"[36] and "now."[37] The struggles of courts to give such common words definite meanings should not be surprising or thought to be unique to law. Charnock (2006) has shown that obscurity of expression is only rarely a barrier to understanding. In contrast, the most difficult interpretive problems involve commonly occurring, plain words. Because common words occur more frequently, they appear in more diverse contexts and develop greater polysemy.

McGreal's objection to ordinary meaning should similarly be dismissed, or at least viewed in a proper context. He is correct that "ordinary conversation" is a poor model for understanding legal texts, but not for the reasons he asserts. Contrary to McGreal's apparent assumption, the semantic meanings of words themselves do not change from oral to written communication. Rather, ordinary conversations are a poor model for the interpretation of legal texts because the context of interpretation of oral statements differs so greatly from the context of interpretation of legal texts. One of the main reasons is that the typical oral utterance is made in a context that contains vital clues that allow for the ascertainment of a speaker's intent. These same clues are not available to the interpreter of a text. The clues include paralinguistic cues such as winking, facial expressions, posture, stance, laughing and gestures, as well as cues from prosody (rhythm, rate, stress, pitch, pitch contour, and intonation of speech), which serve an important role in determining meaning in ordinary conversation. Thus, when legal texts are being interpreted, there are stronger reasons for emphasizing the semantic meanings of the words (i.e., their ordinary meanings) compared to oral conversations where rich contextual clues allow for greater pragmatic inferences about the speaker's intent.

1.5: Legal Interpretation is Restricted in Nature but Sometimes Surpasses Intention and Ordinary Meaning

At the outset, before a more comprehensive conceptualization of the ordinary meaning doctrine is offered in later chapters, it is important to outline some of the ways in which it may be nondecisive of legal meaning because of the nature of language and the existence of legal concerns. As well, the significance of the doctrine depends in part on both the limited existence of authorial intent as well as the restricted nature of legal interpretation compared to that in some other familiar contexts. Chapter 2 addresses in detail why, if the communicative meaning of the textual language is being sought, legal interpreters must construct interpretations based on objective determinants of meaning, such as the conventional meanings of words. That chapter will further explain the constraints on an utterer's intended meaning that must exist in order to recognize that language cannot mean whatever the utterer wishes it to mean, as well as the limited nature of the determinants of meaning available when interpreting texts.[38] For now, the reader should appreciate that the meaning of a text may surpass the intent of its author, even if the actual intent of the author is being sought by the interpreter, making necessary resort to some other standard of meaning (such as ordinary meaning).

Meaning must surpass intent because legal texts such as statutes and contracts are frequently, if not typically, applied to various scenarios that were not contemplated by their drafters, either due to neglect by the drafters or because the situations at issue did not exist at the time of drafting. Neglect by the drafters may be due to various reasons, including the understandable inability to foresee all of the varied situations that may (or may not) fall under the legal document. The words chosen by the drafters may thus be certain, but the intended extensions (i.e., the referential range of application) of the words may be unknown. A theory of meaning, such as intentionalism, typically assumes that there is some fact of the matter as to what the text means. If the necessary fact is authorial intent, however, there may indeed be no fact to uncover, particularly if one is seeking intent directly relevant to the particular interpretive dispute. Could it be said, for example, that the drafters of a statute intended for the term "vehicle" to include airplanes when airplanes had not yet been invented? Or, conversely, that the drafters intended not to include airplanes within the scope of the statute?[39] If "intent" is to be referenced in such a situation, it must be a very general, purposive and speculative sort of intent.[40]

Another obvious way in which the meaning of a text differs from the author's intended meaning occurs when it is not reasonable to expect a member of the intended audience to be able to grasp the utterer's intention. As Tolhurst (1979) explains, it cannot be denied that sometimes authors or speakers fail to write or say what they mean. The coincidence of the author's meaning and a meaning based on conventions of language is only contingent. A mere intention to mean something by an utterance does not guarantee that it will in fact mean what is intended. An author or speaker may, for example, fail to utter the word sequence he intended through a slip of the tongue or pen or may hold inaccurate understand-ings of the possible meaning of the word sequence he utterers.

Intentionalists deny that it is possible for an utterance to fail to mean what the utterer intends, even when the utterer has made a mistake. Some situations, even outside the law, pose difficulties for such a position. Con-sider ordinary conversations. Weberman (1999), taking from Gadamer (2004), argues that the point of the hermeneutical concept *ideality* (*Geist-igkeit*) is that words used in conversation, like words used in writing, have a meaning that transcends the particular content it has in a specific com-municative act. Ideality thus represents the separation of the meaning of a linguistic item from the utterer's intended meaning. Its ideal aspect or sense is that which transcends, unites, and makes possible all specific in-stances in which a linguistic item occurs. Gadamer (2004) thus argues that it is the ideality (*Idealität*) of the word that raises everything linguistic above the transience that characterizes the rest of human existence.

Weberman invites one to consider a scenario involving two people en-gaged in a conversation regarding the role of courts in American political life and whether this role is consistent with democratic ideals. The mean-ing of the word "democracy" will be contextually defined as a contempo-rary American one, yet one of the conversants may consider the word in a more general way that appeals to its usage in another context that dif-fers from the current one. In Weberman's view, listeners will inevitably do so and are entitled to do so without there being any breach of conversa-tional etiquette or necessary misunderstanding. Similarly, conversations can legitimately get carried forward by autonomous utterance meanings that represent what the speaker said rather than what he meant. If, for ex-ample, a speaker insults a listener but does so unknowingly and uninten-tionally, the utterance is still an insult because the utterer's meaning is not the only relevant meaning, or even the most relevant meaning (Weber-man 1999, 323). With respect to conversations, the ideality concept thus offers a reason to be skeptical of the idea that interpretation merely in-volves determining the utterer's intent.

A similar conclusion that a text can also surpass its author's intent must also be made. In fact, sometimes even if the author's intended com-municative meaning were known, the meaning of the text would never-theless transcend it. This is certainly true for literary texts. Levinson (2002) argues that literary works are ultimately more important than, and distinct from, their authors and retain autonomy from the actual mental processes of their creators. While a literary work should be viewed as a communicative utterance, it is a sort of "grand utterance" that should be governed by different ground rules of interpretation than those applied to ordinary conversational utterances. Trivedi (2001) similarly observes that an artist's semantic intentions—the intent to use a word or phrase and mean something by it rather than something else it may mean—may in the case of some artworks only determine part of the work-meaning, not all of it, especially if there are aspects or nuances of work meaning that are not part of the actual artist's intentions about work meaning. With literary contexts, unlike conversational ones, there is a prior and independent interest in the meaning of the work entirely apart from whatever the utterer's intended meaning may stand behind or parallel that work meaning as constituted.

Examples of literary interpretations that surpass an author's semantic intentions are not difficult to identify. To use an example with legal themes, the interpretive difficulties present in Herman Melville's work provide copious grist for interpretations that transcend the author's intended meaning. Hays and Rust (1979) have, for instance, suggested that the novel *Billy Budd* is properly viewed as a reworking of the author's relationship with his sons, while Marx (1953) interprets *Bartleby* as representing Melville's frustration with his own situation as a writer, particularly his disappointment with the reaction to *Moby Dick*.[41] On one view, the numerosity of the interpretations of *Billy Budd* and *Bartleby* is unexceptional (for great works of art, that is) and unsurprising. If a noncommunicative intent theory is being pursued, capturing authorial intent is not the sine qua non of legitimacy, which allows a surfeit of interpretative theories. An interpretation of a literary text is thus, at least arguably, "correct" if it persuades at least some of the intended audience that the interpretation is useful for some purpose, whether as an explanation of the author, story, or human nature, or even as a provocation to the audience.

The examples described above regarding Melville's work might offer easy instances of interpretations that surpass an author's semantic intentions, but they are inapplicable if one is committed to a communicative intent based conception of meaning and theory. Davies (2006) explains that Anglo-American analytic philosophers of art have instead focused their attention more narrowly on analytic, communicative intent interpretations, where the author's intentions relate in some way to the proper interpretation of the author's work. With respect to literature, even under an analytic approach, though, it cannot be denied that interpretations will sometimes surpass an author's semantic intentions. For instance, authors are often willing to accept meanings given to their works that were not explicitly contemplated at the time of writing. Furthermore, they often intend that their works be seen as complex and interpretable in ways that go beyond their own immediate conceptions of them (Davies 2006).

Whatever its value to literature, an analytic approach is appropriate if one is focused on the judicial interpretation of legal texts. In contrast to literary interpretation, legal interpretation is a zero-sum game. In the context of litigation and any specific interpretive dispute, only one interpretation can be privileged (at least at any one time). Designating the authoritative interpretation is necessary. In that sense, only analytic philosophers of art offer approaches that correspond in relevant ways to how legal texts are interpreted. When a legal text is involved, however, even when a judge generally takes a communicative intent approach to interpretation, not every interpretive controversy involves as its final objective the particular historical fact of authorial intent. In many cases, the final objective of interpretation must by its very nature go beyond authorial intent. In addition to inadvertent indeterminacy, mentioned above, one such situation involves authorially intended indeterminacy. It is widely recognized that legal language is drafted with intentional ambiguity and vagueness in order to shift the lawmaking burden to others, primarily agencies and the judiciary. Indeterminacy, both intended and unintended, is so endemic to the interpretation of legal texts that it might be said to constitute a normal state of affairs, rather than being marked as an occasional problem. In situations of intentional indeterminacy, authorial intent is not sufficient to resolve the interpretive dispute, and legal or other nonlinguistic principles must be employed to select an interpretation.[42] In such situations, the ordinary meaning of the language is similarly insufficient to settle interpretive disputes. If vagueness is the issue, the legal interpreter must precisify the text based on nonlanguage reasons, and if (unresolvable) ambiguity is the issue, the interpreter must similarly choose a meaning based on nonlanguage reasons.

Even when an authorial intent sufficient to resolve the interpretive dispute can be at least arguably identified, legal principles often act as constraints on the judicial implementation of that intent. The same is true with ordinary meaning. It should be readily accepted that courts frequently choose interpretations based on concerns specific to the law even when those interpretations may differ from the ordinary meaning of the relevant language. This chapter has already briefly explained that the meaning of language in a legal text is not always predicated on the ordinary meaning of the language. A court may, for example, decide that a statute should be interpreted narrowly in order to further some legal interest, such as concern about the unfairness of retroactive application of laws. The linguistic meaning of the language might not indicate any restriction on the scope of the statute, but the court will provide one based on legal, rather than linguistic, concerns. Later chapters discuss in more detail whether certain interpretive principles help determine ordinary meaning or are more properly classified as principles that are either based on legal concerns or, perhaps in some cases, erroneous views of language.

Another fundamental constraint on ordinary meaning rests on basic rule of law and democratic principles. An important aspect of the rule of law is the judicial desire to maintain consistency with past decisions, which often takes the form of the stare decisis doctrine. With respect to the interpretation of statutes, this commitment to stare decisis sometimes causes courts to focus on the interpretation of prior judicial opinions rather than the communicative meaning of the statute. A further interpretive concept based on rule of law and democratic principles is that the law is the content that legislators vote on in the final passage of the bill, not the various (often unexpressed) intentions and motives that the enacting legislators might possess.[43] According to Justice Scalia (1997, 17), it is undemocratic "to have the meaning of a law determined by what the lawgiver meant, rather than by what the lawgiver promulgated." While the role of legislative intent in statutory interpretation is hotly debated, and many scholars believe that it should play a role in a judge's determination of meaning, there is no sensible position that allows legislative communicative intent to be coextensive with legal meaning in all cases. Such a position would reject, for example, the principle that citizens must have adequate notice of criminal provisions.[44] The intentionalist position that the meaning of a text is determined by the author's intentions thus cannot serve as a theory of legal meaning, although intentionalists would still argue that it can serve as the basis of communicative content meaning.

Other constraints on meaning besides rule of law and democratic theory concepts are employed by judges. In contract cases, the longstanding rule, as explained by Judge Learned Hand, is that a "contract has, strictly speaking, nothing to do with the personal or individual intent of the parties."[45] Parties are entitled to rely on the outward manifestations and conventional meanings of the utterances of the other party, interpreted through an objective, reasonable person standard, instead of some secret meaning intended by only one of the parties, even if that party drafted the contract. These conventional meanings control even if, as Judge Hand explained, "it were proved by twenty bishops that either party, when he used the words, intended something else than the usual meanings which the law imposes upon them."[46] Apart from relying on conventions, a judge in a contract case might select an interpretation on the basis of public policy or out of a desire to protect the nondrafting party.[47] If a statute is involved, the judge might choose an interpretation out of a desire to implement some important legal principle, such as avoiding serious constitutional issues.[48] And, of course, a meaning that would lead to absurd results or, for some judges, results contrary to the purpose of the statute or contract will be rejected in favor of some other meaning. With respect to both literature and legal texts, it must therefore be conceded that a work's meaning sometimes surpasses the author's communicative intentions, and also, of course, the ordinary meaning of the text. These constraints stem from theories of interpretation that do not take as their ultimate objective either the author's intent or the ordinary meaning of the language.

1.6: Distinguishing Ordinary Meaning from Other Doctrines

As the above discussion illustrates, the ordinary meaning concept is influential and applicable to legal texts, even though these texts have unique features and despite the concession that the ordinary meaning (and communicative meaning) of a legal text is not always adopted as the legal meaning of the text. Nevertheless, before a conception of ordinary meaning is constructed, it is important to compare and contrast the ordinary meaning doctrine with the other well-known concepts that have been associated or confused with it. Ordinary meaning is often conflated with other concepts, some of which have negative connotations that should be disassociated from a proper conception of ordinary meaning. Some terms, though, are either appropriately used as synonyms for ordinary meaning or have not been given meanings that differ from how the ordinary meaning doctrine should be conceived. Terms such as "regular usage," "common usage," "natural meaning," "everyday sense," "normal usage," and "common understanding" are relatively innocuous synonyms for ordinary meaning. Appendix A lists some examples of such terms, along with the corresponding Supreme Court case in which the term was used.

1.6.1: Ordinary Meaning and "Textualism"

Unlike the innocuous terms mentioned above, it is important to distinguish the ordinary meaning doctrine from the methodology of interpretation known as textualism, as the two are widely viewed as being overlapping (if not synonymous) concepts. Manning (2010, 1288), a leading textualist, describes textualism as advocating that judges "should seek statutory meaning in the semantic import of the enacted text and, in so doing, should reject the longstanding practice of using unenacted legislative history as authoritative evidence of legislative intent or purpose." In Manning's view, textualism maintains that clear statutes should be enforced as written, even if doing so does not "perfectly capture the background aims or purposes that inspired their enactment" (1288). Over the past few decades, due in part to the advocacy of Justice Scalia and others, the claims of textualism have greatly influenced judges. For instance, judicial reliance on dictionaries has dramatically increased since 1987. Brudney and Baum (2013) explain that, while the United States Supreme Court's use of dictionaries was virtually non-existent before 1987, now as many as one-third of statutory decisions cite dictionary definitions. The authors link the increased reliance on dictionaries to textualism and "its intense focus on ordinary meaning" (Brudney and Baum 2013, 483).

The authors are correct that there is an ostensible connection between ordinary meaning and textualism. Judicial invocation of ordinary meaning has tracked the rise of textualism. As appendix B demonstrates, the Supreme Court has mentioned the term "ordinary meaning" in 418 cases, with 227 of those cases being decided after 1980, which corresponds with the increased influence of textualism.[49] Of course, various reasons could explain some or all of the correlation between the rise of textualism and citation to the ordinary meaning doctrine. For instance, the statutorification of the law, consisting of the proliferation of statutes as well as agency-issued regulations that constitute the law, likely accounts for some percentage of the increased focus on the ordinary meaning of textual language. Compared to common law adjudication where judges have freedom to determine the content of the law, judges are more mindful of their role as "faithful agents" of legislatures when interpreting statutes (Brudney 2013). Thus, increased reference to an objective criterion of meaning such as the ordinary meaning doctrine should not be surprising.

Despite the connection between the two concepts, ordinary meaning is not coextensive with textualism. Most importantly, the unanimity with which judges accept the ordinary meaning doctrine indicates that the two concepts must diverge in important ways. There is no overall methodology of interpretation that has been accepted by judges. Rather, judges use somewhat different approaches to interpretation. With respect to statutory interpretation, scholars tend to recognize three main theories: textualism, intentionalism, and purposivism (Marmor 2012).[50] Textualism maintains that courts should focus on the "semantic import" of the text interpreted in context, but intentionalist and purposivist theories advocate interpretations that are consistent with the intentions of the legislature or the purposes of the statute. While intentionalist judges are by definition not textualists, it is uncontroversial that they accept the influence of the ordinary meaning doctrine (even if they would argue that it is not always decisive). Thus, while many judges disagree with the tenets of textualism, these same judges at least purport to adhere to the ordinary meaning concept, indicating that the two concepts are distinct.

A major distinction between textualism and the ordinary meaning doctrine concerns the claims about interpretation made by textualists. Textualism is an overall methodology of interpretation, unlike the ordinary meaning doctrine, which is only one aspect of a larger process of interpretation. As this book details, the ordinary meaning doctrine represents only the presumptive meaning of a legal text and can be overcome by other considerations, including ones relating to legal concerns or evidence from an examination of the broader context. Thus, the presumptive ordinary meaning of a text may be overcome by evidence of legislative intent. In contrast to the ordinary meaning doctrine, textualism makes certain normative claims about legitimate interpretation that are based on constitutional concerns and the proper role of the judiciary. One such claim, as the Manning quote above indicates, concerns the necessity of adopting the semantic meaning of a text even if doing so may be inconsistent with the intent or purpose of the legislature. Similarly, Scalia and Garner (Scalia and Garner 2012) maintain that it demeans the constitutionally prescribed method of legislating to view a text as just evidence regarding the mental processes of legislators rather than being the law itself.

In contrast to these ideologically based justifications for textualism, ordinary meaning is, as indicated above, properly viewed as a defeasible concept that is appropriately overcome whenever a judge determines that the legislature intended that the statutory words be given a technical or specialized legal meaning, or even some atypical or unordinary meaning. The justification for the ordinary meaning doctrine is based on a generalized belief that drafters of legal texts employ natural language words with their ordinary meanings. Recall the Supreme Court's view that it assumes that the ordinary meaning of statutory language expresses the legislative purpose. The doctrine is thus, at least in large part, not based on an ideological agenda and makes no claims about the constitutional role of the judiciary (other than some loose "faithful agent" commitment).[51] In addition, while textualism makes evidential claims regarding permissible tools of interpretation, such as legislative history, the ordinary meaning doctrine excludes determinants of meaning only if they are orthogonal to the ordinary meaning determination. The ordinary meaning doctrine, at least as defined, is concerned only with the linguistic meaning of the text. Thus, the ordinary meaning doctrine might exclude consideration of legislative history, but only because such consideration is not relevant to the ordinary meaning of the textual language. The rejection of legislative history would therefore not be based on the ideological and constitutional reasons given by textualists.

Finally, despite their approval of the ordinary meaning doctrine, textualists often do not adhere to its import. Specifically, textualists often interpret language in a way that is inconsistent with a proper conception of ordinary meaning, and often seem more concerned with limiting judicial discretion than with adhering to valid principles of language structure and usage. For instance, a main (perhaps *the* main) tool of interpretation used by textualists is the dictionary. Yet, dictionaries often produce interpretations that vary from the ordinary meanings of the words at issue, especially when context is considered. Thus, if textualists do support the ordinary meaning doctrine, and are not utilizing the discretion inherent in textual interpretation to disguise their ideologically motivated interpretations, they should endeavor better to conform their interpretations to what proper ordinary meaning determinations would reveal.

1.6.2: Ordinary Meaning and "Plain Meaning"

Another concept that is often wrongly seen as synonymous with ordinary meaning is the "plain meaning" rule. Defined in a narrow sense, the plain meaning doctrine is relatively uncontroversial, even if inaccurate because if it does not concede that legal considerations can overcome even a "plain" textual meaning. Tiersma (1999), for instance, believes that the plain meaning rule dictates that statutes are to be interpreted using the ordinary meaning of the language of the statute, unless a statute explicitly defines some of its terms otherwise. In addition to describing the plain meaning rule as indicating that unambiguous statutory language should be applied according to its terms, Scalia and Garner (Scalia and Garner 2012, 436) define the plain meaning rule as being "[1]oosely, the ordinary-meaning canon."

Notwithstanding the above statements, the conflation of the two concepts is mistaken, even though they are often used as synonyms. Certainly, beyond any substantive differences, the two terms carry different connotations. In one recent empirical study, administered to nearly one thousand law students, it was found that plain meaning correlated with ideological bias but ordinary meaning did not (Farnsworth, Guzior, and Mulani 2010). As Nourse (2011, 1004) indicates, perhaps that is because "plain meaning" sounds like "dogmatism and self-regard (i.e., 'it is plain because I say so')." In contrast, ordinary meaning "requires the interpreter to put herself in the shoes of a nonlegal audience; it has a built-in form of impartiality, not to mention democratic appeal" (Nourse 2011, 1004). Thus, plain meaning may be seen by some as constituting an internal view of meaning and ordinary meaning an external view of meaning.

A related objection to using the plain meaning rule as a synonym for the ordinary meaning doctrine is that the plain meaning rule has been criticized by scholars for its simplistic view of language. One common criticism is that the plain meaning rule views statutes as being commonly unambiguous and capable of being straightforwardly applied in specific cases based on considerations only of language (Tiersma 1999). A similar critique is that it is unprincipled and merely substitutes for careful analysis an interpreter's ad hoc and impressionistic intuition about the meaning of legal texts. Popkin (2007, 207) states that the plain meaning rule is cited "whenever a judge seizes upon a textual argument that leads to a particular result, whether or not that is the shared understanding of the author and audience." Solan (1993, 95) argues that the "very existence of the plain language rule reflects at some intuitive level a high degree of confidence in people's potential to communicate successfully."[52] He further argues, correctly, that it is tempting for judges explicitly to rely on the idea that textual language has a plain meaning because of the desire to portray that a rule of law is operating, and that the will of the author is paramount. In other words, judges invoke the plain meaning rule in order to frame a ruling as resting on implementation of the author's meaning and not on inherent judicial discretion.

Considering the negative connotations associated with the plain meaning rule, as well as the unfortunate name itself, it is important to distinguish a proper conception of the ordinary meaning doctrine from the plain meaning rule. An additional reason for distinguishing between the two concepts is that the plain meaning rule may in fact stand for a legitimate (even if controversial) but distinct legal proposition in some cases. One study indicated that the plain meaning rule is sometimes used to refer to a specialized but accepted meaning of a term (McGowan 2008). In contrast, the ordinary meaning of a word is conceptually distinct from any specialized meaning. Another view of the plain meaning rule is that it is an evidential rule that provides that if a text is plain as determined solely by the language of the text, a judge cannot consider any outside evidence to decide what the text means (Solan 1999). Under this understanding of the plain meaning rule, the ordinary meaning doctrine is clearly distinguishable. Although the determinants of ordinary meaning may be restricted, the doctrine is not an evidential one (or, at least, should not be viewed as such). Rather, the ordinary meaning is merely the presumptive meaning of a text and can be overcome by other considerations.

Another distinction between the two doctrines was made by Schroth (1998), who notes that the ordinary meaning refers to the sense that an expression usually has in the context at issue, while the plain meaning rule refers to a lack of ambiguity in the text. This distinction is an important one. Unlike the plain meaning rule, the ordinary meaning doctrine should not be seen as exaggerating the clarity of language. Indeed, the ordinary meaning of words, even taken in context, may be vague or ambiguous, and thus not "plain." Further, the determination of ordinary meaning is ineliminably discretionary. The ordinary meaning doctrine therefore cannot reflect or assume a high degree of confidence in people's potential to communicate successfully, at least in a narrow, determinate sense. To the contrary, the doctrine should be viewed as allowing for an epistemically modest view of the determinacy of communication. As this book demonstrates, the ordinary meaning doctrine is particularly important to the interpretation of texts precisely because determining the author's actual intent is not possible, and other methods of determining textual meaning are less compelling.

1.6.3: Ordinary Meaning and "Literal Meaning"

Finally, the ordinary meaning doctrine should also be distinguished from the concept of "literal meaning." In law, there is said to be a "clear preference" for literal meaning (Charnock 2013, 128). Similar to the plain meaning doctrine, the literal meaning concept may stand, basically, for the concept that if the words are clear they must be applied even in situations where the drafter may have had a contrary intention (Tiersma 1999). Not surprisingly, Popkin (2007, 194) observes that literalism is often used as a synonym for textualism. Along with plain meaning, courts have used literal meaning as a synonym for ordinary meaning. Appendix C contains a list of some of the cases (including ones involving the Constitution).

Despite such usage, literal meaning (at least as used outside of law) and ordinary meaning are distinct concepts and should be distinguished when examining legal language. Language is full of nonliteral meanings, such as metaphors, idioms, slang, and polite talk. When such expressions are used, the literal meaning of the expression may differ from its ordinary meaning. Of course, such usages of language are far less common in legal texts (Tiersma 2001). Nevertheless, various expressions are used in legal texts that consistently possess ordinary meanings that differ from their literal meanings.

Undoubtedly, there are various ways to define literal meaning, just as there are various ways to define other terms that will be discussed in this book. Talmage (1994) indicates that literal meaning is commonly identified with the conventional meaning of language. For purposes of this book, the term is similarly characterized as being essentially synonymous with the linguistic meaning of the relevant sentence that is conventional and context independent.[53] Incidentally, this definition of literal meaning has the additional advantage of being consistent with how courts use the term, as they often employ dictionary definitions without consideration of context. Quantifiers (discussed in chap. 3 and described below) and some textual canons of interpretation (discussed in chap. 4) are examples of linguistic phenomena where there is commonly a gap between the ordinary meaning and the literal meaning of the relevant expressions. Thus, the philosophical concept of literal meaning differs from a proper conception of the ordinary meaning doctrine.

1.7: Overview of the Book

Although the ordinary meaning concept is not coterminous with textualism, the plain meaning rule or literal meaning, it is, like those other concepts, necessarily based on an "objective" view of meaning because its content is based on determinants of meaning other than the content of the author's communicative intentions. As indicated at the beginning of this chapter, the constituent question of what makes some meaning the ordinary one and the evidential question of how the determinants of ordinary meaning are identified and conceptualized are thus of crucial importance to the interpretation of legal texts. This book provides a theory that answers the constituent question and a general framework for how the determinants of ordinary meaning (i.e., the evidential question) should be identified and developed. The book explains that the fundamental problem with the common process used by courts for determining the ordinary meaning of texts, such as significant reliance on acontextual dictionary definitions, is that it often does not result in interpretations that reflect the ordinary meaning of the textual language, or only coincidentally does so. One main flaw in the judiciary's approach is a failure properly to consider context. Certainly, there is a tension between the inherent requirement of ordinary meaning that it be generalizable across contexts and the reality that meaning is inherently contextual. A significant aspect of framing the ordinary meaning inquiry, and considering arguments about it, therefore involves considering the contribution that context makes to meaning.

One way to capture generalizable meanings is to conceive of ordinary meaning as being primarily based on semantic meaning. In other words, ordinary meaning could be said to be based on conventions and systematicities of language, rather than by inferential processes tied to the language producer. Further, a distinction between "narrow context" and "wide context" can be made, with ordinary meaning being determined on the basis of consideration of facts from the narrow context. Yet, framing ordinary meaning as being primarily based on semantic meaning, determined from consideration of narrow context, does not eliminate interpretive discretion. When context is considered, the assignment of meaning invariably has an ineliminable element of interpreter discretion that is often quite significant. This is true with respect to various linguistic phenomena. Nevertheless, focusing on the systematicities of language can often narrow the range of interpretive discretion and improve the judiciary's determination of ordinary meaning.

Despite being a fundamental aspect of legal interpretation that is relevant to nearly all interpretations of legal texts, the ordinary meaning doctrine has not been extensively examined by courts or scholars. Because ordinary meaning is not generally a concept in linguistics or philosophy that is the subject of current debate, linguists and philosophers uninterested in legal interpretation are not likely to have considered it in any depth. Meanwhile, those interested in legal interpretation have tended to focus on other interpretive issues. These scholars have focused on such metainterpretive controversies as whether judges should adopt a textualist or an intentionalist approach to interpretation (see, e.g., Manning 2005), narrower issues such as judicial reliance on dictionaries (see, e.g., Thumma and Kirchmeier 1999), as well as examinations of discrete issues such as vagueness (see, e.g., Endicott 2000, 2001). More philosophical approaches have focused on definitions of "meaning" or "interpretation" (see, e.g., Marmor 2008a). It seems, though, that no one has attempted an in-depth examination of the ordinary meaning concept.

This book will fill the gap by offering a theory of the ordinary meaning doctrine that situates it within the realities of how legal texts must be interpreted. When considering ordinary meaning, the reader should understand that it can be approached from (at least) two perspectives. One perspective considers how courts in fact decide the ordinary meaning of textual language. The other perspective considers the best account that can be made of the ordinary meaning doctrine. Encompassed within this account is the normative issue of how courts *should* decide the ordinary meaning of textual language. This book is concerned with both perspectives, but primarily the second. At times, one account may shade into the other. For example, considering how courts *do* determine ordinary meaning can provide insights into how they *should* determine ordinary meaning, as well as how the doctrine might be conceptualized. Conversely, considering how courts *should* determine ordinary meaning must, to be persuasive, evaluate how courts *do* determine ordinary meaning. Of course, it is the actual interpreter that must make the ordinary meaning determination. The actual interpreter must consider various linguistic phenomena in rejecting unordinary meanings and selecting the ordinary meaning. To be useful, the normative question must therefore consider the realities of language and interpretation.

Although meant to be relatively comprehensive in conceptualizing the ordinary meaning doctrine, this book is not intended to be a catalog of every linguistic phenomenon and interpretive principle that may be relevant to ordinary meaning. Rather, it demonstrates the necessity of the ordinary meaning concept, proposes a theory of how ordinary meaning might be conceived, and explores the implications of such a conception. In addition, although the ordinary meaning concept is applied to a wide variety of legal texts, this book will focus on its application to statutes (as this chapter illustrates). Nonetheless, much of the discussion is applicable to the interpretation of other legal texts, and at times broad language such as "legal texts" will be used instead of the narrower term "statutes."

1.7.1: Description of Chapter 2

Chapter 2 develops the claim that the interpretation of legal texts must necessarily be a hypothetical exercise with significant reliance on conventions of language, which largely constitute the ordinary meaning doctrine. In establishing this position, particular attention is given to the claims of intentionalists regarding language and meaning. In a sense, because the ordinary meaning concept is embraced by judges despite widespread differences in jurisprudential ideology and methodology of interpretation, it is possible to develop a theory of it without addressing claims made by the adherents of any particular theory of meaning or interpretation. Ordinary meaning is the default meaning of a legal text, cancellable (often implicitly) for various reasons, including because the author(s) intended some other meaning. As much of this book is concerned with the proper normative and positive conception of ordinary meaning, as well as exploring the determinants of ordinary meaning, it may not seem necessary to join debates about overall definitions of meaning. Notwithstanding these considerations, as has already been mentioned in this chapter, arguments regarding the proper conception of ordinary meaning and its determinants are only coherent in light of an accurate description of the nature and possibilities of legal interpretation, as well as some assumed or explicit definition of communicative meaning.

As any definition of ordinary meaning is only coherent in light of some definition of overall communicative meaning, a proper view of communicative meaning should first be identified before arguments regarding the determinants of ordinary meaning are explored. At the same time, though, just as a chosen definition of communicative meaning should entail, or at least suggest, certain conclusions regarding whether various determinants of meaning are required or prohibited in the interpretive process, the nature of the interpretive process and the availability or unavailability of determinants of meaning may influence conclusions about definitions of communicative meaning. The relationship between the definition of meaning (both communicative and ordinary) and the determinants of meaning is therefore a mutually informative one. The constitutive and evidential aspects of ordinary meaning are informed by the possible definitions of communicative meaning, and, it will be seen, certain understandings of the nature of meaning, language, and interpretation.

1.7.2. Description of Chapter 3

Chapter 3 develops a theory of ordinary meaning and focuses on the tension between the inherent requirement of ordinary meaning that it be generalizable across contexts and the reality that meaning is inherently contextual. One motivation for conceiving of ordinary meaning as generalizable across contexts is to maintain a gap between ordinary meaning and communicative meaning. The chapter outlines the justifications for the ordinary meaning doctrine in order to explain why both communicative meaning (based on objective determinants of meaning as explained in chap. 2) and ordinary meaning should be aspects of legal interpretation. These justifications range from notice to the justificatory nature of legal interpretation. The chapter also discusses the constitutive question of what makes some meaning the ordinary meaning of a text, as well as how the objective ordinary meaning interpreter might be defined.

Currently, the ordinary meaning doctrine is greatly undertheorized, and addressing its determinants in light of an existing, widely recognized framework should help to bring a degree of systematicity to the doctrine that will help explicate it. Thus, in conceptualizing the ordinary meaning doctrine, the chapter introduces and considers Recanati's (2004) division of utterances into three levels of meaning: "sentence meaning," "what is said," and "what is communicated." At the least, ordinary meaning must include the concept of "sentence meaning," which is the most basic level of meaning and portrays language as conventional and context independent (Recanati 2004). Sentence meaning, though, falls short of constituting a complete proposition (i.e., a situation where a complete thought can be assigned to a sentence).[54] Critically, sentence meaning does not include the assignment of references to indexical expressions, which is required for complete propositions. Indexicals are words such as "I," "now," "here," and "today" that require contextual facts in order to fix their references. These words are found in legal texts and sometimes raise difficult interpretive questions. Because sentence meaning does not account for these words, it thus cannot alone serve as a complete theory of ordinary meaning. The notion of what is said, though, is a better candidate for representing the ordinary meaning concept. What is said fleshes out the meaning of the sentence, including assigning references to indexicals. Later chapters describe the components of what is said and how they relate to ordinary meaning.

In addition to the three levels of meaning, in thinking about ordinary meaning, it is useful to consider Scalia and Garner's (Scalia and Garner 2012, 69) view that "most interpretive questions have a right answer," and "[v]ariability in interpretation is a distemper." Scalia and Garner's argument is true only if the determinants of ordinary meaning are determinate in a way that does not allow for interpretive discretion. Yet, a significant aspect of framing the ordinary meaning inquiry, and considering textualist arguments about it, involves considering the contribution that context makes to meaning. One way to capture generalizable meanings and maintain the gap between ordinary meaning and communicative meaning is to conceive of ordinary meaning as semantic meaning, as opposed to viewing the doctrine as one relying primarily on pragmatic processes (which often involve significant inferential reasoning processes). Furthermore, ordinary meaning should be determined based on facts from some definition of "narrow context." These ways of framing ordinary meaning does not, however, eliminate interpretive discretion. It is not possible to remove broader contextual considerations from the assignment of semantic meaning due, in part, to the reality that a "null context" free of contextual input only exists in theory and, in any case, does not produce sufficiently specific meanings. In addition, as discussed throughout the book, the assignment of conventional meaning inherently has an element of discretion.

Courts have often not been careful in considering the contribution that context makes to meaning, even ordinary meaning. For instance, courts often fail to properly consider the complexities that context can add to interpretations of indexicals and rely instead on dictionary definitions. For example, the Supreme Court in *Carcieri v. Salazar*,[55] relied heavily on a dictionary definition of the indexical term "now," which defined the word as "[a]t the present time; at this moment; at the time of speaking."[56] The Court failed to realize the reference-shifting capabilities of indexicals and the need to distinguish between the context of utterance and the intended context of interpretation. The Supreme Court's apparent ignorance of this semantic aspect of "now" unfortunately convinced it that the ordinary meaning of "now" automatically involves the context of utterance. Even under a proper understanding of indexicals, though, an interpreter has significant discretion in determining their conventional meanings. In fact, with respect to indexicals in legal texts, it is questionable whether there is typically likely to be a gap between ordinary meaning and legal meaning (i.e., the authoritative meaning of the text that may be based on legal concerns in addition to linguistic analysis) due to the ineliminable discretion inherent in determining conventional meaning.

1.7.3: Description of Chapter 4

Chapter 4 continues the account of ordinary meaning where chapter 3 ended. Chapter 3 introduced a hierarchy of meaning with "sentence meaning" as the most basic level of meaning, followed by "what is said" and "what is communicated." What is said requires that context be accounted for explicitly, unlike sentence meaning (which was rejected in chap. 3 as the level of meaning synonymous with ordinary meaning). One situation where context must be accounted for explicitly involves the assignment of domains (i.e., the scope of reference) to quantifiers. This linguistic phenomenon falls under the scope of what is said and, it will be argued, ordinary meaning.

A quantifier is an expression that modifies a referring expression in terms of amount. For example, suppose that at a symposium on semantics, Person A asks Person B, "Are there any philosophers?" Person B answers, "Yes, though most people are linguists." Person A understands that Person B's quantifier "most" is limited contextually to those present at the symposium and does not refer to the entire world. Equally, Person B understands that Person A's quantifier "any" is similarly contextually limited. As the example illustrates, the assignment of a limited domain to a quantifier is intuitively connected to the ordinary meaning of an expression, considered in its proper context.

Stanley (2000, 2007) offers a theory of quantifier domain restriction that both comports with empirical adequacy and offers a compelling way to think about the ordinary meaning of sentences that contain quantifiers. Unfortunately, courts have not properly considered quantifier domain restriction when determining the ordinary meaning of textual language. One case that required consideration of a quantifier was *Ali v. Fed. Bureau of Prisons*.[57] Like the *Carcieri* case, the Court in *Ali* emphasized the dictionary definition of the operative word "any" and failed to consider that the scope of most quantifiers is restricted in some way. Notwithstanding the Court's failure to recognize quantifier domain restriction, the assignment of a domain to a quantifier, like the assignment of meaning to other words, is necessarily a discretionary determination.

The discussion of quantifiers (like that of indexicals) illustrates that, for various linguistic phenomena, it is possible to adopt a semantic theory, or at least some theory that emphasizes the systematic nature of language and is seen as arguably semantic by some, that will offer an explanatory account of the phenomenon. The semantic theory can help conceptualize how an ordinary meaning account of the phenomenon can be structured. Nevertheless, there is an ineliminable degree of discretion that makes any ordinary meaning determination discretionary. Moreover, there are no reasons to believe that "common sense" or alignment of background assumptions and knowledge, even if possible, will be sufficient to create interpretive consensus (contrary to Scalia and Garner's arguments, mentioned earlier).

In addition to quantifiers, the chapter also considers whether substantive and textual canons of interpretation are determinants of ordinary meaning. Substantive canons are normatively based presumptions about statutory meaning that are derived from the common law, other statutes, or the Constitution. Textual canons are presumptions that are drawn from the drafter's choice of words, their grammatical placement in sentences, and their relationship to other parts of the "whole" statute. While substantive canons are not determinates of ordinary meaning, some textual canons are, even though they may have to be classified as conversational implicatures and therefore fall under "what is communicated." A conversational implicature is a means of communicating more than what is literally said, and some textual canons can be legitimized under certain theories of conversational implicature. Nevertheless, the discretionary nature of interpretation holds regardless of whether a particular linguistic phenomenon is considered to be, under Recanati's distinctions, "what is said" or "what is communicated." Quantifier domain restriction may be an aspect of what is said and textual canons an aspect of what is communicated, but neither the domain of a quantifier nor the application of a textual canon can be determined without the consideration of context.

Notwithstanding the discretionary nature of interpretation, various useful distinctions can still be made. One is between *ordinary linguistic meaning* and *ordinary legal meaning*. A common characteristic of principles of legal interpretation is that they serve to restrict the domains of legal texts (i.e., their scopes of application), thereby creating a gap between literal meaning and ordinary/communicative meaning. Not all these interpretive principles, however, are relevant to ordinary linguistic meaning. Substantive canons, for instance, generally cannot be considered relevant to ordinary linguistic meaning, as they derive from legal considerations and not linguistic ones and have other attributes (such as vague conditions for application) that render them inapplicable to ordinary meaning. At most, they are determinates of ordinary legal meaning (but the chapter concludes that they cannot be so designated). As indicated above, some textual canons can be considered to be determinants of ordinary linguistic meaning. This chapter identifies the *ejusdem generis* canon as one such interpretive principle. Even so, like the other determinants of ordinary meaning, a systematic account of the phenomenon cannot eliminate the discretionary nature of its application.

1.7.4: Description of Chapter 5

Chapter 5 addresses issues relating to lexical semantics, including the contribution of sentential (i.e., sentence level) context to the ordinary meaning of words. Proper consideration of sentential context should convince courts to not rely on acontextual dictionary definitions that often favor inappropriately broad meanings that capture "possible" rather than "ordinary" meanings. One example where proper consideration of sentential context should have changed the interpretation chosen is the Supreme Court's infamous decision in *Smith v. United States*, where the Court held that a person "uses" a firearm "during and in relation to . . . [a] drug trafficking crime" when the person trades the firearm for drugs.[58] The *Smith* decision will be examined and criticized for its reliance on dictionary definitions at the expense of a more sophisticated understanding of how language operates. The decision has been widely analyzed by commentators, but not all the critiques have approached its interpretive questions correctly. Contrary to the claims of some commentators, the interpretive process exemplified in the case includes an ineliminable degree of discretion, but the process should not be viewed as being entirely discretionary. Rather, there are accurate and inaccurate ways of thinking about the ordinary meaning of language and how that meaning is determined. Also, interpreters should prefer accounts of linguistic phenomena that are based on valid linguistic theories and cognitive science insights, rather than appeals to "common sense," even if the two may often correspond in some ways.

   Notwithstanding the various ways in which linguistic phenomena use context to restrict the literal meaning of a provision, general word meanings may be required in situations that do not involve some systematic aspect of context. Legal interpretation frequently involves determining whether an item (either abstract or concrete) falls within the parameters of the verbal concept inscribed in the relevant textual provision. The judicial tendency to view word categories as formed by necessary and sufficient conditions for membership is consistent with the so-called classical theory of concept meaning. The classical theory, though, is inconsistent with research from linguists and psychologists on the prototypical structure of categories. Instead of a simple set of criterial features, categories do not have sharply delimited borders with clear demarcations. Rather, they are often only unambiguously defined in their focal points, and marginal areas exist between categories.

Chapter 5 explains that prototype theory can be accommodated to the need of the legal system for bivalent definitions (i.e., a "yes" or "no" answer to the question of whether an item belongs in a given category), as well as the reduced capacity for empirical research. Even with the limitations inherent in judicial adaptation, prototype methodology is preferable to the classical model of viewing meaning in terms of necessary and sufficient membership criteria. Nevertheless, legal texts often reference intangible categories that either do not exist outside the law or exist only at high levels of generality compared to the needs of the legal system. In such situations, the ordinary meaning of the relevant term either does not exist or is not specific enough to decide many cases (of course, this may also be true in other cases). Instead of relying on the ordinary meaning doctrine, the interpreter should decide the case on other grounds and be explicit about doing so.

1.7.5: Description of Chapter 6

Finally, chapter 6 offers a conclusion. In it, I give a summary of what this book has demonstrated. I also outline the various areas in which future ordinary meaning research can be conducted. For example, examination of the ways in which syntax contributes to ordinary meaning would be useful in analyzing some present areas of judicial confusion. I further explain that courts do not always demonstrate a willingness to use ordinary meaning as an identifiable part of an explicitly delineated, sequential process of reasoning. Nevertheless, judges purport to take language seriously, judicial practices of interpretation have changed over time, and at least some judges will be willing to continue to refine their interpretive methodologies.

CHAPTER TWO

Hypothetical Intentionalism and Communicative Content

2.1: Defining Intentionalism

This chapter develops the claim that the interpretation of legal texts must necessarily be a theoretical and hypothetical exercise that relies on conventions of language, which largely constitute the ordinary meaning doctrine. In establishing this position, particular attention is given to the claims of some intentionalists regarding language and meaning. Certain intentionalist arguments deserve special attention because, if valid, they pose a challenge to any theory that gives the ordinary meaning concept a central role in determining the meaning of legal texts. The ordinary meaning concept is necessarily based on an "objective" view of meaning because its communicative content is not constituted by the content of the author's communicative intentions. In contrast, intentionalism is based on a Gricean conception of communication where the communicative content of an utterance is the content that the speaker intends the hearer to understand by recognizing that very intention (Greenberg 2010).

For various reasons, the claims made by intentionalists must be taken seriously. For one, intentionalism in interpretation has a long history with various famous proponents, including John Locke (Winkler 2009). In more modern times, intentionalist positions continue to receive widespread support by scholars, both in legal contexts and otherwise (e.g., Hirsch 1967; Carroll 1992, 2000, 2007, 2011; Irwin 1999; Michaels 1979; Fish 1999, 2005, 2008; Knapp and Michaels, 1982, 1983, 1987, 1992; Alexander and Prakash, 2004; Iseminger 1992, 1996, 1998; Livingston 1998). Indeed, debates regarding intentionalism with respect to literature and art have recently been extensive, as well as relevant to the interpretation of legal texts. Judge Richard Posner (1988b), for example, has made a connection between the two disciplines of literary theory and legal interpretation.

Of course, intentionalism is not monolithic. Different theories of intentionalism exist, depending on the views and needs of a particular community and the kinds of communications that must be interpreted. For instance, legal theorists who advocate for an intentionalist view of legal interpretation undoubtedly have some justifications for intentionalism that differ from those offered by those who are concerned with literary interpretation. Legal intentionalists may, for example, be concerned with issues relating to the best way of implementing legislative intent and may also be concerned with evidential issues such as the use of legislative history. These concerns and motivations may have no direct correspondence to nonlegal interpretation of texts. Nevertheless, the basic intentionalist position on the nature of language and interpretation is the same, regardless of the type of text at issue.

In particular, the constitutive claim of intentionalism is that the meaning of a conversational utterance or a text is identical to the speaker or author's intended meaning (*meaning thesis*). The epistemic claim is that interpretation consists of determining the speaker or author's intended meaning (*interpretation thesis*).[1] Undoubtedly, part of the allure of intentionalism is that alternatives to its meaning and interpretation theses are not as intuitive. If an author seeks to convey some message via a text, it would seem that successful interpretation would consist of identifying the intended message. It is far less intuitive to accept that someone other than the author can *decide* the meaning of the author's words, as opposed to merely *determining* the author's meaning. Thus, intentionalism makes ostensibly intuitive claims about meaning and interpretation that seem, at the outset, obviously superior to other conceptions of meaning and interpretation.

The appeal of intentionalism may be its intuitive force as a general theory of communication, but one challenge is that consensus may not exist regarding even its basic aspects. For instance, one important aspect of the meaning thesis concerns the question of how "intent" should be measured. One may seek to determine authorial intent, but intent is a multivarious concept, partly because it can be framed at multiple levels of generality. Among other ways, it can be framed as what the legislature (1) "said" (i.e., the literal meaning), (2) "communicated," (3) "meant," or,

at a much more general level of specificity, as (4) how the legislature intended to "modify the content of the law" (Greenberg 2011). The four
categories above can be further refined and elaborated, thus creating numerous possibilities for the definition of actual intent. Thus, for example,
in considering intent the interpreter could seek to identify, along with
many other possibilities, (1) those intentions manifest in the language
of the law itself; (2) what Marmor (2005, 127–29) deems "further intentions," which concern the legislature's intentions that are in addition to
the ones that rules manifest through their formulations; and (3) intentions
concerning the proper application of the law. Still another way of viewing intent, albeit at a high level of generality, is through an "Intentionalist
Stance" (Boudreau, McCubbins, and Rodriguez 2005). Instead of looking
for the actual intent of an author of a text, an interpreter should do what
she does in all other situations in figuring out what the actions of others
mean. That is, the interpreter views the author as a rational agent with
beliefs, desires, and intentions, but the intentions are metaphorical ones
that are imputed to others in order to determine what their actions, statements, or writings mean.

   None of the possibilities above can be deemed to be the only correct view of intent, although presumably most intentionalists would insist on a formulation that is akin to "what is meant" or, if a more purposive orientation is desired, how the legislature intended to modify the
content of the law. Instead of a situation with a "correct" view of intent,
the choice amongst the possibilities described above is entirely theoretical and dependent on nonempirical notions about the most appropriate way in which to frame intent according to whatever criteria the
interpreter deems important (more on the theoretical nature of interpretation later in this chapter). Furthermore, one's choice about the generality at which to define intent entails, or at least makes relevant, other
(theoretical) choices. Thus, a decision to reject a narrow conception of intent based on choices 1–3 above and instead to choose a more purposivist conception of intent, as described in choice 4, makes certain insights
from other disciplines such as political science especially relevant. Thus,
for example, one problem with a broad definition of intent is that it may
not properly account for typical legislative bargains. Rodriguez and Weingast (2007) have claimed that the voting decisions of moderate legislators
have at times been influenced in a negative manner by the prospect of
activist judicial interpretations that are underpinned by notions of legislative intent. This activism involves the judiciary's extension of statutes,

based on broad purposive interpretations, beyond the critical legislators' understanding of what the statutory language voted on meant. Accepting, or rejecting, such scholarship is itself an interpretive decision based on a theory of meaning.

Putting aside the constitutive issue of how to define "intent," the importance of intentionalism to ordinary meaning concerns the intentionalist view of the "correct" interpretation of a text. In the intentionalist model, the determination of authorial intention is indistinguishable from interpretation, which simplifies how intentionalists view the meaning of language (Fish 1999). Consider a common situation where a sentence may express two (or more) linguistic meanings represented by (A_1) or (A_2), and the author intends to express only one of the meanings. In considering the meaning of (A_1) and (A_2) a distinction can be made, at least according to nonintentionalists, among (1) the linguistic meaning or meanings that a sentence S has in a language L, (2) the linguistic meaning or meanings that a sentence S conveys in a language L in its context of utterance, and (3) the meaning that an utterance S in a language L expresses on a given occasion of use. Chapter 3 develops the three levels of meaning in more detail and relates each to the requirements of the ordinary meaning doctrine. For now, the following description is sufficient.

The first category, (1), can be referred to as the word-sequence meaning or "sentence meaning," which is the meaning of a sequence of words taken in the abstract following the relevant language's syntactic and semantic rules. It excludes all information about the context in which the sentence was uttered or written and is treated as a token of a sentence type in a given language. The second category, (2), can be referred to as the "utterance meaning" (or "what is said"), which is the meaning a sequence of words conveys in its context of utterance. The third category, (3), can be viewed in two different ways. One way is to refer to "what is communicated" by the utterance. This level would include what is said, as well as such things as implicatures, which are explained in chapter 4. Chapter 4 will argue that some conversational implicatures, viewed as systematic aspects of language rather than being dependent on actual authorial intent, can be determinants of ordinary meaning. For purposes of this chapter, distinctions between "utterance meaning" and "what is communicated" are not relevant if both are reviewed as depending on objective, rather than intentional, determinants of meaning.

The second way to view category (3) is through "utterer's meaning," which holds that the utterer's intent determines meaning, regardless of whether the meaning was recognized via words and syntactic structures or other publicly available indicators of meaning, or, for some, regardless of whether the meaning was recognized at all by the relevant listeners or hearers. In addition to the categories above, many other conceptualizations of meaning are, of course, possible. Like utterer's meaning, if one abstracts away from the communicative content of a text, other categories of meaning can be said to exist. For instance, Iseminger (1996, 222–23) identifies "ludic meaning" as "any meanings that can be attributed to either a brute text (a word-sequence in a language), or a text-as-utterance, in virtue of interpretive play constrained by only the loosest requirements of plausibility, intelligibility, or interest."

For purposes of this chapter, the focus will be on the distinction between "utterance meaning" and "utterer's meaning." For an intentionalist, utterer's meaning is all that matters (or, more strongly, all that can be said to exist), and, in determining utterer's meaning, one must ascertain the communicative intent of the author. A text can therefore never fail to mean what the author intends it to mean. Moreover, intentionalists argue that, without resort to the author's communicative intent, every text would mean everything its words could potentially mean in the language in which it was written. Thus, any sentence S would always mean both (A_1) and (A_2), as well as perhaps multiple other meanings. In light of these arguments, one would think that an intentionalist should be committed to the view that actual authorial intentions can be determined with "some epistemically respectable degree of warrant" (Iseminger 1996, 320). For these reasons, the intentionalist meaning thesis rejects the traditional distinction between "sentence meaning" (or "what is said") and "utterer's meaning." In addition, intentionalists argue that in legal contexts deviations from intentionalism by judges may sometimes be wise for reasons specific to law, such as "fair notice," but such deviations nevertheless represent a rejection of a statute's true meaning in favor of some artificial meaning.

2.2: The Intentionalist Challenge to Ordinary Meaning

Both the meaning thesis and the interpretation thesis pose a challenge to the ordinary meaning concept. One intentionalist argument is that a rejection of the meaning and interpretation theses requires that any replacement be based on a theory of interpretation, but that such a solution is unworkable because interpretation is an empirical and not a theoretical exercise. A later section of this chapter rejects the intentionalist claim that interpretation is not a theoretical endeavor. Yet, even a demonstration that interpretation is inherently theoretical in nature still leaves unanswered certain intentionalist claims. If, as intentionalists argue, the meaning of an utterance or text is identical to the speaker or author's intended meaning and the goal of interpretation is to uncover this meaning, it is not immediately clear why the ordinary meaning concept should have a prominent role in the determination of meaning. Any evidence, such as independent word meaning found in dictionaries or corpora (or some other objective source of meaning), not connected to the author's actual intent would be irrelevant (Azar 2007). Even worse, if words do not have established or conventional meanings in a language, the ordinary meaning concept would be incoherent since, by its very nature, it assumes that words have conventional meanings. Consider, for example, Fish's (2005, 633) view that the definition of "interpretation" is limited to the search for authorial intent because "words do not carry fixed or even relatively fixed meanings." At the least, it is not clear why evidence of ordinary meaning should act as more than a pragmatic constraint on the "true meaning" of the text, or perhaps serve as a concession that the true meaning of the text cannot be determined due to insufficient indications of authorial intent.

Because of the intentionalist view of language, the importance of the ordinary meaning concept to interpretation can only be realized through an examination of the determinants of meaning and the limits of textual interpretation, and a consequent rejection of the intentionalist meaning and interpretation theses. Part of the examination will require a rejection of the intentionalist notion that it is illegitimate to distinguish between sentence meaning, what is said, and utterer's meaning. This rejection is a result of the constraints on utterer's meaning that must exist in order to recognize that language cannot mean whatever the utterer wishes it to mean, as well as to account for the limited nature of the determinants of meaning available when interpreting texts. Considering these constraints both challenges the intentionalist meaning and interpretation theses and underscores the theoretical nature of legal interpretation. As well, the constraints of textual interpretation, and the rejection of the meaning and interpretation theses, underscore the legitimacy and necessity of the ordinary meaning doctrine. As developed in this chapter, the ordinary meaning of a phrase or sentence must, constitutively, be a properly contextualized, public meaning, rather than an idiosyncratic meaning that can only be discerned, if at all, based on nontextual inferences from intent. Ordinary meaning must therefore be based on theories of linguistic phenomena (including conventions of meaning) external to the author. It relies on, to use Hogan's (1996) term, a notion of "semantic objectivism" that posits that there are facts about what words mean and that these facts are independent of what individual people mean by the words they use.

Intentionalists claim that it is "embarrassingly obvious" that textual meaning and authorial intention are the same thing (Campos 1996). Their position, however, cannot be sustained. The meaning and interpretation theses must be rejected because the interpretive process is not, as intentionalists would ideally conceive it, telemental where a thought is transferred from the author's mind to the interpreter's mind (Harris 2001). Levinson (2002) observes that our interests in literature are communicative ones but are not more narrowly conversational ones. The same is true with respect to legal texts. Texts are dissimilar from oral utterances in various important ways, and these differences are crucial to how texts can be interpreted. Most importantly, it changes how we conceptualize authorial intention. An author's so-called semantic intentions—the intent to use a word or phrase and mean something by it rather something else it may mean—are relevant to what the author means, and indeed may be said to constitute it, but they are not determinative of what the *text* means. Contrary to intentionalist arguments, the interpretive process should not be viewed as involving merely an archaeological excavation-like search for authorial intent. Rather, it should be conceptualized as a theoretical and structured enterprise where, among other things, courts apply linguistic and cognitive science insights to determine the meaning of the text, taken from an interpreter's standpoint.

Because this book is not designed as a general refutation of intentionalism, various claims made by intentionalists will not be challenged and are, in fact, accurate views on meaning and interpretation. For instance, I take no issue with the claim that in ascertaining the meaning of a text the interpreter must consider sources outside the scope of syntax and semantics. Certainly, pragmatic theories should be considered in some cases, even when the ordinary meaning of the text is being determined.[2] I do submit, though, that it is not the case that the interpreter must, or can, directly ascertain the author's actual intentions. Instead, as this chapter demonstrates, interpreters must base their interpretations on objective features of the context of interpretation, including conventions of meaning that may be said to represent the ordinary meaning of the language. In addition, intentionalists may be correct that textualists are closet intentionalists, in a sense, because they make certain assumptions about the text that are not based solely on the text. I show, though, that intentionalists are not actual intentionalists, in a sense, because they must base their interpretations on a hypothetical version of the author's intent. That is, like the case with other interpretive theories, intentionalists must base their interpretations on generalized and unverifiable assumptions about meaning that are not tied to any author's communicative intent.

2.3: Conversational versus Textual Contexts

Even considering intentionalists' mistaken views regarding the meaning and interpretation theses, as well as some questionable claims about language that will be addressed below, perhaps the biggest flaw in the intentionalist view of interpretation is that it does not adequately consider the fundamental differences between the interpretation of verbal utterances and texts. One of the most important, and constraining, realities of interpretation concerns the differences between these separate forms of communication. Grice's intentionalism (more on him below) was built on a model of spoken language, but other intentionalists have dismissed the differences between spoken and written language. In fact, as Davies (2006) notes, intentionalists make the comparison central to their claims. Carroll (1992, 117–18), for example, states that "[w]hen we read a literary text . . . we enter a relationship with its creator that is roughly analogous to a conversation." Carroll (2011, 127) reasons that

> if art interpretation is on a continuum with the interpretative activity that we engage in on a daily basis, then some form of actual intentionalism would seem to follow naturally, since in the normal course of affairs the object of interpretation is to identify the intentions, beliefs, and desires of others. As we observe the speech, gesture, and behavior of others, we typically do so in order to, as we say, read their minds. Moreover, mind reading is indispensable to human life; it makes the co-ordination of our activities possible. For this reason, the everyday interpretation of the words and deeds of our conspecifics aims at the retrieval of what is going on in the minds of others. There seems little compelling reason to think that things stand otherwise when it comes to interpreting the arts, including the literary arts.

Iseminger (1996, 324) argues that actual rather than hypothetical semantic intentions must be crucial to meaning because hypothetical intentions do not "serve our conversational interests." Davies (2006) similarly argues that the flow of communication in a conversation requires the discernment of what the speaker meant, not what she said, and that it is plausible to regard literary artworks as communications from their authors. The discussion below demonstrates that the basic intentionalist position regarding meaning is flawed because it fails to recognize the important distinctions between typical oral conversations and typical texts, as well as how these distinctions should inform the constitutive and evidentiary aspects of textual interpretation.

2.3.1: Intentionalist Uses of Examples from Ordinary Conversations

Often, intentionalists, whether remarking on legal texts or otherwise, will employ examples from ordinary conversations in order to illustrate the obvious correctness of the meaning thesis.[3] In their view, interpretation and understanding is primarily a matter of reconstructing the intentions of a conversational partner. For example, Stanley Fish (2005) invokes the utterance, "Go through the light," which he indicates was made by his father while Fish was driving them toward an intersection with a stop light that had turned red. He describes how a textualist would see this utterance as having a literal meaning ("Don't stop, just barrel on through"), which was generated by the conventional meanings of the words actually used. The intended meaning ("As soon as the light turns green, drive straight ahead; don't turn either left or right"), though, was one that Fish could recognize but also one that his father did not express adequately through his chosen words alone. In part, Fish uses the hypothetical to argue against a distinction between sentence meaning and speaker's meaning.

Fish's example does not demonstrate what he believes it does and, as well, makes the same mistake as textualists often do in believing that the literal or ordinary meaning of a key text is more determinate than what a careful analysis would reveal. First, unless one believes that the concept of literal meaning used in Fish's hypothetical cannot take account of context, a position that no textualist would argue, Fish's view of the literal meaning of "'Go through the light'" is unpersuasive.[4] Considering the context in which it was uttered (and, undoubtedly, in many other contexts), the utterance is ambiguous (or, more properly, vague) because of its indeterminate temporal properties. Although Fish correctly identifies the interpretive possibilities, he does not properly recognize the indeterminacy of the utterance. The utterance commands the driver to go straight ahead, but it does not indicate that this should be done immediately. On one hand, one might surmise that the passenger is telling the driver to run through the red light: "go straight through the red light instead of stopping." Alternatively, and more plausibly, one may interpret "go" as not commanding instantaneous action and the utterance as thus giving the driver only a direction in which to travel: "go straight rather than turn left or right." The literal meaning of "go through the light" does not mandate either interpretation. "Go through," like various other phrases in the language, can mean different things, depending on the context and even within the same context.

While a textualist interpreter may well give the utterance the literal meaning Fish suggests, that would be a mistake of textualism, or the particular interpreter, and not a problem with literal meaning. In any case, one does not need to know the utterer's actual intent in order to interpret the utterance as not commanding the driver to run through the red light. Also, it may be questioned whether this "intent" on which Fish relies is an actual one based on evidence tied to his father or a hypothetical one that is based on Fish's generalized understanding of human motives and rationality.

The more fundamental criticism of examples such as Fish's is that they are inapposite when used to make arguments regarding the interpretation of texts, especially legal texts. When interpreting a text, it is necessary to consider the context of utterance and the context of interpretation and how the separation of these contexts should influence an approach to interpretation. The process of creating a legal text includes, of course, a context that involves the conversion of an idea into a text that expresses it through the "structured composition of words of a natural language" (Duarte 2011, 113). In turn, the context of interpretation, which involves the conversion of the text "into intellectual content, specifically, the linguistic meaning of the sentence," may be quite removed temporally and physically from the context of creation. Properly considering the separate processes of creation and interpretation requires an examination of the significant differences between typical spoken and written language and how those differences should influence how meaning and interpretation are conceived.

2.3.2: The Differences between Texts and Conversations

Although the comparison is a mistaken one, it is understandable that intentionalists would point to oral conversations as the model for the interpretation of texts. Ordinary conversation has long been seen as the prototypical form of language and the baseline against which other genres are compared (Chafe and Tannen 1987, 390). Writing has been styled by some as a "secondary modeling system," dependent on spoken language as the prior and primary system (Ong 2002). Certainly, writing is artificial in that, unlike speech which is fully natural to humans, it does not inevitably well up out of the unconscious (Ong 2002, 81). Instead, it is governed by "consciously contrived, articulable rules" (81). The artificiality and technologically driven nature of writing has, in the past, lead to skepticism about its value. In the *Phaedrus*, for example, Socrates criticized writings as but "a reminiscence of what we know" and praised oral communication as being solely capable of clearness, perfection, and seriousness. Until the work of the famous Swiss linguist, Ferdinand de Saussure (2011), and perhaps even afterwards, there was a general failure to appreciate the systematicity inherent in writing systems. For Saussure, though, rather than directly substituting for oral communication, it was crucial to understand the semiological fact that writing and speech rely on different systems of signs.

The different system of signs used in writing is driven by the separation, in typical texts, of the context of utterance from the context of interpretation. In typical written discourse, in contrast to typical spoken discourse, the context that concerns the physical setting in which an utterance is produced does not correspond to the physical setting in which the utterance is interpreted. This physical context (which Ivanic [1994] terms "Context A") is not shared in typical written discourse because the interlocutors are separated in time and space.[5] The text is thus a closed, unilateral speech act with no opportunity for linguistic replies that can help precisify indeterminate messages. Unlike the case with much oral communication, the reader of a text cannot immediately, or often ever, seek clarification from the writer of the text. This limitation on communicating via text caused Socrates to compare writing with paintings because, like writing, "the creations of the painter have the attitude of life, and yet if you ask them a question they preserve a solemn silence" (Plato, 360 B.C.E., 274–77).

In addition to the unilateral nature of a written communication, vital cues that allow for the ascertainment of a speaker's intent in an ordinary conversation are not available to the interpreter of a text. With a text, the entire message must be expressed in words. Such a message cannot convey the paralinguistic cues that typically assist the listener in a conversation in discerning the speaker's meaning. Thus, important cues such as winking, facial expressions, posture, stance, laughing, and gestures are unavailable to help discern the meaning of the utterance. In addition, with a text the words must obviously be written, making unavailable cues from prosody (rhythm, rate, stress, pitch, pitch contour, and intonation of speech), which serve an important role in determining meaning in ordinary conversation. Along with offering semantic clues, these prosodic cues contribute to the emotive or attitudinal quality of an utterance, and consequently its meaning.

Routine and important aspects of conversational interpretation are thus unavailable to the interpreter of a typical text. The lexico-grammatic choices may be the same in a given oral conversation and in a text, but the message sent by the speaker in an oral conversation can be modified by adjusting the paralinguistic and prosodic cues that are unavailable in textual utterances. Furthermore, the lack of a shared physical context means that, in typical written discourse, there is no possibility for each interlocutor to monitor the other's comprehension and degree of agreement and to adjust utterances accordingly. The lack of a shared physical context should not be underestimated because language comprehension hinges on voice-based and stereotype-dependent inferences about the speaker (Van Berkum et al. 2008). Language comprehension is immediately context dependent and is processed by the same early interpretation mechanism in the brain that constructs sentence meaning based on just the words. Language comprehension thus takes very rapid account of the social context, particularly information regarding the speaker, which indicates the centrality of these contextual cues in the final interpretation given an utterance. Little is known about how the brain actually constructs an interpretation (Van Berkum 2008). Nevertheless, research indicates that the linguistic brain uses heuristics, particularly regarding the speaker, to arrive at the earliest possible interpretation. Instead of the standard two-step model of language processing where listeners first compute a local, context-independent meaning for the sentence and then determine what it really means given the wider communicative context and the particular speaker, Van Berkum et al. (2008) maintain that research supports a one-step model in which knowledge about the speaker is brought to bear immediately by the same fast-acting brain system that combines the meaning of individual words into a larger whole.

The physical context, particularly that concerning the speaker, which is so crucial to the interpretation of oral utterances but is unavailable to assist readers of text, is, of course, also unavailable to assist writers. Ong (2002, 100) observes that the lack of verifiable context is what makes writing normally so much more agonizing an activity than oral communication. The writer's audience is, in a sense, a fiction, and the writer must set up a role in which absent and often unknown readers can cast themselves. The situation calls for much greater precision in verbalization where the individual words, and their combination, are called on to do more than in an oral conversion. The writer must communicate a message without sending paralinguistic or prosodic cues, requiring a great deal more circumspection about the possible meanings the text may have for theoretical interpreters in various contexts.

Intentionalists and others might point out, correctly, that notwithstanding the lack of a shared physical context, it does not follow that all meanings in a text must be carried *solely* by the lexico-grammatical choices made by the author. In fact, some contextual evidence is available to the interpreter of a text, as well as to the interpreter of an oral statement. Ivanic (1994) observes that, with written texts, what he terms "context B" information is sometimes accessible, which includes all the circumstances in which the text is produced, its purposes, its content, and its interlocutors, regardless of whether they are physically present. This kind of context consists of people's social purposes and meanings, their social identities and social relationships. Similarly, "context C" information is also sometimes accessible to the interpreter of texts and includes broader and more abstract institutional, cultural, and societal information relating to the context of utterance. Nevertheless, although this type of contextual interpretation is sometimes available to the interpreter of a text, the context in which the text was created is often very different from the one in which it may eventually be interpreted. Properly evaluating the context in which the text was written will therefore be much more difficult than evaluating the context in a conversation, making the process prone to erroneous inferences. Even under ideal circumstances, a consideration of cues from contexts B and C might help ascertain broad authorial intent or purpose but, unlike context A, might not help distinguish between slight variations in meanings, which are prototypically the focus of controversies involving the interpretation of legal texts.

Considering the significant differences between the context available for conversational interpretation and that available for textual interpretation, it follows that the features of textual language should differ in substantial ways from the features of conversational language. Certainly, scholars have recognized that the differences between the features of texts and oral conversations illustrate that writing is not simply visible speech (Harris 2001; Jackson 1995; Biber 1988). Kiefer (2005), for instance, points out that inquiries about meaning and intention are fundamentally different in literary interpretation than in conversational contexts. Beardsley (1992) similarly asserts that there is a special and important sense in which the authors of many literary texts are unavailable and cannot be appealed to independently of the text in order to help resolve interpretive disputes.

Others have suggested that the decoupling of the context of utterance from the context of interpretation results in a foundationally different logic for writing. Indeed, there are powerful arguments that the choice of medium both reflects and influences the ways in which we think (Jackson 1995). The difference between speech and writing is thus not merely the choice between alternative but equivalent media to communicate. To that end, scholars have made various claims about the features of texts as compared with those of conversation. These claims include assertions that texts contain fewer expressions that depend on context to fix the proper reference (Ivanic 1994) and that writing is more highly organized (Akinnaso 1982), as well as more complex, elaborate, and explicit (Olson 1977; Biber 1986). Kress (1989, 46) argues that writing "involves a logic of the nominal rather than of the verbal; of objects rather than processes; of abstraction rather than specificness/concreteness; a logic of hierarchy and of integration rather than a logic of sequence and addition." In contrast, oral language requires significantly more repetition and redundancy in order to enable the listener to comprehend an ongoing conversation (Jackson 1995), and it is the technology of writing that structures "sparsely linear" speech (Ong 2002, 40).

2.3.3: Texts as the Paradigmatic Form of Autonomous Language

Despite the broad claims about the structural features of writing versus speech, Biber (1986, 1988) has, through his empirical work, established that few (if any) absolute differences exist between speech and writing. While most studies have found that writing has a much higher degree of subordination and other markers of "structural complexity," including passive constructions, there is no single feature or dimension that distinguishes all of speaking from all of writing (Chafe and Tannen 1987). The differing features that exist do not, however, occur on a random basis. Instead, different conditions of production, as well as different intended uses, foster the creation of different features of language. There is a wide range of linguistic variation across spoken and written texts that correspond to, for example, features of social class, ethnic group, and formality, and the features of degree of lexical precision are determined by processing considerations (the restrictions of real-time production in speech vs. opportunity for extensive editing in writing) (Biber 1986). Thus, according to Biber and Gray (2010), spoken and written texts should be compared along "dimensions" of linguistic variation, such as formal/informal, interactive/noninteractive, literary/colloquial, restricted/elaborated, and common/specialized. Academic writing, for example, is structurally "compressed," with phrasal (nonclausal) modifiers embedded in noun phrases, which makes it much less explicit in meaning and more difficult for novice readers than alternative styles that employ elaborated structures (Biber and Gray 2010).

It is thus an oversimplification to view written language as intrinsically structurally elaborated, complex, formal, and abstract, and spoken language as the inverse. Rather, the relations among spoken and written texts are complex and associated with a variety of different situational, functional, and processing considerations (Biber 1988). Certainly, it is not difficult to envision many situations where speech possesses many of the characteristics commonly associated with texts. According to Kay (1977), such situations involve "autonomous" speech, which is the kind of speech ideal for technical and abstract communication among strangers. Autonomous or "elaborate" speech is minimally dependent on paralinguistic cues or the contribution of background information on the part of the hearer. Autonomous speech thus transmits information through strictly linguistic channels, thereby placing minimal reliance on the ability of the hearer to supply items of content necessary either to flesh out the body of the message or to place it in the correct interpretive context. The greater the interpersonal distance between speaker and hearer(s), the more autonomous, and less egocentric, idiosyncratic, and contextualized, must be the communicative information.

Some speech can obviously be autonomous, as Kay has explained, but writing is the paradigmatic form of "context-free" or autonomous language because it has been detached from its author (Ong 2002). In contrast to oral communication, writing offers a form of unsponsored language, which is not limited to particular categories of speech act or verbal practice. It is this detachment that explains Saussure's view that writing is not just an ad hoc appendage to speech, but, rather, that writing systems depend on different systems of signs (Harris 1989, 52). The detachment between author and text is described through the concept of "autoglottic space," which refers to the distance between writing and its author and, more particularly, the possibility that the writing may be interpreted by those who have no idea of the identity of the author. In a sense, then, the document "speaks for itself" ("auto-glotta") and is no longer "sponsored" (as is any speech act) by being identified with a particular human source. As Harris (1989) explains, utterances, even if autonomous in Kay's sense, are automatically sponsored by those who utter them, but written sentences have no sponsors and are therefore autoglottic abstractions.

Writing and its inherent autoglottic space and unique systems of signs have been said to enable forms of thought that were previously impossible (Harris 1989, 103). For instance, writing creates a greater capacity for precision and scientific objectivity (Jackson 1995, 86). It allows for a level of abstract verbal conceptualization that detaches words from their sponsors and allows for a new kind of theoretical thinking. For one thing, the restructuring of thought that writing introduces depends on prising open a conceptual gap between sentence and oral utterance (Harris 1989, 104). Such a view is central to the hermeneutical perspective on meaning. The ideality of language is especially associated with writtenness (*schriftlichkeit*). Gadamer (2004) explains that the detachment of writing both from the author and from a specifically addressed reader gives the text a life of its own. The fixed writing raises itself into a public sphere of meaning in which all readers have an equal share in its meaning. Literate cultures, with public spheres of meaning, make it relatively less difficult than in a primary oral culture to "distinguish consistently what is said and what is meant from the person who said it and the occasion on which it was said" (Harris 1989, 104). At the same time, though, the nature of texts make it more difficult to identify what was meant and are the reason why what was meant should not be the primary criterion of meaning.

2.3.4: Unsponsored Legal Texts

The differences described above between the interpretive cues available in a prototypical conversation and those available for a text are relevant to the interpretation of most texts and are particularly relevant to the interpretation of legal texts. For various reasons, legal texts are paradigmatic examples of autonomous texts that differ greatly from the prototypical personal communication context. Unlike the case with a typical oral conversation in which the linguistic brain engages in quick interpretations, interpreters of legal texts can spend a substantial amount of time constructing an interpretation. Yet, other factors make the interpretive process much more difficult.

Consider the interpretation of statutes. Unlike the typical oral conversation, the legislative context is impersonal. Legislators and interpreters do not, generally, know each other personally, making clarification impossible (absent further legislation, of course, which nevertheless cannot be seen as the continuation of a conversation in any authentic sense). Contextual information regarding the legislators' intent is often either not available or is of questionable value. For statutes, the typical source of contextual information termed "legislative history" has been widely attacked as being unreliable and subject to manipulation. Part of the reason is that the legislative process is a far less cooperative one than is the typical communicative context. The common strategic behavior is such that some, such as Marmor (2014) and Poggi (2011), have questioned the applicability of Grice's maxims of cooperation to legislation (more on this in chap. 4). Because of strategic behavior, and other legislative practices, the words of the legislative text may reflect, in a general sense, the intent of the legislature to modify the content of the law but may not have been chosen to implement the legislators' communicative intentions.[6] Further, the relevant interpreters, including judges, may have to interpret the text decades or centuries after it was created.

The differences between legal texts and typical oral conversations have been noted by a handful of scholars. Jori (1993, 2113, 2120) describes legal communication as focusing on impersonal, prescriptive, and linguistic-only signs and legal texts as being intrinsically impersonal in character with most of its features determined by the necessity of communicating messages out of context. Similarly, Jackson (1995, 86) has observed that legal texts are a "central example" of unsponsored communication. In his view, legislation is a genre in which the forms of thought characteristic of literacy have become utterly dominant, and it would be problematic to translate this, for a different audience, into forms of thought structured predominantly by oral patterns. Tiersma (2001, 433) agrees with these views and compares legal texts to messages set adrift in the currents of the ocean because the entire message must be expressed in words and may not be read and interpreted until years after its creation.

Because of their autonomous nature, Tiersma (2001) argues that legal texts need to be more semantically precise than ordinary language so that they can be understood by different people in the same way. Of course, semantic precision is desirable in an abstract sense, and legal texts must be more precise than ordinary conversations, but there are limits to the level of precision that can be expected. In natural language communication, a general sense of an expression's meaning is typically (but not always) sufficient to enable effective communication. In contrast, as the famous philosopher Gottlob Frege explained in this writings (Frege 1980, 113–14; 1997, 259), a system for formal logical reasoning requires sharpness of concepts in order to allow for gap free proofs. Are legal texts similar in nature? Can the creation of a statute be viewed as a program expressed in human language to be executed by humans rather than computers? Kowalski (1992) has observed that the linguistic style in which legislation is normally written has many similarities with the language of logic programming. Yet, notwithstanding the truth of such a claim, the comparison is flawed. Unlike logic programming, legislation is subject to the severe limitations inherent in the use of natural language, with its significant indeterminacy, not to mention the limitations of the legislative process. As this discussion of written texts versus spoken utterances has explained, the autonomous nature of legal texts creates a greater potential for misunderstanding than does oral conversations.[7] This potential for miscommunication is especially acute when the text was written by a committee or long before the relevant interpretation, in part because the relevant background information or knowledge of the circumstances that prompted the writing are less accessible. Combined with the sometimes uncooperative and strategic nature of the legislative process, these realities suggest that requests for greater semantic precision may be an infeasible way to enhance successful communications between drafters and interpreters.

Regardless of the possibilities of greater semantic precision, due to autoglottic space and the unsponsored nature of legal texts, some scholars have suggested that intent should be defined differently when a legal text is being interpreted than it would be with respect to a speaker's utterance in a typical conversation. Tiersma (2001, 440) argues that while "virtually any linguist would agree that the goal of interpretation is to determine what the speaker or author intends to communicate to his audience," an interpreter must recognize that an autonomous text must be interpreted as such. Thus, the interpreter determines the intent of the writer on the basis of what is contained in the text and must assume that that the words have been used in an "ordinary" or "literal" sense. Jackson (1995) similarly argues that statutory language should normally be regarded as unsponsored language via a model of sentence meaning rather than utterer's meaning.

Tiersma (2001) and Jackson (1995) have correctly advocated that many legal texts should be considered unsponsored.[8] While this book will argue that there is often a gap between the literal meaning and the ordinary meaning of a legal text, such a distinction does not undermine the basic premise of Tiersma and Jackson about unsponsored legal texts. The unsponsored nature of legal texts, with their concomitant autoglottic space, should have various consequences, including underscoring the necessity of the ordinary meaning doctrine in legal interpretation. Their unsponsored nature would seem to require that interpreters place sustained, if not exclusive, attention on textual rather than extratextual authorial evidence. More precisely, it would seem to require that textual meaning, as opposed to authorial meaning, be the primary determinant of the communicative meaning of a legal text. Designating legal texts as unsponsored also illustrates the unpersuasiveness of intentionalist arguments that use examples from ordinary conversations. An intentionalist account of interpretation that fails to address the fundamental differences between ordinary conversations and legal texts thus undermines any argument that the meaning of a text is identical to the author's intended meaning and that interpretation consists of discovering that meaning.

2.4: Intentionalist Claims about Language

2.4.1: Fixed Meanings and Intentionalist Claims about the Necessity of Reference to Authorial Intent

Viewing legal texts as unsponsored and not analogous to ordinary conversations supports a theory of interpretation that would give a prominent role to the ordinary meaning concept and its reliance on conventions of meaning, but intentionalists make other arguments about language and interpretation not yet considered that, if persuasive, would undermine reliance on conventions. Fish (2005, 633), for example, argues that the definition of "interpretation" is limited to the search for authorial intent because "words do not carry fixed or even relatively fixed meanings." Fish's position that words do not have even relatively fixed meanings would, if true, seriously undermine any reliance on conventions of meaning. In fact, if taken seriously, it would counsel that authors are the only parties qualified to interpret their own works.

Notwithstanding the ideality of language, assertions about the absence of inherent lexical meaning or the reality of diachronic (i.e., development over time) fluctuations in word meanings do not further an intentionalist agenda. In a narrow sense, any linguist or philosopher of language should agree with certain intentionalist assertions about language. With respect to natural language, it is the users of language that determine whether signs will convey meaning and what meaning the signs will convey (Cruse 1983). That is, the marks on a page that any given community of speakers agrees to interpret as words do not contain any *inherent* meaning. As Jackson (1995, 18–19) observes, neither the sound d-o-g nor the written characters "dog" inherently refer to a member of the subspecies *canis lupus familiaris* (which is itself a conventional term). Rather, the reference is natural, and seemly inherent, to English speakers due to the strength of the convention that "dog" refers to [dog]. Saussure (2011, 67) referred to this phenomenon as the "arbitrary nature of the sign." That is, there is typically an arbitrary connection between a "sound-image," or signifier, and a "concept," or signified. Saussure explained that, "if words stood for pre-existing concepts, they would all have exact equivalents in meaning from one language to the next; but this is not true" (2011, 116). For the most part, the connection between signifier and signified is not rational or natural but is instead conventional. Thus, it would be just as rational for d-o-g to refer to a member of the group of organisms that consist of all gill-bearing aquatic craniate animals that lack limbs with digits (i.e., "fish") as it would for it to refer to a member of the subspecies *canis lupus familiaris*.

While words have the meanings that are assigned to them by the users of language, these meanings are independent of any particular authorial intention. Indeed, as has been observed by some scholars, various combinations of words can create meaningful sentences that have never been uttered at all. The nature of language easily allows for such possibilities. Verbs select the events and nouns select the entities that allow us to individuate happenings and events in the world. Identifying the meanings of verbs and nouns requires distinguishing their meanings from the happenings and entities in the world that they describe in a particular use. The lexicalized, or context-invariant, meaning, determined on the basis of grammatical behavioral patterns in the data, consists of those properties that are shared across all uses of a verb or noun, regardless of context. When a noun is chosen to describe an entity in the world, a claim is being made that the entity has the attributes lexicalized by the noun, though it may also have other attributes. Two nouns may refer to the same entity, but in lexicalizing different attributes, they may construe it as an entity in different ways. Similarly, a single verb can be applied to quite different happenings, and two verbs may lexicalize distinct but partially overlapping sets of attributes yet be able to refer to the same happening out in the world. Nevertheless, when a verb is chosen to describe an event, a comment is made regarding certain attributes present in the chain of happenings in the world being referred to by that verb. For example, Botne (2001) has produced a crosslinguistic study showing that verbs of dying fall into four major types that can be differentiated according to which stages of the dying process they lexicalize. The Acute Type lexicalize the point of death alone, while the Transitional Type lexicalize the onset, the point of death, and the result.

Speakers are thus constrained by the lexicalized meaning of verbs (and nouns). Consider a situation where the speaker wishes to convey that a table has been dried. In choosing an appropriate verb, the speaker must consider that there are verb pairs where each member lexicalizes distinct sets of attributes in the same stream of happenings (Levin and Rappaport Hovav 1995). The speaker could describe the scenario using the verb "wipe" or the verb "dry."

(1)   a. Kelly wiped the table with a tea towel.
      b. Kelly dried the table with a tea towel.

"Wipe" is a manner (as opposed to result) verb that involves nonscalar changes, which means that it is not characterizable in terms of a scale, that is, an ordered set of degrees along a dimension representing a single attribute. The lack of an ordering relation and complexity are the two properties that contribute to making a change nonscalar (Rappaport Hovav and Levin 2010). The vast majority of nonscalar change verbs, such as "wipe," involve a complex combination of many changes at once, so that there is no single, privileged scale of change. If the speaker uses "wiped," as in (1a), the speaker will have said nothing about whether the table has actually been dried, though perhaps some hearers would assume that it has been.[9] Unlike "dry," "wipe," like "scrub," involves a specific pattern of movement of the hand and arm that is repeated an indefinite number of times against a surface but, collectively, does not represent a change in the values of one attribute, nor is any one element in the sequence of movements a necessary starting point of the activity. Thus, absent additional, revealing facts in the context that would add information about the lexicalized meaning of the verb, the speaker cannot use "wipe" and insist that the hearer should understand that the table has been dried.

2.4.2: *Intentionalist Arguments About the Creativity of Language*

Fish and other intentionalists also argue that existing linguistic conventions (if they exist) do not impose any constraints on the ability of individuals to give words new meanings. From a diachronic perspective, it is, of course, correct that the meanings of words can change. Knapp and Michaels (1987) correctly point out that in everyday life people frequently give new meanings to words and phrases and that this is a natural way in which language develops. The existence of linguistic conventions does not preclude these items from obtaining new meanings, as conventions can change. Thus, the philosopher Ludwig Wittgenstein (1953, 18) is correct that one can say "bububu" and mean, "If it doesn't rain I shall go for a walk." Under certain conditions (unusual if a text is involved), a successful communicative effort may even result from these instances of linguistic creativity.

Conceding the uncontroversial fact of linguistic creativity does not, however, entail that individual speakers have autonomy over the meanings of their utterances, nor does it undermine the reality that word meanings are independent of authorial communicative intention. As Wilson (1992) argues, there are an unbounded number of "available" meaningful sentences in any natural language that have never been uttered, and may never be uttered. They are meaningful due to conventions of meaning, and any speaker is part of a linguistic community in which conventions thrive. Meaning may originate in individuals, but conventional meaning derives from individuals as restricted by their group's conventions (von Savigny 1985). While conventional meanings undoubtedly change over time, it does not follow that the rate of linguistic change exceeds efforts to determine a word's conventional meaning at any particular time. If this were true, successful communication via texts, as well as a great deal of oral communication, would be impossible.

Much literary and linguistic analysis is based on the understanding that words have meanings outside of any specific author's intent, and language could not get started if they did not. If signs did not contain meanings outside of authorial intent, literary concepts like symbolism, simile, metaphor, irony, synecdoche, metonymy, exaggeration, and sarcasm, which depend on a gap between sign and signified, would be incoherent. Because of autoglottic space, these concepts are more difficult to discern in texts than in oral conversations. Nevertheless, their effectiveness depends on conventions of meaning. Similarly, if the effort to capture specific authorial intent represented the only permissible definition of interpretation,

there could only be "empirical" failures (as Fish puts it) to discover meaning, but there could be no such concept as ambiguity.[10] At the least, there
would be no such thing as *unintentional* ambiguity. Natural languages
(and especially legal language), though, are considered to be pervasively
indeterminate by linguists (Tabossie and Zardon 1993).

Furthermore, if words had no meaning outside an author's specific intent, there would be no need to distinguish between semantics and pragmatics. At a basic level, though, such a distinction is important and necessary, although the dividing line between the two has been subject to much
debate. One common conception of semantics is that it involves computing truth conditions of utterances compositionally according to the types
of expressions used in the utterances and the ways they are combined.
"Truth conditions" are the "conditions a world must meet in order for a
proposition [i.e., a sentence] to be true" (Murphy and Koskela 2010, 36).
In turn, the principle of compositionality "states that the meaning of a
complex linguistic expression is built up from the meanings of its composite parts in a rule-governed fashion" (Murphy and Koskela 2010, 36).
Thus, a sentence is compositional if its meaning is the sum of the meanings of its parts and of the relations of the parts.

Sentences are not always compositional, however, and violations of
compositionality create a conflict between form and meaning (Moravcsik
2006, 111). For example, idiomatic phrases, such as "He went ballistic," involve meanings that are not captured compositionally by the meanings of
the composite parts. In addition to being an issue within semantics, violations of compositionality are studied within the field of pragmatics, which
concerns information "generated by, or at least made relevant by, the act
of uttering the sentence" (Bach 2002, 284). The proper definition of pragmatics is disputed, and will be addressed in greater detail in chapter 3, but
in a general sense the field attempts to explain how "extra meaning (in
a broad sense) is 'read into' utterances without actually being encoded
in them" (Levinson 1983, 11). Thus, as the descriptions of semantics and
pragmatics illustrate, a fundamental and well-established principle of a
central area of study in linguistics (namely, semantics) is that words have
meanings outside of any specific context.

2.4.3: Further Intentionalist Arguments about Meaning

Notwithstanding the existence of author-independent word meanings,
intentionalists make various related arguments that insist that interpretation of a text is impossible without reference to an author. If, so the

arguments go, reference to an author or authors is a necessary aspect of interpretation then all interpretation is intentionalist in nature (Robertson 2009). Some of these intentionalist arguments are true, sometimes trivially so, but none establish the intentionalist meaning or interpretation theses. Contrary to intentionalist arguments, one can agree that generalized assumptions about authorial intent are unavoidable in any interpretive effort but disagree that ascertaining specific communicative authorial intent is necessary to determining meaning.

One intentionalist argument about the necessity of an interpreter's reference to authorial intent is that the interpreter must either actually know or assume various things about texts. Thus, for example, intentionalists assert that no text by itself declares the language in which it is written (Alexander and Prakash 2003; Knapp and Michael 2005). An interpreter must therefore assume that the Constitution and statutes, and other legal documents, are written in English, thereby giving the interpretation an intentionalist focus. This observation, though, does not add support to any intentionalist arguments and, if anything, undermines them. Simply put, why would a document (at least one that is more than a word or two) *need* to proclaim the language in which it is written?

Deciding that a text is written in English does not depend on assumptions about authorial intent. One does not need to know *anything* about an author, or any broader nontextual context, to discern the language in which a document is written. Sufficient clues about the language of the text can be found in the text itself. Determining the language of a text depends on the interpreter's ability to identify the English language based on syntactic, semantic, morphological, and other linguistic evidence. Under normal circumstances, it is not clear why an author's intent would even be relevant in such a situation, or why an author would bother to make such an intent known. Also, if the author proclaims that a given text is written in language X (say, French) but the syntax, morphology, and lexicon is clearly that of language Y (say, English), in what sense could the author's proclamation sensibly be said to govern? Even if one accepts Knapp and Michael's (2005) hypothetical where two languages (which they term English and "Schmenglish") look exactly alike except for their semantics, there is no doubt that an interpreter could identify a text (again, unless it is very short), with no reference to the author, on the basis of its semantics.[11]

A related argument regarding the inevitability of intentionalism is that an interpreter must acknowledge or assume an author with an intention whenever the interpreter is interpreting a meaningful text (Knapp and

Michaels 1982). Thus, Alexander and Prakash (2004, 976) argue that "one cannot look at the marks on a page and understand those marks to be a text (that is, a meaningful writing) without assuming that an author made those marks intending to convey a meaning by them." Similarly, Fish (2005, 635) argues that "lexical items and grammatical structures by themselves will yield no meaning—will not even be seen as lexical items and grammatical structures—until they are seen as having been produced by some intentional agent." At the outset, it seems as though the argument regarding the necessity of intentions should be summarily rejected. One problem is that the intentionalist arguments beg the meaning of "meaningful." For instance, language is perfectly capable of being analyzed for various purposes without referencing an author, or even assuming that one exists. That is, marks are analyzable as lexical items and grammatical structures without referencing an author in any concrete way. More importantly, though, even if this point is conceded, referencing the existence of an author's general intent to communicate via a text is using the concept of intent at a very high level of generality, rather than in a narrow way to signify the communicative intent of some specific meaning. By itself, the high level of abstraction at which intent is framed makes the fact of intent a triviality. Who would deny that an author of a text had an intention of conveying *some* meaning through the text? For what other purpose are texts created?

Despite the triviality of the intentional author argument, intentionalists intend for a strong inference to be drawn from the indisputable fact that an author has some sort of communicative intention when creating a text. More specifically, for the same reasons that it is impossible to have a text without an author, the intentionalist position is to deny the possibility of a distinction between textual meaning and author's meaning. Thus, Knapp and Michaels (1982, 724) assert that "[t]he clearest example of the tendency to generate theoretical problems by splitting apart terms that are in fact inseparable is the persistent debate over the relation between authorial intention and the meaning of texts." This strong intentionalist inference is not, however, persuasive. A concession that a text has been created by an author with some general intent to communicate does not entail that authorial intention and the meaning of texts are coterminous. Rather, it is possible to concede the relevance of broad authorial intent yet deny the relevance (or at least the decisiveness) of authorial intent to communicate some specific meaning.

As the above arguments illustrate, a fundamental problem for intentionalists is their tendency to conflate distinct aspects of intent with different degrees of generality. Instead, a distinction must be made between intentionally creating something in a simple agentive sense and creating it with a specific intention (Kiefer 2005). Artworks may be intentionally created, but Kiefer questions whether many of them are created with a specific intention. He mentions in this connection examples such as Pollack's action painting (involving a style in which paint is spontaneously dribbled, splashed, or smeared onto the canvas, rather than being carefully applied), minimalist sculpture, and a hypothetical painter who claims he is just painting, period. He argues that if artworks are not created with specific intentions, understanding that they are the product of intentional activity will give us little or no information that could contribute to an appreciative understanding of them.

Similarly, with literary works, consider a division based on the type, and generality, of intention. With respect to these works, Levinson (2002) distinguishes between *semantic intentions* and *categorical intentions*. Categorical intentions, which are actual intentions, relate to the status of works as literature and to their categorical or genre location within literature. A categorical intention is a desire that a text be classified, taken, or approached in some specific or general way, such as literature or art (Levinson 2002, 232). They amount to metasemantic intentions regarding what sorts of meaning are to be sought in given works. Thus, they involve intentions regarding the approximate nature of the work, but not the precise import (Levinson 2002, 314).

The distinction drawn by Levinson between categorical and semantic intentions, as well as his assertion that categorical intentions rest on actual authorial intent, may have flaws, but the arguments underscore the conflation of different types of intent in the intentionalists' arguments.[12] There are multiple levels of generality associated with the concept of intent, as was discussed at the beginning of the chapter. When interpreting a statute, one can, for example, consider intent narrowly as what was said or, more broadly, as how the legislature intended to modify the content of the law (Greenberg 2011). Of course, intent can be framed even more broadly as the intent to author a text with a meaningful content. These different levels of intent are not, however, freely substitutable. An assertion, posed at a very high level of generality, that an author must have had a communicative intention when creating a text does not suggest, let alone entail, that the identity of much more specific intentions can be determined or are relevant to meaning or interpretation. One can concede intent on a metasemantic level yet deny it at more specific levels without any inconsistency. Thus, one can acknowledge, for example, that Congress (almost certainly) had an actual intent to write in English or to enact a binding statute yet deny that any actual authorial intent is relevant to the meaning of a provision that, for example, provides for a sentence enhancement when a defendant uses a firearm in relation to a drug offense.[13]

Further issues complicate intentionalist claims that the meaning of a text is coterminous with authorial intent. Somewhat related to intentionalists' conflation of different levels of intent is their failure to recognize that the supposed "actual" intentions to which they refer are frequently assumed rather than discerned. Often, if an appeal to authorial intent is made, the basis must be a generalized assumption, such as one that authors intend to write in the language that is expected by the audience for which the document is written, not one based on any specific communicative intent. Such generalized, and often fictional, assumptions, however, cannot be seen as intentionalist, within the definition of intentionalism that actual intentionalists defend, but instead are similar to the conventions that intentionalists criticize. A generalized assumption may be framed by the interpreter as something that captures authorial intention, but it is one that is imputed to the author and is thus not an actual intention. Fish (1989, 329) argues that interpretation is not a two-stage process in which the interpreter first finds the context-independent meaning and then consults the relevant context. Instead, the "semantic meaning" cannot be selected independently of a context of assumptions, concerns, priorities, and expectations. This point is correct and was made earlier when describing the work of Van Berkum and the distinctions between oral utterances and texts. In addition, the contribution that context makes to meaning is explored in later chapters and is in fact one of the major themes of this book. But the context that Fish describes must necessarily apply to all interpreters and methodologies. Similar to other methodologies, an intentionalist therefore cannot determine actual authorial intent independent of assumptions, concerns, priorities, and expectations, which are not tied to any actual intent but which will invariably shape and distort that task.

2.4.4: The Collective Intent Problem

Another issue for actual intentionalism that is often glossed over involves the collective intent problem that exists whenever a text has multiple authors (or is seen as being the creation of more than one party).[14] Actual intentionalism is especially difficult to reconcile with contract law. A contract is formed between two or more parties, each with an equal stake in its interpretation. In a situation where one of the parties drafted a written contract, it would be odd to insist that the meaning of the contract was identical to the drafter's intent, without regard to the views of the other party to the contract. If the contract is conceived of as having been drafted by both (or all) of the parties, one must concede that the parties might have sincerely held but differing views regarding the meaning of the terms. Resorting to some objective theory of interpretation is thus appropriate. Not surprisingly, courts do use objective theories of interpretation when interpreting contracts.[15]

Collective intent problems are also present in the interpretation of statutes. As Marmor (2005, 126) describes, "legislation in legislative assemblies is a complex and concerted action involving elaborate procedures." With statutes, any given clause or sentence may reflect various intentions, at different levels of generality, which reflect the many authors and their varied motivations. Some of the members of the legislature may vote for the bill in hopes that it will be interpreted in a broader or narrower manner than its terms would indicate. The identity of the utterer is thus a matter of dispute. Is it the legislature as a unit, all legislators considered collectively, the legislators who voted for the legislation or only those who read it, the drafter(s) of the legislation (even if not legislators themselves?), the sponsor(s) of the legislation, or some other possibility? Furthermore, what about the intentions of the president who signed the bill into law? The myriad of possibilities indicates that there is therefore no singular intention to which an appeal can easily be made, although some scholars have argued for various proxies for communicative intent. The proxies, though, must reflect some theory by which to attribute intent to some group representing the majority of the legislators based on the intent of a subset of that group.[16]

A familiar intentionalist response to the collective intent problem, apart from arguing for a proxy for collective intent, is to emphasize at a high level of generality the intentional aspects of legislation. Posner (1986, 195) makes the claim that a "document can manifest a single purpose even though those who drafted and approved it had a variety of private motives and expectations." Marmor (2014) makes a somewhat different claim, observing that legislation is a speech act that is done intentionally and that if legislatures cannot act with a collective intention then enactment cannot be a speech act either.[17] Marmor argues that, if one doubts that it is possible to attribute collective intentions to a legislature, it would be difficult to assert that judges should take seriously the communicative content of the law rather than simply ascertaining what the law aimed to achieve. But a concern with the communicative content of the law need not rest on any specific intent of the legislature and can be justified, as will be discussed in chapter 3, on other grounds. In addition, Marmor's argument, like those of other intentionalists, including Posner (1986), conflates different levels of generality regarding intent. One may accept at a very general level of intent that a legislature had the intent to enact a statute and did so in order to accomplish some purpose. Such an observation, though, is not necessarily relevant to any particular interpretive dispute (which often occurs at the margins of the enacted law). One can still deny that specific aspects of the communicative intent of the legislature are discernible, if they can be said to exist at all. An intentionalism that is based on something other than generalized intent is not always (and maybe never) possible because the author (or authors) does not always have a specific communicative intention regarding the interpretive dispute at issue. Rather, it is typical that the author or authors failed to form any intent or neglected to consider the issue at all. This is especially true with legislation because, due to the enormous volume of legislation and other reasons, most legislators do not read most of the text of the statutes on which they vote. Even if some proxy for legislative intent is used, such as a committee report, the same problems remain.

2.4.5: Arguments about the Necessity of Reference to Authorial Intent

Apart from the intentionalist claim that an interpreter must, in a general sense, always acknowledge or assume an author with an intention, intentionalists make other arguments regarding the necessity of reference to authorial intent. One of these arguments is that language, being underspecified, is indeterminate without reference to authorial intent, even if one concedes the well-established principle that words have conventional meanings independent of any individual author's specific intention. Consider intentionalist examples used to make the point that authorial intent is necessary for disambiguation. Knapp and Michaels (2005), taking an example from Scalia (1997), argue that the sentence

(2) I took the boat out on the bay

can be interpreted as meaning "I went sailing" (A_1), as opposed to *both* "I went sailing" (A_1) and "I used the horse to carry the dingy" (A_2), only by reference to an author's specific communicative intent. If the point is merely that the meaning of a term or sentence *in abstracto* can be indeterminate, ambiguous, or otherwise uncertain, the point is trivial. An obvious example involves indexicals (such as "I," "now," "here," and "today"), which necessarily have content that is relative to the context of utterance.[18] The reference of "I," for instance, obviously shifts depending on the identity of the speaker. Another common example of context dependence involves quantifiers, which modify a referring expression in terms of amount.[19] Using an example from Wilson (1992), if a speaker asserts, "Every napkin is frayed," it is likely that the seemingly universal quantifier "every" was meant to be restricted to some smaller domain such as "in the house" or "on the table." The linguistic meaning that a sentence *S* expresses acontextually is not, therefore, as a rule sufficient to determine what Wilson terms the "context-loaded linguistic meaning" that S expresses on an occasion of utterance. Every commentator on language must concede this point, which should be uncontroversial.

Intentionalists, though, make claims about clarity and indeterminacy that are broader than the principle that expressions are context dependent. Knapp and Michaels (2005, 655), for instance, argue that if one believes that the meaning of a text is the sort of thing that authors can try to express clearly, and of clarity as something they can either achieve or fail to achieve, then a commitment has been made to the idea that the text means what the author meant by it. They argue that, in (2) if one is not interested in what the author meant by the text, the interpreter might look up "bay" in the dictionary but not have any idea which of the multiple meanings is the most appropriate. Knapp and Michaels claim that the problem would be an ontological one, rather than an epistemic one, because the meanings would be correct. To them, the conclusion is that every text would mean everything its words could mean in the language in which it was written. Thus, the only way a sentence like, "I took the boat out on the bay," can be interpreted to mean, "I went sailing," instead of, "I used the horse to carry the dingy," is by reference to what its speaker means.

The broader intentionalist claims about the necessity of ascertaining specific communicative intent are unpersuasive. While authorial intent, if available and discernible, could, of course, serve to disambiguate language, other evidence can also disambiguate. Under any circumstances, the mental intention of the utterer or author is not directly observable or assessable. Other evidence of intent may also be unavailable to the interpreter. If a text is involved, especially a legal text, prosodic and other author specific evidence may not exist, and the author may not be available for clarification (or it may be inappropriate or unhelpful to seek clarification from the author). For purposes of resolving the communicative indeterminacy of a text, a competent interpreter's rational belief regarding the author's intentions is more plausible than ascertaining those intentions themselves. In such cases, meaning is discerned through determinants that may surpass the author's intentions, such as conventions of language and context (including earlier expressions). Thus, Wimsatt and Beardsley (1946) correctly reject the idea that an author's intent is a valid ground for arguing the presence of a meaning but indicate that this rejection does not cover situations where the intention is found in, or inferred from, the work itself.

Authorial intent found in the work itself may include sentential evidence, which can disambiguate words, and broader textual evidence, which can disambiguate words as well as sentences and paragraphs. Thus, in (2), even without any evidence of specific authorial communicative intent, the sentence, "I took the boat out on the bay," means, "I used the horse to carry the dingy," if, for example, surrounding sentences describe the horse and the hitching of the dingy to the horse. Similarly, it is not difficult to imagine surrounding sentences that would disambiguate (2) to mean that the author went sailing. Thus, contrary to intentionalist assertions about meaning, it can be argued that nontextual evidence of specific authorial intent may be *sufficient* to disambiguate words and sentences, but it is incorrect to assert that it is always *necessary* evidence. Rather, sentential and broader contextual evidence is often sufficient to disambiguate. While an intentionalist would respond that sentential and other contextual evidence is relevant because it helps to identify what the author actually meant, such a response would be inaccurate. Contextual evidence is not evidence of what the author actually meant, but rather evidence that an intended interpreter could use to gauge what the author was trying to convey in employing a given verbal vehicle in the given communicative context.

2.4.6: Intentionalism and Anomalous Meanings

As the above discussion illustrates, discerning actual authorial intentions is not necessary in determining meaning, and these intentions are typically unavailable in any case. Interpreters must rely instead on conventions of meaning and other objective determinants of meaning. Intentionalists at-

tempt to integrate conventions of meaning into an intentionalist framework by arguing that, if an interpreter views a text as having a clear conventional meaning, it is because the interpreter either assumes or knows
that the author intended to employ those conventions (Robertson 2009).
As argued earlier, an interpreter relying on a generalized assumption that
an author intends to employ conventions should not be seen as actual intentionalism. Rather, such an act is itself the creation or application of a
convention, not the evaluation of evidence that would reveal actual communicative intent. Intentionalists argue, though, that while conventional
meanings and context may be relevant evidence to a choice between two
or more meanings, an interpreter can never rely on conventional meaning
alone (or, one would assume, syntax or other text related information) to
determine the meaning of a text. The reason is that the speaker may have
intended some anomalous meaning. Thus, in any given situation, an interpreter cannot know whether any word or sentence has the conventional
meaning or some unconventional meaning unless reference is made to the
intention of the author.

Knapp and Michaels (1987), for instance, argue that conventions have
no intrinsic power to give a text a meaning that makes sense for an interpreter to select as an alternative to, or in addition to, the author's intended
meaning. Such a position suggests that it is always (or at least usually)
possible to discern an author's actual intended meaning without regard
to conventions and other generalized assumptions about intent. But unless the author and interpreters are members of the same speech community, sharing a lexicon and similar rules of grammar, linguistic communication is impossible. Considering the unsponsored nature of many texts,
with their inherent autoglottic space, a position that it is routinely possible
to determine authorial communicative intent without the aid of conventions and other generalized assumptions is naïve (at best). Conventions
exist, at least partly, because they are devices necessary to interpretation,
especially the interpretation of legal texts. Often, there is little other relevant evidence on which to rely.

Apart from the practical necessity of reliance on conventions, a determination that the author intended some unconventional meaning is inherently problematic. Of course, if there is accessible public evidence of such
an intention, such as a stipulated definition or persuasive contextual information, determining that an unconventional meaning was intended can
be uncontroversial. Imagine, though, that an author intends for the text to
have an unconventional meaning but gives no explicit indications of this

intent. In such a situation, intentionalists still insist that the meaning of the text conforms to the author's intent. In fact, they argue that although it is sensible to use conventional meanings in order to achieve successful communications with others, doing so is a pragmatic decision, rather than a meaning constraint, and is determined by the outcome one wants to achieve. Intentionalists must therefore be committed to the following proposition: a text T means p, even in situations in which the audience is justified in concluding that the text means q, if and only if the author intended it to mean p. Tellingly, the intentionalist position does not recognize that the author's actual semantic intentions may have been unsuccessfully implemented, making the text mean something other than what the author intended it to mean.[20]

The insistence that an utterance or text means just what its author intends it to mean, even if the audience is justified in giving it some other meaning, is unconvincing. The problem is that the intentionalist argument about the potential of anomalous meanings ignores essential constraints on meaning, thereby making communicative success mysterious. By privileging the speaker's intent, intentionalism adopts Humpty Dumpty's philosophy: "When I use a word," Humpty Dumpty said, in rather a scornful tone, "it means just what I choose it to mean-neither more nor less" (Carroll 1971, 190–91). With authorial intentions as the basis for meaning, a speaker's uses of expressions refer to anything the speaker chooses. Humpty Dumpty is claiming the right to change the meaning of a word not through ex-ante public stipulation but through a private mental act. Given speaker confusion, carelessness, mistake, or a disordered mental state, the possibilities for anomalous meaning are vast. As Gorvett (2005) argues, if intentionalism is accepted there would appear to be nothing preventing bizarre referring expressions, such as using "I" to refer to one's uncle, boss, or the Pope (assuming the Pope is not the author). While intentionalists argue that such bizarre referring expressions are perfectly acceptable as a linguistic matter (in the sense that there are no inherent language-based constraints on the dynamic use of language), hearers have little access to what people have in mind apart what they say or write. Hearers, thus, cannot accurately use an interpretive method that depends on the hearer's ability to have independent insight into the speaker's intentions. Interpretation would be potentially unsolvable if hearers were required to have knowledge of the speaker's intent in order to ascertain the content of the context. In order for interpretation to proceed via a reliable method, the interpreter must have access to the determinants of meaning, independently of what proposition the speaker attempts to express.

2.5: Moderate Intentionalism

2.5.1: Description of Moderate Intentionalism

Faced with the damaging Humpty Dumpty problem, some intentionalists nevertheless maintain the meaning thesis even when the author's intention fails. Whether an intentionalist insists on the meaning thesis depends on that individual's view of communication theory. Consider Grice's (1969, 151) view that "*U* meant something by uttering *x*" is true if and only if, for some audience *A*, *U* uttered *x* intending

I.   *A* to produce a particular response *r*,
II. *A* to think (recognize) that *U* intends (I),
III. *A* to fulfill (I) on the basis of his fulfillment of (II).

According to Grice, the interpreter of a conversational utterance asks himself the question, "What intentions best explain the utterance of my (actual) interlocutor? In other words, what does she have in mind that would lead her to say precisely this?" One view of Grice's theory is that the utterer cannot end up meaning something other than what he intends to mean. He may fail to mean anything, but he cannot mean the wrong thing.

There is a different view of intentionalism, though, that is similarly based on communication theory. In order for an author to have a semantic or other intention, the author must believe that the intention has some chance of being fulfilled (Donnellan 1968). If so, a stipulation that the work must support the artist's intention follows from Grice's analysis of meaning outlined above where *A* must intend his utterance to be recognized as so intended (Carroll 2011). Hirsch (1967, 31) calls the limits that convention places on meaning the "Humpty-Dumpty effect" and indicates that, "when somebody does in fact use a particular word sequence, his verbal meaning cannot be anything he might wish it to be," but is sometimes "excluded from language by the linguistic norms that actually obtain." Consequently, Hirsch defines meaning as "whatever someone has willed to convey by a particular sequence of linguistic signs and which can be conveyed (shared) by means of those linguistic signs."[21] Davidson

(1986) similarly argues that one cannot intend to accomplish something by a certain means unless one believes that the means will, or at least could, lead to the desired outcome. Under such an understanding of communication, Davidson (1986) notes that there is no doubt that Humpty Dumpty was entirely aware that Alice would fail to interpret "There's glory for you" as meaning "there's a nice knockdown argument for you." Hence, Humpty Dumpty's utterance cannot mean what he says it means.

In ways similar to Hirsch and Davidson, various other intentionalists have sought to avoid the Humpty Dumpty problem by focusing on theories of successful communication, thereby modifying the meaning and interpretation theses and, in their view, distinguishing the interpretation of art and texts from the comprehension of ordinary linguistic communications. These intentionalists, often calling themselves "moderate intentionalists" (or "weak intentionalists"), have introduced constraints on actual intentionalism that require that the correct interpretation be one that is compatible with the author's actual intentions and that is also "supported" or "manifestly realized" by the work or "meshes" with it (Carroll 2000, 2011; Stecker and Davies 2010; Livingston 2005; Iseminger 1992; Stokke 2010). According to the theory, actual intentions play an ineliminable role in specifying meaning (Stecker 2006). Moderate intentionalists concede, however, that an author may intend his text to mean something but fail to give it that, or perhaps any, meaning (Goldsworthy 2005). Where the author's intention is not realized, the work does not mean what was intended and the interpretive efforts focus on constructing a meaning that is different from the one that was unsuccessfully intended (Davies 2006). In such cases, the meaning of the work is its textual meaning (Carroll 2011). Moderate intentionalism thus attempts to "unify" intentionalist and conventionalist determinants of meaning by maintaining authorial intentions as the focus but limiting those intentions to successful ones. At the same time, these moderate intentionalists contemplate a clear distinction between "utterance meaning" (i.e., "what is said") and what the author means (Iseminger 1996, 321).

While moderate intentionalists agree that constraints on authorial intent must exist, they suggest slightly different formulations of those constraints. All the formulations refer to a different kind of meaning than utterance meaning, which focuses solely on objective criteria of meaning. One common formulation of moderate intentionalism refers to an "uptake constraint" (Stokke 2010). Stecker, for example (2006, 429), proposes that an utterance means X if

I.   The utterer intends X;
II.   The utterer intends that her audience will grasp this in virtue of the conventional meaning of her words or a contextually supported extension of this meaning permitted by conventions; and
III. The first intention (I) is graspable in virtue of those conventions (identified in II) or permitted extensions of them.

The issue in these formulations concerns the strength of the uptake condition, identified in III. In order to for the uptake condition to be satisfied, a key question is whether the author's intent must be the one *most likely* to secure uptake from the appropriate audience, or is it successful if the work *can* be read in accordance with the intended meaning even if other meanings are more likely to be attributed to the work by the audience (Davies 2006).

Other tactics are possible if one wants to remain an actual intentionalist, rather than a moderate intentionalist, but still address the Humpty Dumpty problem. One possibility is to have a system that explicitly associates meaning with utterer's meaning and successful communicative intent with the meaning an interpreter would give the text. Akerman (2009), for example, argues for a distinction between the *correct interpretation* and the *reasonable interpretation*. The correct interpretation is determined by the speaker's intention. The reasonable interpretation is determined by external standards and is the interpretation the audience may legitimately take to be the correct one. Akerman argues that there are two routes to the "correct" interpretation, which is the meaning intended by the speaker. One way is to have direct access to the determinants of the meaning. The other is to take the external evidence into account and infer the values of the parameters from this evidence. Although the relation between the determinants and the evidence is different between the two cases, there is typically a reliable connection between them. In Akerman's view, cases of mismatch occur when relevant intuitions about the determinants track the *reasonable* interpretation rather than the *correct* interpretation. In such cases of mismatch, communication is likely to fail, and the speaker is to blame. But this does not show that the correct interpretation is the one that the audience would be likely to arrive at, rather than the one intended by the speaker.

Similar to Akerman, Predelli (2002) defends a theory that distinguishes between meaning and interpretation. Under Predelli's theory, reference is a relationship between a word and an object, but one that does not require or entail successful communication. A distinction must thus be made between a term referring to a referent and a term being *used* to refer. That a word refers to an object does not mean that it can necessarily be used to communicate a thought about that object. In Predelli's picture, the role of the speaker's intention is to determine the context with respect to which the word should be interpreted. A speaker can intend her use of a word to be evaluated with respect to any context whatsoever. While the word always refers pursuant to the utterer's intent (and thus the intent provides the "correct" meaning), it cannot always be used to refer to any context whatsoever. Instead, the hearer's ability to interpret the utterance limits a word's possible referring uses.

Table 2.1 reflects the two intentionalist theories introduced above. Notice that intentionalist theories such as Akerman's and Predelli's accept the notion of utterance meaning. It is not clear, however, how the Akerman and Predelli distinction between the "correct" interpretation and the reasonable or hearer's interpretation is a useful one. Specifically, it is not clear why in a case of unsuccessful communication the author's intended meaning is the correct one even though the audience is justified in choosing a different meaning. For one, as explained earlier, the meaning of the text can transcend the author's communicative meaning. Thus, what is said has autonomy from what the author meant by the words. More generally, the meaning of texts, like utterances, is not reducible to the author's intentions because language is governed by nonintentional social and linguistic conventions that act as constraints on meaning.

2.5.2: Moderate Intentionalism and Circularity

Moderate intentionalists understand the importance of conventional constraints on meaning but fail to recognize that the determinants necessary to interpret a text should not directly include the speaker's perceived communicative intention (Gauker 2008). Any position to the contrary is confronted by a dilemma. If a text T means p if and only if the author intended it to mean p, then intentionalists adopt Humpty Dumpty's philosophy where simply intending an utterance to have a specific meaning would be sufficient to give it that meaning. Furthermore, the position is circular. The author intends a text T to mean p, and T means p because the author intended T to mean p. Inserting a constraint, as moderate intentionalists have done, undermines the intentionalist meaning and interpretation theses, but it does not solve the dilemma. Consider the typical

TABLE 2.1. **Two intentionalist theories of interpretation**

Akerman (2009)	Speaker intention → Direct access to determinants → Correct interpretation External evidence → Infer values → Reasonable interpretation
Predelli (2002)	Speaker intention → Term refers to the referent → Correct interpretation Speaker intention → Term is being used to refer → Hearer's interpretation

moderate intentionalist constraint where a text T means p if and only if the author intended it to mean p *and* that intention has been successfully realized in the text. If only successfully realized communicative intentions serve as the criterion of textual meaning, a circularity problem still results. The reason is that successful communicative intentions cannot be given a coherent sense that does not presuppose an independent notion of work meaning to which a communicative intention can be compared to determine whether it has been successfully realized (Levinson 1996). One way to avoid circularity is to stipulate that a communication is successfully realized when (a) the author intends that an appropriately backgrounded audience discern P in T, and (b) such an audience discerns P in T. Such a stipulation, though, renders successful intent superfluous as a criterion of meaning since (a) + (b) offers a sufficient explanation of it (Trivedi 2001).

Davies (2006) argues that the circularity argument begs the question of authorial intentions by assuming that, because utterance meaning can be determined independently of utterer's meaning, intentions are irrelevant to interpretations. Carroll (2011) similarly argues that moderate intentionalism makes utterance meaning theoretically dispensable because utterer's meaning along with word and sentence meaning are sufficient to avoid the Humpty Dumpty problem. These arguments do not, however, successfully address the problems raised above. Once intentionalists concede that the meaning thesis needs modification and that there are convention-based constraints on a text meaning whatever its author intended, it is intentionalists who must justify why actual intentions are still integral to meaning. This is especially true considering that the moderate intentionalist "unified view" is more cumbersome and less elegant than an interpreter-based alternative that would focus only on utterance meaning. In addition, the intentionalist view does not adequately contemplate situations where a text can have meaning even though the author does not have specific semantic intentions. Davies (2006) argues that intentions are still relevant because interpretations target successfully realized utterer's meaning, not only utterance meaning, and we are interested in the fit with utterance meaning as one way of considering whether utterer's meaning is successfully realized. This justification, though, is orthogonal to the determination of meaning and focuses instead on interests extraneous to it, even if important or interesting.

2.6: Hypothetical Intentionalism

2.6.1: Interpretation of Texts Is by Its Nature Hypothetical

Instead of conceiving of meaning as something that is separate from successful communication (as a distinction between the "correct meaning" and the "reasonable meaning" would do) or as consisting of utterer meaning plus interpreter recognition of same (as moderate intentionalists would have it), textual interpretation, and the communicative meaning of the text, should be based on a model of utterance meaning that recognizes the realities of the evidentiary question. One can assert that the constitutive, or meaning, thesis must focus on actual authorial intent, but such a theory flounders, at least in cases involving textual interpretation, when faced with the evidentiary question of what evidence the interpreter typically relies on in answering the constitutive question. Intention is a fundamental aspect of determining utterance meaning, but intention must be viewed from the interpreter's perspective, not the author's. An utterance can thus only be said to mean what it means conventionally due to the strong and direct social constraint on meaning (Talmage 1996). With the recognition of social constraints, utterance meaning can be viewed as the intention that a member of the intended audience would be most justified in attributing to the author based on the knowledge and attitudes that he possesses in virtue of being a member of the intended audience (Tolhurst 1979). Intention thus stays central to the interpretive project because interpreters must decide whether the author intended to mean p through T. Under an interpreter-based approach, what a work in fact means remains the focus of inquiry, but intent is hypothetical (Levinson 2002).

A few literary scholars, including Levinson (2010) and Tolhurst (1979), have recognized that an interpreter-centered approach, which they term "hypothetical intentionalism," is the most defensible form of intentionalism. A basic tenet of hypothetical intentionalism is that a text should be viewed as an utterance, produced in a public context by a historically and culturally situated author. The meaning of the text is its utterance meaning as opposed to either a textual meaning or an utterer's meaning. Levinson (2010, 139) describes the utterance meaning as being determined on a "pragmatic model according to which what an utterance means is a matter, roughly, of what an appropriate hearer would most reasonably take a speaker to be trying to convey in employing a given verbal vehicle in the given communicative-context."[22] Thus, while the interpreter makes a hypothesis regarding authorial intent to convey a meaning to an audience, the hypothesis is based on evidence external to the author.[23]

2.6.2: Aspects of the Interpreter and Author

One issue regarding hypothetical intentionalism concerns the degree to which it makes various aspects of the interpretive process hypothetical versus "actual." One component is the status of the interpreter. Should the interpreter be conceived of as ideal or omniscient, as some suggest, or, as Trivedi (2001) argues, competent but fallible? If one is addressing actual interpretive systems such as judicial interpretation of legal texts, rather than hypothetical or constructed ones, an infallible interpreter would typically be posited, even though the judicial implementers of that interpreter are of course fallible. Chapter 3 discusses the characteristics of the idealized interpreter of ordinary meaning in more detail, aspects of which are relevant to the determination of communicative meaning, and addresses such issues as what level of linguistic knowledge the interpreter is presumed to possess.

At this moment, the more interesting component concerns the status of the author. Levinson (2010) claims that hypothetical intentionalism focuses on the actual author rather than a hypothetical author, even though meaning is not determined by actual authorial intent but rather by optimal hypotheses about authorial intention. In contrast, Nehamas (1981, 1986) argues for a hypothetical intentionalism that posits a fictional or hypothetical artist or author. Trivedi (2001) argues that it is ontologically unnecessary to postulate a fictional author to account for work meaning. This is so because the actual author can still be the reference where work meaning is determined (through the work, including its context and conventions) as something the author could have intended to communicate to the audience, as opposed to what he did intend to communicate. Stecker and Davies (2010) counter that the author in hypothetical intentionalism is in reality hypothetical given that the theory rejects as irrelevant the actual author's intentions at the point where they come apart from what his public persona is most likely to have intended.

Stecker and Davies are correct that the author in hypothetical intentionalism should be seen as hypothetical, but that is so because all the viable theories of textual interpretation posit an author that is to some degree hypothetical. Once the focus is on a nonomniscient interpreter's view of meaning, as opposed to the author's intended meaning, it is difficult to see how tinkering with the epistemic question of the determinants of meaning (as moderate intentionalists such as Stecker and Davies do with their focus on private determinants of meaning) can make the author actual rather than hypothetical. In other words, once the meaning thesis has been (properly) rejected, there is no "pure," nonhypothetical possibility. Indeed, as has already been argued, even actual intentionalists must accept a large degree of hypothetical speculation in their interpretations. Alexander and Prakash (2004) argue that positing an idealized author raises various interpretive issues that must be addressed, such as whether the author uses primary definitions of words or secondary definitions and whether his grammar and punctuation are perfect. Yet, these issues must also be addressed, typically on the basis of no *actual* evidence regarding the author's practices, by actual intentionalists. The interpretation of texts could not get started, in most cases, if the interpreter did not assume that the author intended to give the words in the text a meaning that would be known to the other members of the speech community (or intended to follow certain grammatical rules). Regardless of the particular theory, the interpretive process, including the author and authorial intent, is thus based at least in part on conventions, which are made up of assumptions and generalizations about meaning. Any given interpretation is thus based, at least in part, on determinants of meaning that are unconnected to actual authorial intent.

2.6.3: Legal Texts and Hypothetical Intentionalism

The view of interpretation as hypothetical fits well with the realities of how legal texts must be interpreted. Greenawalt (2000, 1620), although arguing for the relevance of "mental states," asserts that "no viable approach to legal meaning can wholly exclude reader understanding approaches." The concession is warranted. The meaning of legal texts must be based on optimal hypotheses about authorial intention rather than on actual authorial intent. Considering the unsponsored nature of legal texts, with their inherent autoglottic space, and the necessity of relying, in least in part, on generalized assumptions about authorial intent, a claim that actual intent is being sought is, in virtually all instances of interpretation, a fiction. With such texts especially, interpreters must assume that authors intend to comply, in general, with conventions of meaning. Otherwise, to be interpretable, each text would need to be accompanied by a dictionary created by the author that could be used to decode the text. Of course such a dictionary would itself inevitably need to be interpreted. An intentionalist might point to a supposed direct source of authorial intent, but specific assistance from such sources is not always available. With statutes, one might point to the legislative history of a particular provision, but any relevant information is usually stated at a high level of generality, making any specific inferences drawn from it hypothetical in nature. Even when the legislative history is relatively specific, the collective intent issue must be addressed, and there is no way of dealing with it without imputing intent—and thus making the interpretation hypothetical—to some of the members of the legislature.

A view of the interpretive process as focusing on a hypothetical author who complies with conventions of meaning fits with the dominant theories of legal interpretation. For the reasons indicated above, any intentionalist practice of legal interpretation will be, in essence, comparable to Levinson's hypothetical intentionalism. Despite the asserted goals of textualism, the theory also cannot ignore communicative intentions, especially considering that textualists argue that context and pragmatic factors may properly be considered. Flanagan (2010) follows the arguments of others in asserting that these considerations indicate that the textualist interest in literal meaning, rather than authorial intent, might be fictional. This conclusion is not necessary, however. A more accurate view of textualism is that it posits a hypothetical author (seen from the viewpoint of a reasonable interpreter) who complies with conventions of meaning. Consider Marmor's (2012, 10) description of textualism:

> What the law says is at least partly determined by what a reasonable hearer, knowing all the relevant background, would infer that it says. In other words, textualism can concede the idea that legal interpretation aims to ascertain the communication intentions of the legislature, as long as it is granted that the relevant communication intentions are understood objectively—that is, as they would be grasped by a reasonable hearer.

The description is similar to the textualist Manning's (2003, 2392–93) description of meaning as "how a reasonable person, conversant with the relevant social and linguistic conventions, would read the text in context." Others, including Solan (2005a) have described the similarities between textualist and intentionalist approaches to interpretation.

Of course, there are fundamental differences between textualism and intentionalism, such as textualism's focus on literal rather than utterance meaning as the correct meaning of a text. As a linguistic matter (as explained in chaps. 3 and 4), textualists seem more likely than intentionalists to confuse literal meaning and ordinary meaning. Furthermore, textualists are more likely than intentionalists to reject the possibility that some of a text's contents are determined by relations between its purely interior elements and matters lying beyond its boundaries. Intentionalists are thus more willing than are textualists to conclude that the textual meaning does not represent the correct communicative meaning of the text. In addition, some have claimed that textualists prefer to interpret statutory provisions as establishing rules, as opposed to more open-ended standards, that narrow judicial discretion in their application (Marmor 2012; Nelson 2005). Textualist preferences for determinate texts and legal rules with objective meanings and interpretive rules that can be easily and objectively applied can come at the expense of adhering to sound interpretive principles. These preferences include, among other things, the placing of significant weight on dictionary definitions and an inclination to (inaccurately) portray these definitions as though they establish necessary and sufficient conditions for the term (an issue extensively discussed in chap. 5).

In addition to the above distinctions, textualists and intentionalists differ in their views regarding various other evidential aspects of interpretation. Certainly, there are at least theoretical differences between textualists and intentionalists about the proper weight that, in general, should be accorded various interpretive devices. One notorious evidential dispute involves the consideration of legislative history, which textualists, for various reasons, either refuse to consult or hold in low esteem as a source of information that should help resolve interpretive disputes. One view of the textualist position is that, to the extent it rejects consideration of legislative history or in contracts cases testimony from the contracting parties, it can be said to ascribe meaning based on a restricted set of evidence, therefore making it vulnerable to allegations of rewriting texts. Nevertheless, in both intentionalism and textualism, because access to the actual communicative intentions of the author are unavailable, interpretation must rely on generalized assumptions about intent, such as the assumption that authors of legal texts intend for their words to have their ordinary meaning. Thus, in both methodologies, properly conceived, legislative intent must necessarily be determined from the perspective of the interpreter, and reference to authorial intent is of a hypothetical nature.

Similar to intentionalism and textualism, a purposivist approach to interpretation also posits a hypothetical author. The hypothetical nature of purposivism is obvious. A purposivist interpreter does not attempt to determine the actual intentions of the legislators, but rather may ask something along the lines of what a reasonable legislature wanted to achieve, or would have wanted to achieve if it had foreseen the issue, by enacting the legislation at issue (Marmor 2012). A focus on the legal effects intended by the legislature may seem to render conventions of meaning unimportant, as conventions focus narrowly on communicative meaning while purposivism purports to view language at a higher level of generality. Yet, it is difficult to claim that the communicative meaning of the text does not act, at the least, as a constraint on the available interpretations that a purposivist judge is willing to consider. In some areas of law, such as criminal statutes, it must be acknowledged that the communicative meaning of the text is given priority.

Furthermore, the various methodologies also consider aesthetic or coherence type considerations when choosing an interpretation, increasing the hypothetical character of the interpretation. For instance, purposivism purports to focus on the outcomes that any given interpretation will produce, which is analogous to the value-maximizing view of literary interpretation advocated by Davies (2006), which holds, roughly, that the correct interpretation of a literary work is that which maximizes the artistic value it can be seen to possess. Other theories of interpretation also allow for aesthetic considerations. Hypothetical intentionalism, for instance, views the best hypothesis of meaning as one that allows for consideration of aesthetic beliefs (i.e., an interpretation that makes the work artistically better), even if the hypothesis must still be epistemically optimal (i.e., what is most likely to be true given the evidence). Similarly, even textualism, which more than any other interpretive theory purports to eschew policy considerations, will consider how a given interpretation fits into the body of law as a whole and will avoid interpretations that will lead to absurd results.

2.7: Interpretation and Theory

2.7.1: Intentionalist Claims about Interpretation and Theory

One of the main goals of the above discussion in this chapter was to demonstrate the falsity of the intentionalist argument that genuine interpretation cannot be anything other than a commitment to the meaning a text's author or authors intended. The rejection of this intentionalist position has implications for how interpretation is conceived, which will be re-

flected in the rest of this book. One important concomitant effect of rejecting the intentionalist meaning and interpretation theses should be a
realization of the theoretical nature of interpretation. Not surprisingly, for
some intentionalists interpretation is not a theoretical endeavor. For these
intentionalists, theory refers to the attempt to govern interpretations of
specific texts by appealing to general accounts of interpretation (Knapp
and Michaels 1982, 1983, 1987, 1992; Fish 1985).[24] Knapp and Michaels
(1992) argue that since there are no limits on what a speaker can intend
her language to mean, it is incoherent to attempt to devise a general interpretive method that would resolve interpretive controversies. Instead, the
object of every interpretive controversy involves the particular historical
fact of authorial intent. The problem, according to Knapp and Michaels,
is that there is no general way to determine what any particular historical
fact might be, and no general belief about interpretation offers any help
in determining the meaning of any particular text.

Fish (1999) similarly argues that interpretation is not something one
can have a theory about because no theory can instruct one on how to
proceed, make decisions, and evaluate evidence. For Fish (2008, 1140), because interpretation involves only an attempt to realize authorial intent,
the interpretive process involves "no approach, no method, no theory, just
good old-fashioned empirical inquiry in the course of which you mine for
evidence, put it together when found, and build it into an account of the
author's intention and therefore of the meaning of his, her or their text."
Fish (1985, 115) distinguishes between empirical generalizations, which
cannot be deemed theoretical, and a general hermeneutics, which can.
Fish does allow that textualism constitutes a theory because it offers instructions for reaching correct or valid interpretive conclusions. He denies, though, that it is a theory that gives instructions that can be followed
because the "distinction between text and context is impossible to maintain and cannot be the basis of demarcating alternative theories with their
attendant consequences" (119).[25]

2.7.2: Ordinary Meaning and Empiricism

Contrary to intentionalist claims, interpretation is a theoretical endeavor,
even if one accepts the intentionalist meaning and interpretation theses,
but it is even more clearly so when those theses are rejected. While it
might be readily apparent that the constraints on adopting communicative meaning for legal texts stem from some theory of interpretation, such

as fair notice in criminal cases, even the determination of the communicative content of a text must rest on theoretical notions. The range of available theoretical notions, however, is necessarily limited. Theory, with respect to the interpretation of legal texts at least, cannot easily be based on an overarching methodology that can systematically account for all the nuances of interpretation. Interpretation is too contextual to allow for a prescribed step-by-step methodology that would instruct judges on how to weigh and reconcile the various interpretive tools that may be relevant in any given case (Slocum 2010). For one, determinacy is a relative notion that depends on the standard of proof required by the interpreter. In addition, no methodology can give precise instructions on when, in a given case, a particular interpretive principle should be applied. Thus, many interpretive principles have very general triggering instructions, such as being applicable unless the context indicates that application of the principle would be inconsistent with legislative intent.[26] Further, if the interpretive principle at issue is applicable, no theory can give precise instructions on how it should be combined with other interpretive principles, some of them pointing to a different interpretation, or whether the combination has met the required standard of proof. As a result, interpretive instructions cannot be more precise than either broad principles or contextually-sensitive presumptions.

Notwithstanding the impossibility of a highly determinate, comprehensive theory of interpretation, the interpretive process is one filled with theoretical judgments that cannot be simply characterized as empirical generalizations. As was covered earlier in this chapter, contrary to intentionalist assertions, there are communicative limits on what a speaker can intend her language to mean. Yet even putting these constraints aside, it cannot be said that interpretation involves merely empirical inquiry. While theory concerns views about the world that are conjectural, empirical generalizations must be based, at least in part, on actual fact. These sorts of empirical generalizations are not possible, however, with respect to many crucial aspects of legal interpretation. Interpretation *can* be based on empirical findings in the sense that a method of handling a linguistic phenomenon may be based on ways in which people use language (as the frequent gaps between literal meaning and ordinary meaning discussed in later chapters demonstrate). In a larger sense, though, overall interpretations, or methods of interpretation, cannot be empirically verified. A legal interpretation cannot be confirmed by appeal to an author or authors, making empiricism a difficult project. There are no studies indicating whether any given interpretive principle produces results consistent with original legislative intent, nor could there be. Furthermore, like other linguistic phenomena, the conventional meaning of words may be subject to empirical inquiry, but conventional meaning is never the only consideration for a legal interpreter. All interpretations are thus in some sense conjectural regarding their targeted standard of meaning, and any future-looking generalizations about meaning are similarly conjectural, not empirical, in nature.

Despite the conjectural nature of the process, in a system such as law where multiple interpretations that are very similar must be made, coherent, nonarbitrary interpretation requires that certain future-looking generalizations be made that give structure to the interpretive process. Such future-looking generalizations are necessary with respect to any type of textual interpretation. De Man (1982, 5) describes theory as "the rooting of literary exegesis and of critical evaluation in a system of some conceptual generality." Of course, as de Man points out, "[e]ven the most intuitive, empirical and theoretically low-key writers on literature make use of a minimal set of concepts (tone, organic form, allusion, tradition, historical situation, etc.) of at least some general import" (5). As with literary interpretation, legal interpreters cannot operate without recourse to concepts of general import. These interpretive principles generally cannot be labeled as empirical in nature (in the sense that they can be confirmed to conform with authorial expectations), even though sometimes styled by judges as such, because they are not subject to any empirical findings, and it is difficult to imagine that they could be.

It is true that some interpretive principles created by courts may not be considered by congressional drafters when drafting legislation. Bressman and Gluck (2013, 2014) have made significant contributions to jurisprudence through such findings. These sorts of studies might well lead to conclusions that certain interpretive principles are based on naive and incorrect assumptions about the drafting process. For example, they may call into question interpretive principles that cannot be tied to normal language usage outside of the legislative context. Such studies, though, are at best indirect reflections of even hypothetical congressional intent and cannot show that any individual interpretation is incorrect.

At a functional level then, a judge's interpretation of multiple texts over time necessarily presents issues of commonality that entail, even if subconsciously, the creation and maintenance of at least small-scale interpretive theories. Consider the legislative history of a statute, seen by intentionalists as a direct source of actual authorial intent. Does consideration of a statute's legislative history *in fact* help to reveal legislative intent?[27] Is it probative evidence if one adopts a hypothetical intentionalism standard? Why, or why not? In addition, as a general matter, are all sources of legislative history of equal persuasive value or are some more inherently persuasive or authoritative than others? Is, for example, a statement from the sponsor of a bill more persuasive than a conflicting committee report? A court cannot consistently consider legislative history when interpreting statutory language without, in some way, answering these questions, and more besides. Moreover, the answer to these questions will not likely be based on any empirical findings but, rather, the judge's own theoretical views about the legislative process and the usefulness of legislative history. It is possible, of course, that there could be some empirical findings that might inform a judge's decision of how to treat legislative history. These empirical findings might relate to some aspect of how the legislative process works but, again, would not likely offer any certain proof of whether any particular source of legislative history can be said to reflect congressional intent (even if intent is considered from a hypothetical perspective).

When the interpretation of statutes is involved, even if the goal is to implement actual authorial intent (which, as the discussion above demonstrated, is not a persuasive standard), the search for meaning cannot stop at consideration of a statute's legislative history (which is primarily, after all, more marks on paper to be interpreted according to some *theory* of interpretation). No judge would rely solely on legislative history and not consider the relevant text of the statute. A focus on text, however, also reveals numerous issues that, because of their recurring nature, are properly seen as theoretical in nature. For instance, should the interpreter assume, in the absence of any other directly relevant evidence, that the same words in different parts of a section (or in different sections) of a statute or contract have the same meaning? Or should the interpreter ignore such "evidence" of intent altogether? Judges do, in fact, apply such a tool of interpretation when interpreting statutes in the form of the *in pari materia* canon.[28] Similarly, if there is no other evidence on the matter, should the court assume that an ordinary or a technical word meaning was intended? Of course, as has already been examined, the consistent answer given by courts is that words and phrases are to be given their ordinary meaning. This practice derives from a theory of how legislatures use language, which is not based on any particular empirical study or analysis of legislative intent (at the least, the practice would predate any such study). Rather, it is based on views about the rule of law, democratic principles, and the idea that legislators should be seen as using language in the same way as the general public, who will be governed by the statutory language and thus should be able to understand it.

In addition, focusing on small-scale theoretical issues, such as the relevance of legislative history or political science, prompts revelations, in an inductive sort of way, about the nature of interpretation. Intentionalists such as Fish (2005, 643–44) indicate that intentionalism is "simply the right answer to a question (what is the meaning of a text?) and not a method."[29] Fish and other intentionalists thus claim that interpretation is a definitional and not a methodological question, but scholars understandably conflate the two because the definition of interpretation as the discovery and implementation of authorial intent (even hypothetical intent) is trivial standing alone. The conflation of methodology and definition is ineluctable if one intends to think about interpretation at anything more concrete than a metalevel. At a concrete level of consideration, a dialectic exists between the definition of interpretation and the chosen methodology of interpretation. Just as the definition of interpretation shapes and constrains methodological questions, the strengths, and especially the weaknesses, of the tools of interpretation (the specifics of any methodology) help shape the definition of meaning. Most importantly for this project, the answer to the question of the determinants of the meaning of texts, and the limitations of these determinants, should play an important role in deciding the constitutive question of the appropriate standard for declaring the meaning of a text. For legal texts, just as the definition of interpretation can shape and constrain the determinants of meaning, the limitations of the determinants of meaning can also shape and constrain the concepts of meaning and interpretation. Thus, if no determinant of meaning can reliably be shown to reveal actual authorial intent (and not just generalizations about intent), one may question whether interpretation can sensibly be oriented to such a standard.

*   *   *

As argued above, the interpretation of texts, especially legal texts, is endemically theoretical. The intentionalist theses that the meaning of a text is identical to the author's intended meaning (meaning thesis) and that interpretation consists of determining the author's intended meaning (interpretation thesis) even if accepted do not entail that interpretation is empirical and not theoretical. A legal interpretation must be based on some overarching theory of meaning and intent, as well as small-scale theories about which interpretive tools are relevant to the chosen goal of the interpretive effort and what combination of tools can been deemed sufficient to conclude that the goal has been reached. Furthermore, in some areas, such as with literary and legal texts, the ultimate goal of the interpretive process may differ from or exceed the identification of communicative intent. Considering the impossibility of empirical data establishing the correctness of any one version of authorial intent or of many of the interpretive tools used by courts, as well as the reasons for applying such tools, the choices made by courts must be considered theoretical and not empirical.

2.8: Objections to Objective Views of Interpretation

2.8.1: The Wrong Result Argument

I have shown that the interpretation of texts, especially legal texts, depends on conventions and assumptions about meaning that make the interpretive project hypothetical in nature. Notwithstanding the inevitability of a hypothetical approach to interpretation, various objections have been raised that suggest that such a view of interpretation leads to incorrect outcomes, is arbitrary, or seriously undermines the persuasiveness of a hypothetical communicative intent approach to interpretation. Consider the following possibility. A text T means p, but p is not intended and the audience of T is justified in believing that p is not intended. Stecker and Davies (2010) argue that, if an audience is justified in believing that p is not intended by the author of T, then it will not hypothesize that the author had that intention and hence, according to a hypothetical intentionalist account, T won't mean p. The problem is that, ex hypothesi, T does mean p. Therefore, hypothetical intentionalism gives the wrong result in such cases.

The flaw in the Stecker and Davies hypothetical is that, noncommunicative constraints aside, if hypothetical intent is being discerned, it is not possible that a text can mean p when the audience is justified in believing that p was not intended. Of course, when noncommunicative constraints are involved, it is possible for the correct interpretation to be one that is neither the utterer's meaning nor the meaning believed by the interpreter to be the correct communicative content meaning. This result is common with legal texts. As illustrated earlier, there are various legally based constraints on communicative meaning that result in a legal text being given an interpretation other than its communicative meaning. For example, a legal text may otherwise mean p, but a judge will feel justified in believing that p was not intended if that interpretation would produce absurd results. Such a determination is not necessarily based on a conclusion about actual communicative intent but rather is based on a generalized assumption that authors do not intend absurd results. Outside of such scenarios, if the interpreter attempts to determine what a speaker was trying to convey in employing a given verbal vehicle in the given communicative context, a text will mean p when the interpreter takes a speaker as successfully conveying p in a given communicative context. Of course, an interpreter may speculate that the author's communicative intentions, whatever they may be, were likely unsuccessfully realized, and thus the communicative meaning of the text differs from that intended by the author. This possibility should be a concern, though, only if one accepts the intentionalist meaning thesis, and therefore Humpty Dumptyism.

2.8.2: The Arbitrariness Objection

A different objection to an objective view of interpretation is that by focusing on conventions one is trading the arbitrariness inherent in the utterer's intent view of meaning for the perhaps greater arbitrariness inherent in the audience's view of meaning. Observations about the arbitrariness of conventions, even if accurate, do not, of course, refute a claim that all realistic methodologies of interpretation must rely, at least to some degree, on conventions of meaning. Thus, the argument, even if true, does not undermine the influence of the ordinary meaning doctrine and its reliance on conventions. Nevertheless, if the ordinary meaning concept is to be accurately considered and developed, criticism of interpreter reliance on conventions must be considered.

For instance, Carroll (2011) argues that with hypothetical intentionalism there is a problem of indeterminacy because even ideal interpreters are regularly apt to produce different, nonconverging, and even conflicting hypotheses about the meaning of a text. The indeterminacy argument is partially accurate. One view of the hypothetical intentionalism perspective is that there may be no fact of the matter about what hypothesis the interpreters will reach. A hypothetical account often involves the rejection of a single "true" meaning in favor of a range of truthlike values, such as "plausible" meanings (Margolis 1976). Of course, this view of meaning is not antithetical to the law. Critical pluralism is, in fact, reflected in the Supreme Court's famous *Chevron* doctrine.[30] Pursuant to *Chevron*, a governmental agency is given judicial deference in cases of statutory indeterminary with regard to its choice of statutory interpretations from among a range of reasonable interpretations and is permitted to change its favored interpretation over time if it decides that a different interpretation better fits its policy goals.

With utterer's meaning there is, by definition, only one correct meaning, and the determinant of meaning (author's intent) is epistemically straightforward, even if as a practical manner author's intent endemically remains unknown. On the other hand an objective methodology of interpretation can always generate a more or less precise meaning (i.e., endemically it will be discernible), but that meaning will often involve contested determinants of meaning, making it epistemically uncertain. Different interpreters may thus give a different meaning to the same language, even when in general agreement about the proper methodology of interpretation. Also, there is an ineliminable element of discretion inherent in many instances of interpretation, particularly if one is focused on the communicative meaning of the text, making the interpretation chosen arbitrary from a language standpoint. As de Man (1982) argues, the grammatical decoding of a text leaves a residue of indetermination that cannot be resolved by grammatical means, however extensively conceived.

The problem with the above arbitrariness of conventions argument is that it fails to adequately acknowledge the inevitable disputes that arise when an author's intentions are being determined. Even some intentionalists understand that any intentionality found represents at the most a probable intent (Azar 2007). As Henket (1989) has observed, no matter how careful the interpreter or the number of particulars taken into consideration, any intentionality discovered will always be based on conjecture. Further, intentionalists often fail to appreciate that communications, even oral ones, often fail when viewed from an intentionalist perspective. Keysar (2007) has shown that listeners interpret what speakers say from their own perspective, which is a systematic cause of misunderstanding and miscommunication. Similarly, speakers are typically not sensitive to how an utterance may be ambiguous to a particular addressee and are not able to monitor for ambiguity effectively (Keysar and Henly 2002).

To be persuasive, then, the arbitrariness of conventions argument would have to establish, which they have not done, that disputes regarding actual authorial intent, even when the author does not intend some idiosyn-

cratic meaning, are less pervasive than disputes regarding hypothetical authorial intent. Furthermore, while advocates of hypothetical intentionalism
must concede that a convention and interpreter based approach to interpretation naturally allows for disputes about meaning, the arbitrariness of
conventions objection fails to consider the difference in the degree of arbitrariness between intentionalism and hypothetical intentionalism. With
intentionalism, an author can have language mean anything she wants, with
no external constraints. The arbitrariness inherent in such an approach is
thus absolute. In contrast to actual intentionalism, hypothetical intentionalism relies on external and verifiable evidence, at least to some degree. An
interpreter does not choose an interpretation by fiat but must justify the
choice of one interpretation over another on the basis of the consideration
of relevant conventions. In that sense, a convention-based approach is not
the substitution of one type of arbitrariness for another different, and perhaps greater, type of arbitrariness. Rather, it is the substitution of an objective approach with some degree of ineliminable discretion for an approach,
actual intentionalism, with absolute discretion and arbitrariness.

   Although ultimately unconvincing, the arbitrariness argument applies
equally to moderate intentionalism, which similarly involves conventions
that place constraints on meaning. Carroll (2011), though, argues that
there will be far fewer cases of indeterminacy under the moderate intentionalist view than under the hypothetical intentionalist view. Carroll's
argument is implausible if one compares the typical formulation of moderate intentionalism with that of hypothetical intentionalism. With moderate intentionalism, two levels of indeterminacy must be contemplated.
The interpreter must first determine the author's intent, which is frequently, if not always, uncertain. The second level of indeterminacy occurs
when the interpreter must determine the textual meaning of the work to
determine whether it is consistent with the author's intent. If anything,
considering the two separate inquiries, the moderate intentionalist position adds indeterminacy to interpretation.

   The indeterminacy problem is, arguably, more genuine, however, if it
is focused on determinants of meaning. Hypothetical intentionalism, as
compared to a naïve textualism, solves some problems of underdetermination by causing interpreters to focus attention beyond the text to the
publicly available information concerning the context of utterance. This
would be true, of course, only if textualists properly identified a text as
having an indeterminate meaning instead of inaccurately ascribing clarity to the text (as they are prone to do). Despite this problem, if such con-

textual consideration reduces indeterminacy by disambiguating or pre-cisifying problematic text, arguably a consideration of the mental state of the utterer would yield even greater determinacy. Carroll (2011) observes that hypothetical intentionalism will not consider private avowals, such as diaries, private letters, etc., of intent as being relevant in the interpreter's hypotheses about the author's intention. In contrast, moderate intention-alism will accept private avowals of the author's intention.[31] There would therefore be more cases of indeterminacy under hypothetical intentional-ism if it is in fact true that a greater number of determinants of meaning would lead to reduced indeterminacy. This would be true, however, only if the private avowals helped to explicate the public avowals. For example, with statutes, the analogous "private" avowals would be the relevant legis-lative history. It is questionable, though, whether legislative history en-hances the accuracy of the interpretive process. If, like some other private avowals, it conflicted with the public avowals or failed to help explicate them, there would be no basis for a claim that moderate intentionalism would lead to less indeterminacy than would hypothetical intentionalism.

2.8.3: The Rewriting Claim

A related claim to the one above is that an intentionalist interpretation represents the true meaning of a text while other methodologies, such as hypothetical intentionalism, involve a rewriting of the text (Robert-son 2009; Fish 2008, 1133–34, 1144–45). The rewriting claim, however, has things backward. It is the intentionalist meaning thesis that involves re-writing, not hypothetical intentionalism. If the author's perceived inten-tions are deemed to be controlling, the interpreter ceases to be an inter-preter of the actual text and instead becomes the interpreter of a different and hypothetical work that would have been produced if the author's in-tentions had been successfully implemented (Currie 2005, 124–27). At best, the intentionalists have succeeded in establishing that the rewriting claim depends on one's perspective regarding interpretation and meaning.

In any case, there is no clear distinction between interpreting and re-writing law. Undoubtedly, all judges engage in frequent rewriting of legal texts to further certain important principles, such as the rule of law, and in these situations judges are also motivated to minimize the extent to which they are seen as rewriting. Many influential interpretive principles, consis-tently relied on by judges, are based on generalized assumptions and are difficult to definitively characterize as involving rewriting, even if they are inconsistent with the ordinary linguistic meaning of the text. For example, is it an instance of rewriting a text when a judge relies on a very strong presumption that Congress does not intend to enact legislation with retroactive effects or extraterritorial jurisdiction? Such presumptions are undoubtedly based on noncommunicative policy reasons, but courts have also claimed that they represent legislative intent (Slocum 2010). Further, is it an instance of rewriting when a judge assumes legislative compliance with principles that are not policy based but which have not been shown to be compatible with legislative intent? For instance, judges typically assume legislative compliance with various rules of grammar and punctuation in spite of a lack of evidence that the legislature considered the rules when drafting (and, in some cases, despite a lack of evidence that the rules are consistent with normal language usage). Indeed, many of the principles of interpretation applied by judges are hypothetical in nature and represent what an ideally rational and careful legislature would mean by the text chosen, rather than being tied in any way to the actual intent of the actual legislature.

Greenberg (2010) offers two notes on the problem of inaccurate (or, more accurately, hypothetical) interpretive principles. The first is that the problem is not as relevant for intentionalists because intentionalism does not make interpretive principles constitutive of communicative content. Certainly, this position is accurate, but it merely underscores that actual intentionalism offers a definition of meaning, the constitutive question, but has little to contribute to interpretation, the epistemic question. The failure of actual intentionalists to adequately address epistemic questions undermines their answer to the constitutive question. Greenberg's second point is that if the applicable interpretive principles depend on considerations other than strictly communicative ones, such as rule of law issues, the communication theory's claim to solve problems of legal interpretation entirely on linguistic considerations fails. This second point overstates the claims of communication theorists, who do not generally claim that legal interpretations should be made solely on the basis of communicative principles. Instead, communication theorists seem most interested in either building theories of the communicative content of legal texts, as opposed to claiming that the communicative content must also be the legal meaning, or in deconstructing judicial opinions that claim to interpret legal texts on the basis of communicative principles.

Greenberg makes a related claim that, if actual intentionalism is abandoned in favor of some objective theory, such as hypothetical intentionalism, it is not clear why the communicative content of statutes should have a significant degree of importance (Greenberg 2010). Greenberg (2011) argues that there are good reasons to choose a meaning other than a statute's communicative content, such as a meaning that promotes justice, welfare or rule of law concerns. In contrast, communication theorists have nothing to say about why communicative content is a better candidate for a statute's contribution than the content of a legislature's legal intentions, or some other theory of content. Further, the argument goes, the current interpretive principles are controversial, and courts differ on which interpretive principles are appropriate. Thus, if the applicable principles must be generally conformed to, the communication theory will be of little help to legal interpreters.

As has already been discussed, Greenberg is correct, of course, that current interpretive principles are controversial and unsystematically applied by courts and that, if an objective approach is followed, communicative content can be defined in different ways. It does not follow, though, that the communicative content of a statute needs some special justification to be relevant to interpretation, or that an objective theory places a communicative content approach to interpretation on questionable footing. If one of the goals of a theory of interpretation is to systematize and give rationales for actual legal interpretation, Greenberg's analysis is a bit odd considering that courts do not apply an actual intentionalist approach to interpretation yet place great weight on the communicative meaning of the text. It is true that the communicative content of a statute is not coterminous with a statute's legal content. At the same time, though, it must also be conceded that the communicative content of a statute is relevant to a statute's legal content. For one, the rule of law demands that the communicative content of a statute be relevant, if not decisive, to the interpretation of many types of statutes, particularly criminal ones. In addition, from an interpreter's standpoint, the communicative content of a statute acts, at the least, as a constraint on legal meaning. No critic of objective approaches to interpretation can persuasively argue that the communicative content of the text is unrelated to the legal meaning of the text, or even that it is of little importance to the interpretation chosen by the judge.

2.9: Conclusions about Intentionalism and Ordinary Meaning

This chapter has attempted to lay the groundwork for the broad claim of the book that the ordinary meaning concept should be viewed as a central aspect of the communicative meaning of a legal text. The communicative meaning of a text is its true meaning, not merely a pragmatic constraint on it. Further, the communicative content of a legal text is relevant to the legal content of the text, if not decisive of it. Such views are possible only if one accepts an objective approach to interpretation. Under an objective view, the meaning of a text is the meaning that a competent interpreter would give it by means of a method of interpretation that the interpreter could reliably employ on the basis of features of the situation of which the interpreter is aware (Gauker 2008). Intended meaning can therefore constitute work meaning only if it is accessible to the relevant interpreter (Stecker 2006). An author's perceived actual communicative (semantic) intentions cannot therefore directly serve as one of the criteria of communicative meaning.

Basing the communicative content of a text on objective features of the relevant context avoids the Humpty Dumpty problem, where words mean anything an author intends them to mean. Even apart from the Humpty Dumpty issue, conventions of meaning must underlie all theories of legal interpretation. Such a conclusion is obvious with objective theories of interpretation, but it is also true with actual intentionalism. When interpreting legal texts at least, actual intentionalists must endemically rely on conventions of meaning. Analogous to the intentionalist claim that textualists must make assumptions about a text that are not based solely on the text, actual intentionalists must make assumptions about the author that are not based on actual evidence of the author's communicative intent. Even if one assumes that a text means what its author intended it to mean, the relevant interpreter must be capable of ascertaining this intended meaning. Because utterances are typically made in order to communicate some intended meaning that is accessible, interpreters typically assume that the author intended to follow conventions of meaning. These generalized assumptions about meaning are not tied to the author's actual intent but instead are the basis of the fundamental concept that words in legal texts are to be given their ordinary meaning.

CHAPTER THREE

The Constitutive and Evidential Aspects of Ordinary Meaning

3.1: Communicative Meaning and Ordinary Meaning

3.1.1: Framing the Constituent and Evidential Aspects of Ordinary Meaning

At this point, we know that linguistic communication via a text involves an interpreter determining the meaning of the author's inscription on the basis of various interpretive tools, most of which are based on conventions of meaning or other principles resting on generalized assumptions about language usage. In essence, the interpreter must determine the meaning of the text on the basis of the words used and their composition, as well as the relevant context. A typical author in typical circumstances is motivated to exploit external factors in order to provide the interpreter with sufficiently clear evidence that will enable the interpreter to interpret the inscription as intended. In fact, the author cannot reasonably expect the interpreter to recognize the intended meaning unless the author believes that sufficient cues exist and are available to the interpreter to determine the intended meaning. Notwithstanding these typical motivations, it cannot be denied that an endemic aspect of texts (especially legal texts) is that mismatched communications will exist where the intended meaning and the interpreted meaning do not correspond. In such situations, and therefore more generally, actual intentionalism offers an unsatisfying answer to the constitutive question of what makes it the case that a writing has a certain communicative meaning. By its very nature, actual intentionalism similarly cannot answer the constitutive question of what makes it the case that a writing, or some subset of a writing, has an ordinary meaning. An ordinary meaning, at least in theory, is a purely linguistic meaning (as opposed to a meaning based on legal concerns), and actual intentionalism does not offer a theory of how such meanings are determined.

Rejecting the intentionalist meaning thesis, which is theoretically simple and intuitive, leaves the ordinary meaning constitutive question unanswered. One possible answer, of course, is that provided by hypothetical intentionalism, which was introduced in chapter 2. Recall that under a hypothetical intentionalism account the meaning of a text is determined by what an appropriate hearer would most reasonably take the author to be trying to convey in employing a given verbal vehicle in the given communicative context. While such a formulation offers a definition of the communicative content meaning of a text, it must be rejected as a definition of the ordinary meaning of a text. The primary reason is that communicative meaning as a constitutive matter cannot in all cases be coterminous with ordinary meaning. Under a hypothetical intentionalism view, the focus is on the communicative content of the text considering the given communicative context. In contrast, as developed below, the ordinary meaning determination should not allow consideration of the full communicative context of the utterance. If it did, the concept of ordinary meaning would be incoherent and unnecessary, as the focus would be on an interpretation given a specific communicative context rather than on the ordinary meaning of the language at issue.

If the actual intent of the author is not relevant, legal concerns are similarly disregarded (at least in theory), and hypothetical intentionalism is not an acceptable theory of ordinary meaning, how does one answer the constituent question of what makes some meaning the ordinary one? Further, what are the determinants of ordinary meaning? Are the personal beliefs of the judge, based on intuitions or "common sense" gleaned from a lifetime spent among normal language users, the proper determinants of ordinary meaning? Perhaps, as addressed below, it is not surprising that a more objective source of meaning is often deemed necessary by judges. One obvious source of expert-determined meaning, divorced from authorial intent or specific contextual influence, is the dictionary. It is intuitive why judges would want to consult dictionaries to determine the ordinary meanings of words. A dictionary definition is not created for the purpose of litigation, is external to the judge, and is not widely viewed as being created on the basis of ideological biases. Also, the difficult work of defining the word in question has already been performed by an expert. The judge merely has to consult a dictionary and select the appropriate meaning for the case.

Consulting a dictionary definition may thus be a convenient method of determining ordinary meaning, but does a dictionary definition necessarily represent the ordinary meaning of a word? Chapters 4 and 5 examine various cases that involve the (in)accuracy of dictionary definitions, and chapter 5 explains how judges misuse dictionary definitions. For now, consider the meaning of "now." In *Carcieri v. Salazar*,[1] a recent Supreme Court case critiqued later in this chapter, the meaning of "now" was pivotal to whether the Secretary of the Interior had the authority to accept in trust land for use by the Narragansett Indian Tribe. The Supreme Court relied on a dictionary definition that defined "now" as "[a]t the present time; at this moment; at the time of speaking."[2] The Court's decision raises various issues integral to ordinary meaning. For instance, does, as the Court seemed to believe, "now" always mean "at the time of speaking"? As demonstrated below, the answer is clearly "no."

If not a dictionary definition, then, what is evidence of ordinary meaning? If conventions of meaning are integral to ordinary meaning, how are these conventions determined? Furthermore, what exactly is the object of an ordinary meaning determination? Is the object of meaning the relevant word, sentence, paragraph, document (or statute), or something even broader? In other words, should a court focus on the meaning of a word, such as "now," in isolation or is such a focus improper? Relatedly, are all contextual considerations relevant, no matter how far removed from the object of meaning? If so, there would seem to be no distinction between the communicative meaning of a text and the ordinary meaning of its language. If contextual considerations are to be limited then, what is the principle that should limit them and how should they be limited? Finally, is it likely that courts are able or willing to exclude legal considerations when determining the ordinary meaning of textual language? An examination of these questions, essential to ordinary meaning, is presented below, along with a critique of the Court's opinion in *Carcieri* in light of the discussion.

3.1.2: The Necessity of Ordinary Meaning

Often, courts seem to understand, on some level at least, the distinction between ordinary meaning and communicative meaning. These courts will first determine the ordinary meaning of the relevant text before de-

ciding, based on consideration of wider contextual cues, whether the legislature had an intention to give the language a meaning other than its
ordinary meaning. For instance, the Supreme Court in a recent case (described near the beginning of chap. 1), *Taniguchi v. Kan Pacific Saipan,
Ltd.*,[3] first determined the ordinary meaning of the word "interpreter"
and then indicated that an unordinary but sometimes used meaning of
the word, which includes document translation, would not control "unless
the context in which the word appears indicates that it does." [4] Similarly,
in *Johnson v. United States*,[5] the Court rejected a conventional meaning of
"revoke" in favor of an unconventional one, determined in part by broad
considerations of purpose and legal consequences. The Court remarked
that while it was

> departing from the rule of construction that prefers ordinary meaning . . . this
> is exactly what ought to happen when the ordinary meaning fails to fit the text
> and when the realization of clear congressional policy . . . is in tension with the
> result that customary interpretive rules would deliver.[6]

Typically, though, even though judges might agree that there is a distinction between ordinary meaning and communicative meaning, as explained in this chapter and in chapter 4, courts do not carefully distinguish
between ordinary meaning determinations and communicative meaning
determinations.

Notwithstanding the tendency of courts to conflate the two concepts,
there is no doubt that the ordinary meaning concept does not offer a complete theory of the communicative content of a legal text. In light of the
advocation in chapter 2 of hypothetical intentionalism, this may invite
questions about the role of ordinary meaning in the interpretive process.
The arguments in chapter 2 regarding intentionalism and language support the hypothetical intentionalism account of communicative content. If
the hypothetical intentionalism view represents the communicative content meaning of a text, a further gradation of meaning requires some justification. Fortunately, there are various justifications for the role of ordinary meaning in the interpretive process. These justifications may be seen
as incremental in nature in the sense that the ordinary meaning concept
tends to further or advance the reasons compared to an interpretive re-
gime that did not include the ordinary meaning concept, but may not be
completely successful in realizing the goals that justify its existence.

One reason for the doctrine is that a presumption of ordinary meaning advances the principle that legal texts should be interpreted according to standards of communication that give texts readily discernible meanings. While it may be acceptable in certain situations for a court to choose a meaning that differs from the ordinary meaning of the text, the ordinary meaning concept represents the notion that, in general, a provision's meaning should be discernible based on a relatively limited consideration of context. Readily discernible texts are important because laws should give notice to those to whom they apply so that those affected can plan their affairs. As Justice Holmes famously wrote in *McBoyle v. United States*,

> Although it is not likely that a criminal will carefully consider the text of the law before he murders or steals, it is reasonable that a fair warning should be given to the world in language that the common world will understand, of what the law intends to do if a certain line is passed. To make the warning fair, so far as possible the line should be clear. [7]

In Justice Holmes's view, the "fair warning" principle should prevail even if policy indicated that the provision should have a broader scope or even "upon the speculation that if the legislature had thought of it, very likely broader words would have been used."[8] While it is an important and long-standing aspect of the rule of law, the fair warning principle is not equally applicable across all contexts. Tiersma (2001), for instance, has argued that the notice justification is stronger in some contexts, such as criminal laws, than in others, such as provisions that are applicable only to a highly specialized, sophisticated group.[9]

In addition to the fair warning principle, based on conventions of meaning and restricted contextual relevance, other legal principles are often invoked in support of the principle that the ordinary meaning of the textual language should determine legal meaning. For instance, one popular textualist argument, derived from constitutional concerns, is similar to the notice argument made above but focuses on the constitutionally prescribed legislative process. Essentially, the argument draws inferences from the fact that the statutory text is the only legislative output that is subject to the constitutionally mandated process for transforming legislative policy goals into legally authoritative rules. The "law" therefore consists of the text that was enacted and not the purposes that some legislators might have had in mind when enacting the text. If there is a divergence between the meaning of the enacted language and unenacted intentions, the enacted language must control (Scalia and Manning 2012). Interpreters should therefore assume that legislation was drafted meticulously (Scalia and Manning 2012). Under such an assumption, it seems clear that the ordinary meaning of the text should be the primary determinate of legal meaning.

Another justification for the ordinary meaning doctrine is epistemic in nature. Courts, as well as various scholars, typically state that the words of the text (and the ordinary meaning of those words) are the surest, safest evidence of the author's actual intentions (Benson 2008).[10] Certainly, it can be argued that people generally choose words that express their intended meaning. Nevertheless, one justification for ordinary meaning is based on uncertainty about the ability of interpreters to accurately discern meaning apart from the ordinary meaning of the words. This view is somewhat analogous to the epistemic view of vagueness, closely identified with Williamson (1996), which holds that the extensions (i.e., the referential range of application) of predicates are sharply defined but cannot be determined. The communicative meaning (or the actual intentions of the author) of a text may exist, but interpreters may not have confidence in their ability to accurately assess contextual evidence outside of that associated with the ordinary meaning of the textual language. This uncertainty may not preclude interpreters from considering wide contextual evidence of meaning, but it may make them reluctant, at least explicitly if not implicitly, to dismiss ordinary meaning in favor of some other interpretation. Certainly, it requires interpretive resources to obtain nontextual evidence, such as legislative history or other indicia of intent, with uncertain increases in interpretive accuracy. Vermeule (1998, 2006) makes a similar point in arguing that any interpretive value added by the consideration of legislative history is not justified by the cost of doing so.

Despite the various principles used to support the ordinary meaning doctrine, the presumptive meaning created by the doctrine can be overcome on whatever basis the court finds persuasive. If, for example, an intentionalist judge believes that the ordinary meaning of the relevant language conflicts with legislative intent, the judge can simply find that an unordinary meaning was intended.[11] Such a decision, though, requires an explanation, thereby illustrating the justificatory nature of legal interpretation. In general (and unlike ordinary conversations), courts do not simply announce or assume a particular interpretation but, rather, the process of reasoning is explained. With regard to some objective of interpretation, such as the determination of communicative meaning, courts explain how the evidence met the relevant standard for determining the meaning (often, but not always, defined as the "correct" interpretation). An ordinary meaning determination therefore adds explicit structure to what might otherwise be a comparatively open-ended judicial explanation if only the communicative or legal meaning of the text were being determined.

Notwithstanding its defeasibility, the presumption of ordinary meaning thereby sets a useful default, which requires that deviations from it be explained and justified, or that the underdetermined nature of the language be identified. Of course, courts might erroneously evaluate the relevant language, such as by exaggerating its definiteness. Judges are nevertheless accountable in the sense that they must give reasons for their decisions (Seidman 1988). The ordinary meaning concept enhances accountability by providing an anchoring point for deciding whether arguments about meaning are accepted or rejected. Certainly, courts frequently engage in statutory interpretation (or contract or constitutional interpretation) without mentioning ordinary meaning or one of its synonyms. This does not distinguish the ordinary meaning doctrine from other principles of interpretation, which are also habitually ignored by courts, at least in the sense that a judicial opinion may neglect to address a relevant interpretive principle.[12] In fact, it is likely that in most situations the ordinary meaning of textual language would be a primary consideration for courts implicitly, even if not explicitly. If a court takes the language of a legal text seriously, which it will invariably purport to do, it must give some linguistic meaning to the textual language. It would be odd for a court to immediately give the language some unordinary meaning, and specialized legal meanings obviously extend to only a small portion of the language in any legal text. Even if done incorrectly, the necessity of considering the ordinary meaning of language in legal texts cannot be avoided.

As the above discussion indicates, a significant justification for the ordinary meaning doctrine concerns the sequential nature of judicial interpretation. A sequential process where ordinary meaning is first determined and then accepted as the legal meaning of the text or, conversely, rejected in favor of an unordinary meaning is preferable to an alternative where the communicative meaning or legal meaning is decided without considering the ordinary meaning of the text. Determining the ordinary meaning of the text provides an important methodological commonality amongst judges that would not otherwise exist. A frequent comment about legal interpretation is that there is no generally agreed upon methodology of interpretation (Rosenkranz 2002). The two main methodologies of interpretation, textualism and intentionalism, differ in how they answer the constitutive and evidential questions, and they thus disagree about the definition of communicative meaning. Further, judges do not agree on which contextual aspects of meaning are relevant, or their persuasive value in general or in any given case. Even interpretive principles that have not been explicitly disavowed are often haphazardly applied by judges, or ignored altogether. Yet, both intentionalist and textualist judges use the ordinary meaning concept, establishing an area of agreement regarding a fundamental principle of interpretation.

Of course, it is common for a statute to have language that underdetermines its legal meaning, rendering the notice justification unachievable to some degree. Even in these situations, the ordinary meaning doctrine has significant value. Contrary to the claims of some legal experts (which will be elaborated below), who see ordinary meaning as decisive of legal meaning and the result of consensus, an accurate analysis of the ordinary meaning of the text at issue can underscore the underdetermined nature of some legal texts. Such a result would therefore frame the scope of judicial discretion explicitly, adding to the justificatory nature of legal interpretation. Even so, the notice justification persists and is often satisfied. If the necessity of notice of a provision's meaning is crucial, as it is for certain statutes, a strong presumption may exist that the ordinary meaning is the legal meaning. Thus, as indicated above, the presumption of ordinary meaning as legal meaning should be strongest for criminal provisions (and similar kinds of statutes) where notice and due process principles are necessary and weaker when the provision concerns highly sophisticated parties, such as agencies, with a high degree of knowledge of the legislative process.

3.2: Constitutive Aspects of Ordinary Meaning

3.2.1: The Problem of Designating Some Meaning as the Ordinary Meaning

As the above discussion indicated, there are reasons based on legal concerns, ranging from notice to the justificatory nature of legal interpretation, for maintaining the ordinary meaning doctrine (as opposed to simply determining the communicative or legal meaning of the text). The actual distinctions, however, between ordinary meaning and communicative meaning should be based on linguistic rather than legal concerns. Courts contrast ordinary meaning with technical meaning and legal meaning (although often only implicitly), and at least sometimes with unordinary meaning. Distinguishing technical meaning and legal meaning from ordinary meaning does not raise the same linguistic issues as does distinguishing ordinary meaning from other types of meaning, such as communicative meaning or unordinary meaning. In situations involving words with specialized technical or legal meanings, courts determine whether the legislature intended to give these words their technical or legal meanings instead of their ordinary meanings, if any. Of course, even if a technical or legal meaning is deemed to have been intended by the legislature, the court must determine the ordinary technical or ordinary legal meaning of the words. Designating a word as requiring a legal or technical meaning does not therefore avoid giving it its ordinary legal or technical meaning.

In contrast to the distinction between ordinary meaning and legal or technical meaning, identifying ordinary meaning, as opposed to some unordinary meaning, is a purely linguistic matter. For example, an unordinary meaning is one that can be said to be unusual or idiosyncratic. But how is an ordinary or unordinary meaning so designated? Waismann (1951, 122), writing about the "ordinary use of language" by philosophers, raises the following issues about the determination of ordinary meaning:

> But how ought one to determine what this ordinary use is, e.g. in a case of doubt? What ought one to do—to ask people? Any people? Or only the competent ones? And who is to decide who is "competent"—the leading circles of society, the experts of language, the writers just in vogue? And supposing there are people generally considered incompetent—what if they disagree?

Recall, from the beginning of chapter 1, Justice Scalia's creative source for empirical research. In Justice Scalia's view,

> the acid test of whether a word can reasonably bear a particular meaning is whether you could use the word in that sense at a cocktail party without having people look at you funny. The Court's assigned meaning would surely fail that test, even late in the evening.[13]

Of course, Justice Scalia's suggestion was likely meant to be more humorous than serious and likely reveals a preference for relying, at least in part, on "common sense" intuitions about ordinary meaning (although, as explained below, he criticizes judicial interpreters who rely on their own sense of language).

One way to conceptualize the constitutive question of what makes some meaning the ordinary one is by framing it in terms of the interpreter's role, rather than as a general empirical question. That is, an interpreter-focused answer may be given regardless of whether the judge is determining the ordinary meaning of the text or its ultimate communicative meaning. Thus, similar to the hypothetical intentionalism account, one might answer the constitutive question by asserting that a meaning is ordinary if it is deemed to be so by some hypothesized interpreter. The test cannot, of course, involve reference to the actual interpreter. It would be circular to aver that a meaning is ordinary simply by virtue of the actual interpreter proclaiming it as such. For one, especially when deciding on the ordinary meaning of a text, it is essential to recognize that competent and intelligent interpreters can disagree about its ordinary meaning but that some interpretations are wrong and not merely different but equally valid (Armstrong 1990). There is therefore a necessary distinction between what is in fact the case and what any given individual believes to be the case (Neale 2008).

3.2.2: Defining the Ordinary Meaning Interpreter

If a meaning is not the ordinary one by virtue of the fact that the actual interpreter has so proclaimed it, an idealized interpreter must be defined. But what are the characteristics of this interpreter? Some would pluralize the relevant interpreter, emphasizing that meaning is tied to an interpretive community and how that community would interpret the language at issue. Chapter 1 addressed the issue of whether the special nature of legal texts renders the ordinary meaning doctrine a misnomer. While the answer to that question should pretty clearly be "no," the specialized audiences for which legal texts are created may be relevant to their interpretation. Famously, Fish (1980) has taken the position that textual interpretation is based on the views and interpretive practices of the relevant interpretive community. Some legal scholars and judges have made broadly similar arguments. Judge Frank Easterbrook, for example, believes that the "significance of an expression depends on how the interpretive community alive at the time of the text's adoption understood those words" (Scalia and Garner 2012, XXV). Justice John Marshall believed that a text's "words are to be understood in that sense in which they are generally used by those for whom the instrument was intended."[14] Blatt (2001, 630) has offered a more detailed ontology, arguing that "[s]tatutes engage the following three distinct communities: the policy community of specialized professions found in government bureaucracies, the political community of elected politicians, and the public community of the general electorate."

It is not clear how focusing on an interpretive community's view of ordinary meaning differs from viewing it in terms of an idealized interpreter (who, in any case, is typically said to represent a class of people and not one person), but it may be seen as a way, for some at least, of avoiding the obligation of defining the characteristics of the idealized interpreter. Certainly, courts have been reluctant to imbue the interpreter of ordinary meaning as one possessing elevated language skills. To do so might seem inconsistent with the "reasonable person" standard, which is the prototypical standard of conduct employed in law. The notion of the reasonable person has been labeled "common law's most enduring fiction" (Moran 2010, 1233) and is often referred to as the typical, average, and ordinary person. Unsurprisingly, when they mention the interpreter's role in connection with ordinary meaning, courts have tended to refer to how an "ordinary person" would interpret the provision.[15] Sometimes, courts are more specific. With insurance contracts, for example, various courts have explained that the correct interpretation is one "which would be attached by an ordinary person of average understanding if purchasing insurance."[16]

The ordinary person referred to by courts seems to be relatively similar to how nonlegal scholars have described their idealized interpreter, although some scholars are explicit in envisioning their interpreters with at least somewhat elevated language skills. Wilensky (1989, 173), for example, refers to the "sensible speaker/hearer" as a normative language user who is a "typical if idealized member of a language community." The construction is designed to capture not an idiosyncratic property of some speaker but rather a more generalizable assignment of meaning to a sentence given world knowledge. Others have offered similar formulations, such as Kay's (1987) conception of the "ideal reader," Levinson's (2010) "appropriate hearer," and Shapiro's (2006) "competent speaker of English." The idealized interpreter seems to have a relatively high degree of linguistic ability. For example, Wilensky's (1989, 172) sensible hearer has (1) the cultural, as well as the linguistic, knowledge required to be a competent language user of a particular language community; and (2) skill at exploiting her knowledge, together with any available contextual information, to interpret sentences to arrive at their intended meanings. Importantly, the sensible speaker/hearer is a "non-deviate" language user. Similarly, Shapiro's (2006, 137) "competent speaker" is "someone that understands the language" and indicates that most readers of his book are "clear cases of competent speakers."

With legal texts, using a designation like "competent speaker" or "ordinary person," or some synonym referencing an average member of the community, to reflect the degree of sophistication of the interpreter is difficult to reconcile with how courts interpret statutes. Courts endemically employ interpretive principles that are not aspects of the ordinary meaning of the text (as argued in chap. 4) but that are also beyond the knowledge of the competent speaker or ordinary person." Courts will, for example, apply canons of interpretation, such as the canon of constitutional avoidance, which directs courts to select less persuasive, but "plausible," interpretations if doing so will avoid a serious constitutional issue (Slocum 2010). Similarly, courts will avoid giving a statute extraterritorial effect unless the statute clearly provides for such scope. Courts will also consider how a possible interpretation of a provision will fit into the statutory scheme as a whole. Plainly, an "ordinary person" is not likely to make any of these determinations when interpreting a text. It is not even clear that the ordinary person would consider the grammatical or semantics focused canons that courts consider, which may be seen as being aspects of the ordinary meaning determination. Courts will, for example, consider a principle such as the rule of the last antecedent, which provides that when a modifier is set off from a series of antecedents by a comma, the modifier should be interpreted to apply to all the antecedents. Would an ordinary person attach such significance to the presence or absence of a comma? Similarly, the rule against surplusage directs courts to avoid interpreting a provision in a way that would render other words, sections, or provisions of the act superfluous or unnecessary. Again, though, would an ordinary person be bothered by the presence of superfluity and be motivated to interpret a provision so as to avoid it? [17]

As the above examples illustrate, the ordinary person is attributed with greater knowledge, particularly of the specific concerns of the legal system, than the ordinary person would realistically possess. If the ordinary person is assumed to have knowledge of all interpretive rules, relevant laws (which might be needed in order to ensure coherence between the provision at issue and other relevant provisions), and other relevant legal concerns, the person would indeed not be "ordinary." Even if the focus is solely on linguistic knowledge, which is closer to the context relevant to ordinary meaning determinations (as explained below), the ordinary person standard does not accurately portray the level of sophistication that judges use when interpreting statutes. More accurate than some of the bare appeals to the ordinary person is Scalia and Garner's (2012) description of the idealized interpreter. Scalia and Garner indicate that the "fair reading method" (which seems to be a synonym for ordinary meaning) involves the "application of a governing text to given facts on the basis of how a reasonable reader, fully competent in the language, would have understood the text at the time it was issued" (Scalia and Garner 2012, 31).[18] The actual interpreter must possess "aptitude in language, sound judgment," the ability to conduct "historical linguistic research," and, of course, the ability to suppress "personal preferences regarding the outcome" of an interpretive determination (31).

As Scalia and Garner's description suggests, the idealized interpreter is plainly more linguistically sophisticated than is the ordinary person whose judgment is being measured. For one, as chapter 5 explains when examining the nature of definitions, the ordinary person as a competent language user may have the correct intuition regarding the meaning of a term but may not be aware of the basis of the intuition. Judges, though, have a justificatory obligation. It is generally not quite sufficient to base an interpretation of a provision on a bare appeal to what a reasonable person would undoubtedly think, although courts frequently do this with individual words. Undoubtedly, this justificatory motivation is one major reason why close examination of dictionary definitions is so prevalent among judges. The judicial reliance on dictionary definitions has been widely criticized, however, and other ways of determining the meanings of words have been suggested. These other possibilities for determining word meaning, such as the results from prototype analysis or corpora research, are obviously beyond the kind of analysis an ordinary person would likely perform, although they might result in interpretations that are consistent with those that would be made by an ordinary person.

Greenawalt (2010, 9) indicates that interpreters must decide whether the "objective" person should be the "average person," the "reasonable person," or the "most astute person (with capabilities exceeding those of ordinary people)." With respect to statutory interpretation, and undoubtedly for other legal documents such as constitutions, the idealized interpreter is astute, and an accurate description is something along the lines of "sophisticated determiner of how ordinary people use language." This modified view of the answer to the constitutive question should not necessarily create concern. Just as a judge knows more about the legal considerations that influence meaning than would a lay person, so too should the judge know more about language. The modified view does entail, though, that the process of legal interpretation for the most part has little to do with the views of the ordinary person, even if the interpreter's determination of ordinary meaning is consistent with what an ordinary person would think. It also casts doubt on any notion that there is a gap between what the actual interpreter believes to be the case regarding an issue of meaning and what the actual interpreter, via the idealized interpreter, determines an ordinary person would believe to be the case.

3.2.3: Ordinary Sentence Meaning

Formulating some view of the idealized interpreter of ordinary meaning addresses only part of the constitutive question of what makes some meaning of a legal text the ordinary meaning. Another important aspect of the constituent issue concerns the proper object of interpretation. With philosophy of language and linguistics, the typical focus is on sentences as the relevant units of meaning. Part of the problem with the current judicial approach to interpretation, though, is that courts often frame the ordinary meaning inquiry as involving an individual word instead of the relevant sentence. Even though judges agree that context is relevant, too often they treat the interpretive inquiry as though it merely involves the acontextual meaning of an individual word such as "vehicle," "use," or "deliver."

Sometimes the same case will illicit conflicting judicial views on the proper object of interpretation. Consider a recent Supreme Court case. In *Yates v. United States*,[19] the court had to determine whether a federal criminal statute, 18 U.S.C. § 1519, was violated by the action of having fish thrown overboard to avoid being found in violation of a separate provision that required the immediate release of grouper less than twenty inches long. Section 1519 provides:

> Whoever knowingly alters, destroys, mutilates, conceals, covers up, falsifies, or makes a false entry in any record, document, or tangible object with the intent to impede, obstruct, or influence the investigation or proper administration of any matter within the jurisdiction of any department or agency of the United

States . . . , or in relation to or contemplation of any such matter or case, shall be fined under this title, imprisoned not more than 20 years, or both.

The majority considered the surrounding words, and broader context, to limit the key phrase "tangible object" to "only objects one can use to record or preserve information, not all objects in the physical world."[20] In a dissenting opinion, though, Justice Kagan, purporting to use "conventional tools of statutory construction" to "lead to a [] conventional result," argued that "[a] "tangible object" is an object that's tangible" and, thus, "the ordinary meaning of the term "tangible object" in § 1519, as no one here disputes, covers fish (including too-small red grouper)."[21] To the majority, though, it was not particularly relevant whether in the abstract the ordinary meaning of "tangible object" includes "fish." Rather, the question at issue was whether the meaning of the relevant provision, § 1519, included "fish" within its scope.

Often the focus on word meaning instead of sentence meaning stems from the judiciary's overreliance on dictionaries, which offer acontextual word meanings. Instead of an exclusive focus on word meaning, as Jackson (1995, 43) has recognized, a distinction must be made between the meaning of words and the meaning of sentences. Defining ordinary meaning in terms of sentence meaning helps to mitigate the tension between the inherent nature of contextual consideration by an interpreter and the necessity of definitional generalizability. Thus, ultimately the relevant inquiry is not the ordinary meaning of words such as "use," "vehicle," "deliver," or "tangible object," which encompass numerous and varied senses. Rather, what is relevant is the ordinary meaning of the sentences in which the words appear.

One alternative to a focus on sentence meaning is to assert, according to Canale and Tuzet (2013, 36), that "the basic unit of meaning [is] not the sentence, but the relations among sentences." Obviously, the relations among sentences might reveal that the communicative meaning of a text differs from its ordinary meaning. Such an observation does not establish, though, that the basic unit of meaning is not the sentence. As explained above, there are advantages to a sequential kind of interpretation that starts with something more basic than an entire document, or even multiple sentences. Still, while the ordinary meaning focus should be on the relevant sentence rather than individual words or the entire document (or statute), this focus should not be taken as a precise standard. The point is that acontexual searches for individual word meanings lead to inaccurate ordinary meaning determinations, but a focus on an entire document (or statute) or body of law would result in a search for communicative meaning and not ordinary meaning. Thus, for example, the issue whether two independent clauses joined by a semicolon should count as one sentence for ordinary meaning purposes is not an interesting issue for this project to resolve.

3.3: Evidential Aspects of Ordinary Meaning

3.3.1: Views on Interpretive Consensus

The constitutive question of ordinary meaning has been answered by explaining that the ordinary meaning determination should focus on the meaning that the idealized interpreter, a sophisticated determiner of how ordinary people use language, would give the relevant sentence considering the context deemed to be relevant. The more complicated issue is the evidential question of what justifies the actual interpreter in believing that a sentence has a certain ordinary meaning. In considering evidential issues, the focus must be on the distinctions between ordinary meaning and unordinary meaning and between ordinary meaning and communicative meaning. In defining the border between ordinary meaning and communicative meaning, it is useful to consider how textualists view ordinary meaning and its role in textual interpretation.[22] For textualists such as Justice Scalia and Judge Easterbrook, ordinary meaning is a fundamental aspect of their conception of language and interpretation. Scalia and Garner state that the "ordinary-meaning rule is the most fundamental semantic rule of interpretation" (Scalia and Garner 2012, 69). The ordinary meaning rule is decisive, in Scalia and Garner's view, because "most interpretive questions have a right answer," and "[v]ariability in interpretation is a distemper" (Scalia and Garner 2012, 6). Further, the rule discourages or eliminates ideologically motivated interpretations because "judges who use the fair-reading method will arrive at fairly consistent answers" (6). The textualist position in essence is that interpretive methodologies that focus on text, such as ordinary meaning, produce consensus in interpretations across judges because they minimize judicial discretion. For instance, Judge Easterbrook asserts that the more the interpretive process strays outside a law's text, the greater the interpreter's discretion (Scalia and Garner 2012, XXV).

At the outset, without much elaboration required, various aspects of the textualist positions taken above are of questionable validity. Note the erroneous, but perhaps understandable, assumption that judicial consensus means that correct answers have been reached. Of course, it is possible to achieve consensus on the basis of incorrect, but widely accepted, understandings of language and interpretation, especially within a single community (such as judges). In addition, even a cursory examination of the textualist position reveals that textualist claims about discretion are unpersuasive and that discretion is to a large degree ineliminable even under the textualist view of proper interpretation. For instance, Scalia and Garner, in their book, list fifty-seven "fundamental principles" of interpretation, including the ordinary meaning doctrine. In some cases these fundamental principles will conflict, requiring a judicial judgment about which principle should prevail.[23] More importantly, even when they do not conflict with other interpretive doctrines, many of the principles require judicial discretion about whether and how they should be applied. As Scalia and Garner (2012, 51) themselves concede, the fundamental principles are "presumptions about what an intelligently produced text conveys" and not "'rules' of interpretation."

Also, it is unclear to what extent "most interpretive questions have a right answer." In some sense this assertion is true. Most objects in the world, for instance, are clearly not "vehicles," thereby creating an infinite number of "right answers" to interpretive questions that would never be asked. Interpretive questions asked in litigation, however, tend to be much more difficult, often being decided on the basis of reconciling conflicting interpretive clues and drawing inferences about statutory purpose. In essence, these sorts of interpretations involve significant discretion. Appendix D contains a list of fifty-five recent statutory interpretation cases in which the Supreme Court mentioned "ordinary meaning." In thirty-eight of these cases, there was a dissenting opinion on the interpretive issue before the court, and in some of the cases a split of opinion among the lower courts. Certainly, the Supreme Court, for the most part, considers difficult cases, as Greenawalt (2013) points out when examining judicial disagreement over interpretive matters.[24] It what sense, then, can a split of opinion on interpretive issues reflect a judicial "distemper"? Certainly, there are various methodological deficiencies in judicial decisions that may contribute to disagreement over the relevant interpretive issue. Frequently, though, disagreements reflect justifiable differences in opinion that would exist (but perhaps on different grounds) even if judges applied the same "correct" methodology of interpretation.

3.3.2: Empiricism and Ordinary Meaning

As the above description of the textualist position regarding ordinary meaning indicates, there is an obvious tension between "correct" meanings and discretion, assuming that in this case discretion refers to the multiple meanings a contested provision can legitimately be given. If interpretations follow highly structured, determinate paths, discretion would be comparatively minimized and consensus maximized. The textualist claim about interpretation, but more importantly about ordinary meaning, thus depends in part on the degree of discretion inherent in its determination. The issue, relating to the evidential aspects of ordinary meaning, would be relatively more straightforward if ordinary meanings were just utterance meanings that occur with a certain frequency. As Rorty (1985, 464n4) indicates, a distinction can be made "between two sets of intentions—the ones normally had by users of a sentence and some special ones had, or possibly had, by an individual user." If the issue is empirical, Waismann (1951, 122) asks, "Is perhaps the right way of tackling the question just this—to write down a long list of actually observed uses, taking note of the frequency of each use, and distilling the whole into a statistical table?"[25]

While empirical work of various kinds can greatly add to our understanding of ordinary meaning, the sort of empirical study suggested by Waismann is not sufficient to act as the evidentiary basis for ordinary meaning. This is especially true considering that the object of the ordinary meaning determination is the sentence and not individual words. The ordinary meaning of a sentence cannot typically be identified as that meaning which occurs with a certain frequency. For one reason, while it is possible to "write down a long list of actually observed uses" of individual words, doing so with sentences is not possible because of the infinite variation with which words are arranged. One exception involves sentences with idiomatic meanings, which are understood as such based on their precise formulation. Thus, if A says to B, "C has a chip on her shoulder," B understands based on hearing the idiomatic phrase "X has a chip on his/her shoulder" in the past, perhaps many times, that A intends to convey that B has some sort of grievance that readily provokes disputation. Another reason why frequency research based on sentences is not sufficient is because there are an unbounded number of potentially meaningful sentences in any natural language that have never been uttered (Wilson 1992). They are meaningful in part due to (1) the principle of compositionality (i.e., how the meaning of a complex linguistic expression is built up from the meanings of its subsentential elements in a rule-governed fashion) and (2) the principle of recursivity (i.e., how we can move from a finite base of rules and vocabulary to an understanding of an unlimited number of sentences) (Davidson 1967). Thus, it is entirely possible, and indeed normal, to decide that a sentence that had not previously ever been uttered nonetheless has an ordinary meaning.

3.3.3: Ordinary Meaning and Context

Because of the implausibility of frequency research being sufficient to answer issues of ordinary meaning, the doctrine must be investigated in terms of compositionality, recursivity, and other linguistic evidence. On one view, the meaning of a sentence is its interpreted syntactic structure. The content of a sentence is determined compositionally and is a function of the content of the sentence's constituents (for our purposes, think of "constituents" as words) and their syntactic relations. On the other hand, it is widely accepted that an interpreter generally is influenced by extralinguistic knowledge and that it is not possible to interpret language without consideration of context in some sense (Recanati 2006a). Indeed, Cappelen (2007) argues that, if the context associated with the utterance is varied enough, by changing such things as the audience, conversational context, and the background knowledge, etc., any sentence can communicate different propositions. As the above discussion suggests, a significant aspect of framing the ordinary meaning inquiry, and considering textualist arguments about it, involves considering the contribution that context makes to meaning.

Courts generally have no difficulty with the bare idea that when determining the ordinary meaning of a term consideration should be given to the context in which the word is used.[26] The concept of context, though, raises difficult issues for textualists. Textualism advocates a methodology of interpretation that is claimed to promote judicial restraint and, as Scalia and Garner claim, consensus. Context, though, is a variable concept that is difficult to limit, and the relevance and persuasiveness of contextual elements are typically subject to various, reasonable positions. When context is considered, not all interpreters will understand it in the same way, or give equal weight to its various components. So a concession that context is integral to interpretation is difficult to reconcile with an assertion that most interpretive questions have a "right" answer or produce widespread consensus.

Despite the tension between interpretive consensus and the consideration of context, textualists are motivated to concede the relevance of context. They have had to defend their methodology against charges that it has an unsophisticated view of language, including a failure to acknowledge the pervasiveness of vagueness and polysemy. Textualists are now eager to aver their sophisticated understanding of language. Scalia and Garner (2012, 70), for example, criticize the judicial interpreter who is "tempted simply to rely on his or her own sense of the language" and indicate that it would be a "mistake not to consult" "lexicographers and usage commentators" on certain issues of meaning. Manning (1999) similarly asserts that textualists have relied on insights from philosophy of language. Even so, such opinions are not likely unanimously shared by textualists. For instance, Vermeule (2006, 4), although not mentioning linguistic insights, argues that "judges should stick close to the surface-level or literal meaning of clear and specific texts."

Part of the textualist strategy has been to disassociate their theory from "plain meaning" judges who have been widely criticized as having an unnuanced view of language. These plain meaning judges are accused of interpreting language in an acontextual way and of exaggerating its clarity. Hence, Manning (2003, 2456), a leading textualist, seeks to differentiate modern textualists from "their literalist predecessors in the 'plain meaning' school."[27] Manning (1997) asserts that textualist judges routinely draw interpretive insights from sources outside of the statutory text. In fact, his definition of textualism explicitly incorporates consideration of context. Manning (2003, 2392–93) indicates that, in determining the meaning of a statute, textualists "ask how a reasonable person, conversant with the relevant social and linguistic conventions, would read the text in context." Similarly, Justice Thomas, a devoted textualist, has indicated in opinions that "[s]tatutory language has meaning only in context."[28]

Despite the textualist belief in the pervasiveness of contextual influences on meaning, there is an intuitive tension between consideration of context and the ordinary meaning of language. By its very nature, an ordinary meaning must be generalizable and not a special meaning for a particular context. Otherwise, a court would be merely determining the communicative meaning of the text, and there would be no methodological or conceptual gap between ordinary meaning and communicative meaning. On the other hand, words are naturally polysemous and considering the ordinary meaning of a word in isolation without allowing context to help select a meaning would not advance the interpretive endeavor in any useful way. The interpreter would be left with either ambiguity or a very general, indeterminate meaning, similar to that described by Wilensky (1989) below.

As the textualist position illustrates, there is widespread agreement that context is a necessary component of meaning, and that it is relevant to both ordinary meaning and communicative meaning. Scalia and Garner (Scalia and Garner 2012, 70), for instance, indicate the relevance of context both to ordinary meaning and to communicative meaning, stating that "one should assume the contextually appropriate ordinary meaning unless there is reason to think otherwise. Sometimes there *is* reason to think otherwise, which ordinarily comes from context." The broad, general consensus that context is integral to meaning, though, is not sufficient to differentiate the kind of context relevant to the determination of ordinary meaning and that relevant to communicative meaning. Considering that an ordinary meaning should be generalizable in some way, it seems right that determining the ordinary meaning of language should not involve the same consideration of context that is involved after the ordinary meaning has been sought and the interpreter is deciding whether an unordinary meaning was intended, how ambiguity should be resolved if there is no one ordinary meaning, or how vague text should be precisified. Some context may thus be relevant to communicative meaning, legal meaning, or other determinations but not to ordinary meaning.

3.3.4: The Distinction between Semantics and Pragmatics

One possible conception of context would be to recognize some division between a narrow kind of context relevant to ordinary meaning and a wide kind of context relevant to communicative meaning. Neither textualists nor anyone else has formally proposed such a division. For instance, regarding the interpretation of legal texts, Scalia and Garner (Scalia and Garner 2012, 33) indicate that context includes a "word's historical associations acquired from recurrent patterns of past usage, and a word's immediate syntactic setting—that is, the words that surround it in a specific utterance." As an exclusive description, this would indicate a relatively narrow conception of context. Scalia and Garner also indicate, however, that it is proper to consider "purpose demonstrated from reading the text in context" (Scalia and Garner 2012, 38). They describe the "fair reading method" as requiring "an ability to comprehend the purpose of the text, which is a vital part of its context. But the purpose is to be gathered only from the text itself, consistently with the other aspects of its context" (33). Consistent with other scholars and courts, however, Scalia and Garner do not draw any distinctions between the context relevant to the determination of ordinary meaning and that relevant to communicative meaning.

In thinking about context, and the extent to which ordinary meaning can be adequately framed as involving conventions of meaning and some degree of contextual invariability, it is useful to consider the distinction between semantics and pragmatics and how that distinction informs conceptions of interpretation. Scalia and Garner, probably colloquially, refer to ordinary meaning as a "semantic" rule of interpretation (Scalia and Garner 2012, 69). As detailed below, the distinction between semantics and pragmatics is important to legal interpretation because of the issues of discretion and context invariability. If the ordinary meaning of a sentence is coextensive with its semantic meaning, discretion would be limited compared to a version where pragmatics is integral to meaning. If, instead, pragmatics is typically or always relevant to ordinary meaning, the gap between ordinary meaning and communicative meaning would be much more difficult to define in a systematic or coherent manner.

There is considerable debate regarding the definitions of semantics and pragmatics and where the semantics/pragmatics borderline crosses for specific linguistic expressions. Part of the debate concerns the wide, and sometimes contradictory, range of ways in which philosophers and linguistics have used the terms "semantic" and "pragmatic." A long-standing view is that semantics accounts for linguistic phenomena by relating, via the rules of the language and abstracting away from specific contexts, linguistic expressions to the world objects to which they refer (Ariel 2010). Under this account, semantics is compositional and convention based, and sentence meanings are derived from a null context (more on this below). A semantic meaning is thus one based on decoding and not intent determining (Ariel 2010).

In contrast to semantics, pragmatics is not compositional, accounts for linguistic phenomena by reference to the language user (producer or interpreter), and involves inferential processes (Ariel 2010). The traditional view is that pragmatics takes as input the semantic contents of sentences uttered in contexts (Soames 2008a). After identifying the semantic content of an utterance, pragmatic principles are generated. Context is thus centrally involved in explaining how pragmatics complements semantics. Pragmatics takes account of contextual factors, such as the mutual knowledge shared by the speaker and addressee, and the relevant unit is a sentence-context pair. The focus of pragmatics is the speech act and how meanings can be given to human utterances. The interpreter seeks to identify the utterer's intention in making the utterance by considering what the utterer said and the way he said it. Thus, to provide an interpretation for the utterance is to identify the reason for it and the agent's particular intention. Pragmatics is thus concerned with whatever information is relevant to understanding an utterance, even if such information is not reflected in the syntactic properties of the sentence.

The semantics/pragmatics distinction can serve as part of the framework for thinking about the varied ways in which ordinary meaning can be defined and how the possible definitions relate to issues of discretion. Along the semantics/pragmatics spectrum are those who argue that the communicative contents uttered by speakers are generally not coterminous with the semantic contents of the sentences they use, as well as those who argue the opposite. On one end of the spectrum is the contextualist view that there is always some pragmatic explanation for how, in any given case, sentence meaning can underdetermine what the speaker means (Bach 2002). A sentence's linguistic meaning may not (and some would say never does) reflect the meaning it has when it is uttered, and the gap between semantic meaning and actual meaning is explained by contextual facts. The meaning of sentences can therefore vary and what determines meaning is not limited to facts about the words alone but also includes facts about the circumstances in which the sentence is uttered. Thus, the "context of utterance" is crucial (Bach 2002).

The result of the contextual inputs is that semantic meanings are defeasible and there is no limit to the amount of contextual information that can affect pragmatic interpretation. The proposition that the interpreter would intuitively believe to be the proposition expressed by the communication may therefore contain an element that is not the value of any constituent in the sentence uttered, nor introduced by composing those values. Instead, the element is considered to be an "unarticulated constituent," making the element part of the statement made even though it corresponds to nothing in the uttered sentence. Because of these broad contextual effects on meaning, the contextualist view of meaning has been described by opponents as not providing detailed, formal explanations of how interpretation works when it exploits context.

In contrast to the contextualist view is the semantic view of interpretation that emphasizes the compositionality and systematicity of language. Semanticists emphasize the semantic content of a sentence, which is de-

rived by taking the semantic contents of the parts of that sentence, relative to that context, and composing them in accord with the composition
rules governing the syntactic structure of that sentence. The content of
the sentence a writer inscribes, being semantic, is independent of the writer's communicative intention. When one reads an inscription, one needs
to understand the sentence the writer inscribed in order to figure out the
communicative intention with which he inscribed it. Understanding the
sentence, though, is independent of context except insofar as there are elements in the sentence whose semantic value are context relative (an example of this are indexicals, which are described below). Recognizing the
writer's communicative intention is a matter of figuring out the content of
that intention on the basis of contextual information in the broad sense.

Some scholars sympathetic to the semantic view of language emphasize that language is systematic, allowing interpreters to readily understand information from sentences that the interpreters have never before
encountered. If this process were not possible, successful communication
would be mysterious. Mystery is not, of course, an adequate account of
language and interpretation. On the semantic account, then, context sensitivity is not an impediment to a proper account of linguistic meaning.
Sentences cannot therefore have thin context-independent meanings. As
Stanley (2007, 18) argues, "[i]f context could affect the interpretation of
words in such a manner that the content they express relative to a context would be inconsistent with their context-independent meaning, that
would threaten the systematic nature of interpretation." In Stanley's
(2007, 208) broad definition, content is semantic if it is constrained by linguistic meaning. Successful interpretation involves assigning denotations
(i.e., meanings) to the constituents of the sentence and combining them
in accordance with composition rules that do not vary with extralinguistic
context. Stanley concedes that, even if the grammar and standing linguistic meanings of all the words in a sentence are known, there is still a gap
between that knowledge and the information about the world conveyed
by an utterance of that sentence (2007, 2). Nevertheless, Stanley argues
that "extra-linguistic context is never called upon to expand the content
determined by the context-independent meaning of a term in a context"
(2007, 18). It can, of course, serve to narrow meaning, as the examination
of quantifiers and other linguistic phenomena will demonstrate.

It is not necessary to the exploration of ordinary meaning to take sides
on how to define the pragmatics versus semantics distinction. The question of which view of meaning (contextualist vs. semantic) is correct is
largely empirical in nature (involving questions of how language works

and is processed) and beyond the scope of this book. Nevertheless, the contextualist/semantic positions regarding meaning help illustrate ways in which the ordinary meaning doctrine can be conceived. Intuitively, the semantic view of meaning is connected to the ordinary meaning doctrine in the sense that an ordinary meaning should be one that is generalizable and systematic and not based on the particular intent of the author (even an intent seen from a hypothetical intentionalist point of view). Often, a meaning that is compositional and not substantially affected by context could not be said to be one that is unordinary. In order to outline how the gap between communicative meaning and ordinary meaning might be conceived, this book will emphasize a semantic view of language. As will be illustrated, however, even a semantic view of the various linguistic phenomena that will be examined cannot elide the fact that core aspects of interpretation are ineliminably discretionary.

3.3.5: The Null Context

Even under a semantic view of language, interpreters are inevitably influenced by their knowledge of the world. Semanticists recognize this reality, and textualists concede generally that context is relevant to interpretation. In considering a semantic account of ordinary meaning, though, it is necessary to consider the extent to which context-independent word meanings can be conceived. As well, in defining ordinary meaning and how the semantics/pragmatics divide relates to it and to communicative meaning, it is useful to consider how the semantics/pragmatics divide relates to the different levels of meaning commonly used by scholars.

In general, scholars have distinguished between "sentence meaning," "what is said," and "what is implicated" (Recanati 2004). The terms can be put in a hierarchy of communication, as follows:

sentence meaning

vs.

what is said

vs.

what is implicated.

Recanati describes sentence meaning as conventional and context independent. The sentence meaning is that interpretation of a sentence that can be made in the "zero" or "null" context. The null context represents the idea that the sentence meaning depends entirely on the meanings of its constituents and its syntactic structure.

The concept of sentence meaning and the null context is controversial. For purposes of ordinary meaning, it would be desirable if a distinction could be made between a meaning that could be assigned to a sentence using only grammatical and lexical knowledge and a meaning that could be assigned by supplementing this information with contextual knowledge. Searle (1979) argues, though, that we must abandon either the idea that literal meanings establish truth conditions, or the notion that literal meanings can be determined independent of context.[29] For the interpretation of legal texts, the notion of truth conditions is not particularly relevant. Essentially, Searle is arguing against the idea that complete meanings, such as would be required in legal cases, can be determined in a null context. The null context concept is thus relevant to legal interpretation because it is connected to the larger concept of context, which, as explained above, is important in defining ordinary meaning and thinking about judicial discretion. In any case, an important assumption about sentence meaning is that it represents an actual meaning but in a null context. It is questionable, though, that there is such a thing as a true null context, as opposed to only informationally impoverished contexts. Wilensky (1989), for instance, suggests that it is a mistake to assume that because a sentence is considered in isolation (i.e., the null context) a meaning can be determined based only on linguistic knowledge.

Consider the following examples (from Searle 1980):

(1)   The cat is on the mat.
(2)   Cut the grass.
(3)   Cut the cake.

The preposition "on" can be used to identify a variety of different physical situations. At the least, it can mean "lying upon, "balancing upon," "hanging from" (e.g., "the fixture on the ceiling"), and "vertically supporting" (e.g., "the notice on the bulletin board"). Wilensky (1989) notes that a "central meaning" of "on" that would encompass all the situations might be something like "supported by." The problem is that, while the dictionary definition offers many meanings, a use of "on" in (1) means only one of the more specific relations. Similarly, for (2) and (3) the sentence meaning is the same, but the contribution to the communicated meaning is sig-

nificantly different. Searle argues that "cut" makes a different contribution in (3) than in (2) because if the facts revealed in response to the
command in (3) that the agent ran the cake over with a lawn mower, the
hearer would not have interpreted the speaker correctly. Assuming that
"cut" is not being used ambiguously, it must be the case that the literal
meaning of the sentences must take context into account.

Even accounting for the criticism that Searle confuses sentence meaning with sentence use, Searle's examples pose a problem for meaning.
Wilensky (1989) explains that, however specifically we are willing to postulate word senses, interpretations will be even more specific. As indicated
above, this is obvious with respect to "on" in "The cat is on the mat." Similarly, if it is stipulated that "cut" means "slice," the interpretation of "Cut
the salami" and "Cut the cake" will still be different. Sentences like (1)–
(3) therefore have a meaning that is different from what would be assigned the uses of the sentences in the null context. The null context assumption is that the sentence meaning is utterance meaning in the null
context. The problem is that "sentence meaning" is much more abstract
than "literal meaning." The sentence meaning is not really a meaning because the meaning that can be computed using the grammar and lexicon
may never be in itself a suitable candidate for the meaning of an utterance. The mistake is to assume that, because we heard a sentence in isolation (i.e., the null context), we are computing a meaning based only on
linguistic knowledge. Even though there may indeed be a semantic object
computable from the grammar and lexicon without recourse to context,
the interpretation of this sentence when no external context is supplied
(the null context) is likely to depart from this object.

Even before considering the other ways in which meaning depends on
context, the null context scenarios illustrate the problematic nature of at-
tempting to separate context from meaning. Even assuming that meaning
is compositional, world knowledge intrudes on knowledge of syntax and
linguistic meaning. Utterances occur within a certain context, and acontextual meaning is an unobservable, theoretical concept (Charnock 2013).
Only some conclusions about language follow from such an observation,
though. Recanati (2004, 56), for example, argues that semantic interpretation is not determinate enough to deliver complete propositions but,
rather, only semantic schemata. Recanati is mistaken that semantic interpretation cannot deliver complete propositions, even if sometimes there
is a gap between the communicative content uttered by a speaker and the
semantic content of the sentence used. Further, the null context scenario

does not by itself compel a conclusion that some wide contextual scope must operate at all levels of meaning. It does not, for example, show that systematicities in languages do not exist, but rather illustrates the need for such examination. For instance, as chapter 5 explains in connection with an infamous Supreme Court case, in some situations what varies from utterance to utterance is not a term's semantic properties but how those properties interact with those of the words with which it is associated. The phenomena involved are, arguably, too systematic to be relegated to pragmatics.

3.4: "Sentence Meaning," Indexicals and Ordinary Meaning

3.4.1: Description of "Sentence Meaning"

Apart from the issue of the problematically abstract nature of the meanings produced in a null context, a separate problem for the "sentence meaning" category as an account of ordinary meaning is that it does not account for even semantically triggered contextual evidence. Linguistically mandated processes that require resort to context should uncontroversially be seen as being a part of ordinary meaning. A further problem is that the ordinary meaning is the presumptive meaning of the legal text and therefore needs a theory of meaning that represents complete propositions that can serve as the meaning of a text. As will be explained below, because sentence meanings do not satisfy this requirement, they are not synonymous with ordinary meanings.

An examination of indexicals will illustrate how even semantically triggered linguistic categories are problematized by context. The traditional view of indexicals is that they exhibit more regularity than do many other context-sensitive terms. Yet, the traditional view of indexicals has been widely attacked by philosophers, who have undermined the claims of invariant meaning. Nevertheless, there are semantically-based theories of indexical meaning that can serve as the ordinary meaning of indexicals. Thus, the context-sensitive nature of indexicals is not fatal to the assignment of ordinary meaning because although the content of an indexical varies according to context, it has a fixed meaning across all contexts. Recognizing a semantic account of the ordinary meaning of indexicals, while also outlining how the communicative meanings can be determined, will maintain the gap between ordinary meaning and communicative meaning. As with other linguistic phenomena, though, even determining the ordinary meaning of indexicals allows for considerable interpreter discretion. Part of the discretion associated with a semantic view of indexical meanings is that the semantic view readily allows judges to choose ordinary meanings based on legal rather than linguistic judgments.

As indicated above, because it does not include contextual considerations, the sentence meaning category excludes the concept of "saturation." Saturation is the process that completes the meaning of a sentence and makes it "propositional through the contextual assignment of semantic values to the constituents of the sentence whose interpretation is context-dependent" (Recanati 2004, 7). Appeal to context is necessary for the sentence to express a complete proposition because one (or more) of the constituents (i.e., words) requires that its reference be determined through the consideration of context. In Recanati's view, saturation covers such things as indexicals, genitives (e.g., "John's book"), and nominal compounds (e.g., "burglar nightmare"). Indexicals, for example, are classic examples of constituents that must be contextually assigned a reference for the given sentence to be fully propositional. These words, such as "I," "now," "here," and "today," thus have content that is relative to the context of utterance. Thus, the sentence

(4)   He is a good linguist

does not express a complete proposition unless a referent has been contextually assigned to the pronoun "he." Because saturation of this sort is necessary in order to make a sentence fully propositional, it is a mandatory contextual process.

3.4.2: A Supreme Court Case, Carcieri v. Salazar, Illustrating that Indexicals Are Relevant to Legal Interpretation

To some it might seem odd that such significant space will be devoted below to the examination of indexicals considering the widespread avoidance of in-depth examinations of them by legal scholars.[30] Undoubtedly, legal scholars generally do not view indexicals as raising particularly important issues of legal interpretation. Marmor (2008b, 426), for example, has stated that, "[b]ecause it is widely recognized that the use of [indexicals] renders the content of the expression profoundly context-dependent, legal formulations normally try to avoid them." Similarly, Rickless (2005,

524) states that "theorists of adjudication can safely ignore the phenomenon of explicit context sensitivity," because indexicals and demonstratives
do not appear in legal texts.[31] It is true that litigation involving the interpretation of indexicals is not as common as that involving other linguistic phenomena such as ambiguity and vagueness. It is not the case, though,
that the drafters of legal texts always avoid indexicals, and it will be shown
below that the reference shifting associated with indexicals is similarly applicable to definite descriptions. When indexicals have appeared in legal
texts, courts have struggled to properly consider the complexities that
context can add to the interpretation of indexicals. As a result, as in many
other areas of legal interpretation, there is often an overreliance on dictionary definitions.

As introduced at the beginning of this chapter, *Carcieri v. Salazar*[32] illustrates a typical way in which courts have approached the interpretation of indexicals, as well as the gap between ordinary meaning and communicative meaning. *Carcieri* involved the Narragansett, who occupied
much of what is now the state of Rhode Island at the time of European
colonization of New England.[33] In the 1970s, the Narragansett filed suit to
recover ancestral land, claiming that Rhode Island had misappropriated
tribal territory in violation of the Indian Non-Intercourse Act.[34] Following
enactment of the Rhode Island Indian Claims Settlement Act (the Act),[35]
the tribe received title to eighteen hundred acres of land in Charlestown,
Rhode Island.[36] In 1983, the Narragansett Tribe's ongoing efforts to gain
recognition from the United States government finally succeeded.[37] After
obtaining federal recognition, the tribe began urging the secretary of the
interior ("secretary") to accept a deed of trust to the eighteen hundred
acres conveyed to it under the Act.[38] In 1988, at the tribe's behest and pursuant to section 465 of the Indian Reorganization Act ("IRA"),[39] the secretary took the eighteen hundred acres into trust on the tribe's behalf.[40]
In 1998, the secretary notified the state of Rhode Island, its governor, and
the town of Charlestown, Rhode Island, that he intended to accept in trust
a parcel of land for use by the Narragansett Indian Tribe in accordance
with his claimed authority under the statute.[41]

Litigation arose after the secretary's notification. The litigation cen-
tered on whether the secretary had statutory authority under the IRA to
accept in trust land for use by the Narragansett Indian Tribe. Section 465
of the IRA expressly authorizes the secretary to take land and hold it in
trust "for the purpose of providing land for Indians."[42] Section 479 of the
act defines "Indian" as follows:

The term "Indian" as used in this Act shall include all persons of Indian descent who are members of any recognized Indian tribe *now* under Federal jurisdiction, and all persons who are descendants of such members who were, on
June 1, 1934, residing within the present boundaries of any Indian reservation,
and shall further include all other persons of one-half or more Indian blood
(emphasis added).

The governor of Rhode Island et al. contended that the term "now"
in the statute refers to the time of the statute's enactment and permits
the secretary to take land into trust for members of recognized tribes
that were "under Federal jurisdiction" in 1934. In contrast, the secretary
argued that "now" is an ambiguous term that can reasonably be construed
to authorize the secretary to take land into trust for members of tribes
that are "under Federal jurisdiction" at the time that the land is accepted
into trust.

In ruling against the secretary, the Supreme Court reversed the rul-
ings of the district court and the US Court of Appeals for the First Circuit. The district court had found that the statute clearly favored the secretary's interpretation. Like the district court, Justice Thomas, writing for
the Court, found the text of the IRA to be unambiguous, except in the
opposite direction. Justice Thomas reasoned that the Court should begin
with the ordinary meaning of "now," as understood when the IRA was
enacted. Justice Thomas first quoted a dictionary definition that defined
"now" as "[a]t the present time; at this moment; at the time of speaking."[43]
He also quoted *Black's Law Dictionary*, which similarly defined "now"
and which also indicated that "'[n]ow' as used in a statute ordinarily refers to the date of its taking effect."[44] Justice Thomas then claimed that
the dictionary definition of "now" was consistent with how the Court had
interpreted "now" in statutes both before and after passage of the IRA.[45]

Justice Thomas further reasoned that in the original version of § 465,
which provided the same authority to the secretary, Congress explicitly
referred to current events.[46] In addition, elsewhere in the IRA, Congress
expressly referenced future events by using the phrase "now or hereafter."[47] In the Court's view, Congress's failure to include the phrase "or
hereafter" provided further textual support for the conclusion that "now"
referred solely to events contemporaneous with the act's enactment.[48] The
Court also noted that the secretary's current interpretation was at odds
with the executive branch's construction of the provision at the time of
enactment.[49] The Court responded to the argument that "now" is ambigu-

ous by indicating that alternative meanings do not render a word ambiguous, "particularly when 'all but one of the meanings is ordinarily eliminated by context.'"[50] Because the Court found the statute to be clear and that the provision therefore "speaks for itself," it refused to consider the policy implications of its decision.[51]

In a concurring opinion, Justice Breyer noted that the statute's language was not by itself determinative because, "[l]inguistically speaking," "now" could refer to either the time of enactment or the time the secretary exercises his authority to take land "for Indians."[52] Justice Breyer pointed to other statutes where "now" had been interpreted as referring to the time of exercise of delegated authority, as well as when a will becomes operative.[53] Justice Breyer concurred with the Court's decision because the legislative history of the statute, which the Court did not consider, convinced him that "now" in the provision should be interpreted as referring to the time of the statute's enactment. He also reasoned, similarly to the district court, that § 479 "may prove less restrictive than it at first appears," because a tribe "may have been 'under Federal jurisdiction' in 1934 even though the Federal Government did not believe so at the time."[54]

Table 3.1 lists, in order of discussion, the evidence relied on by the majority in its opinion in *Carcieri v. Salazar*. Some of the questions posed at the beginning of the chapter regarding ordinary meaning have already been addressed. For instance, the object of ordinary meaning is the sentence, rather than an individual word or an entire document. In addition, the ordinary meaning interpreter has been described as something akin to a "sophisticated determiner of how ordinary people use language." Nevertheless, many of the questions are yet to be answered. The Court's opinion in *Carcieri* offers an excellent vehicle through which such an examination might take place.

As is typical, the Court in *Carcieri* asserted that it would interpret the statute according to the ordinary meaning of its language, but did the Court accomplish its task? One notable aspect of the decision, in light of Scalia and Garner's (Scalia and Garner 2012, 69) view that "[v]ariability in interpretation is a distemper," is the Court's insistence on the clarity of the provision despite the district court and First Circuit decisions (which the Court overruled). The district court concluded that "[t]he plain language of § 479 does not impose [the] limitation" for which the state had argued.[55] The Court held that the first part of the definition of "Indian" contains two separate requirements: (1) that an individual be a "mem-

TABLE 3.1. **Order and reasoning of the Supreme Court's opinion in** *Carcieri v. Salazar*

Dictionary definitions	Quotes from *Webster's New International Dictionary* and *Black's Law Dictionary*, which indicated that "now" referred to the time of enactment
Precedents	Two previous decisions that focused on the time of statutory enactment rather than subsequent events
Prior version of provision	Express reference to current events indicated that the time of enactment was the correct focus
Linguistic usage	Use of "now or hereafter" in other provisions indicated that "now" by itself referred to the time of enactment
Administrative interpretation	Executive branch's construction of relevant provision at time of enactment undermined its subsequent interpretations
Policy views	Clarity of relevant provisions rendered consideration of policy views inappropriate

ber[] of [a] tribe[] in existence in 1934," and (2) that the "tribe subsequently attain[] federal recognition."[56] That recognition occurred after the IRA's enactment was not relevant to the district court.[57] According to the Court's analysis, "now" in § 479 references the date of enactment, June 18, 1934. So long as the Narragansett existed as a tribe in 1934, the tribe falls under the scope of "Indian" and "tribe" as defined in § 479 because federal recognition is no more than "recognition of a previously existing status."[58] In turn, the US Court of Appeals for the First Circuit reached the same result as the district court, though it held differently as to the referent of "now." While the district court found the term unambiguous, the First Circuit found the act's text to be "sufficiently ambiguous in its use of the term 'now.'"[59] The First Circuit reasoned that "now" means "at the present time," but noted that there is ambiguity as to whether to view the term "now" as operating at the moment Congress enacted it or at the moment the secretary invokes it. The reason for the ambiguity was that Congress sometimes uses the word "now" to refer to a time other than the moment of enactment.[60]

Notwithstanding the interesting fact of conflicting court interpretations of the key provisions, the usefulness of the Supreme Court's opinion to this book's project of conceptualizing ordinary meaning is how it determined the ordinary meaning of "now." Justice Thomas relied on two dictionary definitions of "now," along with some other evidence (as indicated in the above table). As posed at the beginning of this chapter, is the ordinary meaning of "now" invariably "at the present time," as Justice Thomas seemed to believe? Part of the following discussion will explain why the answer is "no." It might seem counterintuitive that a court may not be able to simply rely on a dictionary definition as the ordinary meaning of a word. But Justice Thomas did not, of course, rely solely on the dictionary definition. The object of the ordinary meaning analysis should be the relevant sentence, but what contextual considerations are relevant? For instance, Justice Thomas referenced a prior version of the provision at issue, but is such evidence relevant to ordinary meaning? What about the Court's precedents, which Justice Thomas also discussed? What about the legislative history of the provision, which was examined in Justice Breyer's concurring opinion? These sources of meaning are often deemed to be relevant to the interpretation of statutes, but are they relevant to the determination of ordinary meaning?

3.4.3: The Traditional View of Indexicals

Despite the consensus that an indexical has a context-dependent reference, there is debate regarding the extent to which indexicals possess context-invariant meanings. The traditional view regarding indexicals, attributed to David Kaplan (1989) and followed by Justice Thomas in *Carcieri*, is an intention-free formal account that posits that indexicals have linguistic meanings that are, in essence, conventions regarding their use. Under this view, the context-sensitive nature of indexicals is not problematic because, although the content of an indexical varies according to context, it has a fixed meaning across all contexts. According to Kaplan, the *character* of an indexical expression provides a rule of use that determines its *content* (i.e., referent). Simplifying somewhat, characters can be represented as functions from contexts to referents. The contexts are collections of the parameters required by the particular functions (Predelli 2011).

Simple indexical expressions, such as "I," are treated by Kaplan as rigid singular terms with constant semantic values. Because the content is context dependent, "I" may refer to distinct individuals with respect to different contexts. It is therefore sensitive to the identity of the appropriate contextual parameters. For any context c, the intension (i.e., meaning) i_c for "I" with respect to c is the function yielding "the agent" of c as that expression's semantic value. This view of indexicals is such that "I am here now" is "true whenever uttered" based on semantic reasons. Kaplan

(1989, 509) states that the phrase is "deeply, and in some sense ... universally, true. One need only understand the meaning of [it] to know that it cannot be uttered falsely." The traditional view thus posits that the sentence

(5) I am here right now

can never be uttered falsely, and thus its inverse

(6) I am not here right now

can never be uttered truthfully.[61] As Romdenh-Romluc (2006, 2008) indicates, this traditional account of first-person thought makes the following further claims:

(7) The reference-determining context is the context of utterance.
(8) An utterance of "here" refers to the location of the utterance.
(9) An utterance of "now" refers to the time of the utterance.

3.4.4: Challenges to the Traditional View of Indexicals

The traditional view of indexical utterances has been broadly attacked by modern commentators. Along with others, Nunberg (1993) explains that the theories developed by Kaplan and others do not offer solutions to various situations in which statements containing indexicals are made. These challenges have shown that the traditional claims about indexicals in (7)–(9) cannot be maintained. Some of the situations used to undermine the traditional view of indexicals involve devices for later broadcasting (termed instances of "deferred reference" by Sidelle 1991). Consider a situation where Colleen is an executive and Bill is her secretary.[62] For some reason, Colleen will not be in her office for a week but does not change her telephone answering machine. Without Colleen's knowledge, Bill changes the (computerized voice) message to include the following utterance:

(10) I am not here right now.

The utterance undermines the traditional view of indexicals by proving the falsity of (6).[63] An utterance of "I" does not always refer to the utterer.

Colleen is not the utterer since she did not create the message or even arrange for it to be created. Rather, Bill is the utterer. While Bill is the utterer of (10), the referent of "I" was intended by Bill to be Colleen and would undoubtedly be interpreted by callers as such. Further, the deferred communication aspect of (10) reveals that (7) and (9) are also false. The reference-determining context is not necessarily the context of utterance.

Other examples involving "now" illustrate that the traditional view is not a sufficient theory for determining the references of indexicals considering the variety of circumstances that have to be evaluated in determining meaning. As Corazza (2004) explains, speakers and authors often use present tense locutions to refer to past or future events. For example, cases involving so-called historical time involve situations where the reference of "now" would not pick out the time of utterance. Thus, a teacher lecturing about the Nazi invasion of Paris might say,

(11) *Now* Hitler takes control of Paris.[64]

In (11), like (10), "now" obviously does not refer to the time of the utterance. Instead it refers to the time when the Nazis invaded Paris. Similarly, in the following utterance,

(12) In 1834 Jon visited his mother, the once famous actress, *now* an old, sick woman[65]

"now" does not pick out the time of the utterance. Rather, the reference is to 1834, when Jon visited his mother.

It is clear that indexicals are even more context specific than many scholars have assumed. In addition to the scenarios involving (likely) successful communications, as exemplified in (9)–(12), efforts to undermine the traditional view of indexicals have often employed examples of mismatched communications where a discrepancy exists between the meaning intended by the utterer and the one likely to be given the utterance by the listener. Notwithstanding the typical motivations of the speaker to communicate effectively and the listener to interpret accurately, instances of mismatched communications exist where the intended meaning and the interpreted meaning do not correspond. In such situations, the character of an indexical expression does not provide a rule of use that will invariably determine its content. Rather, as is the case with "I," "now," and other indexicals, features of the relevant context may indicate that the traditional rule of use is inappropriate.

3.4.5: Post-Kaplan Approaches to Indexicals

As the above discussion illustrates, it cannot be said that the "character" of an indexical expression provides a rule of use that will inevitably determine its "content" (i.e., referent). In light of widespread attacks on the traditional view of indexicals, scholars have proposed various frameworks to account for how the references of indexicals are determined. One group of theories explicitly accounts for indexicals in terms of the broad contextual considerations that influence their references. If one is considering the communicative meaning of indexicals, what Cohen and Michaelson (2013) term the "doxastic control theories" offer the accounts that most closely approximate how courts might evaluate the available evidence that is relevant to the references of indexicals. The proposed frameworks fall along familiar lines, similar to the division described in chapter 2 between actual intentionalists and hypothetical intentionalists.

Under the intentionalist model advocated by Akerman (2009) and Predelli (2002), which was explained in chapter 2, the proposition expressed by a sentence containing indexicals is dependent on the speaker's intentions.[66] The speaker's intentions determine the context for interpretation (and values) and thereby determine the correct interpretation and the proposition expressed. Akerman argues for a distinction between the correct interpretation (which is determined by the speaker's intention) and the reasonable interpretation (which is determined by external standards). In Akerman's view, cases of mismatch occur when relevant intuitions about the determinants track the *reasonable* interpretation rather than the *correct* interpretation. Predelli (1998, 114) argues that multiple contexts are needed for the correct interpretation of indexicals. In Predelli's picture, the role of intentions is to determine the context with respect to which the indexical should be interpreted. A speaker can intend her use of an indexical to be evaluated with respect to any context whatsoever. While the indexical always refers pursuant to the utterer's intent (and thus the intent provides the "correct" meaning), it cannot always be used to refer to any context whatsoever. Instead, the hearer's ability to interpret the utterance limits an indexical's possible referring uses. Table 2.1 in chapter 2 reflects the two intentionalist theories of indexicals discussed.

3.4.6: Objective Views of Indexicals

The intentionalist accounts of indexicals, exemplified by Predelli and Akerman, are insufficient for the same reasons as were given in chapter 2 for communicative meaning. Other scholars writing about indexicals have opposed the intentionalist accounts described above for some of the reasons described in chapter 2, particularly the Humpty Dumpty problem. A speaker's intention to give an indexical a certain reference, no matter how unlikely to normal language users (i.e., the reasonable person), cannot be deemed a sufficient (or necessary) condition for the "correct" interpretation. Instead, some scholars have proposed various objective theories that are within the doxastic control theories because they involve the determination of indexical reference through audiences' expectations rather than fixed linguistic conventions.

Gauker (2008), for instance, proposes that the determinants of the context necessary to interpret a sentence never include the speaker's intention.[67] Gauker argues that "the proposition an utterance expresses will be a proposition that a competent hearer would be able to assign to it by means of a method of interpretation that the hearer could reliably employ on the basis of features of the situation that the hearer could normally be aware of" (361). The relevant features are external accessibility criteria such as salience, prior reference, relevance, charity, pointing, and location in a series (364–65). Other criteria are possible. The criteria "can be elaborated in ad hoc ways, so long as those elaborations are intelligible in light of commonly recognized relations" (365). The criteria determine the context pertaining to the utterance, which in turn determines the reference of the indexicals and demonstratives used in the utterance. Thus, the "proposition an utterance expresses will be a proposition that a competent hearer would be able to assign to it by means of a method of interpretation that the hearer could reliably employ on the basis of features of the situation that the hearer could normally be aware of" (361).

Romdenh-Romluc (2006) similarly focuses on broad contextual cues and rejects the view that the relevant context is fixed by conventions delivered by the utterance setting. According to Romdenh-Romluc (2002, 38), the "context with respect to which indexical reference is determined is the context A identifies using the cues that U intends her to use." A is assumed to be a competent and attentive hearer whom the speaker is addressing.[68] Thus, the speaker may exploit the beliefs, desires, history, and interests of A. These cues that U intends A to use to identify the context are ones that A can reasonably be expected to recognize as being relevant, even if these are not the cues that U actually intends her audience to use to identify the relevant context. Although the conventional ways of using indexicals will have some bearing on what an audience can

TABLE 3.2. **Objective doxastic theories of indexical interpretation**

Gauker (2008)	Setting → Accessibility criteria → Context → Correct interpretation
Romdenh-Romluc (2002)	Setting → Audience cues → Context → Correct interpretation

understand, the ability of an audience to grasp what is meant by an utterance is not limited by conventions which have already been established (2006, 272).

Table 3.2 reflects the objective doxatic theories of indexicals introduced above. The doxastic control theories, which emphasize the multiplicity of contexts, may be effective in establishing the communicative meaning of an indexical in any given case, but they problematize the issue of how it can be said that an indexical has an ordinary meaning. The flaw in the above theories, at least with respect to ordinary meaning, is that although they recognize that conventional meaning is relevant, they do not attempt to capture observed regularities associated with indexical reference. Although the communicative meaning of an indexical is contextually based and involves consideration of various facts, it does not follow that the ordinary meaning of an indexical must do so. Michaelson (2014) correctly observes that an important goal of semantic theory should be to capture the strong default interpretations of terms like indexicals. This goal is obviously important to ordinary meaning. Kaplan's characters, after all, are also "set by linguistic conventions" (505). Kaplan's theory, though, fails because it recognizes only one sort of context (contexts of utterance) and one sort of character rule (rules for that sort of context). A revision of the theory on semantic grounds is therefore necessary in order to offer an account of indexicals that can serve as their ordinary meaning.

3.4.7: Indexicals and Conventions

As indicated above, a semantic account of indexicals that doubles as an ordinary meaning account must focus on default interpretations. Determining the default interpretation of indexicals involves conventions, which arise in response to situations in which a desired outcome depends on multiple agents being able to coordinate their actions over time (Michaelson 2014). There are a few basic strategies for dealing with the observed regularities associated with indexical reference in light of the attacks on Kaplan's theory of the semantics of indexicals. Two of them will

be discussed. The first approach accepts the basic Kaplan view of indexicals but modifies it to some extent. Cohen (2013), for example, distinguishes between the context of production/inscription (c^i) and the context of audition/tokening (c^t) and argues that "here" and "now" refer to
the place and time c^t rather than, as Kaplan does, the place and time of
c^i. Cohen's proposal would give the correct references for answering machine situations, while Kaplan's, of course, does not. As Michaelson (2014)
argues, though, Cohen's proposal gives the wrong results for inscriptions
such as postcards, which typically use "now" to refer to c^i. Consider, for instance, a case in which Traveler mails a postcard on which he has inscribed
the following:

(13) It is beautiful here now.

It seems obvious that in (13) "here" and "now" refer to the place and time
of the context of inscription, not to the place and time of interpretation
which might be weeks (or longer) in the future. Kaplan's semantics pre-
dicts this result, but Cohen's does not.

   A different approach recognizes that any fixed character (or meaning
rule) given to indexicals can be shown to give the erroneous reference in
some cases and responds by advocating a flexible approach to conventions. For instance, Corazza, Fish, and Gorvett (2002, 11) argue that "for
any use of the personal indexical, the contextual parameter of the agent
is *conventionally given*—given by the *social or conventional setting* in
which the utterance takes place." By considering the notion of the setting
of an utterance, the conventionalist account considers a wide variety of
presemantic facts, including "the language being spoken, the physical environment and other factors as relevant to determining our contextual parameters" (11). These features might include such things as, for example,
"speaking English, belonging to a given community, hearing an answering machine message, sarcastically imitating someone, acting in a piece of
theatre" (12). According to Corazza, Fish, and Gorvett's conventionalist
view, there is a convention to the effect that "I" on a post-it note attached
to someone's office door refers to the usual occupant of that office. The
convention is "illustrated by the fact that we do not have any difficulty in
coping with someone's pre-recorded answer-phone message" (12). The
conventionalist account, thus, yields the intuitively correct reference, as
opposed to the intentionalist account, which does not always do so.

   Michaelson (2014) brings a slightly different perspective than does

Corazza, Fish, and Gorvett (2002) to the recognition of indexical conventions. He advocates a framework where, similar to Kaplan's views, indexicals remain context sensitive. The contexts, though, are typed and character rules are allowed to vary relative to context type. Michaelson argues that the character rules associated with each indexical remain constant: "I" returns the agent, "here" returns the location, and "now" returns the time of the context. What counts as an agent, location, or time, however, is allowed to vary with the type of context under consideration. The formal notion of character thus remains unchanged—functions from a regimented set of features of contexts to objects—but the informal characterization of characters as broader rules of reference is allowed to vary relative to the context type. The features associated with being an agent, time, or location shift, relative to a context type but not the formal rules. It is thus not the formal rules associating indexicals with a particular feature of a context that shift, relative to a context type, but rather the features associated with being an agent, time, or location.

Michaelson makes a distinction between face-to-face contexts and other contexts. In contexts involving certain sorts of recording technologies, agency, location, and time are instantiated by different sorts of things than they are in face to-face contexts. In situations involving recording technologies, the character-shifting account evaluates indexical reference relative to the context of interpretation, not the context of production. The justification for the distinction has to do with the conventions governing the different types of communications. With recording devices, there may have been multiple ways that indexicals were used when the devices were initially introduced. Once a regularity is established, however, speakers will have an incentive to comply with the regularity in order to communicate successfully.

Michaelson takes a cautious approach to the recognition of indexical conventions. Michaelson acknowledges that fixed and recognized conventions may not exist for indexicals that do not involve the prototypical Kaplan face-to-face communications but also do not involve specific types of recording technology. Of course, the interpreter can weigh the cues, as other theories have explained. Michaelson wonders, though, whether a plausible explanation of the relation between these varied phenomena and indexical interpretation can be had in terms of a singular convention. The problem is that these cases are extremely diverse, and no intention-free description of them seems available to unify them into a single sort of interpretive problem—in response to which a convention

TABLE 3.3. **Convention-based theories of indexical interpretation**

Cohen (2013)	Characters → Context of audition/tokening → Correct interpretation
Corazza, Fish, and Gorvett (2002)[a]	Setting → Conventions → Context → Correct interpretation
Michaelson (2014)	Kaplan character rules → Context type → Correct interpretation

[a] Gorvett (2005, 296) follows Corazza, Fish, and Gorvett (2002) in rejecting a focus on the intentions of the utterer and arguing instead for the relevance of "social conventions of language." Gorvett advocates a convention-based account that attempts to restrict an audience from grasping certain nonstandard uses of indexicals while allowing them to grasp others. Specifically, Gorvett (299) argues that a "speaker's referential intentions are restricted by her expectations about the referring act, including her expectations regarding the audience's ability to 'get' the reference."

might in fact arise. Still, some have illustrated different ways that reference shifting can occur outside of a conversational context. For example, Mount (2008) observes that reference-shifting uses of language are standard in some "official" contexts, like board game instructions. Establishing the existence of conventions in other contexts is undoubtedly possible, but doing so would be an empirical exercise rather than a theoretical one.

Table 3.3 reflects the convention-based theories of indexicals introduced above.

3.4.8: The Ordinary Meaning of Indexicals and the Distinction between "Narrow" and "Wide" Context

If the approach to the semantic meaning of indexicals involves default meanings according to conventions of language, the character rules of meaning must be relativized to different sorts of contexts. An indexical must be evaluated according to a rule that is determined by what sort of communicative channel is used to deliver the message at that context. The Kaplan set of rules may offer the semantic meaning of indexicals in face-to-face contexts, but a different set of rules must determine the reference when an indexical is used in a different context. Further, for ordinary meaning, the default character of indexicals should be univocal. Positing ambiguity would violate the constraint that the ordinary meaning is the default meaning of the text. Still, the approach described above is not sufficient to represent communicative meaning. Any framework that involves convention-based default interpretations must recognize that the communicative meaning of a legal text may deviate from the recognized conventions and that sufficient evidence might exist that indicates that the deviation was intended.

One useful way to frame the distinction between ordinary meaning and communicative meaning is through the consideration of the type of context relevant to each determination. Along with other linguistic categories, the ordinary meaning of indexicals must be framed in a way that includes some consideration of context. Additionally, as indicated above, for the ordinary meaning concept to be meaningful there must be a gap, at least in some cases, between ordinary meaning and communicative meaning. This requires some division of context into that relevant for ordinary meaning determinations and that relevant for communicative meaning determinations. One way of conceptualizing the respective contexts is to consider the distinction made by Bach (2002, 2005, 2007), Recanati (2006a), and others between "narrow context" and "wide context." Such a distinction is similar to the distinction made by Perry (1997) and others between semantic and presemantic uses of context.

According to Stokke (2010, 385), narrow context concerns "those aspects of context that determine reference" (the metaphysical role), while wide context concerns those aspects of context "that the audience uses in reasoning about the speaker's intentions" (the epistemic role). Narrow context is therefore concerned with capturing what a sentence expresses relative to the relevant facts from the narrow context and is independent of the content of the speaker's communicative intentions. One use of narrow context concerns information specifically relevant to determining the semantic values of context-sensitive expressions such as indexicals. For context-sensitive expressions, "narrow context" includes the indices of agent (needed to fix the reference of "I"), time (to fix the reference of "now" and "today"), location (to fix the reference of "here" and "there"), demonstrative (to fix the reference of demonstratives like "this" and "that"), and possible world (to fix the reference of "actual"). With these context-sensitive expressions, the interpreter consults facts from the narrow context and is concerned only with determining the references of the words in accordance with the applicable conventions.

In contrast to narrow context, "wide context" is concerned with capturing what a speaker expresses by uttering a sentence in a particular context and is said to operate at a pragmatic level. Recall from chapter 2 that the constituent question of how to define the communicative meaning of a relevant text can be answered in different ways. According to objective theories of communication, such as hypothetical intentionalism, the determinants of meaning do not include the author's intentions in writing the relevant text. Even a moderate intentionalist like Stokke (2010) concedes that the author's intentions in writing the relevant text are not a part of the collection of information the audience uses in order to ascertain the author's intentions. Stokke (2010, 387) refers to this limitation as "The Argument from Inaccessibility," because it "starts from the observation that the speaker's intentions, just by their very nature, are not directly accessible to her audience." For Stokke (387), the wide context "*constrains* the range of intentions that a speaker can 'reasonably' have in the first place" (emphasis in original).

The use of wide context thus serves an epistemic role because it comprises the full range of information the audience will use in order to ascertain the author's intentions on a particular occasion (Stokke 2010). Of course, as indicated above, even under wide context the determinants of meaning do not directly include the author's intentions. Rather, the evidence considered is indirect, even if the inquiry is framed in terms of the author's intent. According to Corazza, Fish, and Gorvett (2002), indirect evidence includes things relating to the setting in which the communication takes place (such as acting in a piece of theater). Facts relevant to the legal setting will of course differ from those relevant to a literary setting and may include such things as the legislative history of the relevant provision and inferences from related provisions. Consideration of wide context in such a manner allows the legal interpreter to fill the gap, if one exists in the particular case, between ordinary meaning and communicative meaning.

Up to this point in the discussion, the conception of narrow and wide context described above offers a plausible method of helping to distinguish between ordinary meaning and communicative meaning. At least one aspect of the distinction between narrow and wide context made by various philosophers and linguists must, however, be reconsidered, at least when legal texts are being interpreted. Specifically, it concerns the classification of evidence regarding the meaning of words. Some scholars, such as Corazza, Fish, and Gorvett (2002), argue that it is a matter of wide context whether a given word is used with a particular conventional meaning. These scholars distinguish between "presemantic" and "semantic" facts. In their view, the issue of conventional meaning is similar to other facts like speaking English, belonging to a given community, or hearing an answering machine. These facts are presemantic because they are not part of what one says and usually aims to communicate but, rather, are facts of the setting in which the linguistic exchange takes place. The facts therefore do not determine what the terms "mean." Instead, they determine which terms are "used."

Whatever its virtues for some purposes, the presemantic/semantic distinction outlined above is unpersuasive in the legal context. While the semantics/pragmatics distinction helps to elucidate important concepts like determinacy and interpretive discretion, the presemantic/semantic distinction does not further an understanding of ordinary meaning. In order to be relevant, concepts or categories must relate to ordinary meaning or the ordinary meaning/communicative meaning distinction. The narrow context/wide context categories are useful because facts relevant to ordinary meaning fall under narrow context, and facts relevant to communicative meaning fall under wide context. If a fact relates to the identification of the conventional meaning of a word, it is a fact from the narrow context, even if it is found outside of the text. Certainly, as chapter 5 addresses, if the applicable meaning of a polysemous word is at issue, sentential context can be relevant in selecting the contextually appropriate ordinary meaning. In such situations, the relevant facts are from the narrow context, even if they relate to how the term at issue is "used" and not what it "means," and even if the relevant facts are found outside of the text.[69] Similarly, facts relating to the determination of a word's conventional meaning (and not just *which* conventional meaning is being used) are properly viewed as part of the narrow context even if found outside of the text. In these situations, a judge might consult a dictionary, empirical study or corpus in order to determine the extension of the ordinary meaning of a word. Although the inquiry might be far-reaching, any facts discovered are from the narrow context, because they relate only to general knowledge about the relevant words used and not specific facts about the communicative meaning of the text (as would be found from the legislative history of the provision).

With respect to indexicals, there may be different conventions that apply to different legal texts, as discussed further below. Determining the type of legal text involved is a matter of fixing the setting in which the communication takes place. As such, the determination involves narrow context, similar to the determination of the semantic meaning of a nonindexical word. On one view, the determination is analogous to Levinson's (2002) view, described in chapter 2, that a categorical intention represents a metasemantic desire that a text be classified in some specific or general way. It represents an intention regarding the approximate nature of the work, but not the precise import. Once the particular text is classified and the appropriate convention determined, linguists and philosophers agree that the narrow context is then consulted to determine the reference of the relevant indexical (which, again, may require recourse to facts outside of the text). Of course, wide context may be analyzed to determine whether the communicative meaning of the text differs from its ordinary meaning. Thus, the interpreter may be convinced by facts from the wide context that the conventional meaning of the indexical does not represent its communicative meaning in that particular context.

The distinction between narrow context and wide context thus allows for a plausible account of ordinary meaning both with respect to words covered by the saturation concept and more generally in determining the conventional meanings of nonindexical words. As well, it provides for a gap between ordinary meaning and communicative meaning. The relevant Kaplan convention, along with the narrow context facts, determines the ordinary meaning of the indexical and its reference. The ordinary meaning of the indexical is its presumptive meaning, which might be stronger or weaker depending on the foreseeability of cancellation. For the indexical "I," for example, if the applicable convention provided that the utterer is the agent and therefore the referent the presumption that the convention is the correct meaning would be quite strong. Every utterance of "I" would thus presumptively be of the same type in the sense that the character of the term remains the same. Of course, the interpreter must also consider the wide context to determine whether the communicative meaning of a term, whether indexical or nonindexical, differs from its ordinary meaning. If the wide context indicates that the presumptive meaning was not intended, the communicative meaning would control.

3.4.9: Challenges to the Objective View of Indexicals

The above account of ordinary meaning and communicative meaning faces various difficulties. With indexicals, as well as other words, one obvious difficulty concerns the determination of whether a convention exists and how narrowly or broadly it should be defined. Predelli (2002) criticizes the conventionalist approach on the basis that it will lead to the addition of an implausibly large proliferation of conventions to our ontology, as each unique situation will require a different convention or conventions. According to Predelli (2002, 313), pursuant to a conventionalist theory, we would need relevant conventions concerning the use of indexicals in "postcards, answering machines, recorder messages, written diaries, post-it notes attached to one's office door, day-dreaming, and re-enactments, etc." A similar concern could be raised for legal texts, as multiple conventions may need to be recognized.

The persuasiveness of Predelli's argument depends in part on how a convention is framed. Predelli views conventions as being quite narrow and highly specific. He claims, for example, that different conventions would be necessary for "today" as used on post-it notes saying, "I am not here today," and "Today the dean is getting on my nerves," where the former is written on Monday to inform readers of the note on Tuesday that the author is not in on Tuesday, and the latter is written on Monday only to record the author's annoyance on Monday (314). In response, Gorvett (2005, 306–7) argues that conventions are established regularly among language users, so the proliferation of conventions is not really as implausible as Predelli thinks. Further, Predelli's criticism may not be devastating to the determination of conventions for legal texts, even if persuasive generally. Any proliferation of conventions for legal texts is not likely to outstrip the proliferation of the varying substantive rules applicable in any given situation and is thus unlikely to be unmanageable. While Predelli's arguments regarding the proliferation of conventions are not damaging to a proposal that indexicals in legal texts should be seen as having conventional meanings, uncertainty would undoubtedly arise, as with any legal rule, regarding the level of generality at which the conventions are framed. If conventions are conceived of at a high level of generality, a problem separate from the proliferation issue would emerge. In general, the higher the level of generality at which a convention is conceived the greater the likelihood that there will arise disagreements regarding its application.

The relationship between generality and rules (whether the rule is a "convention" or given some other name) can be illustrated through the following two possible rules:

(14) Minors must be home at 10 p.m.
(15) Minors must be home at the time a reasonable person would think is appropriate.

The first rule, rule (14), is relatively narrow and specific and, assuming literal interpretation, its application is, at least comparatively, fairly straightforward.[70] In contrast, rule (15) admits of multiple interpretations due to its context dependent terms that allow for different judgments about meaning. In any given situation, it is not immediately obvious what a "reasonable person" would think was an "appropriate" time for a minor to be home. In addition, like the idealized interpreter in ordinary meaning determinations, the reasonable person who is to set the appropriate time would be an abstraction (and perhaps a composite based on a given community's views) and not based on any actual individual. This aspect of the convention would add an additional layer of uncertainty. Judicial opinions regarding the application of rule (15) would inevitably vary.

Other flaws have been attributed to a convention based theory of indexicals. One argument is that a conventional view might successfully prevent the "correct" reference from being anything the speaker chooses it to be, but it fails to account for the use of indexical expressions in non-idiosyncratic but novel ways. A conventionalist theory relies, of course, on the invocation of a convention (or set of conventions), which is an established manner of doing something. As Romdenh-Romluc (2006) argues, such a theory entails some time period between the first usage and the establishment of the convention. Thus, under a conventionalist model, there will be an unavoidable lag between the first usage and the establishment of an applicable convention. While this argument might limit the scope of the conventional theory of indexicals, it is not clear that it poses a problem for the interpretation of legal texts. One reason is that the interpretation of indexicals is sometimes problematic for courts, as illustrated below, but it is not likely that indexicals are used in novel ways in legal texts. In addition, courts can look to wide context to determine whether an existing convention does not fit the facts of the interpretive dispute.

3.5: Ordinary Meaning and Legal Meaning

Another problem with the conventional account of indexicals is that ordinary meaning determined by a judge may sometimes differ from a possible communicative meaning, but it may not always differ much from legal meaning. Recall that the legal meaning of a text is its authoritative meaning, which may be based on legal concerns in addition to linguistic analysis. The reason why there may be no gap between ordinary meaning and legal meaning is that, unlike other categories of words, the conventional meaning approach relevant to indexicals does not impose constraints external to the law, as the relevant convention may be tied to the type of legal text at issue. The result is that judges will be tempted to base their view of conventions on the correct legal outcome rather than the conventions used by drafters (of course, this is also a problem for the other interpretive rules used by courts). In addition, the issue of reference shifting in legal texts due to the passage of time extends beyond indexicals and includes definite descriptions that are context dependent. These reference-shifting issues may not have obvious parallels outside the legal context, making ordinary meaning in those cases similarly difficult to distinguish from legal meaning.

Consider reference shifting in wills. The usual rule is that the word "now" in a will relates to the time when the will becomes operational (i.e., at death or at probate) because of the type of medium a will is understood to be. Yet, this convention may not be sufficient for all the indexicals, as well as other terms, used in wills. Imagine that in 2001 Madre leaves her farm to her children in her will through the following language:

(16) I hereby leave my farm to my children.

Madre's child Daudre is born in 2002. Madre's child Sonder is alive at the time of the formation of the will but dies in 2008. Madre has three other children that were born prior to 2001 and die subsequent to 2015. Madre dies in 2015. To whom does Madre's farm pass? The answer depends on the extension of "my children." The phrase functions like an indexical in that its character stays the same but its reference changes over time. The result is that a court must answer the following questions. Does a predeceased child, such as Sonder, still fall within the extension of "my children"? What about a child, such as Daudre, born after the formation of the will?[71]

The extension of "my children" thus changes over the term of Madre's life. One issue, then, regarding the interpretation of (16) involves the proper context of interpretation. The two temporal choices with respect to the context of interpretation are (1) when the will is executed or (2) at the testator's death. As explained above, in most cases outside texts, the context for interpretation is set at the time of utterance. This is especially true with respect to a statement that is worded as a present tense commissive act, as is the case with (16).[72] The issue of the proper context of interpretation invokes, again, the answering machine scenarios. In fact, a will is in some ways similar to the answering machine examples. Certainly, even though the bequests are made in a present tense voice, the terms of the will are not intended to be fulfilled at the time of its execution.[73] Rather, like an answering machine message that asks the hearer to leave a message, its instruction is not meant to be implemented at the time of the original utterance. Unlike the making of an answering machine message, however, the statement in a will does have a present effect. When executed, it has a legal status. The utterances in a will are, in a sense, made twice (at the time of execution and at the time of distribution), although the import (legal and otherwise) of the utterances differs. The utterances must be made in order to execute the will, and they must also be made in order to distribute the property according to the testator's wishes.

As the answering machine scenarios illustrate, the context of utterance does not have to correspond, temporally, with the context of interpretation. Instead, sometimes interpretation is to be deferred from the time of utterance. An intentionalist account may not be able to adequately address such a situation. In addition to its other detriments (which were described in chap. 2), the intentionalist position fails to recognize that there is sometimes no correct interpretation of indexicals available under an intention based theory. The intentionalist position may offer an account of the mismatch between speaker intent and reasonable interpretation, but this duality does not recognize that a speaker might not have possessed an intent regarding the interpretive issues that must be decided. Indeed, it is not hard to imagine that Madre at the time of her statements in (16) never contemplated that one of her children might predecease her (or that she might have another child). Certainly, the relevant legal authorities would provide a stipulated definition for "my children." Notwithstanding such stipulation, Madre might not have formed any intent with respect to the disposition of her property in the event of a predeceased child. Thus, even though Madre had a general desire that she wished her children to receive her property when she died, and an interpreter might rightly hypothesize that she certainly would have wanted her property to be split amongst all her children, under the intentionalist view there could be no "correct" interpretation with respect to the issue that must be decided.

In any case, it is undeniable that the indexical term "hereby" in (16) is meant to refer to a later time period, namely the time of interpretation. Nevertheless, establishing a time of interpretation that is separate from the context of utterance does not mean that all the words in the utterance must have the same context of interpretation. In fact, there is no reason why "hereby" and "my children" may not have different contexts of interpretation. "Hereby" is a case of deferred context, but the context of interpretation for "my children" may differ from its time of interpretation. It is thus entirely coherent to conceive of a class-gift interpretive rule that has the context of interpretation separate from the time of interpretation for at least some of the words. What is *not* clear, however, is that the context of interpretation of "my children" must correspond with its first time of utterance. Furthermore, any conventions used for "my children" and other indexicals would likely be created by judges based on their view of the proper legal outcomes and not based on a purely linguistic inquiry about communicative conventions.

As the above discussion illustrates, even under a semantic view of indexicals, broad discretion exists for the interpreter both in determining conventions and in considering the broad context to determine whether the convention fits the facts of the case or instead should be rejected in favor of a different meaning. In addition, if legal interpreters decide that different conventions apply to different categories of legal texts, as is likely, there would undoubtedly be uncertainty regarding the boundaries of those categories. Further, it is not clear that there would be wide consensus regarding the proper referent of any given indexical. Considering the variety of relevant facts under the wide context, a more likely premise is that there would be widespread disagreement. The likelihood of such a situation undermines the textualist argument that most interpretive questions have a right answer and that using a semantic method of interpretation would achieve consensus amongst interpreters. The failure of textualists to realize the uncertainty inherent in language is especially acute in this examination of indexicals, where greater consensus exists regarding their context invariability than with other categories of words.

3.6: Revisiting The Supreme Court's Decision in *Carcieri v. Salazar*

In light of the above explanation of indexicals and reference shifting, it is now appropriate to return to the Court's decision in *Carcieri v. Salazar* and address some of the issues that were raised when the case was first described. Indeed, there are several notable aspects of the Court's opinion that are relevant to both ordinary meaning and legal interpretation more generally. Recall that in *Carcieri* the meaning of "now" was pivotal to whether the secretary of the interior had the authority to accept in trust land for use by the Narragansett Indian Tribe. Among other evidence, the Supreme Court relied on a dictionary definition that defined "now" as "[a]t the present time; at this moment; at the time of speaking."[74]

The most noteworthy aspect of the Court's decision was the combination of its declared adherence to the ordinary meaning doctrine and its failure to offer much of an account of the ordinary meaning of "now." The Court selected one definition of "now" from *Webster's New International Dictionary*, but the dictionary definition did not advance in any way the ordinary meaning analysis. The meaning (or character in Kaplan terms) of "now" is not in dispute. The Court, though, seemed confused about this fact. Later in the opinion the Court reasoned that "the susceptibility of the word "now" to alternative meanings "does not render the word . . . whenever it is used, ambiguous," particularly where "all but one of the meanings is ordinarily eliminated by context."[75] The issue is not, however, whether "now" is ambiguous. Rather, it is whether what counts as the relevant "time" is deemed to vary because of the type of context under consideration. Thus, the ordinary meaning of an indexical like "now" cannot be satisfied by the kind of dictionary definition on which the Court relied. Note that, in any case, the Court failed to notice that the dictionary definition referred to "the time of *speaking*" (emphasis added). The case, of course, involved a text and not a conversation.

Even assuming that it was using the Kaplan semantic rules for indexicals, as reflected in the dictionary definition, the Court did not realize, at least explicitly, that the dictionary definition left some discretion that is likely to be resolved through extralinguistic understandings. Specifically, what exactly is the "time of 'speaking'"? Like a will, a statute involves a context of inscription, context of utterance, and context of interpretation. Is the time of speaking when the statute was drafted or when it was enacted into law? The question cannot be directly answered by merely considering a dictionary definition. In addition, a further complication may arise if the effective date of a statute is subsequent to the date of its enactment. The correct answer may be when the statute was enacted into law, but such a conclusion is not one based on linguistics. Rather, it is based on an understanding of the legislative and legal systems.

As explained above, instead of simply relying on a dictionary definition when determining the ordinary meaning of an indexical, the interpreter must determine the proper convention given the relevant communicative channel. The Court did arguably rely on a convention when it cited to *Black's Law Dictionary* for the proposition that "now" as used in a statute ordinarily refers to the date of its taking effect. Whether a *Black's Law Dictionary* definition, which did not cite any cases or other authority, is sufficient authority for a convention of meaning is questionable. The Court, appropriately, sought to confirm from its precedents whether the ordinary meaning of "now" in a statute is the date of its taking effect. The Court cited two cases, but neither one offered much support for its position. Neither case offered a general explanation of the meaning of "now" or purported to be determining its ordinary meaning.

Further, the Court ignored Justice Breyer's argument that indexicals in some statutes have been interpreted to refer to the time when the statute is applied. In fact, the Court could have considered whether multiple conventions exist for specifications of time in statutes. If, for example, a statute is designed so that an administrator is required to make judgments about its application to individuals (as was the statute at issue in *Carcieri*), temporal indexicals may be interpreted as of the time of the administrator's judgment. Such a convention would be consistent with the part of the definition of "now" from *Black's Law Dictionary*, which Justice Thomas neglected to quote, stating "the word is sometimes used, not with reference to the moment of speaking but to a time contemporaneous with something done." Indeed, some legal provisions would seem to make sense only if the indexical is interpreted as referring to a time of administration subsequent to the date of enactment. For instance, 25 U.S.C. § 3744(b) (2006), provides that "The Secretary shall work with all appropriate Federal departments and agencies to avoid duplication of programs and services *currently* available to Indian tribes and landowners from other sources" (emphasis added). Can the indexical "currently" be given an ordinary meaning that indicates a reference to the date of enactment, as presumably it would be if the Court were interpreting the provision and relied primarily on dictionary definitions? Such an interpretation would direct the secretary to disregard the duplication of programs and services introduced subsequent to the enactment of the statute but focus on programs and services (even if only briefly) that may have been terminated subsequent to the enactment of the statute.

Another striking but unsurprising aspect of the Court's decision was its failure to distinguish between ordinary meaning and communicative meaning. After its announcement that it was determining the ordinary meaning of the provision and its discussion of the dictionary definitions and precedents, which go to the conventional meaning of "now," the Court shifted to a wide contextual search for communicative meaning without explicitly changing its focus. The rest of the Court's arguments are not relevant to ordinary meaning, but are arguably relevant to communicative meaning. For instance, the Court referred to the language in the original version of § 465 and claimed that it explicitly referred to events current at the time of enactment. Apart from the limited usefulness of such evidence, the argument is not relevant to the ordinary meaning of "now." Rather, it represents an attempt to determine the communicative meaning of the text through an appeal to wide context. Similarly, the Court's efforts to draw meaning from the fact that Congress used the phrase "now or hereafter" in other provisions in the IRA, with the desired inference that Congress intentionally used such language to draw a distinction in meaning, represent an effort to determine the communicative meaning of the text, not its ordinary meaning. Note that the Court was not claiming that a regularity in language usage exists with its focus on "now or hereafter" (and was not equipped to make such a claim in any case), but instead was making a point about how Congress had used language in related provisions. Lastly, its reference to administrative interpretations of the statute is not relevant to ordinary meaning or even particularly relevant to communicative meaning for a Court that purports to focus on congressional intent and was not explicitly considering whether to defer to the agency's interpretation of the statute.

The above commentary is not intended to establish that the Court decision was incorrectly decided. Rather, it demonstrates, using a prototypical Supreme Court decision, the characteristic ordinary meaning reasoning of the Court. It offers yet another illustration that textualist arguments regarding interpreter consensus are overstated. It also illustrates the typical judicial failure to offer an adequate account of ordinary meaning and how courts conflate ordinary meaning and communicative meaning. Although pointed out by the district court and the First Circuit, the decision also ignored the various ways in which the statutory meaning was underspecified. Perhaps the most egregious aspect of *Carcieri* is the Court's exaggeration of the clarity of § 479, which brings to mind the familiar criticism that textualists habitually exaggerate the clarity of texts in order to camouflage the underlying policy choices courts make when interpreting texts. The Court explicitly refused to consider the competing policy views regarding the purpose of § 479 because "Congress' use of the word 'now' in § 479 speaks for itself and 'courts must presume that a legislature says in a statute what it means and means in a statute what is says there.'"[76] A more honest assessment would have acknowledged the uncertainties in the case.

3.7: Conclusion

This chapter described the tension between a view of ordinary meaning as a level of meaning that is generalizable across contexts and the reality that meaning is ineliminably contextual. A motivation for conceiving of ordinary meaning as generalizable across contexts is to maintain a gap between ordinary meaning and communicative meaning. One way to capture generalizable meanings and maintain the gap between ordinary meaning and communicative meaning is to conceive of ordinary meaning as semantic meaning that is determined based on facts from the narrow context. This way of framing ordinary meaning does not, however, eliminate interpretive discretion.

First, it is not possible to remove contextual considerations from the assignment of semantic meaning due, in part, to the reality that a null context free of contextual input does not produce sufficiently specific meanings. Second, the assignment of conventional meaning inherently has an element of discretion. As this chapter illustrated, even when determining the conventional meaning of indexicals, which were traditionally considered to be context invariant, an interpreter has significant discretion. In fact, with respect to indexicals in legal texts, it is questionable whether there is typically likely to be a gap between ordinary meaning and legal meaning (i.e., the authoritative meaning of the text that may be based on legal concerns in addition to linguistic analysis). Further, some, including Recanati (2006a), question whether the references of indexicals (as well as definite descriptions like "my children") can be assigned on the basis of consideration of narrow context only. While, in many cases at least, reference assignment can be made on the basis of narrow context, it is questionable whether courts will be motivated to maintain a distinction between the initial ordinary meaning determination and the subsequent consideration of communicative meaning. Nevertheless, for the reasons indicated at the beginning of this chapter, courts *should* be motivated to do so.

CHAPTER FOUR

Ordinary Meaning, "What Is Said," and "What Is Communicated"

4.1: "What Is Said"

4.1.1: Two Ways of Conceptualizing "What Is Said"

Chapter 4 continues the account of ordinary meaning where chapter 3 ended. Chapter 3 introduced a hierarchy of meaning with "sentence meaning" as the most basic level of meaning, followed by "what is said" and "what is communicated." Because it is the presumptive meaning of the legal text, ordinary meaning requires a theory of meaning that represents complete propositions (i.e., a situation where a complete thought can be assigned to a sentence). Although sentence meaning is conventional and context independent, and thus intuitively a good framework for ordinary meaning, it does not account for even semantically triggered contextual evidence. Linguistically mandated processes that require resort to context, though, such as the assignment of reference to indexicals, should uncontroversially be seen as being a part of ordinary meaning. While the ordinary meaning of indexicals, being constituted by conventions, can be viewed as semantic rather than pragmatic, indexicals do not fall under sentence meaning. Sentence meaning thus does not offer an adequate account of ordinary meaning. A different level of meaning is required in order to offer an adequate account.

Unlike sentence meaning, "what is said" requires that context be accounted for explicitly. What is said is context dependent and results from fleshing out sentence meaning in order to make it propositional. Widespread disagreements exist regarding the definition of "what is said," however. A main concern is the extent to which what is said should represent

TABLE 4.1. **The availability principle**

Subpersonal level	Consciously available
"Sentence meaning" + Contextual ingredients of what is said	"What is said"

the meaning that a normal interpreter would give an utterance. On the contextualist view, what is said must "be analyzed in conformity to the intuitions shared by those who fully understand the utterance—typically, the speaker and the hearer, in a normal conversational setting" (Recanati 2004, 19). Meaning is thus defined in terms of what "a normal interpreter would understand as being said, in the context at hand" (19). Recanati asserts that what is said is therefore subject to the "availability constraint," which provides that what is said "must be intuitively accessible to the conversational participants" (20). A representation of the availability principle is provided in table 4.1. Note that both sentence meaning and the contextual ingredients of what is said are computed at a subpersonal level. In contrast, what is said is consciously available to the interpreter as well as the pragmatic processes necessary to determine "what is communicated," as will be explained later.

Other views of the proper way to categorize meaning are in opposition to Recanati's conceptualization. For instance, so-called minimalists are often seen as the counterpoint to contextualists like Recanati. The distinction between the two has been described as deriving from the distinction between the descendants of those who advocated formal approaches to meaning and the descendants of those who advocated speech act theories of meaning (Borg 2007).[1] In Recanati's (2004) view, minimalists (the descendants of those who advocated formal approaches) define what is said as minimally different from sentence meaning as possible. "What is said" is thus to be the result of little to no pragmatic processing. Those extra constituents of meaning, which are not necessary for propositionality, are external to "what is said." Minimalists view "what is said" as departing from the conventional meaning of the sentence and as incorporating contextual elements only when necessary to "complete" its meaning and make it propositional. Saturation (which, as discussed in chap. 3, involves completing the meaning of context-dependent words in a sentence, such as indexicals, through the consideration of context) is the only contextual process allowed to affect "what is said," because it is a "bottom-up" process that is triggered and made obligatory by a linguistic expression in the sentence.

As indicated above, contextualists (those favoring a speech-act approach) such as Recanati argue that what is said should conform more closely to what intuitively seems to be said than what the minimalist conception of what is said provides. Even the contextualist view, though, maintains that, despite its pragmatic character, what is said is constrained by the input from sentence meaning. That is, what is said must be closely related to the conventional meaning of the sentence. Thus, according to Recanati (2004), the sentence, "I am French," can express various propositions but they all have to be compatible with the semantic potential of the sentence. The sentence cannot therefore mean "kangaroos have tails." In contrast, "what is communicated," a concept taken from Grice (1989), is also context dependent but is not constrained by sentence meaning. It includes pragmatic process such as conversational implicatures, which, as discussed below, are a means of communicating more than is literally said. Thus, if sufficient background information exists, "I am French" may implicate "kangaroos have tails." Although sentence meaning is clearly a constraint on what is said, under the contextualist account it is not an entirely straightforward matter how the literal meaning of a sentence contributes to what is said. There is evidence, for example, that a hearer may recognize the need to assign a metaphorical interpretation to a word without first processing the entire sentence in which the word occurs to recover the proposition literally expressed (Borg 2007).

Instead of looking at things from the linguistic side and equating what is said with the minimal proposition one arrives at through saturation (which describes the minimalist position), contextualists believe that a more psychological stance is required that would equate what is said with the conscious output of the complex train of process which underlies comprehension. For contextualists, what is said corresponds to the primary (truth-evaluable) representation made available to the subject as a result of processing the sentence (Recanati 2004, 17). In contrast, "what is communicated" involves what can be secondarily derived from what is said. In order to fill in the details of what is said and what is communicated, Recanati (2004) distinguishes between two sorts of pragmatic processes. The first, "primary pragmatic processes," are contextual processes, like saturation, which are subpersonally (i.e., not the result of conscious processing) involved in the determination of what is said. Thus, they involve situations where the speech participants themselves are not distinctly aware of the processes through which the context-independent meanings of the expressions used are enriched or otherwise adjusted to fit the situation of use. In the minimalist view, the contextual primary pragmatic processes included in the contextualist version of what is said are not necessary for a sentence to be a complete proposition and are thus excluded from the definition of what is said. Yet, as indicated above, for a contextualist like Recanati, these aspects of meaning are constitutive of what is said, because when they are not considered the sentence meaning is no longer something accessible to the participants to the conversation.

In contrast to primary pragmatic processes, "secondary pragmatic processes" are "postpropositional." Secondary pragmatic processes cannot take place unless some proposition p is considered as having been expressed, for they proceed by inferentially deriving some further proposition q (the implicature) from the fact that p has been expressed. Primary pragmatic processes, however, are "prepropositional" because they do not presuppose the prior identification of some proposition serving as input to the process. Secondary pragmatic processes are conscious in the sense that normal interpreters are aware both of what is said and of what is implied and are capable of working out the inferential connection between them.[2] They are ordinary inferential processes that take the interpreter from what is said to what is communicated, which is something that "(under standard assumptions of rationality and cooperativeness) follows from the fact that the speaker has said what she has said" (Recanati 2004, 17). The notion conforms, roughly, to conversational implicatures. The implicatures correspond to further conscious representations inferentially derived from what is said. As such, the hearer must be able to recognize what is said and what is implied by saying it. In contrast, recall that primary pragmatic processes are not conscious in that sense. Normal interpreters need not be aware of the context-independent meanings of the expressions used, nor of the processes through which those meanings are enriched or otherwise adjusted to fit the situation of use.

Recanati's (2010) view of the minimalist and contextualist approaches is summarized in table 4.2. As Borg (2007) notes, the debate that the table reflects is between those who think that sentences (relativized to contexts of utterance) possess genuine, truth-evaluable content (i.e., a semantic view of meaning) and those who think that it is only at the level of the utterance that it makes sense to talk about real meaning (i.e., a pragmatic view of meaning). Recanati attributes the first position to minimalists and the second to contextualists. Because it relies on more systematic accounts of meaning, the minimalist definition of "what is said" would be

TABLE 4.2. **Recanati's (2010) view of the minimalist and contextualist approaches**

Minimalist approach	Contextualist approach
Sentence meaning	Sentence meaning
+	+
Prepropositional pragmatics	Primary pragmatic processes
—saturation	—saturation + free enrichment[a]
= What the sentence says ("what is said")	= What is said
+	+
Postpropositional pragmatics	Secondary pragmatic processes
—e.g., implicatures	—e.g., implicatures
= What is communicated	= What is communicated

[a] "Free enrichment" typically consists in making the interpretation of some expression in a sentence contextually more specific than its literal interpretation. The concept is further elaborated in chap. 4.

a more desirable account of ordinary meaning than would the contextualist view of "what is said." The minimalist view of "what is said," though, cannot serve as a definition of ordinary meaning. Minimalists, as they readily admit, envision a divide between semantic content and speech act content (Borg 2007). Borg (340) indicates that the minimalist conception is not equivalent to what people uttering sentences normally communicate. In contrast, the ordinary meaning of a legal text serves as its presumptive meaning and thus must resemble the meaning that people uttering the language would normally communicate. In other words, similar to Recanati's availability principle, an ordinary meaning must correspond to the meaning an idealized, normal interpreter would give the text given the relevant context.

4.1.2: Minimalism and Ordinary Meaning

One defense of minimalism is that minimal propositions can be seen as the content deferred to when information about the context of utterance is insufficient, unreliable, or in some way unstable (Borg 2007). The argument is that, where one knows next to nothing about the speaker and the surrounding context, one can still know that the speaker asserted the proposition expressed by the sentence uttered. This position does not, however, seem justified in many cases. Consider one of Recanati's examples below:

(1) Everybody went to Paris.

Literalism holds that universal quantifier words such as "any," "everybody," and "most" quantify over everything (Stojanovic 2008). Therefore, without consideration of what Recanati terms the optional, pragmatic notion of enrichment (explained below), which is not part of the minimalist conception of "what is said," the meaning of (1) is that every existing person went to Paris. Even with little contextual evidence, though, the literal meaning of (1) is different from that which "untutored conversational participants" would ascribe to it (Recanati 2004, 11). It has become customary to treat terms such as "everybody" as a restricted quantifier, creating situations where there is a gap between intuitive meaning and literal meaning. Relying on examples like (1), contextualists convincingly argue that there is an unjustified gap between the interpretations generated by the minimalist definition of "what is said" and the intuitive truth conditions that untutored conversational participants would give the same utterances.

As shown by examples like that above, minimalism does not provide a framework that gives a sufficient account of ordinary meaning. An ordinary meaning must be intuitively accessible to the idealized ordinary person interpreter. The minimalist accounts of "what is said" do not satisfy this requirement. On the other hand, the contextualist view of meaning, with the large role given to pragmatic processes, similarly cannot give an adequate account of ordinary meaning. Fortunately, even though the theory is successful in establishing that the minimalist account of "what is said" does not correspond to the meanings that would be intuitively accessible to conversational participants, the contextualist criticisms of minimalism do not establish that a pragmatic account must be given to the linguistic phenomena that chapter 3 and this chapter examine. To the contrary, as chapter 3 illustrated, a semantic framework can be given that for purposes of ordinary meaning can offer a sufficient account of indexical meanings. Similarly, this chapter will demonstrate that a semantic account can be offered that can account for the other important linguistic phenomena that constitute "what is said."

4.2: Quantifier Domain Restriction and Ordinary Meaning

4.2.1: The Supreme Court and Quantifiers

One important linguistic phenomenon that this chapter will explain is something often referred to as quantifier domain restriction, which (1) and the accompanying explanation illustrates. For legal texts, the issue is whether the literal meaning of a so-called universal quantifier is also its ordinary meaning (and, inevitably, the legal meaning chosen by the court). Quantifiers are frequently used in legal texts and, unsurprisingly considering the frequent inappropriateness of interpreting quantifiers consistently with their literal meanings, interpretive questions have been raised regarding their domains (i.e., their scopes of reference). The Supreme Court has decided several cases that have involved questions of quantifier scope. The default view of the Court seems to be that the "natural" meaning of quantifiers is the literal meaning and that courts should look for explicit textual language in order to limit the scope of universal quantifiers. Thus, in *United States v. Gonzales*,[3] for example, the Court sought explicit language in a federal sentencing statute in order to restrict "any other term of imprisonment" to federal sentences.[4] In interpreting the provision as including state sentences, the Court emphasized the "naturally . . . expansive meaning" of "any" and refused to consider legislative history due to the "straightforward statutory command."[5]

In some cases the Court has restricted the domain of the relevant quantifier, but often the restriction is motivated by interpretive principles that are based on legal concerns. For instance, in *Small v. United States*,[6] the Court restricted the scope of a statute containing the phrase "convicted in any court" to include only domestic, and not foreign, convictions. The restriction, though, was motivated by the interpretive presumption against extraterritorial application of legislation.[7] Similarly, in *Nixon v. Missouri Municipal League*,[8] the Court interpreted a statute authorizing federal preemption of state and local laws prohibiting the ability of "any entity" to provide telecommunications services as not including a state's own subdivisions. States were thus allowed to prohibit local municipalities from providing telecommunications services. The quantifier domain restriction, though, was at least partly motivated by the interpretive principle requiring that Congress be clear when it intends to constrain a state's traditional authority to order its government.[9]

In some cases, the Supreme Court has restricted the domain of a quantifier without the motivation of a separate interpretive principle. In *Gutierrez v. Ada*,[10] for instance, the Court restricted the domain of a statute containing the phrase "in any election" as referring only to the election of the governor and lieutenant governor and not to the simultaneous general election. In restricting the domain of the quantifier, the Court emphasized that the section containing the quantifier also contained six express references to an election for governor and lieutenant governor. The

Court reasoned that the section was therefore intended to refer only to that election.[11]

4.2.2: Describing the Court's Decision in Ali v. Federal Bureau of Prisons

As the above section illustrates, quantifiers (more so than indexicals) are frequently found in legal texts and raise difficult interpretive questions for courts. Before examining how courts should determine the ordinary meaning of quantifiers, this section will describe for purposes of later critique a representative Supreme Court case, *Ali v. Federal Bureau of Prisons*,[12] which turned on the meaning of a quantifier. The facts of the case involved Ali, a federal prisoner at the United States Penitentiary in Atlanta, Georgia.[13] During his transfer to the United States Penitentiary Big Sandy in Inez, Kentucky, several items belonging to Ali went missing.[14] The missing items included two copies of the Qur'an, a prayer rug, and religious magazines.[15] After exhausting his administrative remedies, Ali filed a complaint alleging, inter alia, violations of the Federal Tort Claims Act (FTCA), 28 U.S.C. §§ 1346 *et seq.*[16] In the FTCA, Congress waived the United States' sovereign immunity for claims arising out of torts committed by federal employees.[17] In § 1346(b)(1), the FTCA authorizes

claims against the United States, for money damages . . . for injury or loss of property . . . caused by the negligent or wrongful act or omission of any employee of the Government while acting within the scope of his office or employment.[18]

The FTCA exempts from this waiver certain categories of claims, including an exception in § 2680(c) which provides that § 1346(b) does not apply to

[a]ny claim arising in respect of the assessment or collection of any tax or customs duty, or the detention of any goods, merchandise, or other property by any officer of customs or excise or *any other law enforcement officer* (emphasis added).

The Bureau of Prisons claimed that Ali's claimed was barred by the exception in § 2680(c) concerning governmental liability.[19] The district court agreed and dismissed petitioner's FTCA claim for lack of subject-matter jurisdiction.[20] The First Circuit affirmed.[21] The First Circuit's decision added to the split among the Courts of Appeals regarding the proper scope of the exception in § 2680(c). Six Courts of Appeals, including the First Circuit, interpreted § 2680(c) as encompassing all law enforcement officers.[22] In contrast, five Courts of Appeals interpreted § 2680(c) as limited to officers performing customs or excise functions.[23]

The Supreme Court, with Justice Thomas writing the opinion, affirmed the First Circuit's decision and interpreted § 2680(c) as encompassing all law enforcement officers. The Court began its analysis by asserting that the "[r]ead naturally, the word 'any' has an expansive meaning" and quoted a dictionary definition (via one of its previous decisions) that defined "any" as "one of some indiscriminately of whatever kind."[24] The Court then cited to other decisions where it had defined "any" expansively.[25] The Court reasoned that using "any" to modify "other law enforcement officer" is "most naturally read to mean law enforcement officers of whatever kind," emphasizing that "any" is "repeated four times in the relevant portion of § 2680(c)."[26] In addition, the Court emphasized that amendments to § 2680(c), although not applicable to Ali's claim, indicated that Congress viewed the section as having a broad meaning.[27]

*   *   *

Like with indexicals, described in chapter 3, the Supreme Court in *Ali* seemed to believe that the ordinary meaning of a word can be determined primarily through its dictionary meaning (although the Court also relied on other evidence). Can the ordinary meaning of a quantifier like "any" be determined via a dictionary definition? Certainly, it is clear that the reference of a quantifier (i.e., its domain) is often narrower than its literal meaning. Is this restricted domain simply an aspect of communicative meaning, leaving the semantic, ordinary meaning undisturbed? As the discussion below illustrates, it is a mistake to believe that determining the ordinary meaning of an indexical can be done by simply looking up the word in a dictionary.

4.2.3: A Description of Quantifier Domain Restriction

As a linguistically mandated process, including saturation (which involves indexicals as well as other context-dependent phenomena) within the scope of ordinary meaning should be uncontroversial. While it is not similarly linguistically mandated, the linguistic phenomenon of "free enrichment" must also be deemed to be within the scope of ordinary meaning, although its inclusion may be more controversial. "Free enrichment," which is a species of what Recanati (2004) terms "modulation," typically consists in making the interpretation of some expression in a sentence contextually more specific than its literal interpretation. One type of "free enrichment" is "strengthening," which, in Recanati's terms, involves restricting the application of a predicate by contextually providing further conditions that are not linguistically encoded. Like saturation, the contextualist view of free enrichment is that it is a "primary pragmatic process" because, unlike "secondary pragmatic processes," it is *not* a conscious process in the sense that normal interpreters are aware both of what is said and of what is implied and are capable of working out the inferential connection between them.[28] Importantly, though, unlike saturation it is an optional and context-driven (top-down) process. As such, it often relies on more than sentential (i.e., sentence level) context.

In Recanati's view, free enrichment (and, more specifically, strengthening) is the process that accounts for the contextual restriction of quantifiers (i.e., quantifier domain restriction). Recanati uses the example

(2)   Most students are male.

to illustrate quantifier domain restriction. The sentence is intended to assert that most students *in my class* are male. The additional ingredient *in my class* is optional because there is a possible "absolute" reading of (2) in which no such contextual restriction of the domain occurs. In fact, the contextualist view asserts that there is no level of meaning which is both propositional (i.e., a situation where a complete thought can be assigned to a sentence) and unaffected by top-down factors (i.e., without the possibility of some unarticulated constituent being contextually provided). In other words, the proposition that the hearer would intuitively believe to be the proposition expressed by the communicative act contains elements that are not the value of any constituent in the sentence uttered, nor introduced by composing these values.[29] Instead, these elements are provided directly by context through, in Recanati's view, an unconstrained pragmatic process. The analysis of *in my class* is therefore that it is part of "what is said," even though it corresponds to nothing in the uttered sentence. Rather, as explained above, it is part of "what is said" as a result of the primary pragmatic process of free enrichment, which is triggered not by something in the sentence but simply by the context.

Clearly, the literal meanings of (1) and (2) do not correspond to the ordinary meanings of the phrases, but the contextual account of quantifier domain restriction does not offer a satisfying account of the ordinary meanings. Restricted quantifier domains are an aspect of "ordinary meaning" (because considering the restricted domain creates a proposition that the hearer would intuitively believe to be the proposition expressed), yet the contextual account, which views the linguistic phenomenon as being pragmatic in nature, does not offer the kind of systematic framework that is optimal for an adequate ordinary meaning analysis. Another, albeit less important, related reason also exists for rejecting the contextualist account of quantifier domain restriction. It is that the contextualist account, which relies on unconstrained pragmatic processes (i.e., free enrichment), offers an unconvincing semantics for quantifier domain restriction.

Stojanovic (2008, 2012) notes that the empirical data presented in the semantic literature show that the majority of speakers understand the restricted meanings of utterances such as (1) and (2) to be true. One might assert that speakers' intuitions are not a good guide to semantic content, but track some other, pragmatic level. Stojanovic (2012, 139) rejects that alternative in favor of a "criterion of empirical adequacy" which holds:

> If the majority of competent speakers are inclined to judge that a given sentence, as used in a given context, is true, then the truth value that the *semantic* (emphasis added) theory predicts for that sentence, with respect to the appropriate assignment of values to the relevant contextual parameters, had better be True.

The criterion of empirical adequacy would counsel that both the literalist and contextualist solutions to quantifier domain restriction should be rejected in favor of a semantic theory that comports with empirical adequacy. The solution would also comport with the need for any theory of ordinary meaning to also be consistent with empirical findings.

4.2.4: A Descriptive Semantic Theory of Quantifier Domain Restriction

Between the extremes of minimalism and the radical contextualism espoused by Recanati, which focuses on optional or free pragmatic processes, are mainstream contextualist scholars. These scholars argue for a variety of positions in which there exists some lexical, syntactic, or semantic level where a contextual restriction over the domain of quantification is represented (Stojanovic 2008). Stanley (2000, 2007), for example, offers a theory of quantifier domain restriction that both comports with empirical adequacy and offers a compelling way to think about the ordinary meaning of sentences that contain quantifiers. Stanley (2007, 117) rejects the minimalist account of meaning and offers a semantic analysis of quantifier domain restriction, which he terms "nominal restriction."[30] Stanley proposes a semantic framework where each nominal expression is associated with a domain variable. Relative to a context, the domain variable is assigned a set. The semantic relation between the extension (i.e., the referential range of application) of the nominal expression and the set is a set-theoretic intersection. A sentence such as

(3) Every bottle is empty

can communicate the proposition that "every bottle in Hannah's house is empty," because, relative to the relevant context, the domain variable associated with "bottle" is assigned the set of things in Hannah's house. In Stanley's view, "every bottle is empty" communicates the proposition that "every bottle in Hannah's house is empty," because, relative to this context, it semantically expresses this proposition.

Stanley uses the term "logical form" to refer to the output of the syntactic process that is visible to semantic interpretation. A logical form is a lexically and structurally disambiguated ordered sequence of word types, where word types are individuated both by semantic and syntactic properties. Logical forms are phrase markers. In this theory, nominal expressions are associated with domain variables. Thus, nominal expressions such as "bottle" cohabit a terminal node with a domain variable. According to Stanley's account, which he terms "Nominal Restriction Theory (NRT)," the logical form of a sentence such as

(4) Every man runs

would look like that depicted in figure 4.1. The value of "i" is an object provided by the context, and the value of "f" is a function provided by the context that maps objects onto quantifier domains. The restriction on the quantified phrase "every man" in (4), relative to a context, then would be provided by the result of applying the function that context applies to "f" to the object that context supplies to "i."

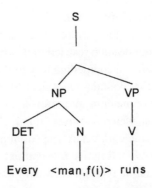

FIGURE 4.1. Logical form of "Every man runs." Value of "i" is an object provided by the context, and value of "f" is a function provided by the context that maps objects onto quantifier domains. DET, determiner; N, noun; NP, noun phrase; S, subject; V, verb; and VP, verb phrase.

As the logical form indicates, domain variables are independently meaningful expressions that incorporate with nouns and do not occupy their own terminal nodes. As a result of the theory, quantifier domain restriction is due to the presence of domain variables in the actual syntactic structure of sentences containing quantified noun phrases. Each nominal co-occurs with variables whose values, relative to a context, together determine a domain. Under NRT, the intuitive restriction on quantificational determiners such as "every," "any," and "all" is not because of a restriction on the quantificational expressions themselves, but instead to a restriction on the nominal complements of these determiners.

As described above, Stanley offers a semantic account of quantifier domain restriction that emphasizes compositionality and the systematic nature of language. Unlike the contextualist account, where context makes some nonspecific contribution to meaning, Stanley's account, as explained above, includes domain variables in the actual syntactic structure of sentences containing quantified noun phrases. Nevertheless, Stanley's theory only offers an answer to the descriptive problem of quantifier domain restriction. A descriptive semantic theory assigns semantic values to the expressions of the language and explains how the semantic values of the complex expressions are a function of the semantic values of their parts (Stojanovic 2012). For Stanley, the "descriptive problem" of context dependence for an expression e relative to a context c is the problem of deriving the interpretation of e relative to c, given a prior characterization of what features of the context c have a bearing on the interpretation.

The account is highly abstract in the sense that the posited domain variable does not specify what in the context makes it the case that an object is the denotation of the relevant nominal (i.e., how the relevant restriction was determined).

The "foundational problem," which Stanley does not purport to address, of context dependence for an expression e relative to a context c, is the problem of making these specifications. A solution to the foundational problem specifies what it is about the context in virtue of which certain entities (be they objects, properties, or propositions) play the role they do in the interpretation of an occurrence of e (Stojanovic 2012). In other words, it answers the question of what makes it the case that the language spoken by a particular individual or community has a particular descriptive semantics. For instance, the debate in chapter 3 regarding intentionalist versus objective theories of indexical meaning addressed the foundational problem of assigning meaning to indexicals. Certainly, the descriptive approach taken by Stanley is useful in the sense that it offers an account of how quantifier domain restriction can be said to be semantic. Nevertheless, considering how this descriptive account is linked to a foundational account of ordinary meaning requires that various decisions be made that are not assisted by the descriptive account.

4.2.5: A Foundational Theory of Quantifier Domain Restriction

Adapting to the requirements of ordinary meaning a semantic theory of quantifier domain restriction is more difficult than it was for indexicals. With indexicals, as chapter 3 explained, each indexical can be said to have a character or conventional meaning. Through narrow context, the conventional meaning is applied to the indexical in order to identify the correct reference. Of course, the conventional meaning is not always the correct meaning, and "wide context" (which includes any contextual evidence deemed relevant by the interpreter) can be consulted to determine whether the communicative meaning of a particular indexical differs from its ordinary meaning. With quantifier domain restriction, the distinction between ordinary meaning and communicative meaning is less clear. Although Stanley (2000, 2007) argues that there is syntactic evidence of quantifier domain restriction, the argument responsible for domain restriction is implicit in a way not shared by indexicals. A quantifier domain is not bound by semantic rules in the same way as is the determination of the reference of an indexical, because indexicals rely on conventional meanings in a way that quantifier domain restriction does not. The semantic rule alone does not determine the reference of the quantified expression in the light of the context of utterance. For quantifier domain restriction, then, any distinction between ordinary and communicative meaning turns on the scope of contextual reference.

The communicative meaning of the quantifier domain is not difficult to frame. Doing so invokes the debate described in chapters 2 and 3 between intentionalist theories of meaning and objective theories of meaning. For instance, Bianchi (2006) approaches the foundational problem of quantifier domain restriction by distinguishing between the objective perspective on context (OPC) and the intentional perspective on context (IPC). The OPC defines context in terms of the relevant states of affairs occurring in the world. The context is objective and mind transcendent and includes facts that are particularly relevant to the conversational aims of the interlocutors, whether they are aware of these facts or not. In contrast, the IPC defines context in terms of intentional states of the participants or their shared assumptions. For the reasons given in chapters 2 and 3, the OPC is the appropriate stance in which to view the communicative meaning of legal texts. Under an OPC view of domain restriction, the communicative meaning of a sentence containing a quantifier phrase would be determined in a similar way as the communicative meaning of a sentence containing an indexical. In both situations the "wide context" would be considered to determine whether an unordinary meaning is appropriate.[31]

A more difficult question is how the ordinary meaning of a sentence containing a quantifier phrase should be determined. In light of the lack of a conventional meaning that can straightforwardly be applied to contextual facts to determine reference, and thereby ordinary meaning, it may be questioned whether any distinction can or should be made between the ordinary meaning and communicative meaning of sentences containing quantifier phrases. One answer to this question is to consider again what motivates the existence of the ordinary meaning doctrine. As chapter 3 explained, one important motivation based on the principle of notice is the idea that those reading the text of the provision at issue should be able to readily discern its meaning. The ordinary meaning concept thus represents the notion that, in general, a provision's meaning should be discernible based on a relatively limited consideration of context. Of course, the degree of understanding (especially if one includes in the concept of understanding awareness of the consequences of a law) may depend on the reader's knowledge of law, but that does not nullify the notice principle.

The notion of notice thus supports the distinction between narrow context and wide context. While wide context concerns any contextual information that is relevant to determining the speaker's intention, including extralinguistic evidence, narrow context must of course be more limited. As explained in chapter 3, narrow context refers to a limited notion of context that concerns information specifically relevant to determining the semantic values of the quantified phrases. As such, it should depend on some notion of linguistic cotext, such as the relevant sentence and surrounding sentences. Certainly, at the very least, it should be limited to knowledge shared by speaker and addressee, which would likely be limited to information in close proximity to the provision at issue. Like the case with indexicals, though, even consideration of narrow context allows for the interpreter to select a domain restriction at least in part on the basis of desirable legal outcomes and principles, making a distinction between legal meaning and ordinary meaning difficult to maintain.

4.2.6: The Flawed Nature of the Supreme Court's Decision in Ali v. Federal Bureau of Prisons

It is fair to conclude that the Supreme Court has at times exhibited a poor understanding of quantifiers, especially the linguistic reality that the ordinary meaning of a quantifier often deviates from its literal meaning. In particular, the opinion in *Ali* reflects a considerable degree of confusion about quantifier phrases. Note the Court's view that it was giving an unrestricted scope to the phrase, "any other law enforcement officer," indicating that the phrase means "law enforcement officers of whatever kind."[32] It also repeated its reasoning that "'any other law enforcement officer' does in fact mean any other law enforcement officer."[33] Despite the Court's absolute language, it was of course implicitly restricting the domain of "any other law enforcement officer." Considering that § 1346(b)(1) authorizes claims only for acts of employees of the federal government, including foreign or state law enforcement officers in the list of exemptions in § 2680(c) would obviously be nonsensical. The Court would of course reject any interpretation that would include foreign law enforcement officers or even state law enforcement officers, even if the literal meaning of "any other law enforcement officer" would include them.[34]

The Court's opinion demonstrated further indications of confusion regarding the nature of quantifiers. One example was its indication that it viewed the interpretive dispute in bivalent terms of ambiguity/no ambiguity, stating that it was "unpersuaded by [Ali's] attempt to create ambi-

guity where the statute's text and structure suggest none."[35] Like indexicals, the interpretive issue concerning quantifiers is not of course whether
the conventional meaning is ambiguous but rather whether, and how, the
scope of the quantifier phrase is to be restricted from its literal meaning.[36] The Court's reliance on its precedents for the meaning of "any" was,
for similar reasons, misplaced.[37] Unless the objective was to establish that
quantifiers in legal texts never have a restricted domain, which would be
a truly implausible claim, considering how the Court evaluated the context of other statutes does not have the persuasive value that the Court
seemed to attach to it.

The Court also engaged in the typically specious but commonly used
tactic of arguing that if Congress had desired the interpretation the Court
was rejecting, Congress could have chosen different statutory language.
In the Court's view, Congress "easily could have written 'any other law
enforcement officer *acting in a customs or excise capacity.*'"[38] Of course,
almost any statute could be drafted more explicitly to clearly address the
particular interpretive dispute facing a court. But such an observation
is typically beside the point. Unless it is based on a valid linguistic insight about language usage (which the Court made no attempt to demonstrate), the "could have drafted differently" argument always cuts both
ways. As Justice Kennedy observed in his dissenting opinion, had Congress intended the Court's interpretation, "in all likelihood it would have
drafted the section to apply to 'any law enforcement officer, including
officers of customs and excise,' rather than tacking 'any other law enforcement officer' on the end of the unenumerated categories."[39] A more fundamental error in the reasoning, though, is that it seemed to presume that
users of language always explicitly rather than implicitly restrict the domains of quantifiers.

Among its various errors, the most fundamental flaw in the Court's interpretation in *Ali* was its failure to recognize that the ordinary meaning
of a sentence containing a quantifier phrase typically involves a certain
domain that is restricted. As Stanley (2000, 2007) has demonstrated, a semantic account can be given of this linguistic phenomenon. The logical
form of the relevant phrase from § 2680(c) would look like that in figure
4.2. Following Stanley's theory of nominal domain restriction, "officer" is
associated with a domain variable. If the Court had sought to determine
the ordinary meaning of § 2680(c), it would have attempted to determine
from the linguistic cotext (i.e., the narrow context) the extent of the domain restriction. In some cases, this could plausibly be done. In *Gutierrez*

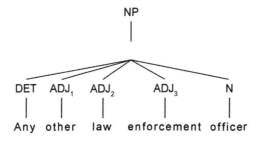

FIGURE 4.2. Logical form of "any other law enforcement officer." Value of "i" is an object provided by the context, and value of "f" is a function provided by the context that maps objects onto quantifier domains. ADJ1, adjective 1; ADJ2, adjective 2; ADJ3, adjective 3; DET, determiner; N, noun; and NP, noun phrase.

v. Ada,[40] the Court was able to restrict the domain of the quantifier based on the language of the relevant provision, which contained references to the object (i.e., the election of the governor and lieutenant governor) to which the quantifier was to be restricted. In many other situations, though, the text of the relevant provision may not contain sufficient contextual information as to the proper domain of the quantifier. In such situations, the restrictions will come from broad context and thus be part of communicative meaning, thereby possibly creating a situation where the ordinary meanings (but not the communicative meanings) of quantifiers in legal texts bear a closer connection to their literal meanings than do communications outside of legal texts.

In addition, as was explained in chapter 3 with indexicals, the required contextual consideration is irreducibly discretionary (absent, of course, some explicit limiting phrase). With indexicals, the discretionary element involves the identification of the governing convention and its application. Further, with indexicals in legal texts, judgments regarding conventions are not likely to be made without consideration of legal concerns. With quantifiers, the discretionary element is a bit different but no less pervasive. Determining the value of the domain variable, and thereby its ordinary meaning, does not involve the determination of a convention but rather a judgment about the influence of cotext. In comparison with indexicals, where there should be external evidence regarding the existence of a convention, judgments that an interpreter gave the wrong semantic meaning to the quantifier phrase are more difficult to make. Thus, in *Ali*, even where there was substantial evidence that the domain of "any" should be more restricted than the Court recognized, the relevant domain is essentially a judgment call by the interpreter, and hence discretionary. This observation does not validate the Court's reasoning, of course, which demonstrated a poor understanding of quantifier phrases that might lead to unpersuasive interpretations in future cases.

Despite the Court's failure in *Ali* and other cases to properly address the issue of quantifier domains, this confusion is not universal amongst the justices. Chief Justice John Marshall in 1818, when referring to a statute with the quantifier "any," indicated that "general words must . . . be limited to . . . those objects to which the legislature intended to apply them."[41] Justice Breyer, in particular, has on multiple occasions demonstrated an understanding of quantifiers. In *Small v. United States*,[42] Justice Breyer recognized that

> In ordinary life, a speaker who says, "I'll see any film," may or may not mean to include films shown in another city. In law, a legislature that uses the statutory phrase "any person" may or may not mean to include "persons" outside "the jurisdiction of the state."[43]

In *Ali* in his dissenting opinion, Justice Breyer similarly explained how the ordinary meaning of a quantifier often differs from its literal meaning. Justice Breyer reasoned that

> The word "any" is of no help because all speakers (including writers and legislators) who use general words such as "all," "any," "never," and "none" normally rely upon context to indicate the limits of time and place within which they intend those words to do their linguistic work. And with the possible exception of the assertion of a universal truth, say by a mathematician, scientist, philosopher, or theologian, such limits almost always exist. When I call out to my wife, "There isn't any butter," I do not mean, "There isn't any butter in town." The context makes clear to her that I am talking about the contents of our refrigerator. That is to say, it is context, not a dictionary, that sets the boundaries of time, place, and circumstance within which words such as "any" will apply.[44]

In this passage, Justice Breyer correctly observes that speakers typically rely on context to restrict the domain of quantifiers and that the domain of quantifiers is usually restricted in some way. Justice Breyer also correctly argues, in response to the court's reliance on the dictionary definition of "any," that a dictionary definition giving the literal meaning of "any" should not be determinative in interpreting the statute.

Of course, confusions still remain. Justice Breyer errs in arguing that, "[a]s with many questions of statutory interpretation, the issue here is not the meaning of the words. The dictionary meaning of each word is well known. Rather, the issue is the statute's scope."[45] The ultimate issue is, of course, the statute's scope, but the "meaning of the words" is crucial to that scope. While Breyer is correct that dictionary definitions with literal meanings are not sufficient, he fails to acknowledge that context is crucial in determining the *meaning* of the words (and that a literal dictionary definition does not necessarily represent the meaning), and is not some external constraint on the meaning. This confusion is not as fundamentally flawed, however, as the textualist position, exhibited in the majority opinion in *Ali* as well as the dissenting opinion in *Small,* where Justice Thomas (joined by Justices Scalia and Kennedy) similarly insisted that, by restricting the domain of the quantifier, the Court distorted "the plain meaning of the statute and depart[ed] from established principles of statutory construction."[46] It is unfortunate that it is the textualists on the Court who claim to take the nature of language seriously and purport to adhere to a methodology that makes textual meaning dispositive in most cases, but, at the same time, exaggerate the determinacy of language by applying an impoverished method of textual meaning. Through an over-reliance on dictionary definitions, textualists seem not to appreciate the frequent gaps that exist between literal meaning and ordinary meaning, as well as the contribution that context makes to ordinary meaning.

4.3: Temporal Preposition Phrases and the Scope of a Statute

4.3.1: A Description of Temporal Preposition Phrases

As the *Ali* case and above discussion illustrate, the linguistic scope of a sentence can be decisive in determining the meaning of a legal text. Linguistically valid sources for domain restriction are thus of great importance. One such example, quantifier domain restriction, is a systematic aspect of language that can be given a semantic account. Quantifier domain restriction has received particular attention in the philosophical and linguistic literature, but other linguistically-based restrictions on the domains of sentences are also possible. For instance, consider the difficult issues involved with the temporal domains of sentences. As Pratt and Francez (2001) observe, it is widely acknowledged that even simple assertive sentences like

(5) Mary kissed John

make an existential claim that an event of a certain type (i.e., Mary kissing John) occurred within some contextually determined interval. Temporal preposition phrases (TPPs) include situations where explicit temporal indications are provided. Thus, for example, in the sentence

(6) Mary kissed John during every meeting

the existential quantification present in (5) falls within the scope of the universal quantification (i.e., "every") over meetings.

To deal with the various issues relating to TPPs, Pratt and Francez (2001) developed the concept of a temporal generalized quantifier, which is a device that allows for meanings to be equipped with a variable representing the temporal context. Pratt and Francez argue that sentence meanings and TPPs must incorporate a temporal context variable. The temporal context variable originates in the meanings of nouns and verbs. The theory advocates a relational view of both noun meanings and (undetermined) sentence meanings, in which an added "context" argument constrains the occurrence time of the familiar "object" argument.

Demonstrating a systematic and semantic basis for domain restrictions on sentences containing temporal preposition phrases may be important for various reasons, but similar to quantifier domain restriction, it complicates ordinary meaning. Like with any linguistically-based domain restriction, some examples of TPP illustrate the distinction between literal meaning and ordinary meaning. Of course, the ordinary meaning is underdetermined compared to the literal meaning. Similar to quantifier domain restriction, a variable can be introduced as being part of the semantics of the relevant phrase or sentence, but identification of the relevant domain is essentially a discretionary exercise that depends on the interpreter's evaluation of the relevant context. Also, like quantifier domain restriction, it is difficult to distinguish between the ordinary meaning and the communicative meaning of sentences that contain TPPs. Presumably, a similar distinction would need to be made between "narrow context" and "wide context."

4.3.2: Linguistically-Based Contextual Constraints on the Domains of Statutes and the Supreme Court's Decision in Zadvydas v. Davis

Despite the above concerns, there is an important distinction between labeling a domain restriction as originating from language rather than from an interpreter creating an interpretive principle on the basis of concerns specific to the law. Formalizing to some degree the treatment of TPPs would thus establish that temporal restrictions on the domains of sentences are a natural aspect of language and, with respect to legal texts, not an instance of an interpreter-created principle. Such an analysis could change the focus of an interpretation. Consider the Supreme Court's decision in *Zadvydas v. Davis*.[47] The *Zadvydas* case involved the indefinite detention of Zadvydas, a resident alien who was born to Lithuanian parents in a displaced persons camp in Germany in 1948, and also the indefinite detention of Ma, a resident alien who was born in Cambodia in 1977.[48] Both Zadvydas and Ma had been ordered deported by immigration courts after having been convicted of serious crimes.[49] The Immigration and Naturalization Service (INS) was unable to find a country willing to accept either Zadvydas or Ma.[50] Zadvydas and Ma, and hundreds of others similarly situated, filed habeas corpus petitions challenging their continued detention.[51]

The government claimed that it had authority under 8 U.S.C. § 1231 (a)(6) to indefinitely detain aliens like Zadvydas and Ma who had been ordered to be deported but could not be transferred to other countries. Section 1231(a)(6) provides as follows:

> An alien ordered removed [1] who is inadmissible . . . [2] [or] removable [as a result of violations of status requirements or entry conditions, violations of criminal law, or reasons of security or foreign policy] or [3] who has been determined by the Attorney General to be a risk to the community or unlikely to comply with the order of removal, *may be detained beyond the removal period and, if released, shall be subject to [certain] terms of supervision* (emphasis added).[52]

The Ninth Circuit held that § 1231(a)(6) authorizes detention after the removal period of ninety days only if there is a realistic chance that the alien will be deported.[53] The court ordered that Ma be released. In contrast, the Fifth Circuit held that Zadvydas's continued detention was authorized.[54] The Tenth Circuit ruled similarly in a different case.[55] The Supreme Court granted certiorari in order to resolve the circuit split and held that § 1231(a)(6) does not authorize indefinite detention.

As an interpretive matter, the *Zadvydas* case is interesting because the text of § 1231(a)(6) contains a TPP, "may be detained beyond the removal period."[56] Instead of exploring the possibility of a contextual restriction on the temporal domain of "beyond," the Court, in an opinion written by Justice Breyer, purported to find ambiguity in a different part of the provision. The Court correctly noted that, in arguing for authority to indefinitely detain, "[t]he Government argue[d] that the statute means what it literally says."[57] The Court found, though, that "while 'may' suggests discretion, it does not necessarily suggest unlimited discretion. In that respect the word 'may' is ambiguous."[58] The finding of ambiguity allowed the Court to invoke the canon of constitutional avoidance. The canon of constitutional avoidance directs that, "if an otherwise acceptable construction of a statute would raise serious constitutional problems, and where an alternative interpretation of a statute is 'fairly possible,' . . . [reviewing courts] are obligated to construe the statute to avoid such problems."[59] Through its invocation of the avoidance canon, the Court "read an implicit limitation into the statute."[60] The Court, "for the sake of uniform administration in the federal courts," decided that the aliens covered by § 1231(a)(6) can only be detained for a six-month period unless there is a "significant likelihood of removal in the reasonably foreseeable future."[61]

4.3.3: Assessing the Supreme Court's Decision in Zadvydas v. Davis

Although it undoubtedly reached a humane result, the Court's linguistic reasoning in *Zadvydas* was flawed. It seems likely (and reasonable) that the Court was motivated to find an interpretation of § 1231(a)(6) that would not authorize indefinite detention. The Court's primary doctrine in restricting the scope of § 1231(a)(6), the canon of constitutional avoidance, is a controversial interpretive principle. Critics allege that courts invoke the avoidance canon not to resolve uncertainty regarding a statute's meaning but to choose questionable interpretations of clear statutes. Indeed, one of the primary complaints of Justice Kennedy's dissenting opinion (joined by Justices Scalia and Thomas and Chief Justice Rehnquist) in *Zadvydas* was that the statute was clear and that the Court had engaged in "disingenuous evasion" by adopting an interpretation that "simply bears no relation to the text."[62] Similar criticisms have been made in other cases. For instance, in a follow-up case to *Zadvydas* involving the meaning of § 1231(a)(6), Justice Thomas, in a dissenting opinion, argued that "[a] disturbing number of this Court's cases have applied the canon of constitutional doubt to statutes that were on their face clear."[63] The Court in *Zadvydas* seemed to concede Justice Thomas's characterization (except the "disturbing" part), indicating that it has in the past "read significant limitations into other immigration statutes in order to avoid their constitutional invalidation."[64]

The controversial nature of the avoidance canon made even more unfortunate the Court's misguided assertion in *Zadvydas* that ambiguity in the provision existed due to the auxiliary verb "may." Although the Court's reasoning was not explicit, presumably the Court was contrasting "may" with an auxiliary verb such as "shall," which would mandate continued detention. In fact, there are other provisions covering the detention of aliens that are stated in mandatory terms. For example, 8 U.S.C. § 1226(c) provides that "[t]he Attorney General shall take into custody any alien who" is removable from this country because he has been convicted of one of a specified set of crimes. Plainly, though, the distinction between a grant of authorization in permissive (i.e., "may") or mandatory (i.e., "shall") terms is orthogonal to the temporal domain of the authorization. Contrary to the Court's assertion, the language in § 1231(a)(6) was not ambiguous but, rather, unspecified regarding the temporal domain. By misidentifying the linguistic issue, the Court failed to persuasively identify uncertainty regarding the scope of the detention authority and provided a poor basis for the application of the avoidance canon, which purports to be applicable only in cases of uncertainty.

If the Court had properly identified the issue as centering on the domain of the TPP, its analysis would have been more convincing. Still, it would be difficult to restrict the domain on the basis of narrow context. Unlike the provision at issue in *Ali*, there is little information in the narrow context that would indicate the existence of a restricted domain. Perhaps the best argument is that, because the text of § 1231(a)(6) refers to aliens ordered removed and the ninety-day removal period, detention is authorized only if removal is reasonably foreseeable. But it is surely a stretch to assert that such an interpretation is the ordinary meaning of the provision (i.e., the interpretation an idealized interpreter would give the provision based on a consideration of narrow context).

The Court's adoption of the presumptive six-month period of detention is even less justifiable as the ordinary meaning of the provision. It is also questionable whether the Court's interpretation is the communicative meaning of the provision. Even if broad context is considered, the Court's interpretation was not likely the intended meaning of the provision. The Court pointed to a congressional indication over forty years prior to the enactment of the statute that doubted the constitutionality of detention for more than six months. That is pretty thin evidence, however, on which to decide that the communicative meaning of § 1231(a)(6) included the six-month restriction.[65] In order to adopt a more determinate restriction than the very general "only if removal is reasonably foreseeable," the Court would have had to go beyond the communicative meaning of the text. Whether such a restriction represented a "fairly possible" meaning, as required by the avoidance canon, is questionable. The Court admitted as much when it asserted that it was adopting the six-month limitation "for the sake of uniform administration in the federal courts."[66] Regardless of these considerations, though, undoubtedly the Court's opinion would have been greatly strengthened if it had correctly identified the linguistic problem (the TPP) and then reasoned within the context of identifying the restricted domain of the prepositional phrase.

4.4: Judicially-Created Interpretive Principles and Domain Restriction

As explained above, it is difficult to portray the Supreme Court's interpretation in *Zadvydas* as the ordinary meaning of the statute, or even its communicative meaning. Considerations external to language were clearly motivating the interpretation, as the Court itself indicated when it invoked the canon of constitutional avoidance. Nevertheless, in a general sense the methodology of the Court's interpretation in *Zadvydas* was not aberrational but, rather, consistent with a larger pattern of how courts restrict the domains of statutes (and, in many similar situations, contracts). In fact, there are numerous cases where courts have restricted the domain of a provision, contrary to its literal meaning. In many of these cases, the decisive interpretive principle was one created by courts. It is widely recognized that federal courts have the power (as do, in large part, state courts) to determine the applicable principles of interpretation (Rosenkranz 2002). The rules created by courts cover a broad range of interests, many of them unique to the law, yet a common theme is that when applied they narrow the scope of statutory language.

A classic example of domain restriction involves the recognition of common law exceptions to statutory provisions that do not otherwise provide for them. One famous example discussing these unarticulated constituents is found in Lon Fuller's 1950 article, "The Case of the Speluncean Explorers." In the article, Fuller presents a scenario where five men are trapped in a cave while hiking. Eventually, the group decides that in order to avoid death by starvation one of the men would have to be eaten by the others. The group casts lots to determine which member would be sacrificed. After putting to death and eating one of the group members, the four remaining members are rescued and charged with murder. The criminal provision at issue, N. C. S. A. (n. s.) § 12-A, provides simply that

(7) Whoever shall willfully take the life of another shall be punished by death.
(Fuller 1958, 619)

Although succinct, the provision is misleadingly clear to those not knowledgeable about the legal system, considering the difficulties that the (fictional) individual justices had in deciding the meaning of it.

Fuller's article, which contained five opinions from the justices of the fictional Supreme Court of Newgarth, illustrated the variety of approaches a judge could take to the interpretation of the provision. One set of issues involved whether the literal meaning of the provision represented its legal meaning. Specifically, the question was whether common law defenses to criminal charges were still available notwithstanding the unlimited scope (at least with respect to defenses) of the criminal provision. Under one theory, the defendants needed the benefit of a necessity defense in order to avoid conviction.[67] Although there was no majority of justices willing to recognize a necessity defense, Chief Justice Truepenny commented that self-defense was a recognized defense to § 12-A, even though there is nothing in the wording of the statute that suggested the exception. Thus, the literal meaning of § 12-A exceeded in scope the legal meaning of the provision, which had its domain limited by the availability of at least one implicit defense.

Courts have differed in their recognition of common law defenses to criminal provisions that do not explicitly provide for them. It is plain though that the domain restrictions imposed by judges due to common law concepts are motivated, at least in part, by legal concerns rather than linguistic phenomena. Similar to common law defenses, many other interpretive principles that are motivated by legal concerns are used to restrict the domains of statutes. Some of these principles have been categorized by scholars as substantive canons of interpretation (described below). The pervasiveness of substantive canons, and similar interpretive principles, raises the issue of whether they are determinants of ordinary meaning. Namely, can an interpretive principle motivated, at least in part, by legal rather than linguistic concerns nonetheless be part of the ordinary meaning of a legal provision? As explained below, if the ordinary meaning doctrine is limited to the "ordinary linguistic meaning" of the relevant legal sentence, which would be limited to linguistic principles that apply outside of any legal context, the answer should typically be "no." If one instead considers whether the interpretive principle is part of the "ordinary legal meaning" of the provision, the answer may change, although many of the interpretive principles motivated by legal concerns should not be considered part of the ordinary legal meaning of a given provision.

4.4.1: Substantive Canons of Construction and Domain Restriction

Substantive canons have been described as "essentially presumptions about statutory meaning based upon substantive principles or policies drawn from the common law, other statutes, or the Constitution" (Eskridge and Frickey 1995, 634). They have also been referred to as "normative canons," among other terms (Bradley 1998, 507). The strongest substantive canons are known as "clear statement rules" and require a court to interpret the statute to avoid a particular result unless the statute clearly indicates that the result was intended (Slocum 2003). As their name suggests, clear statement rules require particularly precise indications of congressional intent in order to be overcome. As such, they are similar to linguistic phenomena like quantifier domain restriction, which often produce meanings at odds with the literal meaning of the relevant sentence.

As indicated above, substantive canons are judge created and represent a wide range of concerns that are relevant to the law. Because they are not tied to particular linguistic phenomena, the number of possible substantive canons is theoretically unlimited. Unsurprisingly, the number and relative strength of substantive canons is often a source of dispute, and scholars often advocate for the judicial adoption of a new substantive canon to protect interests the particular scholar believes are important. Table 4.3 lists several of the most prominent substantive canons.

Whether the creation and application of substantive canons is consistent with the proper judicial role in matters of interpretation is a matter

TABLE 4.3. **List and description of substantive canons of construction**

Name of substantive canon(s)	Description
Rule of lenity	Requires that ambiguous criminal statutes be interpreted in favor of the defendant
Canon of constitutional avoidance	Requires that a court adopt a "fairly possible" interpretation if doing so would avoid a serious constitutional issue
Presumption against retroactivity	Clear statement rule that requires that a court adopt a rule only prospectively unless there is a clear indication that retroactive application was intended
Clear statement rules regarding the preclusion of judicial review and habeas corpus jurisdiction	Clear statement rules requiring explicit statutory language in order to divest courts of judicial review or habeas corpus jurisdiction
Clear statement presumption against extraterritoriality	Clear statement rule requiring explicit language in order for a statute to have extraterritorial application
Various federalism canons	Numerous canons designed to protect federalism interests that are threatened by possibly abrogating state Eleventh Amendment immunity, exposing states to generally applicable regulations, or displacing state law in areas of traditional state concern

of much debate, and also beyond the scope of this book.[68] What is notable, though, is that the purpose of all the substantive canons listed above is to restrict the domains of statutes. The domain restrictions are motivated by policies relevant to law, and external to any given statute, and are therefore normative in nature. In contrast, theories that account for linguistic phenomena such as quantifier domain restriction and temporal preposition phrases are empirically based and model the way in which language is used. As such, it would seem that for purposes of ordinary meaning there is a clear distinction between substantive canons and linguistic phenomena like quantifiers and temporal preposition phrases.

One response to the position that substantive canons and similar concepts place artificial restraints (i.e., nonlinguistically motivated) on the domains of statutes is to make an interpretive communities argument. Generally, the argument is that the canons are long-standing conventions, and legislatures draft statutes in light of the canons. Arguably, then, a legislature may therefore assume that it can enact unqualified provisions, and courts will restrict the domains of these provisions if appropriate, thereby making the drafting process more efficient. Legislatures often draft statutes with general language that effectively delegates rule-making authority to courts and administrative agencies. A large number of court decisions and scholarly papers have focused on various aspects of this phenomenon, including the scope of discretion granted an agency or court when a statute contains general language. The focus here, though, is on the comparatively narrow issue of whether unarticulated provisions specific to the law can be said to be contained in statutes. Of course, as the history of courts recognizing unarticulated defenses to criminal provisions illustrates, the answer is that legal texts sometimes contain unarticulated constituents. In a general sense, the possibility of unarticulated constituents is recognized by the Supreme Court's assertion that "[i]t is presumable that Congress legislates with knowledge of our basic rules of statutory construction."[69] In a similar way, Manning (2001, 16–17) argues that

> textualists believe that legislation supposes that legislators and judges are part of a common social and linguistic community, with shared conventions for communication. Accordingly, they argue that a faithful agent's job is to decode legislative instructions according to the common social and linguistic conventions shared by the relevant community.

As such, it could be argued that the ordinary meaning of a literal, unqualified provision includes restrictions imposed by implied defenses and substantive canons, even if the restrictions are motivated by legal concerns and not linguistic phenomena.

4.4.2: Substantive Canons and the Conventional Rules Argument

There are problems with the theory that judicially-created interpretive principles are legitimized as principles of language usage simply by being well established. More specifically, presuming that the legislature is aware of the rules does not establish that substantive canons are conventions relevant to the determination of ordinary meaning. While courts will typically defend a chosen rule on the ground that its application will result in a statutory interpretation that reflects congressional intent, the application of a substantive canon reflects the values of the judiciary, not necessarily those of legislatures.[70] Various scholars have argued that many substantive canons run contrary to likely legislative preferences. Elhauge (2002), for instance, argues that many of the substantive canons are preference-eliciting statutory default rules. These rules are used by courts in ways that may be counter to the desires of the legislature (such as by interpreting a provision in favor of a criminal defendant), resulting in the satisfaction of enactable political preferences once the legislative reaction to the judicial decision has been successfully enacted. Empirical research has indicated that the drafters of legislation are often unaware of the interpretive rules created by courts, including substantive canons, and do not consult them when drafting legislation (Nourse and Schacter 2002; Gluck and Bressman 2013). The background rules argument does not therefore establish that substantive canons should properly be considered to be part of an ordinary meaning determination.

Apart from whether the drafters of statutes consider substantive canons when drafting, substantive canons (and especially clear statement requirements) have been criticized because they assume an unrealistic level of congressional foresight. In part, this is because it is not always possible to anticipate the sensitive issues that may be raised by the application of a statute. For example, with respect to the canon of constitutional avoidance, the law may change and create constitutional issues that were not present at the time of the statute's enactment.[71] Another reason to be skeptical of the background rules argument has to do with language and issues of determinacy. The strongest clear statement rules may set forth relatively determinate conventions. For example, one particularly strong clear statement canon may require "magic words" (i.e., specific language) before a court will interpret a statute as divesting courts of habeas corpus jurisdiction.[72] A provision that purports to curtail all judicial review but does not explicitly include habeas corpus will not be interpreted as divesting courts of habeas corpus jurisdiction. For various reasons relating to the proper judicial function, these superclear statement requirements are controversial, and most clear-statement rules do not require any specific level of clarity. The issue, then, is how clear is "clear"? In any given case it is often difficult to predict how much clarity will be required by courts to satisfy the presumptions created by substantive canons. One reason for this is that the relevant judges may disagree with the existence of a canon on normative grounds and may thus wish to avoid its application or, conversely, may strongly agree with the canon and be motivated to apply it (Spaak 2008). In any case, the answer to the degree of clarity issue may not be something the legislature could have predicted at the time of drafting.

Equally so, there are problems with weaker canons of interpretation. In contrast to a clear statement rule, the rule of lenity, along with other so-called tiebreaker canons, is applicable when a criminal provision is ambiguous. The legal determination of ambiguity is notoriously unpredictable, though, because courts typically conflate ambiguity identification with disambiguation (Slocum 2010). A court will thus typically not determine whether a provision is ambiguous but instead whether it can be disambiguated. A court will therefore refuse to declare that a provision is ambiguous unless the court determines that disambiguation is not possible. Typically, a court will consider, or refuse to consider, various pieces of evidence from the "wide context," making the final determination of ambiguity entirely discretionary and therefore difficult to predict. For example, a court may or may not be willing to consider the legislative history of a statute, depending on the court's views regarding the probative value of such evidence. Even if a court is willing to consider the legislative history, it may not find the evidence compelling regarding the interpretive issue before the court. Further, even if the court finds the evidence to be persuasive, it may conflict with other evidence that is supported by other long-standing interpretive principles.

The application of other substantive canons is similarly difficult to predict. Consider the canon of constitutional avoidance. It is unclear whether it should properly be viewed as a tiebreaker canon that resolves ambiguity or a clear-statement rule that requires that a certain degree of clarity be present in the statutory language. Recall that it is applicable when an otherwise acceptable construction of a statute would raise serious constitutional problems and an alternative interpretation is "fairly possible."[73] The canon has been identified in the past as a clear statement canon, but the Court has recently stated that the avoidance canon's function is to "choos[e] among plausible meanings of an ambiguous statute," as opposed to a clear-statement rule that "implies a special substantive limit on the application of an otherwise unambiguous mandate."[74] This characterization is at odds, though, with the Court's statement in *Zadvydas* that it had "read significant limitations into other immigration statutes in order to avoid their constitutional invalidation."[75] It is also at odds with the Court's use of the canon as much more than a mere tiebreaker. Indeed, the significant strength of the canon has been the subject of controversy as both judges and scholars have criticized courts for applying the canon in order to choose implausible interpretations. In any case, while it may be unclear whether the canon should be classified as a clear statement rule, it is clear that its application is unpredictable and controversial.

Further undermining any ordinary meaning claims is that courts do not typically consider the temporal implications involved when substantive canons are created or when their strength or scope is broadened or narrowed (Slocum 2008). Courts frequently create and modify substantive canons and other rules of interpretation, but generally apply these new or modified rules of interpretation retroactively. In other words, courts do not typically consider whether new or modified rules should be applied only prospectively to statutes enacted after the judicial decisions that created or modified the rules. When a substantive canon is created or is modified by increasing its strength or scope but no consideration is given to whether the new or modified rule should be applied only prospectively, the end result can be an interpretation that the legislature would not have predicted. The failure of courts to consider temporal issues when creating or modifying substantive canons further undermines any assumption that Congress is able to choose statutory language in light of the rules of interpretation that will be applied by courts.

4.5: Ordinary Linguistic Meaning and Ordinary Legal Meaning

The discussion of linguistic phenomena and substantive canons illustrates an important distinction that should be made between the "ordinary linguistic meaning" of a sentence in a legal text and the "ordinary legal meaning" of that sentence. The ordinary linguistic meaning of a sentence in a legal text has been the focus of this project and can be said to constitute part or all, depending on the circumstances, of the ordinary legal meaning of a sentence. Broadly stated, the basic determinants of ordinary linguistic meaning are external to the legal interpreter and the legal system. They reflect linguistic phenomena that exist outside the interpretation of legal texts. Applying a substantive canon of interpretation might be an exercise in determining the ordinary legal meaning of the provision, but it has nothing to do with the ordinary linguistic meaning. On the other hand, the ordinary linguistic meaning of a word or phrase might not be dispositive because the word has a certain meaning in a legal text that differs from its nonlegal meaning. Justice Oliver Wendell Holmes explained that, "[i]f Congress has been accustomed to use a certain phrase with a more limited meaning than might be attributed to it by common practice, it would be arbitrary to refuse to consider that fact when we come to interpret a statute."[76] Courts frequently must determine whether a word bears a special ordinary legal meaning. For example, does the word "assault" in a civil case involving a student playfully jumping on the back of a school employee carry its special legal meaning or its ordinary linguistic meaning?[77]

To be sure, as the examination of indexicals in chapter 3 illustrates, as well as the discussion in this chapter of quantifiers and temporal preposition phrases, it is unclear that the ordinary meaning of a sentence in a legal text can be determined without consideration of the legal context in which the sentence appears, and without concern for the legal consequences of a particular interpretation. Even when the legal context is not considered explicitly, as it would be with indexicals in order to determine the appropriate convention, the legal context would likely at least be considered implicitly by the legal interpreter in virtue of the interpreter's training and motivations. Even so, an interpretation motivated by a substantive canon of interpretation generally does not represent the ordinary linguistic meaning of a text. For substantive canons, rather than contributing to ordinary linguistic meaning, they offer reasons for deviating from it in order to protect other interests deemed to be more important in the particular case. Even if the existence of applicable legal interpretive principles such as substantive canons create conventions regarding the interpretation of statutory provisions, these conventions should be distinguished from the conventions that originate outside of the law. The determinants of ordinary linguistic meaning must be justified on the basis of empirical evidence and knowledge of how language functions. The justifications for other interpretive principles must rest on other grounds, particularly normative ones relating to legal concerns. A substantive canon might be changed to make it stronger or weaker or to make its scope broader or narrower, and any possible objections would not be based on the regularities of language. Rather, any objections would be normative ones, focusing on issues such as the proper judicial role in interpretation and the impact that the changes would have on the content of the law.

Certainly, in some cases it might be difficult to categorize an interpretive principle as being part of ordinary linguistic meaning. Consider a nonlegal prohibition on fighting. Would such a prohibition contain an unarticulated constituent (i.e., an unstated exception) allowing for a self-defense exception? If, for example, a father tells his child not to fight with other kids at school, it might be reasonable for the child to conclude that it is nevertheless permissible to fight in self-defense. A justification for acting contrary to a prohibition might therefore arise in other contexts just as in a legal context, and whether it is an aspect of ordinary meaning would depend on the identification of such a convention. Such possibilities do not, however, undermine the claim that it most, if not all, substantive canons are not aspects of ordinary linguistic meaning.

Similarly, many substantive canons do not contribute to ordinary legal meaning, although, obviously, their application determines the legal meaning of the relevant text. Often, they do not contribute to ordinary legal meaning for the reasons indicated above regarding their vagueness, uncertain application by interpreters, and the lack of use by legal drafters. Some of the strongest canons might, however, contribute to ordinary legal meaning (even if their existence is controversial). In contrast to other substantive canons, the strongest clear statement rules are triggered when specific language is absent from the relevant legal provision. The absence of "magic words" may, for example, justify a court in concluding, as a matter of ordinary legal meaning, that the provision does not strip courts of habeas corpus jurisdiction, even if there is no evidence that the legislature considered the issue.[78] Thus, there is much more certainty regarding clear statement interpretive principles. In addition, the strength and certainty of the principles should alert statutory drafters to their existence and potential applicability. Still, the validity of these interpretive principles would typically rest on normative grounds rather than an argument that they represent the ways in which legislatures use language. Despite the claims of some judges that substantive canons reflect legislative intent, a persuasive defense (which, to be sure, can be made for at least some of them) of the even the strongest substantive canons must, as indicated above, typically be made on normative grounds and not on the basis that they are consistent with drafting practices.

4.6: Conceptualizing the Role of Textual Canons of Construction

4.6.1: A Description of Textual Canons of Construction

In contrast to substantive canons, other fundamental interpretive principles frequently applied by judges are alleged by some to be general principles of language usage and not motivated by legal concerns. One such category of interpretive principles is termed "textual canons," which "set forth inferences that are usually drawn from the drafter's choice of words, their grammatical placement in sentences, and their relationship to other parts of the 'whole' statute" (Eskridge and Frickey 1995, 634). Like substantive canons, quantifier domain restriction, and some temporal preposition phrases, the application of a textual canon will tend to narrow the scope of a statutory provision. Several of the more prominent textual canons are listed in table 4.4, along with corresponding descriptions.

TABLE 4.4. **List and description of textual canons of construction**

Name of textual canon	Description of its function
Rule against surplusage	A statute should be construed when possible so that no clause, sentence, or word is superfluous
Noscitur a sociis	The meaning of words that are placed together in a statute should be determined in light of the words with which they are associated
Ejusdem generis	When general words in a statute precede or follow the designation of specific things, the general words should be construed to include only objects similar in nature to the specific words
Expressio unius est exclusio alterius	When a statute expresses something explicitly (usually in a list) anything not expressed explicitly does not fall within the statute
In pari materia	There is a general presumption that identical words in the same statute have identical meanings
Rule of the last antecedent	When a modifier is set off from a series of antecedents by a comma, the modifier should be interpreted to apply to all of the antecedents
Proviso canon	Clauses limiting another more general clause in a substantive provision are to be interpreted narrowly

Textual canons have received considerable support from commentators, and many of the canons have considerable pedigrees as principles of legal interpretation. Further, some commentators have explicitly tied textual canons to ordinary language usage. For instance, one major treatise on statutory interpretation, Singer (2000, 291), indicates that the *ejusdem generis* canon (which will receive special attention in this chapter) "expresses a valid insight about ordinary language usage." It is textualists, though, who are currently the strongest supporters of textual canons. One reason for the textualist support stems from the contribution of textual canons to textualists' stated preference for neutral, rulelike principles of interpretation, and their corresponding distrust of judicial reliance on legislative history, broad purposive reasoning, and other determinants of meaning that give judges considerable discretion. For instance, Vermeule (2006, 4) argues that, because of the inability of legal interpreters to successfully deduce operating-level rules of interpretation directly from high-level conceptual commitments (such as to legislative supremacy), "judges should sharply limit their interpretive ambitions, in part by limiting themselves to a small set of interpretive sources and a restricted range of relatively wooden decision-rules." Although Vermeule's arguments may be more extreme than those of many textualists, as argued in chapter 3, textualists favor fixed, determinate rules of interpretation that cabin judicial discretion. Rosenkranz (2002, 2088), for example, has advocated that Congress codify principles of interpretation in order to ensure the "central imperative of statutory interpretation: a single, predictable, coherent set of rules."

At a less metalevel, textualists generally defend the linguistic validity of textual canons. For instance, Manning (2011, 2007) views the *expressio unius est exclusio alterius* canon (i.e., the negative implication principle) as "a commonsense approximation of how people use language." Similarly, Justice Scalia (1997, 26) has described textual canons as "so commonsensical that, were [they] not couched in Latin, you would find it hard to believe anyone could criticize them." Justice Scalia and Garner (2012) list various textual canons among their "valid" canons of construction, including the *expressio unius est exclusio alterius* canon (107), the rule of the last antecedent (144), the proviso canon (154), the rule against surplusage (174), the *noscitur a sociis* canon (195), the *ejusdem generis* canon (199), and the *in pari materia* canon (252).[79]

Despite their ubiquity, long-standing status, and justification on language rather than normative grounds, textual canons have received significant criticism. One significant line of criticism concerns their status as genuine, as opposed to pretextual, principles of interpretation. In a famous critique, the legal scholar Karl N. Llewellyn (1950) listed twenty-eight pairs of textual canons and argued that for each canon there was a corresponding canon that conflicted with it. Llewellyn's argument was that courts typically selected one, seemingly determinate, canon to apply to a statute, disingenuously ignoring the conflicting canon, in an attempt to make is seem as though the interpretive question had only one correct answer. In Llewellyn's view (401), in situations involving one of the canons, the interpretation selected by the court required justification on other grounds, such as the "good sense of the situation and a simple construction of the available language." Llewellyn's view was widely viewed as devastating and, according to Macey and Miller (1992, 647), "derailed" "intellectual debate about the canons for almost a quarter of a century."

Although Llewellyn's argument that each textual canon has a conflicting canon has been rebutted by scholars (see Sinclair 2005–6, 2006–7, and 2008–9, for a comprehensive analysis), criticisms of textual canons still persist. One common theme is that textual canons, or at least some of them, set forth erroneous rules about language usage. Dickerson (1975, 234), for instance, questions whether the *ejusdem generis* canon is "lexicographically accurate." Another common criticism, echoing and expanding on Llewellyn's critique, is that much of the judicial use of textual canons is disingenuous. One variant of the claim is that courts often simply ignore applicable textual canons when it is convenient to do so. Another variant is that the process of statutory interpretation is much more nuanced and complex than is accounted for by textual canons. Even some scholars who defend textual canons do not conceptualize them as setting forth determinate principles that guide judges and constrain their interpretations. Sinclair (2005–6, 923), for example, views a citation to a textual canon as "more like a formulaic summary of the end result of a process of reasoning, but a process sufficiently commonplace to justify a canonical formula."

4.6.2: A Role for Textual Canons

While some textual canons may fail to capture how legislatures use language and, like other interpretive principles, may be ignored by courts when convenient, it is important to be precise in considering how textual canons, if valid, should be viewed by commentators and courts. One consequence of failing to properly define the role of textual canons is that, as applied, they can be seen as conforming to the (inaccurate) conception formed by critics of how textual canons operate. This consequence is implicitly encouraged by those who generally support canons but are imprecise about their role in statutory interpretation.

For instance, even supporters of textual canons like Sinclair view the canons as "aids" to interpretation. If a canon is merely described as the "formulaic summary of the end result of a process of reasoning," which recall is Sinclair's formulation, it is not difficult to understand why critics would label judicial citation to canons as pretextual. Scalia and Garner have also been imprecise in their description of how textual canons fit within a methodology of interpretation. For instance, Scalia and Garner (2012, 212) state that, "like the other canons, *ejusdem generis* is not a rule of law but one of various factors to be considered in the interpretation of a text." Scalia and Garner (213) further explain that "*ejusdem generis* is one of the factors to be considered, along with context and textually apparent purpose in determining the scope. It does not always predominate, but neither is it a mere tie-breaker." A slightly different claim, made by

Justice Kagan in a recent dissenting opinion, is that canons like *ejusdem generis* are only relevant to "resolve ambiguity."[80] Such a claim is inconsistent with the principle that *ejusdem generis*, and perhaps other textual canons, help determine ordinary meaning.

The problem with the above descriptions is not that textual canons are more determinate than described but rather that the descriptions are either inaccurate or too imprecise regarding the role of textual canons in the interpretive process. First, critics of canons place too high of a burden on supporters of the canons to prove their consistency and objectivity. It should not be surprising that other considerations sometimes trump the application of a textual canon. As has been addressed throughout this book, courts frequently reject the ordinary or communicative meaning of a text in order to promote or protect other interests. Indeed, as this chapter has discussed, they often reject the ordinary or communicative meaning of a text in favor of a substantive canon. Second, like quantifier domain restriction, a textual canon may be applicable to the statutory language even if it is not dispositive of the interpretive dispute before the court. Thus, the fact that the canon is not dispositive of the legal dispute does not mean that its linguistic principle is not relevant to the meaning of the text.

More fundamentally, like the other linguistic phenomena considered thus far, the role of textual canons in the sequential process of interpretation must be clarified. Textual canons are only coherent if, like other determinants of ordinary meaning, they are viewed as starting presumptions of how language is used, as opposed to "aids" or "factors," or even ways of resolving ambiguity. Describing a textual canon as a mere "aid" or "factor" gives no sense of when the canon should be applied (and perhaps decide a case) or under what circumstances it should be rejected. It suggests that application of the canon is optional, seemingly at the whim of the interpreter. In contrast, viewing textual canons as presumptions (or default meanings) specifies their role in the sequential interpretive process and is consistent with how ordinary meaning concepts like conventional meaning should be treated. Of course, as has been explained above and in chapter 3 when discussing other interpretive principles, courts can consider the wide context of a statute and reject the ordinary meaning. Unlike situations where judges cite canons at the end of a process of reasoning, thereby raising the possibility of pretextual usage, the consideration of broader contextual evidence is a legitimate means of confirming or rejecting the presumption created by the canon at the beginning of the process of reasoning.

If textual canons are to be defended, it must be on the basis that they capture language usage. This is not to say that it must be empirically proved that the relevant legislature considers a given canon when drafting, although such evidence is of course useful. Such a standard, though, would likely be inappropriate in most situations, as people may adhere to certain norms of language use even without consciously being aware of doing so. Instead, like conventional meaning or quantifier domain restriction, it must be the case that the canon represents the way that language is normally used, or at least the way it is used in the context of legal drafting. If a textual canon does not capture general language use, there is no justification for the existence of the canon, considering that there is no normative basis for the canons. Further, canons can be criticized (or eliminated) on the basis that they do not reflect language usage, and courts can be criticized for ignoring or misapplying canons, but textual canons should not be criticized on grounds of indeterminacy. In comparison to other principles of interpretation, they are, in fact, fairly determinate. Certainly, they are more determinate than an open-ended examination of "purpose" or legislative history. In addition, as has already been illustrated, even seemingly determinate linguistic phenomena, such as indexicals, quantifier phrases, and temporal prepositional phrases, allow for significant interpretive discretion.

4.7: The *Ejusdem Generis* Canon

4.7.1: A Description of the Ejusdem Generis *Canon*

In conceptualizing the relationship between textual canons and ordinary meaning, the objective of this chapter is not to analyze in detail every canon but, rather, to illustrate in some detail the process of reasoning by which a textual canon can be said to be a proper aspect of an ordinary meaning determination. One paradigmatic canon, the *ejusdem generis* canon, will be the focus of the analysis. The canon provides that, "if a series of more than two items ends with a catch-all term that is broader than the category into which the proceeding items fall but which those items do not exhaust, the catch-all term is presumably intended to be no broader than that category" (Dickerson 1975, 234). The motivation for the *ejusdem generis* canon is straightforward and intuitive. Lists are pervasive in legal texts, and legislatures often use a general term at the end of a list of specifics in order to ensure that the provision has a broad scope (Tiersma

2005c). Intuitively, though, the general term must be narrower in meaning than its literal meaning would suggest. As will be examined below, the indeterminacy of the *ejusdem generis* canon relates not to whether there is typically a gap between the literal meaning and ordinary meaning of the general term but instead the multiple ways in which the general catchall term (usually an "other" phrase) can be given a limited meaning.

It is not difficult to conceive of examples where the application of the *ejusdem generis* principle seems intuitively correct. For example, a law concerning the regulation of

(8)   gin, bourbon, vodka, rum and other beverages

would not likely (absent some unusual context) be interpreted as including Coke (the soda), even though it is a "beverage." Because of the predilection that legal drafters have for general, "other" phrases following lists of specific items, courts frequently apply the *ejusdem generis* canon in order to narrow the meaning of the "other" phrase. By doing so, they of course create yet another gap between literal meaning and legal meaning (as well as ordinary meaning, as will be explained below). Consider a further "real-life" example, which resulted in litigation. The Illinois legislature granted the Illinois Department of Conservation the power to sell

(9)   gravel, sand, earth or other material

from state-owned land.[81] The Sierra Club filed a lawsuit seeking to enjoin the department from inviting bids for logging a portion of Pere Marquette State Park. One of the interpretive issues in the case involved the scope of "other material." A literal interpretation would give an extremely broad scope to the phrase, including anything that might be deemed a "material" [similar to (8) above where the literal meaning of "other beverages" is quite broad]. The Supreme Court of Illinois, though, applied the *ejusdem generis* canon and held that the provision did not include commercial timber harvested on state-owned land.[82] The court stated that "other materials" "can only be interpreted to include materials of the same general type" as those listed (i.e., gravel, sand, and earth).[83] The court reasoned that it would "both defy common sense and render the other statutes on timber sales surplusage" to include timber within the provision.[84]

Often, the catchall "other" phrase includes a quantifier. Consistent with quantifier domain restriction, the inclusion of a quantifier is not viewed, however, as broadening the scope of the "other" phrase. In *Circuit City Stores, Inc. v. Adams*,[85] for example, an employer brought an action under the Federal Arbitration Act (FAA) to enjoin an employee's state court employment discrimination action and to compel arbitration. Section 1 of the FAA excludes from the act's coverage

(10) contracts of employment of seamen, railroad employees, or any other class of
      workers engaged in foreign or interstate commerce.

Despite the literal meaning of the "other" clause, which would include the employee, the Supreme Court held that the provision included only transportation workers in foreign or interstate commerce.[86] The Court reasoned that "the location of the phrase 'any other class of workers engaged in . . . commerce' in a residual provision, after specific categories of workers have been enumerated, undermines any attempt to give the provision a sweeping, open-ended construction."[87] Of course, as with other interpretive principles, some confusion exists regarding the combination of a quantifier and a general "other" clause. For example, in a recent case a federal district court indicated that the *ejusdem generis* canon "does not apply where there is no ambiguity as to the expansive (or unlimited) nature of the general phrase, such as when the term 'any' precedes the general phrase."[88]

4.7.2: The Ejusdem Generis *Canon and Grice*

As the cases above illustrate, application of the *ejusdem generis* canon will result in an interpretation that narrows the scope of the provision from its literal meaning. In that respect, it is similar to quantifier domain restriction and some temporal preposition phrases, as well as substantive canons. Still, such a similarity does not by itself legitimize the canon. Notwithstanding the assertions that textual canons represent principles of language usage, some theory must be offered as to how the application of a textual canon results in a meaning that is the ordinary meaning of the sentence at issue. At least ostensibly, such a theory is more difficult to construct for textual canons than for linguistic phenomena like indexicals and quantifier phrases, which can be given straightforward semantic conceptualizations.

One possibility is that, as two legal scholars have argued, at least some textual canons can be defended on the grounds that Grice's theory of "conversational implicature" provides justification for their application.

If true, textual canons would seem to fall under Recanati's (2004) third level of meaning, "what is communicated," which, according to Recanati, is similar to Grice's theory of conversational implicature. Recall that what is communicated concerns what Recanati terms "secondary pragmatic processes." In contrast to "primary pragmatic processes," which are included in "what is said" (the second level of meaning), secondary pragmatic processes are "post-propositional." Secondary pragmatic processes cannot take place unless some proposition p is considered as having been expressed, for they proceed by inferentially deriving some further proposition q (the implicature) from the fact that p has been expressed. They are ordinary inferential processes that take the interpreter from "what is said" to what is communicated, which is something that "follows from the fact that the speaker has said what she has said" (17).

Grice's conversational implicatures are oriented toward everyday conversation where people often convey information that goes beyond what is said. Exaggeration and irony are prominent examples of such communications. Recall from chapter 2 that Grice (1969, 1989, chap. 5) explained his theory of utterer's meaning on the basis of the utterer's intention being achieved just by being recognized by the hearer. In thinking about meaning, though, Grice distinguished between what is said, which he understood as being closely related to the conventional meaning of the words uttered, and what is "conversationally implicated," which can be inferred from the fact that an utterance has been made in context. What is conversationally implicated is not coded but, rather, is inferred on the basis of assumptions concerning the Cooperative Principle and its constituent maxims of conversation, which describe how people interact with each other. The Cooperative Principle is the following: "Make your contribution such as is required, at the stage at which it occurs, by the accepted purpose or direction of the talk exchange in which you are engaged" (Grice 1989, 26). The Cooperative Principle works in both directions in the sense that speakers observe it and listeners assume that speakers are observing it.

In fleshing out the Cooperative Principle, Grice proposed four maxims of conversation, which describe specific rational principles observed by people who obey the Cooperative Principle. These maxims enable effective communication and are a way of explaining the link between utterances and what is understood from them. The maxims are listed in table 4.5.

Conversational implicatures arise on the basis that the maxims are being preserved. Grice distinguishes between what a speaker has said by virtue of the conventional meaning of the words used and what a speaker

TABLE 4.5. **Grice's (1989) maxims**

Maxim	Description
Maxims of quality	"Try to make your contribution one that is true." "Do not say what you believe to be false." "Do not say that for which you lack adequate evidence." (Grice 1989, 27)
Maxim of relation (relevance)	"Be relevant." (Grice 1989, 27)
Maxims of quantity	Q1: "Make your contribution as informative as is required (for the purposes of the exchange)." Q2: "Do not make your contribution more informative than is required." (Grice 1989, 26)
Maxims of manner	"Be perspicuous." M1: "Avoid obscurity of expression." M2: "Avoid ambiguity." M3: "Be brief (avoid unnecessary prolixity)." M4: "Be orderly." (Grice 1989, 27)

conversationally implicates by saying those words. A conversational implicature is defined by Grice (1989, 30–31) as follows:

> A man who, by (in, when) saying (or making as if to say) that p has implicated that q, may be said to have conversationally implicated that q, provided that (1) he is presumed to be observing the conversational maxims, or at least the Cooperative Principle; (2) the supposition that he is aware that, or thinks that, q is required in order to make his saying or making as if to say p (or doing so in *those* terms) consistent with this presumption; and (3) the speaker thinks (and would expect the hearer to think that the speaker thinks) that it is within the competence of the hearer to work out, or grasp intuitively, that the supposition mentioned in (2) is required.

Levinson (2000, 15) explains that, among other characteristics, conversational implicatures are defeasible (i.e., cancellable), calculable (i.e., "the more or less transparent derivation of the inference from premises that include the assumption of rational conversational activity"), nonconventional (i.e., "the noncoded nature of the inferences and their parasitic dependence on what is coded"), and reinforcable (i.e., "it is often possible to add explicitly what is anyway implicated with less sense of redundancy than would be the case if one repeated the coded content").

4.7.3: Criticizing Grice's Maxims

Although perhaps useful when reasoning at a high level of abstraction, by themselves Grice's maxims are deficient when used to account for linguistic phenomena. Various scholars have criticized the maxims for their vagueness and other deficiencies. Frederking (1996, 1), for instance, claims that, although "clearly true in some sense," Grice's maxims are "hopelessly vague" and that his categories, at least at the Gricean level of description, have no predictive or explanatory power. Cooren and Sanders (2002) similarly recognize that Grice's theory of implicatures offers valuable descriptions of conversational logic. Cooren and Sanders argue, though, that the theory is vague in specifying how people reason from the content of an uttered proposition to some other proposition it implicates. They argue that implicatures can be made less open-ended and indeterminate. Davis (2007) claims, as have many others for various reasons, that Gricean implicatures are never derivable from conversational principles in the way required. Chierchia, Fox, and Spector (2012) similarly argue that by logic alone it is not possible to derive scalar implicatures (a special type of implicature explained below) in their full strengths from the Gricean maxims.

The vagueness of Grice's maxims is illustrated in the two most prominent attempts to justify application of textual canons, including the *ejusdem generis* canon, under the maxims. Sinclair (1985) wonders about the persuasiveness of the *ejusdem generis* canon. Sinclair reasons that, if there was a way to express the category into which the specific list of examples fall, the legislature, acting in accordance with the maxims of manner and quantity, would have used that instead of the list of examples and general catchall. To assume that there is a general rule that can characterize the specific examples, while at the same time assuming that the legislature was saying as much as it could as clearly and concisely as it could and yet did not specify a general rule, is to assume infelicitous legislation. Sinclair proposes the following maxim of quality applicable to legislative speech: "Do not enact a provision that can be shown not to further the legislative purpose" (397). He argues that this maxim indicates that the *ejusdem generis* canon should be applied "[o]nly if the item in question can be shown to further the legislative purpose in the same way as do the items listed should it be held to come under the statutory provision" (412).

Miller (1990, 1199–200) similarly indicates that the *ejusdem generis* canon "appears to be an application of Grice's second maxim of quantity (do not provide more information than is called for in the conversational setting)." Miller recognizes that with respect to *ejusdem generis* the second maxim of quantity will conflict with the first maxim of quantity (make your contribution as informative as is required for the purposes of the exchange), because the legislature should have specified the relevant category rather than the more generic catchall. For instance, reasons Miller (1200), if a statute bans "cats, dogs and other animals" from a public park, it is not clear why the city would not indicate "pets" if it meant to limit "other animals" to that concept. He ultimately indicates that perhaps the costs of greater specificity outweigh the benefits. Taking Miller's reasoning further, it would also not be clear why the legislature could not at least simply add "similar" before "animals." As illustrated in the *Ali* case, though, it is typically not productive to speculate about how the legislators could have drafted, unless one is tying the observation to some regularity or usage of language.

By relying, without supplementation of a systematic kind, on Grice's maxims, Miller and Sinclair offer attenuated defenses of textual canons such as *ejusdem generis*. If, to consider Sinclair's analysis, "legislative purpose" is to be the guide to interpretation, and is capable of being framed at the level of specificity required to solve actual interpretive disputes, it is not clear what interpretive work the *ejusdem generis* canon performs. It merely offers an intellectual gloss to an interpretation determined on other grounds and offers no predictive value. Further, and importantly to this book's project, Miller and Sinclair's application of Gricean implicatures to textual canons do not establish that canons such as *ejusdem generis* are proper determinants of an ordinary meaning analysis. Similarly, it is not clear from their analysis how textual canons contribute to communicative meaning.

4.7.4: A More Systematic Account of Conversational Implicatures

In order to properly account for textual canons in ordinary meaning determinations, a more systematic approach to language is required. Traditionally, and consistently with Recanati's three levels of meaning, implicatures have been considered to be a wholly pragmatic phenomenon (Chierchia, Fox, and Spector, 2012). On the classical Gricean view, conversational implicatures, including scalar implicatures, are derived on the assumption that the speaker is trying to be cooperative.

Since Grice, various accounts have been offered that provide more systematic analyses of the linguistic phenomena that motivated Grice's conversational implicatures. One aspect of this systematicity is the distinction between "particularized conversational implicatures" (PCIs) and "generalized conversational implicatures" (GCIs). Levinson (2000, 16) describes the distinction between PCIs and GCIs as follows:

a. An implicature *i* from utterance *U* is *particularized* if and only if *U* implicates *i* only by virtue of specific contextual assumptions that would not invariably or even normally obtain.
b. An implicature *i* is *generalized* if and only if *U* implicates *i* *unless* there are unusual specific contextual assumptions that defeat it.

Levinson (22) views the application of GCIs as constituting preferred or default interpretations. In explaining his view of GCIs, Levinson distinguishes between sentence meaning and speaker meaning (or utterance-token meaning), neither one of which captures the features of GCIs. Speaker meaning is a matter of the "actual nonce or once-off inferences made in actual contexts by actual recipients with all of their rich particularities" (22). The speaker-meaning level is inadequate because it underestimates the regularity, recurrence, and systematicity of many kinds of pragmatic inferences. Instead, a third-level "utterance-type meaning" is required, located between sentence meaning and speaker meaning. The third level accounts for GCIs and is based not on direct computations about speaker intentions but rather on general expectations about how language is normally used. As such, it appears to be somewhat similar to Recanati's third level, "what is communicated," although Recanati views implicatures to be wholly pragmatic. In contrast, at the utterance-type level, Levinson views the systematicity of inference as being deeply interconnected to linguistic structure and meaning, making distinctions between semantic theory and pragmatics problematic.

Levinson's (2000, 24) view of GCIs provides a generative theory of idiomaticity that consists of a set of principles that guide "the choice of the right expression to suggest a specific interpretation" and that also offer a theory that will account for preferred (or default) interpretations. The theory (26) focuses on the combination of utterance form and content, in line with general principles, that triggers the inferences. In Levinson's (29) view, inference is cheap and articulation expensive, and thus the design requirements are for a system that maximizes inference. Furthermore, linguistic coding is to be thought of less like definitive content and more like interpretive clue. Levinson sets up his theory through the following hypo-

TABLE 4.6. **Levinson's (2000) heuristics**

Heuristic	Example

Heuristic 1 (Q)
Quantity: As informative as
required: What isn't said, isn't
	"There's a blue pyramid on the red cube."
	Licensed inferences:
	    There is not a cone on the red cube.
	    There is not a red pyramid on the red cube.

Heuristic 2 (I):
Quantity: Not more
informative than required.
What is simply described is
stereotypically exemplified
	"The blue pyramid is on the red cube."
	Licensed inferences (among others):
	    The pyramid is a stereotypical one, on a square, rather
	      than, e.g., a hexagonal base.
	    The pyramid is directly supported by the cube (e.g., there
	      is no intervening slab).

Heuristic 3 (M):
Manner: Be perspicuous.
What's said in an abnormal
way, isn't normal; or marked
message indicates marked
situation
	"The blue cuboid block is supported by the red cube."
	Licensed inferences:
	    The blue block is not, strictly, a cube.
	    The blue block is not directly or centrally or stably
	      supported by the red cube.

thetical (see table 4.6). One is to assume that there is a world consisting of a set of cubes, cones, and pyramids of different colors. The italicized sentences in the boxes in the right column represent utterances. Below the italicized sentences are licensed inferences corresponding to the heuristic in the box in the left column.

In Levinson's view, heuristic 1 is related to Grice's first maxim of quality: Make your contribution as informative as is required. This heuristic depends crucially on clearly established salient contrasts. The reason is that if the heuristic were unrestricted whatever one did not specify would not be the case, and such a powerful heuristic would inhibit one from saying anything in fear of having to exhaustively list everything that is the case. Heuristic 2 is, in Levinson's view, extremely powerful because it allows an interpreter to bring background knowledge about a domain to bear on a rich interpretation of a minimal description. In turn, heuristic 3 is complimentary to heuristic 2. Heuristic 3 allows the communicator to cancel the assumptions that would otherwise follow from heuristic 2's assumption that a normal description indicates a normal situation. A simple description can be assumed to be stereotypically exemplified and thus what is described in a marked or unusual way should be assumed to contrast with that stereotypical or normal exemplification.

Heuristic 1 describes how scalar implicatures are conceived. Consider the utterance

(11) Some of the students did well.

The literal meaning of (11) is that some, and perhaps all, of the students did well. In contrast, the intuitive interpretation, of course, is that not all the students did well. The latter interpretation can be based on the theory of a scalar implicature, the central notion of which is a contrast set, or linguistic expressions in salient contrast, which differ in informativeness (Levinson 2000, 25). The heuristic thus depends crucially on a restriction to a set of salient alternatives. Relevant to the interpretation of (11), there is a scalar contrast set <some, all>, such that saying (11) implicates the rationale that the speaker would have chosen the stronger alternative if she was in a position to do so. Thus, for sets of alternatives, use of one (especially a weaker) implicates rejection of another (especially an otherwise compatible stronger alternate).

In Levinson's (2000, 41) view, a scalar implicature is metalinguistic in the sense that it can only be recovered by reference to what else might have been said but was not. Other systematic theories of scalar implicatures have been offered. Regardless of the specific theory advocated, the various positions all follow Horn's (1972, 1989) proposal to some extent, which focuses on the principle that scalar implicatures come about through a constrained set of relevant alternatives. In typical cases, as illustrated above in Levinson's example, they are lexically constrained by items of the same category whose entailments line them in a scale of increasing informativeness. Examples of Horn's scales are in table 4.7. The scales are characterized by the increasing strength of the items going from left to right. If, for example, all the students did well, then "most," "many," and "some" of them did. The process for the other scales works similarly.

While GCIs are the default mode of reasoning, they are defeasible and can be overcome by the addition of further premises. Thus, the assertion in (11) can be overcome through the addition of a second sentence:

(12) In fact, all the students did well.

Further, and importantly to the *ejusdem generis* canon, Chierchia, Fox, and Spector (2012, 2302) argue that "Horn's suggestions can be extended to other seemingly more volatile/ephemeral scales." The authors consider the following example:

(13) A: Did John mail his check?
    B: He wrote it.

TABLE 4.7. **Horn's (1972) scales**

Scale	Example
Positive quantifiers	Some, many, most, all
Negative quantifiers	Not all, few, none
Numerals	One, two, three, etc.
Modals	Can, must
Sentential connectives	And, or
Gradable adjectives	Warm, hot/cold, freezing, etc.

The suggested interpretation is that B has conveyed that John did not mail the check. The scale considered by the interpreter would be something like {write the check, mail the check}. The authors argue that it is crucial that the relevant options are not *mailing vs. not mailing*, or *mailing vs. stealing*, for otherwise we would only derive ignorance implicatures (i.e., the speaker does not know which is the case). The key point is that the notion of relevance used in implicature calculation is context dependent but constrained through the lexicon (i.e., certain classes of words form lexical scales) and through a monotonicity constraint (i.e., all scales cannot simultaneously include upward and downward entailing elements).

4.7.5: Ejusdem Generis *and Scalar Implicatures*

The scholarly work on scalar implicatures provides a way of conceptualizing the role of the *ejusdem generis* canon. Instead of trying to understand the rationale of the canon through consideration of the vague Gricean maxims, which do not provide any particular insight as to why the legislature did not provide a more specific category instead of a catchall, the notion of the scalar implicature should be used. Importantly, considering scalar implicatures to be a systematic aspect of language usage justifies the relevance of GCIs to legal texts. As described in chapter 2, there are fundamental differences between spoken and written language. Considerations that depend on the dynamics of oral conversations are not necessarily relevant to the interpretation of texts, especially legal texts. Furthermore, various scholars have explored how the legislative drafting process does not follow the assumptions of a cooperative oral exchange, and especially does not adhere to the maxims of quantity or manner. For instance, legal texts are often drafted with intentional vagueness or ambiguity, and legislatures generally do not draft with the level of informativeness that legal interpreters desire. Partly, this is due to the impossibility of predicting the range of factual scenarios to which the statute will need to be applied. Often compounding the problem is the significant gap of time between when a statute is drafted and when it will be interpreted by courts. Focusing on systematicities of language helps address these difficulties. The systematic nature of CGIs and the other insights about language made by Levinson and others (some of whom do not view all conversational implicatures as inferences) indicates that the generalities of language identified by these scholars should apply to both oral conversations and written texts.

Applying the concept of scalar implicatures provides a way of considering the *ejusdem generis* canon while avoiding the infelicitous language problem considered by Sinclair and Miller. As explained above, the *ejusdem generis* canon is based on salient contrasts. A generic scale, as considered by a drafter of a legal text, would look as follows: {specific list, list + "other" clause, general term}.[89] For example, a prohibition might be phrased as a specific list, like the following:

(14) No dogs, cats, or birds allowed.

In (14), the scope of the provision is constrained and does not allow (at least explicitly) for prohibitions outside of "dogs," "cats," or "birds."

Suppose, though, that the drafter believes that "dogs," "cats," and "birds" are the known and primary targets of the prohibition but that other, similar targets exist, even if they cannot all be known at the time of drafting. The drafter might then redraft (14) as follows:

(15) No dogs, cats, birds, or other animals allowed.

Compared to (14), (15) is a stronger statement. In addition to "dogs," "cats," and "birds," "other animals" are prohibited. Of course, the literal meaning of (15) is broad and can be said to include all animals, but its ordinary meaning is narrower. This is illustrated by the option on the far right of the scale, as illustrated below.

Suppose that, instead of (14) or (15), the drafter has the following prohibition:

(16) No animals allowed.

The scope of the literal meaning of (15) and (16) is the same. Both would seem to prohibit all animals, and (15) would seem to include unnecessary surplusage (i.e., "dogs, cats, birds"). When considering scalar implicatures,

though, the ordinary meanings of (15) and (16) may differ. While (15) has
a list of specifics followed by an "other" clause, (16) has a general prohibition. In comparison to (14) and (15), (16) is the stronger statement. The
comparison between (14) and (16) is obvious. The list of specifics in (14)
is narrower in scope than the category "animals" in (16). The comparison
between (15) and (16), while less obvious, also reveals that the scope of
(16) is broader than the scope of (15). The drafter of (15) understands that
(16) is more succinct than (15), if the intent is for (15) to carry its literal
meaning. There is reason, though, to believe that (15) should not carry its
literal meaning. Instead, one of Levinson's heuristics is applicable. Specifically, the drafter intends the "other" clause in (15) to carry its stereotypical meaning. Levinson's heuristic 2 provides that what is simply described
is stereotypically exemplified. Contrary to the analyses of some analysts,
a broad catchall "other" phrase is not due to infelicitous drafting but, instead, exists because simple language has a conventional meaning that
is stereotypically exemplified through the other items on the list. Otherwise, the drafter could simply use the catchall, as in (16), without the list
of specifics. By not explicitly defining the classification, the drafters leave
courts with the flexibility to frame the classification in light of the variety
of cases (some of them undoubtedly unexpected by the legislature) that
come before the court.

4.7.6: Thinking about Whether the Ejusdem Generis Canon Is Part of Ordinary Linguistic Meaning or Ordinary Legal Meaning

The *ejusdem generis* canon may be justified as being based on a convention of language, but it is less clear whether this convention is part of ordinary linguistic meaning or ordinary legal meaning. Like other linguistic
phenomena, it is doubtful that courts choose the general category to limit
the "other" phrase without consideration of legal consequences. Further,
aspects of the canon may be peculiar to the legal system. For instance,
Scalia and Garner (2012) explain that the *ejusdem generis* canon is not applicable when there is a general term that is followed by a list of specific
items. In their view (204), this formulation serves the function of making
"doubly sure that the broad (and intended-to-be-broad) general term is
taken to include the specifics." Scalia and Garner reason that, while the
general before the specific formulation often includes a phrase such as
"including without limitation," the specific before the general formation
never does so. Also, some courts and commentators have argued that the

ejusdem generis canon is not applicable when there is only one specific term followed by a general term. The *Ali* case, discussed above, is an example of this restriction.[90]

On the other hand, unlike substantive canons, the *ejusdem generis* canon can be said to be motivated by linguistic rather than purely legal concerns (although courts are generally motivated to limit the scope of statutes). As indicated above, the Horn theory can be applied to nontraditional scales. "Other" phrases following lists of specific items have not been studied by philosophers or linguistics, but that is perhaps because of the relative scarcity of such clauses outside the legal context. Further, like quantifier domain restriction, the *ejusdem generis* canon often operates to narrow the domain of a statute from its literal meaning, even if the restriction is not relevant to the particular interpretive dispute before the court. For example, Scalia and Garner consider the following sentence that is placed on a sign at the entrance of a butcher shop:

(17) No dogs, cats, pet rabbits, parakeets, or other animals allowed.

Scalia and Garner (2012, 212) argue that "no one would think that only domestic pets were excluded, and that farm animals or wild animals were welcome." They reason that "when the context argues so strongly against limiting the general provision, the canon will not be dispositive" (212). This may be true and would provide a reason for deciding the case on the basis of other interpretive principles, but note that even with this example the canon has a role. No one would argue that, for example, the prohibition would include humans.

As illustrated above, there are valid reasons to conclude that the *ejusdem generis* canon is a determinate of ordinary meaning. While both categories of canons tend to narrow the scope of statutes, textual canons, as opposed to substantive canons, are motivated by linguistic phenomena. Furthermore, the *ejusdem generis* canon can be legitimized through a scalar implicature analysis. As Levinson and others have shown, there is a level of systematicity to GCIs such that the semantics/pragmatics distinction is implicated. While Recanati views implicatures as wholly pragmatic and part of "what is communicated," researchers like Chierchia, Fox, and Spector (2012) question these designations in favor of more semantically oriented theories. Ultimately, for purposes of ordinary meaning, the semantics/pragmatics distinction is not as relevant as the systematicity of the linguistic phenomena. For GCIs, theorists have shown how salient interpretations are determined without the necessity of consideration of the context of the particular situation in which the utterance was made (Jaszczolt 2005).

As Levinson explains, the meanings generated by implicatures are defeasible interpretations that can be overcome by the addition of further premises. This aspect situates the *ejusdem generis* canon well within the theory of ordinary meaning that has been thus far developed. The scalar implicature creates the ordinary meaning, default interpretation using the concept of narrow context. The interpreter can thereafter consider broad context and determine the appropriate meaning to give to the "other" phrase. Similarly, the ordinary meaning selected may be defeated because the list is exhaustive of the general category selected. In these situations, the court may decide that the "other" phrase should carry its literal meaning (resulting in surplusage). Further, in some cases the list of items may be too disparate in kind to identify a general category with which to limit the scope of the "other" clause. In such situations, the ordinary meaning of the "other" clause is not determinable (Scalia and Garner 2012).

The *ejusdem generis* canon may properly be part of an ordinary meaning determination, as the scalar implicature analysis illustrates, but as with the other linguistic phenomena considered, application of the interpretive principle leaves the interpreter with a core of ineliminable discretion. Like the case with other determinants of ordinary meaning, the interpreter has discretion to decide, on whatever grounds she feels are persuasive, to dismiss the persuasive value of the particular determinant or reject the ordinary meaning in favor of a communicative meaning, which might indicate a broader or narrower general category than that selected by considering only the narrow context. Similarly, the *ejusdem generis* canon may conflict with other interpretive principles (including other textual canons) that are also legitimate aspects of an ordinary meaning determination. More specifically, an ordinary meaning determination via the *ejusdem generis* canon is, at its core, highly discretionary. Scalia and Garner (Scalia and Garner 2012, 207) themselves concede that application of the canon is discretionary due to the issue of how broadly or narrowly to define the general class delineated by the specific items listed. The doctrine does not purport to guide whether the court should identify the genus at the lowest level of generality, highest level of generality, or at some other level. Obviously a higher level of generality will give a broader scope to the "other" phrase. This determination is often crucial then in deciding the outcome of the litigation.

In response to claims that application of the *ejusdem generis* canon is highly discretionary, Scalia and Garner (2012, 208) advocate that the interpreter should "consider the listed elements, as well as the broad term at the end, and ask what category would come into the reasonable person's mind." Often, in their opinion, the "evident purpose of the provision makes the choice clear," and the "difficulty of identifying the relevant genus should not be exaggerated." Of course, in general things should not be exaggerated, but advocating the reasonable person standard and the consideration of context does not foreclose the inherent discretion involved in selecting a general category that will account for the specific items listed. There are always multiple ways, at slight but legally significant degrees of difference, in which to define the general category, and often insufficient contextual evidence exists that makes one choice clearly superior to the others. Hence, like the other linguistic phenomena, the inherent discretion involved in the application of the interpretive principle cannot be negated by (bald) assertions that interpreters would invariably agree in their judgments.

Notwithstanding the discretion inherent in its application, the *ejusdem generis* canon is consistent with the other interpretive principles employed by courts. In fact, the function of the *ejusdem generis* canon underscores the common theme that courts employ interpretive principles in order to narrow the scope of statutes. Shapiro (1992) argues that both substantive and textual canons reflect a judicial preference for continuity over change, which comes from narrowing the scope of legal provisions form their literal meanings. This judicial tendency exists outside the application of substantive or textual canons. Consider that even when a broad concept is used, as in (16) with "animals," the legal meaning of the provision will typically be narrower than its literal meaning (regardless of whether a specific canon is applicable). Certainly, difficulties in application would likely arise, such as whether police dogs or guide dogs fall under the scope of the prohibition, and the difficulties will not always fall within the scope of some canon. Instead, without the benefit of a specific canon, these types of situations require courts to consider whether implied exceptions to the seemingly unlimited mandate of the provision should be recognized.

As well, a court may determine that the general term is too broad to fit the purpose of the provision. Such decisions are not likely to be determinations of ordinary meaning but instead decisions that, based on legal concerns, the scope of the provision should be narrower than its literal meaning. In addition, as chapter 5 explains, "animals" would also have to be defined, and the judicial assignment of definitions to words involves significant discretion. For instance, one would expect, absent unusual circumstances, that humans would be excluded from the scope of the statute. The court might decide that the ordinary meaning of "animals" does not include humans. Alternatively, the court might decide that it normally does include humans, but that the *ejusdem generis* canon limits the "other" phrase to nonhuman animals. Such an interpretation represents yet another example of the frequent gap between literal meaning (all animals) and ordinary meaning (nonhuman animals).

4.8: Doubts about the Application of Conversational Implicatures to Legal Texts

4.8.1: Implicatures, Literal Meaning, and Legal Texts

It might seem quite intuitive that the *ejusdem generis* canon (and perhaps other textual canons) is an aspect of ordinary meaning and can be given a Gricean-type explanation. As Carston (2013), a leading pragmatic theorist, notes, textual canons look very similar to the principles/heuristics formulated by theorists of pragmatics for general communication and interpretation. Some prominent scholars, though, have criticized the idea that conversational implicatures are applicable to legislation. Marmor (2008), for instance, argues that, unlike ordinary conversations, it would be "very rare" for there to be cases in which the content the legislature prescribes is not exactly what the text says.[91] In Marmor's view, the reason is that "[a]n essential aspect of what enables parties to an ordinary conversation to express content that is not exactly what their expressions mean, consists in the fact that an ordinary conversation is, typically, a cooperative activity" (429). In contrast, legislation is typically a form of complex strategic behavior and cannot be considered a cooperative activity. Poggi (2011) similarly argues against the applicability of conversational implicatures to legal texts. His main reasons concern the "conflictual behaviour of the addressees and, above all, to the insurmountable indeterminacy of the contextual elements" (21).[92]

For a variety of reasons, the arguments about the inapplicability of conversational implicatures to legal texts are mistaken. Sometimes it *is* obvious that the literal content of a legal text must differ from its legal meaning. Carston (2013) reasons that one might expect a higher degree of explicitness in legal texts than in day-to-day speech, and thus fewer cases of implicatures. This observation may be accurate. The law, though, requires a higher degree of precision than does day-to-day speech, and cases often turn on small nuances of meaning. Conversely, legislatures often draft with intentional ambiguity or vagueness (instead of with great explicitness), but this similarly does not undermine the arguments in favor of the applicability of implicatures. Courts are often motivated for various reasons to select interpretations that deviate from the literal meanings of the relevant texts. Judicial assignments of nonliteral meanings to legal texts are thus commonplace and some of these deviations from literal meaning can be explained as implicatures. Implicatures are triggered by various verbal formulations (such as an "other" clause in the case of the *ejusdem generis* canon), and are not undermined by vagueness or ambiguity elsewhere in the text. Even when application of an implicature would leave a degree of interpretive discretion regarding the meaning of the text, this would (contra Poggi's position) constitute a normal aspect of interpretation and not a reason to reject the applicability of implicatures. Of course, there are a variety of ways to conceptualize implicatures and Grice's maxims. Even if considering conversational implicatures only under a Gricean-type analysis (as Levinson's approach does), Marmor's and Poggi's arguments are not sufficient to establish that conversational implicatures are not applicable to legal texts.

As indicated above, that courts are willing to find that the content the legislature prescribed is different from the literal meaning of the relevant text is a prosaic aspect of legal interpretation, not exceptional. It is not at all unusual for the literal meaning of a legal text to differ from its ordinary linguistic meaning. In fact, it is often obvious that the literal meaning of the text is not coterminous with its ordinary meaning. These situations are not, however, likely to be part of a litigated interpretive dispute. For instance, as explained in the above discussion of *Ali v. Bureau of Prisons*,[93] the literal meaning of the relevant phrase from § 2680(c), "any other law enforcement officer," differs from its ordinary meaning. The literal meaning would include any law enforcement officer in the world (or in existence, if one prefers). Considering that the related provision, § 1346(b)(1), to which § 2680(c) is the exception, authorizes claims against the United States only for acts of employees of the federal government, including foreign or state law enforcement officers in § 2680(c), would obviously be nonsensical. Precisely because such an interpretation is so obvious and pointless to challenge, it would not be litigated. Thus, judicial decisions, which generally resolve (relatively) close interpretive disputes, do not reflect the variety of obvious ways in which the literal meaning of legal texts differs from their ordinary or communicative meanings.

4.8.2: The Cooperative Principle and Legal Texts

One of the main arguments against the applicability of conversational implicatures to legal texts is that the legislative process does not adhere to Grice's Cooperative Principle. Davis (1998, 11) paraphrases the Cooperative Principle as follows: "Contribute what is required by the accepted purpose of the conversation." It is true that legislation, as well as the legislative process, cannot be compared to an ordinary conversation, as chapter 2 argued. Consider Marmor's (2008b, 435) arguments regarding the Cooperative Principle and its inapplicability to the legislative process:

> The Gricean maxims of conversational implicatures are the norms that apply to an ordinary conversation, where the purpose of the participants is the cooperative exchange of information. But the legal case is quite different. The enactment of a law is not a cooperative exchange of information. Therefore, we should not be surprised if some of the Gricean maxims may not apply to the context of legislation and, more problematically, it is often not clear which norms, if any, do apply. The main reason for the difference resides in the fact that legislation is typically a form of *strategic behavior*. In fact, the situation is more complicated: Legislation consists of at least *two conversations*, so to speak, not one. There is a conversation between the legislators themselves during the enactment process, and then the result of this internal conversation is another conversation between the legislature and the subjects of the law enacted.

Marmor's arguments about the legislative process are correct and are consistent with some of the arguments made in chapter 2 about actual intentionalism. The legislative speech act is designed not to be a cooperative exchange of information but instead to generate rules that modify behavior (Soames 2011). These observations about the legislative process do not establish, however, that conversational implicatures are not relevant to the interpretation of legal texts. Among other problems, the arguments made by critics exaggerate the requirements of the Cooperative Principle.

Marmor and Poggi are not the first scholars to criticize the applicability of the Cooperative Principle to a defined set of communications. Even outside the legislative context, the Cooperative Principle has been criticized for the reason that people are not always or generally cooperative, especially in certain circumstances (such as institutional discourse).[94] The criticisms are not, however, always warranted. Lumsden (2008, 1900) explains that the Cooperative Principle can concern "some constrained form of cooperation, a kind of cooperation within the conversation, as opposed to cooperation generally." Similarly, Pavlidou (1991, 12) distinguishes between "formal cooperation" and "substantial cooperation." Formal cooperation is cooperation in the Gricean tradition, which involves acting according to, or contrary to, the conversational maxims. In contrast, substantial cooperation refers more broadly to the sharing of common goals among the communication partners that go beyond the maximal exchange of information. In some cases an extralinguistic goal determines linguistic cooperation, but in other situations an extralinguistic goal of one of the participants is clearly not shared by the other. In fact, Lumsden describes situations in which no significant extralinguistic goals enter into the relevant conversation at all, so the issue of the goals being shared does not arise. The extralinguistic goal, if any, thus does not determine the linguistic goal. Yet, the Cooperative Principle is till applicable.

The Cooperative Principle therefore should be viewed as only requiring linguistic cooperation, as there is no common nonlinguistic goal in some cases where implicatures are applicable. Also, the linguistic cooperation required is itself relatively narrow. The principle thus "does not say anything about the speaker's extralinguistic goals, but is a theory of the ways in which speakers maximize the efficiency of information transfer" (Capone 2001, 446–47). The cooperation expected allows the speaker to rely on the audience to interpret the implicatures, thereby allowing the speaker to communicate more briefly. Thus, the linguistic goal itself can be imprecise and does not require that the linguistic purposes be shared or mutual, but only that the purposes be mutually modeled. As Lumsden (2008) argues, critics should be open to a range of cases displaying variation in the form and nature of the cooperation. Marmor and Poggi thus overstate the requirements of the Cooperative Principle. There is no obvious reason to think that a legislature and the judiciary, the body primarily responsible for giving statutes authoritative interpretations and thus the most relevant cooperative partner, do not engage in the kind of formal cooperation that is sufficient to warrant the application of conversational implicatures.

4.8.3: Other Arguments about Implicatures and Legal Texts

Marmor (2008) makes further, related arguments regarding implicatures that deserve some attention. Specifically, Marmor (2008, 434) argues that, generally speaking, pragmatic implication requires (at least) three conditions:

(1)   *A speaker* who has certain communication intentions.

(2)   A conversational *context* that, at least to some extent, is *common knowledge* and that is shared by speaker and hearer.

(3)   Some *conversational maxims* that apply to the relevant speech situation.

The first requirement should not be troubling. Marmor's objections are persuasive when concerning the possibility of deriving some conversational implicature on the basis of an inference from actual legislative intent. Like the arguments about the Cooperative Principle, however, it is important not to overstate the requirement of communicative intentions. It may be necessary that the speaker has a communicative intention, but it is not necessary to identify any specific communicative intention. If recognizing the speaker's actual communicative intentions was necessary for application of implicatures, the usefulness of the theory would be greatly limited. It would be difficult, for example, to see how implicatures could be applicable to a conversation that involved two strangers, each with little contextual knowledge of the other. Viewing interpretation as hypothetical in nature, as chapter 2 advocated, does not therefore foreclose the possibility of recognizing conversational implicatures.

For similar reasons, it is important not to exaggerate the required common knowledge that is shared by speaker and hearer. The sole relevance of common knowledge in this context is to determine the applicability of implicatures. Assuming that the relevant hearer is the judiciary, it should not be difficult to conclude that, in general, sufficient common knowledge exists to make at least some implicatures generally applicable. Marmor analyzes the Supreme Court's famous decision in *Holy Trinity Church v. U.S.A.*,[95] as part of his analysis of the applicability of implicatures. *Holy Trinity,* though, is not a good example from which to conclude that implicatures are not appropriate to the interpretation of legal texts. *Holy Trinity* involved the question of whether a broad immigration provision that prohibited the facilitation of the immigration of those who would perform "labor or service of any kind" should be interpreted literally, or instead should only be interpreted as including laborers. As Marmor notes, because of the conflicting contextual cues, which include a provision that already contained exceptions to the general prohibition, it is very debatable whether a conversational implicature could be said to apply to the text and thereby narrow its domain. The *Holy Trinity* case did not, however, involve a regularity of language or drafting, making the relevance of a conversational implicature particularly controversial. In contrast to

Holy Trinity, situations involving a regularity of language or drafting present a much more compelling case for the application of an implicature. If, for instance, a legislature uses an "other" clause, it is doing so in a certain general but recurring context. The relevant context is not the particular statute itself, but, rather, the long history of legislative use of such clauses and the long history of courts interpreting them more narrowly than their literal meanings would indicate.

In any case, Marmor's requirements are the mirror image of many of the judiciary's presumptions about interpretation. With respect to substantive canons and textual canons, courts do not require that the context be obvious that they should be applied but rather that it be obvious that they should *not* be applied. Perhaps substantive canons should be excluded from discussion because their presumptions are created by legal concerns and not communicative ones. Textual canons cannot, however, be so readily dismissed. Rather, they are created based on generalized beliefs about how drafters and others use language. If such beliefs are generally unwarranted in lieu of specific evidence of legislative intent that a regularity of language was intended, a court would be equally warranted in refusing to give a word its conventional meaning absent specific evidence that it should do so. If linguistic cooperation is not sufficient to establish drafting regularities, it is not sufficient to establish conventional meaning.

In considering implicatures, it is also important to distinguish between PCIs and GCIs, which were defined above. Marmor and Poggi's arguments are relevant to PCIs but much less so to GCIs. Recall that GCIs, especially as conceptualized by scholars like Levinson (2000), do not depend on particular features of context and operate as a kind of default reasoning, which can be defeated by contextual evidence. GCIs are governed by the specific maxims or heuristics, without the need to appeal to the overarching principle of cooperativeness (Lumsden 2008). They are thus very different from PCIs, which are implicated only by virtue of specific contextual assumptions that would not normally obtain. In that sense, then, GCIs are closely related to conventional implicatures, which should uncontroversially be considered aspects of the ordinary meaning and communicative meaning of legal texts.

It is similarly useful to compare GCIs and conventional implicatures. Blome-Tillman (2013) explains that conventional implicatures are utterance contents that are grammatically encoded and thus triggered by the conventional meaning of (some of) the words used in the utterance. He offers the following examples:

(18) Marie is poor, but she's honest.
   a. Marie is poor and Marie is honest.
   b. Poor people are not usually honest.

The "a" sentence in (18) expresses "what is said" by utterances of (18), while the "b" sentence expresses content that is conventionally implicated. The reason why "b" is a case of implicature is because sincere utterances of (18) appear true to competent speakers just in case its "a" contents appear true—independently of our truth-value intuitions about its "b" contents. Because the perceived truth values of the conventionally implicated "b" proposition seems largely irrelevant with respect to the truth evaluation of utterances of (18), "b" is, on the Gricean approach, merely implicated rather than part of what is said.

Although scholars such as Levinson (2000) have tended to undermine the distinction between conventional implicatures and conversational implicatures, the difference between the two concepts "hinges largely on the property of deniability (cancellability)" (Potts 2005, 28). For example, as was explained above, the conversational implicature "not all" arising from (19)

(19) Some of the students did well.

can be cancelled through the addition of (20).

(20) In fact, all the students did well.

In contrast, consider the following example (taken from Lumsden 2008) that illustrates the noncancellability of conventional implicatures:

(21) Marie is poor, but she's honest. *And poor people are usually honest.

In contrast to the addition of sentence (20) to (19), a perceived contradiction would arise in (21).

As illustrated by the above examples, the "other" clause that is typically at issue when applying the *ejusdem generis* canon cannot be viewed as a conventional implicature, as its implication can be canceled. This fact does not, however, undermine its status as a component of ordinary meaning.[96] Marmor (2008, 424) indicates that "it would be difficult to think of a legal context where semantically encoded implication, if there is one, should not be seen to form part of what the law determines." While GCIs are not lexicalized in the same way as conventional implicatures, there are no sufficient reasons why GCIs should not also be considered part of the ordinary meaning of the relevant sentence.

Poggi's (2011) arguments regarding the indeterminacy of the contextual elements of legislation as establishing the inapplicability of conversational implicatures are also insufficient. Certainly, as this book has emphasized, interpretation of legal texts carries with it an ineliminable element of discretion. Partly, this is due to the nature of language and the interpretive principles applied by courts. In addition, though, interpretive discretion exists because the typical contextual situation, regardless of whether narrow or wide context is considered, contains information that can support more than one interpretation. With an understanding that conflicting contextual information is the default but is nonetheless sufficient to allow for authoritative interpretations of legal texts, it is difficult to maintain that a greater univocality of context should exist before conversational implicatures are applicable to legal texts. In many cases, a discretionary judgment will decide the precise nature of the implicature, as in, for example, determining the scope of the "other" clause when applying the *ejusdem generis* canon. Such a situation, though, is synonymous with how literal meanings are determined.

It is not therefore exceptional that legal texts can have nonliteral meanings. Rather, the interpretive principles applied by courts tend to narrow the scope of statutes, sometimes creating a gap between literal meaning and ordinary meaning. Conversational implicatures are congruent with this judicial orientation and should be treated as such. Marmor and Poggi, as well as the other scholars with similar theories, though, are not the only ones to fail to appreciate the frequent gaps between literal meaning and ordinary meaning. Textualists also seem to believe that recognizing a gap between literal meaning and ordinary meaning is either an instance of judicial activism or an indication that the speaker has made a mistake in expressing herself. Manning (2006, 2015), for instance, indicates that

> an important strand of modern language theory, known as pragmatics, rests on the . . . premise that because human beings sometimes express themselves inaccurately, listeners in a cooperative setting must occasionally tweak the literal meaning of what has been said in order to make sense of an utterance in context.

Of course human beings sometimes express themselves inaccurately, but pragmatics does *not* rest on the premise that human beings express themselves inaccurately. Rather, pragmatics (as well as some semantic theories) recognizes that humans often express themselves succinctly, assuming that context will contribute to the meaning of the words expressed. Thus, use of a universal quantifier (i.e., "all," "any," etc.) in a situation where some more limited scope is intended is not an incorrect or inaccurate use of language. Similarly, use of a general "other" clause is not an incorrect use of language. Instead, users of such expressions assume that interpreters are able to discern the correct, ordinary meaning of the language based on the available context (even if sometimes the interpreter chooses the wrong meaning or has insufficient indications of the correct meaning).

4.9: Conclusion and Further Thoughts about Textual Canons and Ordinary Meaning

This chapter has further elaborated the arguments made in chapter 3. For various linguistic phenomena, it is possible to adopt a semantic theory, or at least some theory that emphasizes the systematic nature of language and is seen as arguably semantic by some, that will offer an explanatory account of the phenomenon. The semantic theory can help conceptualize how an ordinary meaning account of the phenomenon can be structured. Nevertheless, there is an ineliminable degree of discretion that makes any ordinary meaning determination discretionary. Further, there are no reasons to believe that "common sense" or alignment of background assumptions and knowledge, even if possible, will be sufficient to create interpretive consensus. In fact, even an unsophisticated method of interpretation that simply uses dictionary definitions will not produce consensus considering the wide variety of dictionaries and the multiple definitions for any word.

The discretionary nature of interpretation holds regardless of whether a particular linguistic phenomenon is considered to be, under Recanati's distinctions, "what is said" or "what is communicated." Quantifier domain restriction may be an aspect of what is said and at least some textual canons an aspect of what is communicated (although scholars like Levinson might include them in what is said), but neither the domain of a quantifier nor the application of a textual canon can be determined without the consideration of context. Recanati (2004) argues that the semantic values of semantically underdeterminate expressions (which in his opinion is the only thing that semantic interpretation can deliver) vary from occurrence to occurrence, just as the semantic value of indexicals does. In his view, they can only be determined by pragmatic interpretation based on "wide context." While Recanati's argument may be overstated, it is unclear that sensible interpretations can always be made without consideration of wide context, as ordinary meaning would require. If this is so, there is little to distinguish ordinary meaning from communicative meaning, especially if one has an objective view of communicative meaning (as chap. 2 explained).

Notwithstanding the problems identified above, various useful distinctions can still be made. One is between ordinary linguistic meaning and ordinary legal meaning. A common characteristic that principles of legal interpretation have is that they serve to restrict the domains of legal texts, thereby creating a gap between literal meaning and ordinary/communicative meaning. Not all these interpretive principles, however, are relevant to ordinary linguistic meaning. While substantive canons generally cannot be considered relevant to ordinary linguistic meaning, as they derive from legal considerations and not linguistic ones and have other attributes (such as vague conditions of applicability) that render them inapplicable to ordinary meaning, some textual canons can be considered to be determinants of ordinary linguistic meaning. This chapter identified the *ejusdem generis* canon as one such interpretive principle. It must be conceded that, at least sometimes, the literal meaning of a general "other" phrase must differ from its ordinary meaning and be limited to the category that accounts for the specific items listed. Even so, like the other determinants of ordinary meaning, a systematic account of the phenomenon cannot eliminate the discretionary nature of its application.

Although the chapter mainly focused on only one of the textual canons, other textual canons may also be relevant to ordinary meaning determinations. For instance, the rule of the last antecedent, if valid as corresponding to grammatical usage (which is not altogether clear), would obviously be defensible as an aspect of ordinary meaning. Conversely, some textual canons are difficult to connect to ordinary linguistic meaning. Like substantive canons, the proviso canon is motivated by legal rather than language concerns. There is no apparent linguistic reason why the term "provided that" or some synonym should trigger a narrow interpretation of the clause following the proviso. Also, although all the interpretive principles contain an ineliminable element of discretion, a vague and general instruction to interpret a clause narrowly does not have any obvious relevance to ordinary meaning. This is one reason why substantive canons are not determinants of ordinary meaning. Textual canons other than the *ejusdem generis* canon would require further justification and conceptualization before a conclusion could be made that they are properly part of an ordinary meaning determination. For instance, it is not clear that the *in pari materia* canon, which presumes that identical words in the same statute have the same meaning, is motivated by linguistic rather than legal concerns, or that its presumption is useful. The same could be said for the rule against surplusage and the *noscitur a sociis* canon.

With other canons, the deficiencies are obvious. Consider the *expressio unius est exclusio alterius* canon (the negative implication canon), which provides that, when a statute expresses something explicitly (usually in a list), anything not expressed explicitly does not fall within the statute. The canon has been sharply criticized by some commentators. Dickerson (1975, 234), for instance, argues that it is "simply not true, generally, that the mere express conferral of a right or privilege in one kind of situation implies the denial of the equivalent right or privilege in other kinds." Dickerson argues that context will indicate whether a negative implication is warranted. Similarly, in defending the canon, Scalia and Garner (2012, 107) argue that "common sense" will usually indicate whether the canon is applicable. An adequate conceptualization of the canon requires more than an appeal to the alleged commonality of common sense, though. Levinson's (2000) heuristic 1 provides that what isn't said, isn't, which is in line with the *expressio* canon. Levinson (32) warns, however, that the heuristic is wildly underdetermined and must crucially be understood to be restricted to a set of salient contrasts. Note that in his example of the heuristic, described above, Levinson explicitly delineated the salient contrasts. If this is not done, the heuristic is invalid. Obviously, then, the *expressio* canon must be narrower in scope than its broad definition, as given by courts, would indicate. Rather than rejecting its obvious value, or conversely appealing to context or common sense, the correct approach to the canon is to more precisely define the conditions of its applicability. Such a task cannot be undertaken here but is necessary if the judicial claim to take language seriously should itself be taken seriously.

CHAPTER FIVE

Ordinary Meaning and Lexical Semantics

5.1: Lexical Semantics and Context

Thus far, this book has conceptualized ordinary meaning as a theory that, to be coherent, must in some ways stand in contradistinction to the communicative meaning of a text. Principally, an ordinary meaning must be a meaning that depends largely on the systematicities of language, rather than any specific interpretive clues that can be traced to the drafter of the text. This conceptualization of ordinary meaning is challenging to maintain considering the context-dependent nature of meaning. Previous chapters have examined the ways in which linguistic phenomena (including quantifiers, temporal preposition phrases, and principles of language usage found in textual canons) interact with context to restrict the domain of a sentence from its literal meaning. Although systematic linguistic theories can account for the phenomena identified thus far, focusing on the systematicities of language belies the discretionary nature of interpretation. For every systematic account discussed thus far, an ineliminable and significant degree of discretion is associated with the relevant ordinary meaning determination. Further, the ordinary meaning of a text can only be considered a default or presumptive meaning, requiring the interpreter to consult the wide context to determine whether the drafter intended some unordinary meaning.

Notwithstanding the multifaceted nature of interpretation, and the inherent discretion involved in determining meaning, identifying the systematicities of language should be viewed as a valuable contribution to legal interpretation. Doing so can, for example, help demonstrate why it is a mistake to rely in a significant way on a literal dictionary definition of "any" when determining the meaning of a sentence, and why the Supreme Court's failure to properly address quantifier domain restriction greatly undermined the persuasiveness of its interpretation in *Ali v. Federal Bureau of Prisons*.[1] Such a focus can also help demonstrate the proper method of giving meaning to indexicals (which requires more than a dictionary definition) and the proper way of viewing temporal prepositional phrases, as well as explain why most substantive canons are not determinants of ordinary linguistic meaning.[2] Other systematicities of language, not yet identified, are also relevant to the interpretation of legal texts. For instance, sentence-level context can make a significant contribution to word meaning even for words that are not traditionally viewed as being context dependent. This should not be surprising considering that there is agreement amongst semanticists that words carry many dimensions of meaning and that a particular meaning is brought about in a given context.

The contribution of sentential (i.e., sentence level) context to lexical meaning is, uncontroversially, an aspect of "what is said" and thus ordinary meaning. One example where proper consideration of sentential context should have changed the interpretation chosen is the Supreme Court's infamous decision in *Smith v. United States*.[3] As examined later in this chapter, the statute at issue in *Smith* contained "event ellipsis." An "event" is a type of situation in which something happens, in contrast to a "state" where something just is. The federal statute at issue in *Smith*, 18 U.S.C. § 924(c)(1)(A), provides for enhanced punishment if the defendant "uses" a firearm "during and in relation to . . . [a] drug trafficking crime."[4] Although the statute specifies the subject or agent (the defendant), the direct object (the firearm), and requires a connection to a drug-trafficking crime, it is underspecified regarding the event: how the defendant must "use" the firearm within the meaning of the provision.

Expressions with fully specified event structures are rare (i.e., are ellipsed) when the event is commonly associated with the noun (Traxler et al. 2005, 1–2). This underspecification, a paradigmatic example of underspecificity due to ellipsis, has challenged courts in determining the ordinary meaning of the statutory language. For instance, has the defendant violated the provision if he trades a gun for drugs (the situation in *Smith*), or drugs for a gun (which occurred in a later case), during a drug-trafficking crime? If Congress had intended for these actions to fall under the statute, is it likely that the language of the statute would have more clearly indicated so? Or, conversely, is it likely that if Congress had *not* intended for these actions to fall under the statute it would have enacted explicit language limiting the reach of the provision (i.e., explicitly specify the events that would fall under the scope of the provision). As happened in *Smith*, a failure to appreciate ellipsis and sentential context can result in an inappropriately broad interpretation if the interpreter considers one of the relevant words (in this case "use") in an acontextual manner.

Notwithstanding the importance of context, one of the themes of this book is that courts often interpret words acontextually by placing excessive weight on dictionary definitions. In fact, judicial reliance on dictionaries has dramatically increased since 1987 (Brudney and Baum 2013). One of the flaws in the judicial use of dictionaries is that the definitions considered often favor inappropriately broad meanings because they capture "possible" rather than "ordinary" meanings, which, due to the creativity of language, may result in unlimited potential meanings. Courts, however, are motivated to portray the law as though it is objective and determinate, and the manner in which they often use dictionaries enables them to do so. As Solan (2011) has described, judges are typically inclined to define words in such a way as to avoid uncertainty in application. This may involve selecting a dictionary and treating one of the definitions as though it sets forth necessary (required for membership) and sufficient (jointly guaranteeing membership) conditions for the word. Defining the ordinary meaning of words through dictionary definitions, and viewing these definitions as providing necessary and sufficient conditions of meaning, may seem to narrow interpretive discretion. This result is, as earlier chapters have explained, particularly attractive to textualists.

Apart from the fundamentally flawed practice of treating definitions as though they set forth necessary and sufficient conditions (more on this issue below), judicial use of dictionaries is problematic for various reasons. One issue concerns judges' tendency to go "dictionary shopping," which allows them to select the particular dictionary and definition that furthers the judge's personal predilections. As indicated above (and discussed in previous chapters), another problem involves adopting a dictionary definition without properly considering the contribution that context makes to meaning. Halliday and Yallop (2007, 24–25) describe the danger of relying on dictionary definitions to deliver the ordinary meaning of words as follows:

> A dictionary is a highly abstract construct. To do the job of presenting words more or less individually, in an accessible list, the dictionary takes words away

from their common use in their customary settings. While this is in many respects a useful job, the listing of words as a set of isolated items can be highly misleading if used as a basis of theorizing about what words and their meanings are.

Another aspect of dictionaries, related to the necessary-and-sufficient problem, is that they tend to favor definitions that represent technical meanings, which may not accurately reflect the ordinary meaning of the words. Hanks (2013, 8) explains that

> Giving a precise, unambiguous definition for a word is a stipulative procedure, not a descriptive one, and a stipulative definition inevitably assigns the status of technical term to the word so defined, removing it from the creative potential that is offered by fuzzy meaning in natural language.

Thus, dictionaries do not reflect the important distinction between the flexible meaning of terms in natural language and the stipulative definitions of the scientist. If the ordinary meaning of a word is being determined, a strict, quasi-mathematical symbolization of meaning, like that favored by courts, is therefore deeply flawed.

Despite its inherent flexibility, language should be viewed "as a system, and not just as a loose bag of words," according to Geeraerts (2010, 48). Such a view should convince judges that consideration of context, although necessary, is not a wholly discretionary exercise unconstrained by linguistic principles. Often, as indicated above and examined further below, insufficient weight is given to sentential context in determining the semantics of words, often by ignoring the systematic contributions to meaning that the other words in the sentence provide. To be sure, courts purport to follow a contextual approach when defining words. The context considered by courts, though, is typically broader than, and often does not include, sentential context. As reflected by the *in pari materia* canon (one of the textual canons listed in chap. 4), courts consider the relevant context to be how the provision at issue fits into the statutory scheme as a whole. Courts may also of course choose meanings based on the "purpose or object to accomplish" of the relevant statute, or information gleaned from the statute's legislative history. One might, correctly, characterize these contextual considerations as underscoring courts' ad hoc textual interpretations with debatable, and often fictional, assertions about statutory purpose, congressional intent, and uniformity with other statutes. However courts' contextual considerations are framed, the judiciary often fails to realize that words are frequently underspecified and that the sentential context of a word may influence its semantic contribution to the sentence.

5.2: Examples of the Classical Approach to Meaning and a Prototype-Like Approach to Meaning

While this book has already given reasons why a common way in which judges use dictionary definitions is flawed, particularly their application without consideration of sentential context, an additional fundamental concern has been mentioned but not yet been examined. That is, meaning cannot be determined acontextually, but often an important aspect of ordinary meaning is that the boundaries of a word (i.e., its "extension") must be known as a general matter. Further, sentential and other context may not always be decisive, or even particularly informative. Even in these situations, however, courts often do not approach the interpretive questions in the correct manner. As indicated above, a court will frequently rely on a dictionary definition and erroneously treat it as though it sets forth necessary and sufficient conditions for category membership. There are many cases that can serve as examples of the judiciary's adherence to this so-called classical approach to meaning. This section will introduce one particular case, *White City Shopping Center v. PR Restaurants*,[5] which can serve as an illustration of how the judiciary misuses dictionary definitions when deciding issues of categorization.

In part, the *White City Shopping Center* case was selected because its approach to defining words has received considerable attention from notable commentators, including Justice Scalia and Judge Posner. The case involved a Panera Bread restaurant that leased space in a shopping center under a written agreement that prohibited the shopping center from leasing space to any restaurant "reasonably expected to have annual sales of sandwiches" exceeding 10 percent of the restaurant's income. The shopping center subsequently negotiated for a lease of space with a Qdoba restaurant, which sold tacos, burritos, and quesadillas. Panera Bread sued the shopping center for breach of contract. The Massachusetts Superior Court ruled that the shopping center had not breached its contract with the Panera Bread restaurant. The court sought to decide the case in accordance with the ordinary meaning of "sandwiches," indicating that, "[i]f the words of the contract are plain and free from ambiguity, they must be construed in accordance with their ordinary and usual sense."[6] The court found that the term "sandwiches" is not ambiguous and reasoned as follows:

> The New Webster Third International Dictionary describes a "sandwich" as "two thin pieces of bread, usually buttered, with a thin layer (as of meat, cheese, or savory mixture) spread between them" (Merriam-Webster 2002). Under this definition and as dictated by common sense, this court finds that the term "sandwich" is not commonly understood to include burritos, tacos, and quesadillas, which are typically made with a single tortilla and stuffed with a choice filling of meat, rice, and beans.[7]

The court did not base its decision solely on the dictionary definition and "common sense."[8] The court also shifted the burden to Panera Bread, as the drafter of the exclusivity clause, to include a definition of "sandwiches" in the lease or to "communicate clearly to White City during lease negotiations that it intended to treat burritos, tacos, quesadillas, and sandwiches the same."[9] The court similarly reasoned that

> [a]nother factor weighing against PR's favor is that it was aware that Mexican-style restaurants near the Shopping Center existed which sold burritos, tacos, and quesadillas prior to the execution of the Lease yet, PR made no attempt to define, discuss, and clarify the parties' understanding of the term "sandwiches."[10]

*   *   *

Although judicial use of dictionaries is common, on some occasions a court will eschew a dictionary-based analysis in favor of some other manner of determining ordinary meaning. Consider the Supreme Court's long-ago decision in *Nix v. Hedden*,[11] where the Court had to decide whether tomatoes were to be classified at "vegetables" or as "fruit" under the tariff act of 1883. The Supreme Court first stated its usual rule that terms must receive their ordinary meanings rather than their technical meanings. The rest of the decision is notable because it did not place any particular weight on dictionary definitions and instead engaged in a prototype-like analysis (explained in detail below). The Court noted that the dictionary definitions cited by the parties "define the word 'fruit' as

the seed of plants, or that part of plants which contains the seed, and especially the juicy, pulpy products of certain plants, covering and containing
the seed."[12] In the Court's view, though, the definitions "have no tendency
to show that tomatoes are "fruit," as distinguished from "vegetables," in
common speech, or within the meaning of the tariff act."[13] Instead, relying
on the dictionary definitions, the Court reasoned about the proper classification as follows:

> Botanically speaking, tomatoes are the fruit of a vine, just as are cucumbers,
> squashes, beans, and peas. But in the common language of the people, whether
> sellers or consumers of provisions, all these are vegetables which are grown in
> kitchen gardens, and which, whether eaten cooked or raw, are, like potatoes,
> carrots, parsnips, turnips, beets, cauliflower, cabbage, celery, and lettuce, usually
> served at dinner in, with, or after the soup, fish, or meats which constitute the
> principal part of the repast, and not, like fruits generally, as dessert.[14]

In the Court's view, categorization determinations must be based on
"common knowledge," as demonstrated in the above indented quote, because "very little evidence is necessary, or can be produced."[15] Thus, dictionaries are relevant as "aids to the memory and understanding of the
court" but are not decisive of meaning.[16]

*   *   *

Both *White City Shopping Center* and *Nix* raise important issues regarding the determination of word meaning. To be sure, the classical approach
to meaning exemplified in *White City Shopping Center* has its (noteworthy) defenders as the default method of defining words. Scalia and
Garner (2012, 55), for instance, reason that

> [s]andwiches not being a defined term in the lease, the court sensibly relied
> on a reputable dictionary. . . . The injunction [against the shopping center] was
> properly denied on grounds that no reasonable speaker of English would call a
> taco, a burrito, or a quesadilla a "sandwich."

Notwithstanding Scalia and Garner's endorsement, the court's attempt
to define "sandwich" was significantly flawed. Even a quick reading of
the dictionary definition (given above) should convince the reader that
it cannot possibly set forth necessary and sufficient conditions for being

a "sandwich" and cannot serve as any sort of determinate criteria for the word.

Furthermore, what about other, nondictionary sources of meaning? The US Department of Agriculture, for example, describes a burrito as "[a] Mexican style sandwich-like product."[17] Similarly, a hamburger is a "sandwich type product."[18] If something is "like" the category being considered, does that mean it falls within that category? The Department of Agriculture also has separate definitions for "closed" and "open" sandwiches (contradicting the dictionary definition relied on by the court in *White City Shopping Center*), each requiring that the item contain at least a certain percentage of "cooked meat" and no more than a certain percentage of bread.[19] Such definitions raise important issues for legal categorization. Even assuming that the Department of Agriculture has expertise in such matters, should its definitions be considered authoritative for purposes of ordinary meaning determinations?

In contrast to the *White City Shopping Center* court's reliance on a dictionary definition, consider the Supreme Court's reasoning in *Nix v. Heddon*. Can it be considered an improvement? The Court in *Nix* did not rely on a dictionary definition of "fruit" but instead attempted to determine the meaning on the basis of the features of the category, derived from "common knowledge." Can this manner of determining meaning be considered superior to reliance on dictionary definitions? Perhaps it is unfair to focus on the *White City Shopping Center* because of the unfortunate definition of "sandwich" relied on by the Court (notwithstanding Scalia and Garner's affirmation of it). Would a different dictionary definition, still containing necessary-and-sufficient conditions for membership, have made the Court's reliance on it persuasive?

A further complicating problem is that "tomatoes" and "burritos" may be (relatively) easy cases for ordinary meaning because they obviously exist outside the law and are familiar to the general public. Yet, the terms in legal texts often refer to intangible concepts that either do not exist outside the law or exist at too high a level of generality compared to the needs of the legal profession. For instance, "pattern of racketeering activity" is an important term in the Racketeer Influenced and Corrupt Organizations Act (RICO), a well-known federal statute, but the term obviously is a creation of the law. Can an interpreter simply look up "pattern" in the dictionary and straightforwardly apply the definition to the statute? If, as is the case, "pattern" is too general a term for the needs of the law, and adding "of racketeering activity" does not precisify it sufficiently (having no existence outside of the law), how should a court proceed? Does the term even have an ordinary linguistic meaning that can be applied in a case? The answers to the questions in this paragraph, as well as those in the preceding one, will have to wait until the classical theory of meaning and alternatives to it have been explained.

5.3: Categorization

5.3.1: Dictionaries: The Classical Theory of Meaning and Categorization

As the above cases illustrate, legal interpretation frequently involves determining whether an item (either abstract or concrete, as explained later) falls within the parameters of the concept inscribed in the relevant textual provision. Legal interpretation thus involves acts of categorization, which more generally is a psychological process whereby people make judgments about whether an object falls within a given concept. Categories are equivalence classes of discriminable items, and categorization involves the formation of such categories. More precisely, concepts are psychological constructs that mediate that to which a word refers (Taylor 2003). In turn, categories are what concepts are about (Margolis 1994). This chapter will use the terms "concept" and "category" interchangeably.[20]

In addition to being essential to the operation of the law, categorization is an integral aspect of human development. Categorization requires an ability to intellectually accommodate both similarities and differences. Early in their development, humans demonstrate the ability to countenance differences in order to generalize and form categories based on similarities (Sloutsky 2003). In general, categorization is beneficial because it allows for the organization of knowledge through the creation of taxonomies that include smaller classes within larger ones (e.g., Specific Creature → Yorkipoo → Dogs → Animals). As such, categorization is part of the process of inductive generalization, where, for example, knowing that a creature has features similar to recognized members of the category "dogs" enables one to categorize the creature as a "dog."

The judicial tendency to view word categories as formed by necessary and sufficient conditions for membership is consistent with the so-called classical theory of concept meaning. Under the classical theory, all instances of a category share a set of properties (i.e., "defining attributes") in which each attribute is singly necessary for category membership, and possession of the set of attributes is sufficient for category membership (Margolis 1994). Rosch and Mervis (1975, 573–74) describe the traditional view of categorization as follows:

> Much work in philosophy, psychology, linguistics, and anthropology assumes that categories are logical bounded entities, membership in which is defined by an item's possession of a simple set of criterial features, in which all instances possessing the criterial attributes have a full and equal degree of membership.

The classical approach thus assumes that the meaning of a word consists of a set of properties that can be used as a sort of decision procedure to identify all and only the things denoted by the word (Murphy 2010). The criteria for membership are thus clear, and, importantly, there should be no well-known words that do not have a clear-cut category membership. Also, although generally less important to the law, no item is any more representative of the category than any other.

Because the classical theory assumes that word meanings are determinate, it is, at least in the view of some, conducive to the perceived needs of the legal system. By averring that words in legal texts can be defined by necessary and sufficient criteria, judges can avoid alternative views of meaning that complicate and undermine the classical theory. In this way, the parameters of a concept's extension (i.e., its referential range of application) are always capable of being determined with precision, even if determining the extension is sometimes (epistemically) difficult. There may be hard cases where the object in question may be on the borderline of the concept's extension, but such situations do not necessarily cause concern about the accuracy of the criteria for membership within the concept. The classical theory, though, comes at the cost of accuracy about meaning. Instead of a simple set of criterial features, categories do not have sharply delimited borders with clear demarcations. Rather, they are often only unambiguously defined in their focal points, and marginal areas exist between categories.

Some legal scholars have recognized these features of meaning. Famously, H. L. A. Hart (1958) argued that most legal rules have a "core of settled meaning" but are surrounded by a "penumbra of debatable cases." Hart (1958, 607) used the now-ubiquitous vehicles-in-the-park example to make his point:

> A legal rule forbids you to take a vehicle into the public park. Plainly this forbids an automobile, but what about bicycles, roller skates, toy automobiles?

What about airplanes? Are these, as we say, to be called "vehicles" for the purpose of the rule or not? If we are to communicate with each other at all, and if, as in the most elementary form of law, we are to express our intentions that a certain type of behavior be regulated by rules, then the general words we use—like "vehicle" in the case I consider—must have some standard instance in which no doubts are felt about its application. There must be a core of settled meaning, but there will be, as well, a penumbra of debatable cases in which words are neither obviously applicable not obviously ruled out.

Hart is certainly correct, as will be explained below, that a given word often has a settled scope of reference but is also fuzzy at the margins. Although Hart's vehicle-in-the-park hypothetical is famous for its illustration of the difficulties of categorization, he does not provide any real explanation of how an interpreter identifies the "core of settled meaning" or the parameters of the category. In short, he does not explain how a judge might identify criteria for determining membership in a category such as "vehicle."[21] Such identification is crucial, though, to the ordinary meaning doctrine.

In a response to Hart, Fuller (1958, 663) emphasized the contextual nature of interpretation, arguing that

> [e]ven in the case of statutes, we commonly have to assign meaning, not to a single word, but to a sentence, a paragraph, or a whole page or more of text. Surely a paragraph does not have a "standard instance" that remains constant whatever the context in which it appears. If a statute seems to have a kind of "core meaning" that we can apply without a too precise inquiry into its exact purpose, this is because we can see that, however one might formulate the precise objective of the statute, this case would still come within it.

Of course, Fuller is correct that the legal interpreter must determine the meaning of the relevant legal provision and not just a single word within it. This book has emphasized the contextual nature of interpretation, even when ordinary meaning (as opposed to communicative meaning) is being determined. Yet, as explained in chapter 3, a traditional philosophical focus when providing a theory of meaning is to develop a theory that focuses on the meaning of sentences, rather than on either words alone or larger units (such as collections of sentences). The number of potential sentences in any natural language is infinite, and a theory of meaning must advance a compositional approach according to which the meanings of sentences are seen to depend on the meanings of their parts. In other words, the meanings of individual words form the finite base of the language out of which sentences are composed.

Despite the focus on the meaning of sentences and the role of context, part of a compositional approach to meaning should include a focus on the definitions of words. For one, if ordinary meaning is being sought, the relevant narrow context (or, often, even the broad context) may not change the meaning that would be given one of the provision's words considered in isolation.[22] Further, even when the narrow context would be influential, a proper understanding of how words are defined is essential to determining ordinary meaning, as well as communicative meaning. As this chapter argues, part of such an understanding includes the realization that even beyond the discretionary nature of context, the determination of word meaning, even when considered in isolation, involves significant judicial discretion. Thus, the difficulties associated with defining words must also be examined.

5.3.2: A Description of Prototype Theory

The main problem with the judicial desire to portray categories as though they are constituted by necessary and sufficient conditions of membership is that doing so comes at the expense of accurately describing the ordinary meaning of words. Wittgenstein (1953) famously undermined the classical theory of meaning and the mental structures underlying it. By the 1970s, the classical view of categorization began suffering sustained criticisms. In particular, researchers rejected the classical view that category membership involves a set of necessary attributes that are jointly sufficient to delimit the category in contrast with others. Rosch (1973a, 1973b, 1975, 1978) and others such as Labov (1973) are typically credited with severely undermining the classical view. These researchers offered as alternatives to the classical view psycholinguistic theories of how people perceive categories. From her field experiments, Rosch concluded that defining categories in a rigid manner is inconsistent with psychological reality. In contrast to the traditional view, Rosch argued that perceptually-based categories do not have sharply delimited borders with clear demarcations between equally important concepts. In other words, many words are not defined by people in terms of a list of necessary and sufficient conditions that must be satisfied for a thing to count as a member of the relevant category. Instead, categories are only unambiguously defined in their focal points, and marginal areas exist between categories.

Unsurprisingly, prototype theory has had a significant impact on conceptual analysis. Hanks (2013, 340), for instance, has deemed it "[p]robably the most influential development of the twentieth century from the point of view of conceptual analysis." Under prototype theory, categories contain focal points that represent prototypical members of the category. Rosch (1978, 36) notes that "[b]y prototypes of categories we have generally meant the clearest cases of category membership defined operationally by people's judgments of goodness of membership in the category." The attributes of the prototypical members are thus structurally the most salient properties of the relevant concept. A member of the category is in a focal position if it exhibits the most salient features. Thus, for example, the more typically "birdy" a bird is, the more strongly and immediately it is associated with the name of that category. Of course, as Hanks (2013, 341) points out, items that are outside a category may share certain characteristics with members of the category. For instance, even some non-birds (e.g., bats) are somewhat birdy.

Categories can be dived into three levels: "subordinate levels," "basic levels," and "superordinate levels" (Taylor 2003). The basic level is the most informative and can therefore be claimed as the most economical in relation to cognitive processes. These categories are relatively homogeneous in terms of sensory-motor affordances (Gärdenfors 2000). For instance, a chair is associated with the bending of one's knees and a fruit with picking it up and putting it in one's mouth. The basic level categories also have a sort of privileged status that is manifested in ordinary communications. Taylor (2003) indicates that, if there is an apple on the kitchen table, it is likely that the speaker would ask the listener something like "could you please hand me the apple?" The speaker would be less likely to ask the listener to pass "the Golden Delicious" (a subordinate category) or "the fruit" (a superordinate category). Similarly, if asked the question, "What are you sitting on?," most speakers would say "a chair" rather than something from a subordinate category like "a kitchen chair" or from a superordinate category like "furniture." At the subordinate level (e.g., "kitchen chair"), few significant features can be added to that of the basic level. In contrast, at the superordinate level, conceptual similarities are difficult to pinpoint. For instance, a picture of a chair is easy to draw or visualize but not so for furniture, even though the category may be said to have a prototype (Rosch 1978).

Although many aspects of prototype theory are uncontroversial and straightforward, such as the general proposition that some items may be more salient category members than others, prototypicality is a complex phenomenon. It is, in fact, itself a prototypical concept (Posner 1986). Geeraerts (2010) describes the following four characteristics that are often cited as being typical of prototypical categories:

(1) Blurring occurs at the edges of the category;
(2) Not every member is equally representative for a category;
(3) A family resemblance structure is exhibited that may consist of a radial set of clustered and overlapping readings; and
(4) The category cannot be defined by means of a single set of criterial (i.e., necessary and sufficient) attributes.

The four characteristics of prototypical categories offer both "intensional" and "extensional" views of categories. Generally, "intensional" and "extensional" are terms that offer two ways of individuating concepts at the level of individual concept possessors. The first and second characteristics take into account the referential, extensional structure of a category. Recall that the extension of a category is the referential range of application of the category (i.e., the things that fall under the concept term). The first characteristic, formulated in extensional terms, recognizes that the referential boundaries of a category are not always determinate. While a linguistic category may be clear in the center, it may also be fuzzy at the edges. Thus, while some items may be clear members of a category or clear nonmembers, other items may be neither clear members nor clear nonmembers.

The second characteristic highlights the differences of typicality and membership salience of a category. Not all members of a category are equal in representativeness for that category. Rather, categories have stereotypes, which can affect how categories are perceived (Connolly et al. 2007). For instance, informants in experiments take more time to recognize nonprototypical members than typical ones, typical members are more often named than marginal ones, and typical instances of a category are learned earlier than nontypical cases (Geeraerts 2010). For instance, Rosch (1975) conducted experiments in which informants were asked to classify a set of objects that were all contained in the same category according to the extent to which they considered these objects to be good examples of the category. Thus, for the category "furniture," "chairs" are good examples, "drawers" intermediate, and "telephones" low. Similarly, another Rosch (1973) experiment revealed that informants were quicker to identify "robins" and "sparrows" as examples of "birds" than they were to so identify "penguins," "chickens," and "ducks." The last experiment highlights that category membership is not the same thing as typicality. Although a penguin is not a prototypical bird, it is nonetheless generally viewed as being within that category.

In contrast to extensional accounts, the intensional content concerns the representation of the concept in the mind, through knowledge of the features. The third and fourth characteristics of prototypes are associated with the intensional level of a category, where the definitional rather than the referential structure of a category is envisaged. The family resemblance structure concept is associated with Wittgenstein (1953), who argued that the referents of a word need not have common elements to be understood and used in the normal functioning of language. This observation had an important role in inspiring linguists to reconsider the classical notion that words should be defined in terms of necessary and sufficient conditions. Instead, a family resemblance might link the various references of a word. For instance, a family resemblance might take the following form: [AB, BC, CD, DE]. Each item thus has at least one element in common with one or more of the other items. No elements, however, are common to all the items. Thus, there is no necessary element. Items BC and CD have greater "structural weight" than do AB and DE because they share more elements with the other items. This implies that not every element or item is structurally equally important.

The fourth characteristic, obviously related to the third, emphasizes nondiscreteness and the lack of a single definition of necessary and sufficient attributes for a prototypical concept. Wittgenstein (1953), for example, argued that the concept "game" cannot be defined by properties that are shared by all other games. Instead of being capable of being defined by necessary and sufficient conditions, the different members of the category share properties with various other members.

*   *   *

In sum, categories can be subordinate, basic, or superordinate, and some, but not all, categories have the four characteristics described above. These characteristics feature nondiscreteness and nonequality from both extensional and intensional perspectives. Nondiscreteness involves demarcation problems and the flexible nature of categories. Nonequality involves the internal structure of categories and the reality that not all members that fall within the boundaries of a category have an equal status. Instead, a dominant core area might exist and be surrounded by a less salient periphery. Of course, the characteristics are not coextensive and do not always co-occur. Rather, the characteristics involve prototypicality effects that may be exhibited in various combinations by individual words.

5.3.3: Scientific Meaning and Folk Meaning

Despite the general failure of the classical model, some words uncontroversially can be defined in terms of necessary and sufficient conditions. For instance, words that carry scientific or technical meanings may have some prototypical characteristics but nevertheless often are defined by a single set of necessary and sufficient attributes. The categories may thus not have fuzzy criterial boundaries. A "hypotenuse," for example, is defined by a single set of criterial attributes (i.e., a line in a triangle opposite a 90° angle), as are terms like "even number."[23] Perhaps, then, such meanings should be considered to be authoritative. Margolis (1994), for instance, states that the question whether the category "birds" involves singly necessary and jointly sufficient properties "would seem to be a matter for the zoologists to settle" in the absence of philosophical arguments for some other standard. Similarly, Putnam (1975) refers to a linguistic division of labor where "natural kind" terms have their references fixed by the "experts" in the field of science to which the terms belong. Natural kind objects come into being without human intervention, while artifacts are objects intentionally made to serve a given purpose. Essentially, the argument is that in every linguistic community there are some terms with definitional criteria known only to a subset of the speakers who acquire the terms, and whose use by the other speakers depends on a structured cooperation between them and the speakers in the relevant subsets. So, for example, the community of botanists would fix the reference of the term "tomato."

Obviously, most words do not have technical or scientific meanings, and thus expert definition is not relevant for those words. Even with respect to a word that does have a technical or scientific meaning that is determinate, that meaning may differ from the "folk" (as some philosophers call it) or ordinary meaning of the term. Some scholars have argued that the scientific or technical meaning should generally be described as the "true" meaning and the folk meaning as the "mistaken" meaning. Thus, a folk or ordinary meaning that does not correspond with a scientific meaning may be evidence of epistemological confusion or ignorance. Along these lines, Margolis (1994, 84, 85), quoting (Rey 1983, 248), distinguishes between two types of "unclear cases": those involving an item that may be on the borderline of a category (possible with a category like "black cat") and those involving items like "tomatoes," which may be clear instances of fruit "even though people may be (epistemologically) confused about them." Thus, the distinction is between the legitimate and unavoidable unclarity associated with borderline cases and the illegitimate and avoidable unclarity associated with definitional confusion.

Margolis is correct that in some situations category fuzziness may be largely epistemological in nature. For instance, individuals might believe that category membership is an absolute matter but, for various reasons, are confused about the criteria for membership. Such confusion, however, is not a reason to view the folk meaning as illegitimate. Despite the allure of technical or scientific meanings that are determinate, if the notion of ordinary meaning is accepted, uncertainty about intensional properties, as well as a concept's extension, may be constitutive of a term's meaning. Uncertainty and inconsistency about meaning are therefore not reasons to think that the scientific or technical meaning is the authoritative one. Hanks (2013, 342) reasons, persuasively, that:

> there is a hugely importance distinction between the flexible, analogical, prototype-based meaning of terms in natural language and the stipulative definitions of the scientist. Scientific research must, of course, be held in the greatest respect, but that does not mean that we should be allowed to bully each other into accepting the notion that scientists know the "true" meaning of the terms of our language.

As Hanks argues, there is no reason to view a scientific or technical definition as the "true" meaning and prototypical effects as evidence of "confusion," even if respondents in experiments show confusion about criteria for category membership. There is thus no reason to give any particular weight to the Department of Agriculture's definition of "sandwich," as described above, and, in fact, it should be assumed that such definitions generally do not capture the ordinary meanings of the terms they define.

5.3.4: "Fruit" as a Prototypical Concept

Eschewing a scientific definition in favor of a folk understanding of a concept may be consistent with the judicial commitment to ordinary meaning, but such a rejection raises difficult issues of how category membership

can be determined. Specifically, prototypicality effects may be straightforwardly captured, but categorization criteria are not easily developed and
applied. Consider the category "fruit." If a folk understanding of the category is being sought, a classical definition of "fruit," in terms of necessary
and sufficient features, would be inaccurate. Instead, Geeraerts (2010) describes a prototype analysis of fruit according to a "folk model" rather
than the technical, biological definition. While, according to a technical
definition, any seed containing part of a plant is the fruit of that plant,
such a definition does not correspond with the ordinary understanding
of the concept. For one, the definition would include nuts as fruit. In ordinary language, however, nuts and fruits are distinct categories.

Furthermore, under a folk model of fruit, the salience characteristic is
present. Oranges, apples, and bananas are the most typical fruits according to informants in experiments, and pineapples, watermelons, and pome-
granates receive low typicality ratings. The uncontroversial core members
(i.e., the most salient members) of the category cannot, however, be defined in the classical necessary-and-sufficient manner. The common feature, "edible seed-bearing part of a plant" (in contrast to a herbaceous
plant), is a feature that includes vegetable like peapods. Thus, like with
many categories, the common feature, even if necessary, is insufficient to
distinguish the category from items in other categories.

Beyond selecting the most salient members, analyzing the category
of "fruit" under a folk-meaning perspective involves a level of uncertainty. Once it is recognized that necessary and sufficient conditions do
not adequately define the category of "fruit," the initial aspect of a prototype analysis may seem circular. That is, the uncertainty surrounding
the boundaries of the category is relevant to determining the attributes
of the items in the category. Geeraerts (2010) indicates that if there is a
consensus that, for example, "olives" are not fruit, then they should not
be included in the initial prototype analysis of fruit. If, however, they are
considered to be fruit, even if not salient members, they should arguably
be included. To avoid the problems associated with peripheral members,
the analysis can be restricted to items for which there are no doubts about
membership.

Under a prototype analysis of "fruit" in light of the uncertainty mentioned above, not all of the relevant attributes will have the same range
of application, and an attribute may not apply to the category as a whole.
Rather, the attributes that are relevant to the semantic description de-
marcate subsets of the entire range of application of the category. Such

TABLE 5.1. **Componential analysis of the category "fruit"**

	Edible seed-bearing part	Of wood plant	Juicy	Sweet	Used as dessert
Apple	Yes	Yes	Yes	Yes	Yes
Strawberry	Yes	No	Yes	Yes	Yes
Banana	Yes	Yes	No	Yes	Yes
Lemon	Yes	Yes	Yes	No	No
Tomato	Yes	No	Yes	No	No
Olive	Yes	Yes	No	No	No

Note: Adapted from Geeraerts (2010).

a description will take the form of a cluster of partially overlapping sets. Considering only the most salient members, Geeraerts (2010) indicates that the relevant features of "fruit" are the following: (1) edible seed-bearing part of a wood plant (which, recall, is not a sufficient characteristic), (2) juiciness, (3) sweetness, and (4) use as dessert rather than as a main dish. Table 5.1 contains the salient members of the category, "apple," "strawberry," and "banana," along with three other items (the relevance of which will become clear below). A componential analysis gives values for the five attributes described above.

As table 5.1 illustrates, prototype theory explains the representation of word meanings in terms of properties. It accounts for the extension of a category in intensional terms through the respective properties of the items of the category. With "fruit," all the relevant features of prototypicality are present. First, a family resemblance structure is exhibited with a radial set of clustered and overlapping readings. While all the items meet the "edible seed-bearing part" feature, even the items that are clearly fruit differ in their possession of the other features. Hampton (1981, 149) indicates that a polymorphous concept like "fruit" is one where an item belongs in a category if and only if it possesses a sufficient number of a set of features, none of which need be common to all category members. Thus, for example, "sweet" is one of the features of fruit, but some members (such as lemons) do not possess it. "Sweet" is thus a feature that is neither necessary nor sufficient but is nonetheless relevant to the category. Second, not all the members of the category are equally representative. "Apples" are more representative of the category than are some other members, such as "lemons."

Most importantly, as the above analysis indicates, the "fruit" category

cannot be defined by means of a single set of necessary and sufficient attributes. Rather, it is like a prototypical category with sets of properties
or attributes that are characteristic and not defining. Although there is
internal structure in the sense that some members are better examples
than others, no clear boundary separates members from nonmembers. If
category membership is a matter of satisfying a high number of a set of
properties, then items will be members *to the degree* that they satisfy this
set. Items that possess all the properties will be members to the highest
degree, items that have none will be nonmembers, and items that have a
number around the threshold for membership will be members to a low
degree. It follows that there may be borderline cases where unambiguous
categorization is not possible.

5.4: The Difficulties of Prototype Theory and Categorization Decisions

5.4.1: Prototype Theory and Vagueness

By undermining the classical theory of meaning, prototype theory creates
significant challenges for the interpretation of legal texts. For example, if
one accepts prototype categories, it is difficult to argue against the notion
that legal texts contain significant vagueness. As indicated above, a category may have clear members, clear nonmembers, and instances that are
not clearly either members or nonmembers. It is this third possibility that
raises issues of vagueness. In general, it is said that a concept is vague if:

(1) The concept's extension is unclear;
(2) There exist borderline cases where one cannot say with certainty whether an
     object belongs to a group of objects that can be identified as falling under a
     given concept; and
(3) The sorites paradox can be applied to the concept or predicate.[24]

A comparison of the characteristics of vagueness with those of prototypical categories demonstrates that, far from being exceptional, vagueness is an endemic aspect of meaning. In law, though, textual provisions
deemed to be vague are of particular concern, although their prevalence
is typically underappreciated by courts. On a fundamental level, vague
texts raise concerns about the rule of law. One problem is that they can
fail to provide sufficient notice of the content of the relevant provision. In

criminal cases, lack of adequate notice can be reason for invalidation, and an extremely vague provision may be struck down on void-for-vagueness grounds.[25] Thus, a concession that a provision is vague may have consequences for the validity of the provision.

A related concern is with the bivalent nature of legal categorization, which generally requires a "yes" or "no" answer to the question of whether an item belongs in a given category. The resolution of many cases depends on whether an item is a member of the category indicated in a given provision. While representivity might indicate degrees of category membership, it does not by itself provide criteria for determining whether an item is a member of the relevant category tout court. Thus, observing the degrees of representivity in table 5.1 does not determine the threshold for membership in the category. A "banana," for instance, is perhaps slightly less representative of a "fruit" than is an "apple," but no one doubts that a banana is nonetheless a fruit. The situation may be different for other items, though. For instance, a "tomato" has the "edible seed-bearing part" and "juicy" features but is missing other features. Are the features a prototypical tomato possesses sufficient for membership in the "fruit" category? It may be said that "juicy" (which is itself a prototype category) is a characteristic property of fruit because it is one which is possessed by many of the category's exemplars. It does not, however, represent a necessary condition for category membership considering that bananas (and other fruits) are clear members of the category even though they are not juicy. Instead, the intensional attribute information reveals only information that is more common of category members than of other things, but is not true of all category members. As a result, it is nondefining in the sense that it does not provide criteria for membership. Membership criteria, though, are essential to legal interpretation. As indicated above, instead of prototypicality and degrees of membership, the issue important to the resolution of legal cases concerns whether a nonprototypical item is nonetheless a member of a particular category. In the absence of necessary and sufficient criteria for membership, it is not obvious how such determinations can be made with any degree of epistemological certainty.

One possibility for category membership determinations, judicial intuition or "common sense," may be accurate for clear members and clear nonmembers, but there is no reason why judicial intuition should be viewed as accurate for intermediate items, which are frequently the subject of legal disputes. The individual psychological state of the judge does not fix the extension of a concept. Rather, it is the sociolinguistic state of the collective linguistic body to which the interpreter belongs that fixes the extension. Judges, though, are not likely to be adept at making such predictions. Consider the results from experiments. Highly typical candidate items are almost always classified by experiment participants as category members, whereas extremely atypical candidates are almost never so classified. Presumably, possession of relevant cultural knowledge would be sufficient to predict highly typical candidates and atypical candidates. Between the extremes, though, are items that are not consistently classified as either members or nonmembers of the relevant category. For instance, Hampton, Dubois, and Yeh (2006) report that when people are asked to decide whether "rugs," "paintings," or "televisions" are types of "furniture," they are frequently uncertain about the answer. Similarly, McCloskey and Glucksberg (1978) demonstrated that across a range of semantic categories, there was both disagreement and inconsistency in classification. Asked to decide whether a "pencil" is a "tool," some people say "yes" and some say "no." When asked the same question again some weeks later, as many as 30 percent change their answer. Thus, with these intermediate items, subjects disagree in their categorizations of the items and within-subjects inconsistency is high. McCloskey and Glucksberg (1978) argue that within-subjects inconsistency supports the hypothesis that natural categories are fuzzy and that no clear boundary separates members from nonmembers. Thus, unless judges have some special insight into categorization, of which there is no evidence, there is no particular reason to treat their judgments of intermediate items as reliable.

As explained above, a basic prototype analysis, like that given above of "fruit," does not offer a methodology that is sufficient for determinations of category membership. A basic analysis does not address in any detail the probabilistic focus of prototype theory and, in particular, the prototype representation and corresponding criteria of similarity. In order to make category membership determinations, criteria must be established as well as a method of comparing the item's features to the criteria. Judicial intuition about similarity and category membership is not an adequate substitute for developing these concepts. Further, a comparison of prototypical prototype categories and common definitions of vagueness indicates that categories are massively vague. Plainly, further examination and development of the prototype concept is required in order to determine whether the difficulties identified above can be properly managed.

5.4.2: Creating the Prototype Concept

As indicated above, legal interpretation is generally bivalent, making category salience and degree of membership of lesser importance than the question of category membership. Further examination of the prototype concept must thus focus on how categorization decisions can be made and whether criteria of similarity for category membership can be identified. According to Hampton (1995), a prototype concept has three elements:

(1) The prototype representation, which is generally a generalization or abstraction of some central tendency, average or typical value of a class of instances falling in the same category;
(2) A way of defining similarity to the prototype; and
(3) Criteria of similarity for category membership. Instances that satisfy the criteria are members of the category. Those that do not are nonmembers.

As indicated above, a lexical category C does not have definitional structure but has instead a probabilistic structure in the sense that an item falls under C if it satisfies a sufficient number of properties encoded by C's constituents. Or, more precisely if one considers that a basic level itself has a prototype structure, a class C will be a subcategory of superordinate class S, provided that the prototype for C is sufficiently similar to the prototype for S (Hampton 1995). Possessing the similarity criteria is thus both necessary and sufficient for category membership.

Compared to the other two elements, defining the prototype representation is relatively straightforward. As explained previously, a prototype is a cognitive representation associated with a particular word that serves as the reference for categorization. A given word is not associated with a concrete prototype but rather with the mental representation of the prototype. The mental picture is an abstract entity that involves a combination of features rather than a realistic example of a given category. The prototype representation is usually defined as the instance with maximum average similarity to the others in the category (Hampton 1995). If, for example, the focus is on features, the prototype can be defined as the combination of all the features that occur more frequently among category members than in nonmembers.

Membership in the category is based on similarity to the prototype. A meaning of similarity is specified for whatever form of conceptual representation is chosen. If a feature list is used, similarity is defined based on that representation. Rosch (1975) suggests that categorization might be related to the number of category features that an item possesses. Of course, features are not necessarily all equally probative. Differential weighting for the features may be necessary, so that those features that are thought to be more predictive of category membership will receive a higher weight than those that are less predictive. In addition, interactions among features may be necessary to contemplate. For instance, Wattenmaker (1995) found that object categories (as opposed to social categories such as personality traits or occupations) may involve interactions among features. These interactions make some feature combinations more likely than others. Thus, for example, to be a "good hammer," it is better for an object to be small and light or large and heavy than to be small and heavy or large and light.

Even if the probability of categorization is tied to the similarity of features between the prototype and the item in question, the multiple sources of information that must be integrated in order to make categorization decisions make the process an uncertain one (Hampton et al. 2009b). Ramscar and Hahn (2001) argue that the notion of similarity is radically underdetermined because any two items have infinitely many properties in common, as well as infinitely many differences. Thus, similarity *in a given respect* is what is meaningful about similarity, and it is the particular respect that is crucial. Ramscar and Hahn's observations are particularly applicable to similarity judgments made via an intuition-based prototype analysis, which would likely be the kind performed by most judges. A prototype and a criterion of similarity require the contemplation of various features, but the proper structure for the necessary comparisons is often not obvious. Miscategorization can occur, for instance, when items are grouped together based on features that are illogical or that a wide variety of items have in common. Items have a multitude of features, and categorization requires that some of the features be privileged over others.

To illustrate, consider that the analysis of "fruit" above focused on five features, as illustrated in table 5.1. In addition to these five, though, are many others that may also be arguably relevant to categorization. Hampton (1979), for instance, indicates that participants in a study specified the following features of "fruit" in decreasing order of production frequency: (1) Is a plant, organic, vegetation; (2) Is edible, is eaten; (3) Contains seeds; (4) Grows above ground, on bushes or trees; (5) Is juicy, thirst quenching;

(6) Is brightly colored; (7) Is sweet; (8) Has an outer layer of skin or peel; (9) Is round; (10) Is eaten as a dessert, snack or on its own; and (11) Is a protection for seeds. Note that some of the features are broader than those identified by Geeraerts (2010) in figure 5.1, and others were not mentioned by Geeraerts. Consider the tenth feature, "eaten as a dessert, snack or on its own." Could one, for example, conclude that an "olive" is not eaten as a "desert" but is eaten "on its own"? If so, an "olive" would not possess the feature "used as dessert" under Geeraerts' (2010) analysis but would possess the similar feature, "Is eaten as a dessert, snack or on its own." Similarly, at least some olives would not possess the feature, "Is brightly colored," which is not one of the features in Geeraerts's (2010) analysis. Further, it is possible that an olive has a significant feature that would not be represented in the prototype of "fruit."

An interpreter must therefore consider two kinds of distinctive features. One kind of feature is true of the category prototype but not of the item under consideration. A second is true of the item but not of the prototype. Hampton (1995) indicates that an item will be rendered less typical in a category if it possesses distinctive features that are not part of the prototype, even if the features are irrelevant to category membership. Thus, as Rosch and Mervis (1975) indicate, membership in a category is directly proportional to the number of attributes an item shares with other members of the category and inversely proportional to the number of attributes it shares with members of other categories. Like the reasons given above, this second kind of relevant feature represents another reason why an intuition-based prototype analysis is problematic as a probabilistic device to gauge category membership.

In some cases, categorization decisions may not require a determination of whether a given item falls within a given category simpliciter but, instead, whether it either falls within Category A or Category B. In the first situation, criteria for membership must be established as well as a method of comparing the item's features to the criteria. In contrast, the second situation may require that an item be placed in one of two categories, and the two categories are at least contrasting if not mutually exclusive (such as "fruits" and "vegetables"). In this situation, it may be said that an item X is categorized in Category A instead of Category B if its representation is more similar to the representation of Category A than to the representation of Category B (Dupuy 2000). Any attempt to implement differential weighting for features of course complicates the prototype representation that is being constructed and raises questions of the empirical or other basis for the differential weighting. The end result, though, is still that a given item must pass some threshold value to be considered a member of the category (Hampton 1998).

5.4.3: Further Complications with Prototype Theory

Seeking to avoid the uncertainties inherent in intuition-based approaches to categorization, some linguists and psychologists have developed sophisticated statistic models designed to predict the categorization decisions made by respondents in experiments.[26] In contrast, with a nonmodel-based approach, which a legal interpreter would likely follow, difficult qualitative judgments must be made. As has already been discussed, the numerosity of potentially relevant features and the arbitrary nature of the membership criterion are important complications that a nonmodel-based prototype analysis may be unable to adequately resolve. Other issues also complicate the analysis. One problem concerns the differences between biological and artifact kinds. Hampton et al. (2009b) argue that the conceptual structure of the two domains differ in many ways. For instance Keil (1986) found that transforming the appearance of an artifact would change its type, but transforming a biological kind would not. In contrast, a scientific discovery about a biological kind might affect its categorization, but such discoveries do not affect artifact categorization. Similarly, the function of an artifact is an important feature in determining its class (Hampton et al. 2009b). Even if, for example, a central aspect of a prototypical chair is that it is used for sitting on, the fact that a given item was designed to function as a chair may override the fact that the object cannot be sat upon or that it is currently in use as a bedside table. Thus, a broken chair may still be properly viewed as a chair. At the same time, Chaigneau, Barsalou, and Sloman (2004) found that a change in current function always had a greater effect on naming than did a change in original intended function.

It may seem that such difficulties are not relevant to legal interpretation, but such a view would be mistaken. For instance, in *United States v. McKlemurry*,[27] the court had to determine whether a car body without an engine was a "motor vehicle" within the meaning of the National Motor Vehicle Theft Act. Similarly, in *United States v. Bishop*,[28] the court had to determine whether an engine block, without a car body, was a "motor vehicle" under the same statute. Although neither court relied on prototype theory, the kinds of difficulties described in the previous paragraph are part of the reasons why some have claimed that prototype theory does not offer a sufficiently sophisticated view of categorization, even if the classical view of categorization also does not.

Under prototype theory, categories have a somewhat superficial nature, involving features that are readily perceivable, and the process of concept acquisition is a passive one. In contrast, advocates of "theory-theory" (also known as a "naive-theory") argue that concepts are embedded in and structured around naive mental theories (Hampton et al. 2009a). The argument is that theories are the conceptual glue that makes many of our everyday and scientific concepts coherent, and models of concepts that fail to accord theories an important role are missing an account of a crucial phenomenon. Concepts thus possess coherence that makes them non-arbitrary (Murphy and Medin 1985; Medin, Wattenmaker, and Hampson 1987). For example, a category like "fruit" is coherent in the sense that its members bear explainable relations to one another, but the category "things on the ground outside my office" may just be an arbitrary collection of items. Feature-based theories of concepts, though, such as prototype theory, do not explicitly accommodate the phenomenon of coherence because they are inherently unconstrained and, theoretically, allow any set of items to form a category.

The theory-theory position is thus that categorization is based on a theoretical understanding or causal model of the world. Mature categorization cannot develop from simpler perceptual components because even early in development individuals must have conceptual knowledge (i.e., naive theories about the world) that would constrain which perceptual correspondences would be detected and which would be ignored (Sloutsky 2003). A prototype theory might work adequately for quick and unreflective judgments. When a categorization decision requires reflection, however, individuals do not rely on simple similarity comparisons. For instance, if asked whether a dog that is surgically altered to look like a raccoon is a dog or a raccoon, respondents maintain that it remains a dog (see Keil 1989 and Gelman 2003, for discussion). Features thus differ in their conceptual centrality, and centrality is determined by the causal status of the features. While similarity-based accounts, such as prototype theory, hold that inductive generalizations are driven by similarity that is determined by automatically detected perceptual correspondences, the importance of a correspondence might vary across contexts (Sloutsky 2003).

Notwithstanding its criticisms of prototype theory, the value of the theory-theory position is questionable, especially with respect to legal interpretation. According to Hampton et al. (2009), it is uncertain whether the best way to account for categorization is via a prototype model that is based on the degree of match between the features of the item and the represented concept or, instead, via a theory-based model that addresses whether the defining cause generates the observed features. Like prototype theory, the way in which theory-theory accounts for categorization has been criticized. One problem is that theory-based theories rely on the crucial assumption that people are knowledgeable in ways that they often are not. Keil (2006) has described how people frequently overestimate their conceptual competence and that many well-educated people have only the most rudimentary understanding of the causal workings of the world around them. Ultimately, any increase in probabilistic accuracy offered by theory-theory should not be enough to prefer some version of it to some version of prototype theory. Further, like prototype theories, the available theory-theory models contain a high degree of complexity. Without consideration of a complex model, there is no reason to believe that alternatives to prototype theory, such as theory-theory, offer less uncertain analyses of categorization. To the contrary, the more readily perceivable features of prototype concepts make prototype theory a more realistic vehicle for nonmodel-based ordinary meaning analysis.

5.5: Categorization and Ordinary Meaning

As illustrated above, the difficulty of categorization arises not from identifying the most salient members of a category but, rather, from identifying criteria for unambiguously determining category membership. The view that any given concept has necessary and sufficient membership criteria is no longer taken seriously by linguists and philosophers, but once the falsity of the classical account is acknowledged categorization becomes significantly more difficult. If the classical theory is rejected, it will often be the case that the extension of a category will be unclear. The uncertainties are both conceptual and epistemological in nature. If there is epistemological uncertainty, an item might be a borderline member because it is not possible to discover the criteria of membership. The uncertainty thus is a matter of a state of knowledge rather than a state of understanding.

Some have argued that having a concept requires knowing the conditions of membership for the category. Philosophers such as Kripke (1972) and Putnam (1970, 1975) have argued persuasively, though, that semantic competence with a word does not require knowledge of the conditions of category membership. Thus, epistemological uncertainty on an individual level does not typically pose a barrier to using language in ordinary conversations.[29] Legal interpretation, however, often requires that difficult judgments of category membership be made, which requires a different level of understanding. In addition, legal interpretation requires that the interpreter be able to determine collective (i.e., ordinary meaning) usage regarding these difficult membership determinations. Wittgenstein (1953) may be correct that when questions of proper application arise there is no higher authority than a word's use by competent speakers, but it is aggregate use that matters, not the (bare) opinion of one person. Epistemological uncertainty about the collective view of a linguistic community regarding the extension of a concept is, in contrast to individual uncertainty, problematic for ordinary meaning determinations. Recall from chapter 3 that a meaning is ordinary if it is deemed to be so by some hypothesized interpreter. The hypothesized, or ideal, interpreter has a relatively high degree of linguistic ability. For instance, Scalia and Garner (2012, 31) argue that an interpreter must possess "aptitude in language" and the ability to conduct "historical linguistic research." The hypothesized ordinary interpreter might thus be described as a "sophisticated determiner of how ordinary people use language." This characterization does not, however, endow a legal interpreter with the ability to lessen the conceptual uncertainties associated with categorization.

Under the currently dominant judicial approach to interpretation, discerning collective usage is unproblematic. The interpreter can simply discern the necessary and sufficient conditions (even if fundamentally flawed) of category membership from a dictionary, possibly by transforming a general description into a necessary and sufficient test of membership. Under a more accurate view of language, however, like that described in this chapter, the conditions of membership within a category are not as easily available to the ordinary meaning interpreter. Judges are not in a position to determine the ordinary meaning of categories with a high degree of epistemic certainty if they are merely relying on their own perceptions of language usage. Judges can position themselves as representative members of society and apply the "sophisticated determiner of how ordinary people use language" standard, but, as explained above, there is no reason to believe that they have any special insight into categorization. Hanks (2013) explains that there is a natural human tendency to build categories by analogy. This tendency, however, is accompanied by a further tendency to idealize category membership on the basis of intensional properties. Respondents are able to list prototypical examples of common categories but, of course, are often uncertain about borderline items. Giving a definition in intensional terms, though, is a different matter. Typically, responses by everyday language users to a request for a definition are overrestrictive (e.g., "Fruits are something you eat, they grow on trees, they are sweet and juicy") (Hanks 2013, 341). Even if a judge is deemed to possess a sophisticated understanding of how ordinary people use language, there is little reason to believe that the judge is able to overcome these common tendencies unless she truly has an understanding of the concepts discussed in this chapter.

A judge's casual impressions about categorization are very different from the kind of rigorous empirical analysis that would be performed by a linguist. Undoubtedly, this difference helps to explain why judges so frequently rely on dictionary definitions. A dictionary definition represents empirical work that has already been performed by a trained professional. If a dictionary definition is insufficient though to give the ordinary meaning of a given word, especially with respect to marginal cases, the empirical question becomes much more difficult. Recall that one crucial aspect of categorization is that criteria of similarity for membership must be established. If a folk meaning is being sought, category membership becomes a probabilistic matter of determining some threshold sufficiency of properties that members of the category tend to have. When membership is seen as bivalent rather than as a matter of degree, as it typically must be in legal cases, determining the correct threshold is a stipulative matter. If it is assumed that there are random and individual sources of variation in categorization, then the group measure of how many subjects say X is in category Y may be taken as a measure of the degree to which X is considered to belong in Y. Considering that public usage or opinion is being sought, it is possible in theory to conduct experimental research and gather the results of categorization decisions and compare them to the designated threshold of category membership. For example, in the McCloskey and Glucksberg (1978) experiments, "tomato" had an intermediate level ranking for "fruit" (5.17 out of 10). The modal response was "yes," but 20 percent of the participants said "no," and there was a high degree of within-subjects inconsistency. Even with such uncertainty, it could be said that there was sufficient consensus that a tomato is a fruit, even though it is obviously not a prototypical fruit and a large percentage of the public may disagree with the designation.[30]

If evidence from surveys is not available, as it normally would not be in legal cases, the judge must consider other avenues of obtaining external validation of her intuitions. One possible source would be a language corpus, which is a large and structured set of texts often used for linguistic research. The American National Corpus, for example, is a text corpus of American English containing twenty-two million words produced since 1990. Other corpora are also available. Even a nonsystematic use of a language corpus offers a better foundation for a judicial assertion about language than does a bare reference to "common sense." For example, evidence that an "airplane" is never referred to as a "vehicle" might help confirm an analysis, whether prototype or otherwise, that a provision referencing a "vehicle" does not include airplanes.[31]

Even with evidence from corpora, an intuition that a category is fuzzy may reflect the limited epistemic situation of the interpreter. This limited epistemic situation creates conceptual uncertainty about how appropriate criteria for category membership might be determined. The conceptual question is related to the constituent question of what makes some meaning the ordinary one, but, unlike the case with some linguistic phenomena such as indexicals and universal quantifiers (examined in chaps. 3 and 4), the problem of categorization involves greater uncertainty than merely a degree of interpreter discretion within a given framework. Rather, if a nonmodel-based analysis is used, the very framework of analysis is inherently uncertain, regardless of the sophistication of the interpreter. As explained above, without a model it is uncertain which of the many features are relevant to categorization and how the features should be weighed. The constitutive theory of ordinary meaning may assume that there is some fact of the matter as to what the text means, but this fact may not be discoverable (at least with any degree of epistemic certainty) in many cases. In fact, it is not clear that judges can even reliably differentiate between intermediate items, for which category membership is problematic, and items that are clear members or clear nonmembers.

Legal interpreters must understand the conceptual and epistemological uncertainties involved in categorization and accept that these uncertainties undermine to some degree the successful application of prototype theory to legal texts. Namely, it seems that nonmodel-based approaches to prototype theory are the only realistic options for courts, and the gathering of survey evidence is typically infeasible. Nonetheless, even a flawed prototype analysis is typically superior, at least as a matter of ordinary meaning determination, to the practice of relying on a dictionary definition and treating it as though it sets forth necessary and sufficient conditions for category membership. Further, a prototype-like analysis can be supplemented through empirical research, such as evidence from corpora. Thus, as illustrated below, a rejection of the classical theory of meaning does not entail that interpretation must be seen as entirely discretionary and unmanageable.

5.6: Revisiting *White City Shopping Center v. PR Restaurants*

Returning to the *White City Shopping Center* case in light of the preceding explanation of prototype theory and the (flawed) classical theory of meaning, the deficiencies in the court's approach to interpretation are readily apparent. Recall that in the case the court had to decide whether a "burrito" is a "sandwich" and relied prominently on a dictionary definition (as well as "common sense") in holding that a burrito is not a sandwich. One of the more fundamental mistakes made by the court was the unclarity with which it framed the interpretive question. Recall that the court quoted a dictionary definition of "sandwich" and then concluded that "[u]nder this definition and as dictated by common sense, this court finds that the term "sandwich" is not commonly understood to include burritos, tacos, and quesadillas."[32] One possibility is that the court was determining whether some prototypical item within the subordinate level category "burrito" is considered by the public to fall within the basic level category "sandwich." Under this question, the dictionary definition of "sandwich" consulted by the court, which focused on the features of the category, was of unclear relevance. At the least, the court did not attempt to explain how the features related to the public's perception of how a burrito should be categorized. The dictionary definition could thus not serve *directly* as a basis for the court's claim that the term "sandwich" is not commonly understood to include burritos. The court could have relied on other evidence, of course, such as corpora analysis or the results from some survey. The court could also have engaged in a more creative kind of empirical analysis. Solan (2013), for example, observes that American menus found online do not list tacos under the category of sandwiches.[33] Instead of considering any external evidence, though, the court was left with its unelaborated citation to "common sense" as compelling its conclusion.

Alternatively, the court could have been analyzing whether the features of a prototypical burrito are sufficiently similar to the features of a prototypical sandwich so that one could call a burrito a sandwich. As explained above, this prototype analysis would offer a probabilistic view of whether a burrito falls within the sandwich category. In such a situation, the dictionary definition, which focused on features, would be of obvious relevance but of dubious accuracy. Recall that the court relied on a dictionary definition that describes a sandwich as "two thin pieces of bread, usually buttered, with a thin layer (as of meat, cheese, or savory mixture) spread between them." The court, as well as Scalia and Garner (2012), seemed to consider the dictionary definition as having set forth necessary and sufficient conditions for membership in the category "sandwiches." As so interpreted, though, the definition is quite unpersuasive. As Judge Posner (2012) has correctly observed

A sandwich does not have to have two slices of bread; it can have more than two (a club sandwich) and it can have just one (an open-faced sandwich). The slices of bread do not have to be thin, and the layer between them does not have to be thin either. The slices do not have to be slices of bread: a hamburger is regarded as a sandwich, and also a hot dog—and some people regard tacos and burritos as sandwiches, and a quesadilla is even more sandwich-like.[34]

Solan (2013) similarly criticizes the *White City Shopping Center* court's analysis of the "sandwich" category. Solan notes that Wikipedia refers to a "sandwich wrap" even though it is made with a "soft flatbread rolled around a filling." The Wikipedia entry, as Solan notes, also indicates that the "sandwich wrap" "probably comes from California, as a generalization of the Tex-Mex burrito."[35] Of course, it is not clear that Wikipedia is a reliable source of information about meaning. The same entry that Solan references also asserts that "[a] wrap is different from a sandwich: a sandwich has two distinct layers which are the top and bottom pieces of bread. A wrap, on the other hand, is one piece that completely surrounds the content of the wrap."[36]

As noted above, in addition to the dictionary definition and "common sense," the court in *White City Shopping Center* also based its interpretation on other evidence, including the failure of Panera Bread to include in the contract a definition of "sandwich." Judge Posner (2012) finds these points to be more persuasive than the dictionary definition, but they are merely burden shifting arguments with questionable persuasive value, especially as to the categorization issue. If a burrito *is* a sandwich, it is not clear why the drafter of the provision should have to explicitly stipulate that it is so. Among other reasons, a burrito is only one of many items that fall under the category. Must the drafter include an exhaustive list of items that are sandwiches? The court seems to have suffered from the common mistake of focusing on the dispute before it and inflating its likelihood in comparison to the many other possible disputes. On the other hand, if a burrito is *not* a sandwich, obviously only a stipulated definition that included burritos would benefit Panera Bread. Such an observation, though, is not relevant to whether a burrito is a sandwich. A third possibility is that the court was indicating (albeit implicitly) that in cases of doubt regarding category membership the drafter is obligated to specify all the items in the intermediate category that may or may not be members. Certainly, this reasoning might help resolve the case, but it is of questionable persuasive value. In addition, the point is not relevant to the lexical issue of the meaning of "sandwich."

5.7: Revisiting *Nix v. Hedden*

The flaws of the classical approach to definition, exemplified by the *White City Shopping Center* case, have been described in this chapter, but any alternative to the classical approach must be superior in ways that can be successfully implemented by courts. An approach that relies on prototype theory but without a statistical or mathematical model depends on the intuitions of the interpreter. Yet, those intuitions can be supplemented with various kinds of empirical evidence, including corpora (and, of course, research by linguists and philosophers). The resulting ordinary meaning interpretation is likely to be superior to that produced by relying on a dictionary definition that is treated as though it sets forth necessary and sufficient criteria for category membership. At the least, it should make judges more aware of the uncertainties of definition and, in turn, more cautious about deciding cases without consideration of broader purpose and consistency with other values such as coherence with other legal provisions.

In contrast to the White City Shopping Center case, there were some positive aspects of the Court's decision in *Nix v. Hedden*. For instance, the Court recognized the difference between a technical meaning and an ordinary meaning and the distinction between scientific definitions of "fruit" and "vegetable" and how these terms are used in ordinary discourse. Further, the Court did not place undue weight on a dictionary definition or construe the definition as providing necessary and sufficient conditions for category membership (although it seemed to believe that the features

it identified provided at least sufficient conditions for category membership). On the other hand, the Court's opinion is weak in important ways.
For one, the Court seems to believe that the determination of ordinary
meaning is a matter of common sense. This assertion is unfortunate for
various reasons. A belief that ordinary meaning rather than technical
meaning should be sought does not entail that ordinary meaning is something that all legal interpreters can determine without much delibera-
tion or external guidance. To the contrary, as this book has demonstrated,
many judicial decisions are based on fundamental errors that could have
been rectified through a greater understanding of language, not through
self-referential appeals to "common sense."

Furthermore, and more importantly, the Court's prototype-like analysis was in some ways unconvincing. The Court referred to the "common
language of the people" but gave no evidence for its rather conclusory
analysis. It identified two features of vegetables: (1) they are "grown in
kitchen gardens"; and (2) they are "usually served at dinner" but, unlike
fruits generally, not as dessert. The Court did not, however, attempt to define fruit, other than to note that fruits are generally served as dessert (a
questionable assertion in 2015, if not in 1893). This one feature is obviously not sufficient to identify an item as a fruit. Consider the eleven features of fruit identified in Hampton (1979) or the five features identified
in Geeraerts (2010), both discussed above. Would, for example, a "lemon"
not be considered to be a fruit because it is not served as dessert (at least
by itself, which would seem to be required by the Court)? What about
"olives," considered by some to be a fruit? The Court's failure to attempt
any kind of sensible definition of fruit undermined its conclusion that a
tomato is not a fruit.

The two features identified by the Court are neither necessary nor sufficient to identify an item as a "vegetable" but are they sufficient to distinguish a "vegetable" from a "fruit"? Note that, as explained above, the
Court's task of categorizing was made easier by the fact that it was determining whether an item belonged in one of two categories. One problem,
though, is that the range of items that are grown in "kitchen gardens," one
of the two criteria, is not entirely clear. There are a number of exotic vegetables that may not be grown in many (or any) kitchen gardens. Further,
some things clearly designated as fruits are grown in kitchen gardens.
Some of these fruits may be served during dinner. "Fruit salad," for example, is a dish consisting of various kinds of fruit that is often served at
dinner. The dish can, however, also be served as dessert, which may be

said to exclude the items from being considered vegetables (although the answer is not at all clear from the Court's analysis). Another problem is that some vegetables may not often be served during dinner. Fennel, for example, may be a part of dishes served at dinner, but it is not served by itself without other ingredients (including spices). Can it be distinguished from the avocado, considered by many to be a well-known fruit, which can also be served at dinner (with or without other ingredients)? Avocados may be used in desserts, but that could also be said for other vegetables (such as the sweet potato).

It is difficult to deny that the Court's analysis is flawed in the sense that counterexamples to the two identified features of "vegetables" can be found (although unacknowledged by the court). The two features do not offer a sufficient basis for distinguishing between "vegetables" and "fruits." Still, the Court's analysis in *Nix v. Hedden* compares favorably to the court's analysis in *White City Shopping Center v. PR Restaurants*. Even if flawed, the prototype analysis in *Nix* better approximated the ordinary meaning of the terms at issue than did the dictionary definition that the court relied on in *White City Shopping Center*. Further, under the classical approach (with its necessary and sufficient conditions for category membership), it is not clear why the interpreter would need to seek empirical evidence to support a definition. In fact, doing so would seem to undermine the illusion of determinacy created by the definition. In contrast, an alternative to the classical view like prototype theory embraces the indeterminacy of definitions and the desirability of empirical evidence.

5.8: Intangible Categories and Other Definitional Difficulties

As illustrated above, prototype theory can be applied to both natural kinds and artifacts, and empirical evidence from corpora and other sources can supplement the analysis. Recall that artifacts are objects intentionally made to serve a given purpose, and natural objects come into being without human intervention.[37] Many legal provisions contain terms, though, that refer to things that are not concrete objects. Some of these terms do not exist outside the law, which makes the determination of meaning a difficult proposition, particularly if the legislature does not provide stipulated definitions.[38] In fact, this situation, which is common, is analogous to a type of indeterminacy that is different from the kinds of vagueness associated with borderline cases or a concept's extension. In general, a term or provision is underdetermined if it fails to "give enough detail for the purpose at hand" (Sorensen 1989, 175). Engberg and Heller (2008) refer to this as "communicative underdeterminacy." Similarly, Ludlow (2014) distinguishes between underspecificity and underdeterminacy. Meaning underspecification involves situations where it is undetermined which of several determinate meanings were intended. For example, one way of treating ambiguity is to assert that the term, such as "bank," has a single lexical entry with an underspecified meaning because it has not been specified which of the typical meanings was intended. Of course, as chapter 2 and this chapter have discussed, sentential context often can help specify the correct meaning. In contrast to underspecification is underdetermination, which does not suppose that there are determinate word meanings to specify. Instead, the word meanings are yet to be fully fleshed out and will never be fully fleshed out.

In many cases, communicative underdeterminacy is relatively easy to identify. For instance, the statement

(1)   some event will happen at some time

is vague in the lack-of-detail sense. Both "some event" and "some time" are, for most purposes, insufficiently informative in a way that needs little elaboration. The statement in (1) represents more than just a category with a fuzzy boundary. Rather, the indeterminacy extends beyond the boundary of (1). If required to provide guidance, (1) will require significant nonlanguage-based precisification.

Legal texts contain a significant amount of communicative underdeterminacy, but much of it is less obvious than the underdeterminacy in (1). The example in (1) contains language that is obviously vague in most contexts. In turn, legal texts often contain terms that are problematic for interpreters in the same ways as (1), but which are less obviously underdeterminate. Specifically, the terms in legal texts often refer to intangible concepts that either do not exist outside the law, as indicated above, or exist at too high a level of generality compared to the needs of the legal profession. As explained in the next section, the features associated with intangible concepts raise difficult issues for ordinary meaning determinations. Significantly, the underdeterminacy requires substantial nonlinguistic judicial judgment to precisify the concepts sufficiently to satisfy the needs of the law. In other words, although courts typically maintain that an interpretation is based on the ordinary meaning of the relevant language, other facts must necessarily determine the meanings of the relevant provisions.

A separate but related problem concerns the common situation where concepts are combined. The issue of defining a complex concept extends beyond intangible concepts to include natural kinds and artifacts but is addressed here because of the additional difficulties it raises for defining intangible concepts that do not exist outside of the law. Conceptual combination is often illustrated using the "pet fish" example. Something is a "pet fish" if it is both a "pet" and a "fish." One might think that something is a stereotypical pet fish if it is a stereotypical pet and a stereotypical fish. The problem, though, is that a good example of a pet fish (perhaps, a guppy) is neither a prototypical pet (i.e., some breed of dog) nor a prototypical fish (perhaps, a trout) (Connolly et al. 2007). The example raises the issue of whether the two concepts, "pet" and "fish," can be combined in a straightforward way in order to create a complex concept that inherits the stereotypes of the constituents. As the pet fish problem indicates, complex concepts require some theory as to how the separate concepts, each with its own prototype structure, can be expected to combine.

One theory, the default to the stereotype prediction (DS), is that the prototype corresponding to a combination, say an adjective and a noun, inherits the properties of the prototype corresponding to the noun of the combination (Jönsson and Hampton 2008). Thus, the prototype corresponding to "uncomfortable sofa" shares all of the properties of the "sofa" prototype, excluding those properties that concern comfort (Jönsson and Hampton 2008). A competing theory is that the combinatorial process does not involve propagation of the prototypical properties of the separate concepts to the combined concept. Instead, world knowledge is required in order to make informed judgments about the likely properties of the combined concept (Jönsson and Hampton 2008). Even DS, which posits that properties are inherited by complex concepts, concedes that it is not a straightforward process and that other factors might influence the characteristics of the complex concept (Jönsson and Hampton 2008). For example, some studies have indicated that participants do not assume, even as a default strategy, that complex concepts inherit the properties of their constituents. Furthermore, this effect is greater for atypical modifiers (Connolly et al. 2007). Thus, the sentence,

(2)   Baby Peruvian ducks have webbed feet

is deemed by subjects to be less likely to be true than the sentence,

(3)   Ducks have webbed feet.

*   *   *

As the above discussion indicates, the kind of intangible categories often found in legal texts raise difficult interpretive issues. Most importantly, some of the terms do not exist outside the law. These sorts of concepts often result in a kind of underdeterminacy that grants judges significant interpretive discretion. This discretion is particularly present in situations involving complex concepts, where it is not always clear how the constituent concepts should combine. One important source of information, world knowledge, has a greatly attenuated relevance when a complex concept that does not exist outside of the law is at issue. As the next section illustrates with the statutory phrase "pattern of racketeering activity," in such situations courts still purport to apply the ordinary meaning concept but often struggle in constructing how the ordinary meaning of the relevant concept should be conceived.

5.8.1: RICO's "Pattern" Requirement

One notorious example of communicative underdeterminacy involves the Racketeer Influenced and Corrupt Organizations Act (RICO).[39] For good reasons, the RICO statute has been the subject of extensive criticism. A major reason for the criticism is due to the perception that the statute's key terms are greatly underdetermined in a way similar to that in (1) above.[40] Predictably, the Supreme Court has struggled to define RICO's terms and has been inconsistent in its view of RICO's determinacy. At times, the Court has created additional elements that cannot easily be tied to the ordinary meaning of the statutory terms, even though the Court has proclaimed that it is merely determining the ordinary meaning of the terms. At other times, though, it has rejected additional elements or restrictions on the basis that the ordinary meanings of the terms do not include such restrictions.

RICO prohibits "any person" from: (1) acquiring an "enterprise" with money derived from a "pattern of racketeering activity";[41] (2) acquiring an "enterprise" through a "pattern of racketeering activity";[42] or (3) operating an "enterprise" through a "pattern of racketeering activity."[43] The definition of "racketeering activity" in § 1961(1) includes a number of federal offenses and state crimes and is relatively straightforward.[44] In contrast, determining the meaning of the "pattern of racketeering activity" phrase is not a straightforward matter. The statute defines the term as follows:

"pattern of racketeering activity" requires at least two acts of racketeering activity, one of which occurred after the effective date of this chapter and the last of which occurred within ten years (excluding any period of imprisonment) after the commission of a prior act of racketeering activity.[45]

Notwithstanding the statutory definition, the phrase "pattern of racketeering activity" can be viewed as a prototypical instance of vagueness due to underdeterminacy. Crucially, the definition does not offer sufficient criteria for the establishment of a "pattern." The definition provides only the minimum necessary conditions for the existence of a pattern and implies ("at least two acts") that further requirements are necessary. The two stipulated requirements, (1) at least two acts of racketeering activity that are committed (2) within ten years of each other, are insubstantial and do not serve to define the meaning of "pattern" in any significant way. The two elements are obviously necessary but plainly not sufficient by themselves to constitute a "pattern." How could a pattern exist, in any context, with fewer than two instances of conduct?

The "pattern of racketeering" definition thus leaves crucial, and quite specific, questions unanswered that cannot be decided by simply determining the ordinary meaning of "pattern." For example, do two predicate acts always constitute a pattern? The answer is pretty clearly "no." If not then, how many are necessary? Must the predicate acts be related? If so, in what ways must the acts be related? Perhaps less obviously, must two separate schemes be proven in order to constitute a "pattern"? Undoubtedly, some precisification can be made of "pattern" when considered with the sentential context "of racketeering activity," but this precisification would involve significant discretion to shape doctrine based on nonlanguage justifications.

In fact, the Supreme Court has precisified the "pattern" requirement, although it has been reluctant to admit doing so.[46] In *Sedima, S.P.R.L. v. Imrex Co.*[47] and *H.J. Inc. v. Northwestern Bell Tel. Co.*,[48] for example, the Court addressed the pattern requirement, with the later *H.J. Inc.* decision confirming and expanding the *Sedima* holding. In *H.J. Inc.*, the Court indicated that it was guided by the "ordinary meaning" of "pattern."[49] It referenced the *Oxford English Dictionary* definition of "pattern" as an "arrangement or order of things or activity."[50] Yet, the Court implicitly recognized that neither the stipulated definition nor the dictionary definition, offering a general definition for a very general concept, provided sufficiently specific criteria that would enable courts to distinguish a "pattern of racketeering activity" from mere acts of racketeering activity. In fact, the Court conceded that "[t]he text of RICO conspicuously fails anywhere to identify . . . forms of relationship or external principles to be used in determining whether racketeering activity falls into a pattern for purposes of the Act."[51] The Court noted that in drafting RICO Congress followed a "pattern of utilizing terms and concepts of breadth" and that "developing a meaningful concept of "pattern" within the existing statutory framework has proved to be no easy task."[52]

Realizing that the ordinary meaning of "pattern" would not offer specific enough criteria for the purposes of RICO, the Court in *H.J. Inc.* precisified the "pattern" requirement by relying on the legislative history associated with RICO, as well as the terms of a separate statute. From the legislative history of RICO, the Court picked out the phrase, "continuity plus relationship," and determined that these two elements are both necessary and sufficient to constitute a pattern. The Court determined that the "relationship" element is similar to that found in a provision elsewhere in the Organized Crime Control Act of 1970 and requires criminal acts that "have the same or similar purposes, results, participants, victims, or methods of commission, or otherwise are interrelated by distinguishing characteristics and are not isolated events."[53] In turn, the Court indicated that "continuity" "is both a closed-and open-ended concept, referring either to a closed period of repeated conduct, or to past conduct that by its nature projects into the future with a threat of repetition."[54] Even this (incoherent) definition of "continuity" needed precisification, with the Court indicating that

> A party alleging a RICO violation may demonstrate continuity over a closed period by proving a series of related predicates extended over a substantial period of time. Predicate acts extending over a few weeks or months and threatening no future criminal conduct do not satisfy this requirement.[55]

Even if dismissing the narrow versus wide context principle (introduced in chap. 3) that helps to distinguish ordinary meaning from communicative meaning, and assuming that the meaning of "racketeering activity" is certain in terms of what types of crimes qualify, it cannot be said that the Court was determining the ordinary meaning of "pattern" or "pattern of racketeering activity." The legislative history considered by the Court was not relevant to the ordinary meaning of "pattern," but rather (at most) revealed the views of the legislature regarding the requirement in light of the statutory purpose. As Justice Scalia argued in his dissenting opinion in *H.J., Inc.*, a "pattern," even a "pattern of racketeering activity," does not require as a matter of language conduct that extends over a "substantial period of time."[56] Solan (1993, 105) has similarly demonstrated that common sentences can "use the word 'pattern' in the context of a series of events that took place over a very short period of time." Thus, while the court's attempts to precisify the "pattern" requirement may have been well intended, even if haphazardly performed, the interpretations were driven by nonlinguistic motivations and do not represent the ordinary meaning of the provisions.

5.8.2: RICO's "Enterprise" Requirement

Unlike "pattern of racketeering activity," "enterprise" is a concept that exists outside the law. In RICO, the concept was given a stipulated definition, which is staggeringly broad. Section 1961(4) defines "enterprise" as "includ[ing] any individual, partnership, corporation, association, or other legal entity, and any union or group of individuals associated in fact although not a legal entity." It is difficult to imagine that the stipulated definition, which includes "any individual" and "any group of individuals associated in fact," is not broader than the ordinary meaning of "enterprise." Notably, other than the list of things that are to be included within the "enterprise" concept, the definition does not offer any criteria for membership in the category. Solan (1993, 107) argues that

> there is nothing the least bit clear about what the word "enterprise" means in RICO. While we do have a sense of a typical enterprise, I would be extremely hard pressed to state the necessary and sufficient conditions for membership in the class of enterprises.

Solan's criticisms are accurate only if it is agreed that § 1961(4) is not to be read literally and that, like "pattern of racketeering activity," there are necessary criteria for membership that are not specified in the definition. The difficulty is that, in contrast to the "pattern of racketeering activity" stipulated definition, it is not clear whether § 1961(4) is intended to offer a sufficient definition of "enterprise." If, for example, "any individual" (or "any group of individuals associated in fact") is to be regarded as an "enterprise" under RICO, regardless of the circumstances, the definition in § 1961(4) is quite clear. The problem with such an interpretation is that it helps to establish RICO as a statute with a dangerously broad reach. Not surprisingly, most of the Supreme Court's interpretations of "enterprise" have focused on whether § 1961(4) provides an exclusive definition or, instead, whether the ordinary meaning of "enterprise" requires criteria that are not manifest in the stipulated definition.

One case where the Supreme Court purported to determine the ordinary meaning of "enterprise" but instead focused on the exclusivity of the stipulated definition was *United States v. Turkette*.[57] In *Turkette*, the Court declined to recognize an implicit criterion for membership in § 1961(4). The Court purported to give "enterprise" its ordinary or "plain" meaning and declined to require that the "enterprise" requirement be limited to "legitimate" enterprises, saying that:

> On its face, the definition appears to include both legitimate and illegitimate enterprises within its scope; it no more excludes criminal enterprises than it does legitimate ones. Had Congress not intended to reach criminal associations, it could easily have narrowed the sweep of the definition by inserting a single word, "legitimate."

Similarly, in *National Organization for Women v. Scheidler*,[58] the court held that the RICO statute did not require that the racketeering enterprise harbor an economic motive or that the predicate acts of racketeering spring from one. The Court pointed out that nowhere in the RICO statute is there a requirement of such a motive.

The Supreme Court's reasoning in *Turkette* and *Scheidler* is specious, at least as a methodology of determining ordinary meaning.[59] The Court failed to acknowledge (and perhaps did not recognize) that a stipulated definition, like that in § 1961(4), does not preclude criteria that are implicit in the definition and are aspects of the term's ordinary meaning. In fact, by indicating that Congress could have inserted the word "legitimate," the Court seemed to assume the opposite. If, hypothetically, the ordinary meaning of "enterprise" is limited to "legitimate" entities, the word "legitimate" would of course not be necessary in a stipulated definition, making the Court's observation that the word "legitimate" did not appear in the definition rather off point. A more legitimate approach to the interpretation would involve the determination of both the ordinary meaning of the stipulated definition and the ordinary meaning of the term at issue (i.e., "enterprise"). Only if the interpreter is convinced that the stipulated definition is exclusive or is inconsistent with the general ordinary meaning of the term should the ordinary meaning not be relevant.

The Supreme Court has continued to interpret the "enterprise" term broadly, even when considering the relationship between § 1961(4) and other RICO provisions. For instance, in *Cedric Kushner Promotions, Ltd. v. King*,[60] the Court held that a person (in this case Don King) who is the president and sole shareholder of a corporation can be a "person" for RICO purposes even when the corporation is the "enterprise." The Court engaged in a fairly straightforward, literal interpretation, reasoning that a natural person is "distinct from the corporation itself, a legally different entity with different rights and responsibilities due to its different legal status. And we can find nothing in the statute that requires more "separateness" than that."[61] The Court emphasized the literal meaning of the "person" and "enterprise" terms, reasoning that "[1]inguistically speaking," an employee (the "person") can conduct the affairs of a corporation (the "enterprise") through illegal acts, and "linguistically speaking," the employee and the corporation are separate entities.[62]

5.8.3: An Attempt to Apply Prototype Theory to RICO

The Supreme Court's inconsistent mix of literal interpretation and precisification does not represent a coherent attempt to determine the ordinary meaning of RICO's terms. Note that the Court's attempts to determine the "plain" meaning of the terms mostly involved dictionary definitions and assumptions that RICO's definitions are exclusive. Among other problems, such an approach does not address the "pet fish" problems that arise when a complex concept is being interpreted. It is not clear though that a more sophisticated approach to ordinary meaning could have made the provisions any more determinate than have the Supreme Court's interpretations, although a more sophisticated approach would have resulted in greater coherence. Perhaps surprisingly, however, at least one court has attempted to apply prototype theory to RICO's terms in an effort to make its terms more determinate. In *Fitzgerald v. Chrysler Corp.*,[63] the Seventh Circuit held that, although the corporation Chrysler could be a "person" under RICO, affiliates and agents of Chrysler could not be considered to be an "enterprise." Judge Posner, writing for the court, worried that

> Read literally, RICO would encompass every fraud case against a corporation, provided only that a pattern of fraud and some use of the mails or of telecommunications to further the fraud were shown; the corporation would be the RICO person and the corporation plus its employees the "enterprise."

The court noted that other courts had already determined that an employer and its employees cannot constitute a RICO enterprise and that such an exclusion "doesn't emerge from the statutory language; it emerges from a desire to make the statute make sense and have some limits."[64] The court explained that with a broadly worded statute like RICO there "there is a danger of its being applied to situations absurdly remote from the concerns of the statute's framers."[65]

In order to avoid "absurd applications" of RICO, the court declared that it would apply prototype theory as follows:

> first [] identify the prototype situation to which the statute is addressed. That need not be the most common case to which it is applied; the prototype may be effectively deterred because its legal status is clear. The second step is to determine how close to the prototype the case before the court is—how close, in other words, the family resemblance is between the prototypical case and the case at hand.

The court then determined that

> The prototypical RICO case is one in which a person bent on criminal activity seizes control of a previously legitimate firm and uses the firm's resources, contacts, facilities, and appearance of legitimacy to perpetrate more, and less easily discovered, criminal acts than he could do [without having taken over the firm].[66]

A "step away" from the prototypical case is

> one in which the criminal uses the acquired enterprise to engage in some criminal activities but for the most part is content to allow it to continue to conduct its normal, lawful business—and many of the employees of the business may be unaware that it is controlled and being used by a criminal.[67]

In the "next step" away,

> the criminal seizes control of a subsidiary of a corporation and perverts the subsidiary into a criminal enterprise that manages in turn to wrest sufficient control or influence over the parent corporation to use it to commit criminal acts.[68]

On the basis of the "prototype" and two category members, the court declared that it "could not find any support for . . . applying RICO to a free-standing corporation such as Chrysler merely because Chrysler does business through agents, as virtually every manufacturer does."[69]

Judge Posner might have used prototype-like reasoning in *Fitzgerald* and arguably reached a persuasive interpretation if considering only the optimal reach of the statute, but it should be clear that the analysis was not directed toward determining the ordinary meaning of "enterprise." Although Judge Posner indicated that his prototype method of determining the meaning of "enterprise" was consistent with a "plain language" approach to interpretation, Judge Posner's focus was on the prototypical target of RICO and not the prototypical instance of "enterprise." One focus has to do with the purpose of the statute and the other with the ordinary meaning of the term "enterprise" outside the RICO context. The court's discussion focuses solely on the "prototypical RICO case" and other cases that are a "step" or two steps from the prototypical case. Nowhere is there an attempt to determine what "enterprise" means generally, outside the RICO context.

Apart from whether the prototype analysis was used to determine the ordinary meaning of "enterprise," Judge Posner's analysis glossed over the most difficult aspects of using prototype theory to determine the meaning of legal terms. Recall that determining typicality does not simultaneously identify the threshold to be used for category membership. Instead, the two determinations are related but distinct. Posner's prototype analysis merely described the prototypical RICO case, plus two others that are apparently sufficiently similar to fall within the scope of RICO, and explained that the case at issue was sufficiently removed from the three cases so as not to fall within the scope of RICO. The opinion does not develop criteria, though, for determining whether a marginal case nevertheless falls under RICO, unless "not more than two steps beyond the prototypical case" can be considered the criterion for category membership. If so, why is two steps the proper standard instead of "three steps" or "four steps"? Whatever the source of the criterion (whether from legislative history or some other source), an answer to this crucial question seems necessary. As a consequence of the court's reasoning, though, later courts within the jurisdiction are not left with much of a framework for applying the "enterprise" concept.

5.9: Problems with the Supreme Court's Current Approach to Word Meaning and Sentential Context

5.9.1: Sentential Context and the Interpretation of 18 U.S.C. § 924(c)(1)(A)

As this book has illustrated, in many situations accurately determining the meaning of a word is dependent on the surrounding context. Indexicals, examined in chapter 3, are a prototypical example. Other words, such as quantifiers (examined in chap. 4), are also widely seen (as least by linguists and philosophers) as having their referential scope (i.e., their domains) determined by the surrounding context. A different class of words, typically verbs, also derives their meanings from context, typically sentential context. The situation is somewhat analogous to the earlier discussed underdeterminacy associated with intangible concepts that either do not exist outside of the law or exist at too high a level of generality compared to the needs of the legal profession. Yet, in some cases it is possible for these words to have relatively definite ordinary meanings by deriving a stereotypical, ordinary meaning through combination with the other words in the sentence. Further, linguistic evidence of these combinations does not necessarily depend on prototype theory but, rather, on other theories of meaning that are arguably superior (or at least supplemental) in explaining the contribution that sentential context makes to meaning.

As outlined at the beginning of this chapter, one example where proper consideration of sentential context, and the cognitive science insights that help explain its contribution to word meaning, should have changed the interpretation chosen is the Supreme Court's infamous decision in *Smith v. United States*.[70] Recall that the *Smith* case required the Court to interpret a federal statute, 18 U.S.C. § 924(c)(1)(A), that provides for enhanced punishment if the defendant "uses" a firearm "during and in relation to . . . [a] drug trafficking crime."[71] Remarkably for a routine criminal statute providing a penalty enhancement and presenting no constitutional issues, § 924(c)(1)(A) has been interpreted by the Supreme Court on multiple occasions. In *Smith*, where the defendant traded a gun for drugs, the Court held that the statute does not require that the firearm have been used as a weapon. The Court explained that when a word is not defined by statute, as most are not, courts normally construe it in accord with its "ordinary or natural meaning."[72] The Court stated that exchanging a firearm for drugs "can be described as "use" within the everyday meaning of that term."[73] The Court consulted two dictionaries regarding the word "use" and concluded that it means "to employ" or "to derive service from."[74] The Court rejected the argument that "uses" has a reduced scope in § 924(c)(1)(A) because it appears alongside the word "firearm."[75] The Court reasoned that "it is one thing to say that the ordinary meaning of "uses a firearm" *includes* using a firearm as a weapon," "[b]ut it is quite another to conclude that, as a result, the phrase also *excludes* any other use."[76] Thus, because "one can use a firearm in a number of ways," "[t]hat one example of "use" is the first to come to mind . . . does not preclude us from recognizing that there are other "uses" that qualify as well."[77]

Because of the broad meaning of "use," the Court concluded that the statute's language "sweeps broadly, punishing any 'us[e]' of a firearm, so long as the use is 'during and in relation to' a 'drug trafficking offense.'"[78] Therefore, the Court reasoned, "it is both reasonable and normal to say that [the defendant] 'used' his MAC-10 in his drug trafficking offense by trading it for cocaine."[79] In the Court's view, if Congress had intended that the firearm must have been used as a weapon in order for the enhanced punishment to apply, it could have included the words "as a weapon" in the statute.[80]

In dissent, Justice Scalia criticized the Court's failure to properly consider context in determining the ordinary meaning of "use." First, Justice Scalia pointed out the "elastic" nature of the word "use."[81] Second, Justice Scalia pointed out, correctly, that "[t]o use an instrumentality ordinarily means to use it for its intended purpose."[82] Thus, "to speak of 'using a firearm' is to speak of using it for its distinctive purpose, *i.e.*, as a weapon."[83] Justice Scalia reasoned that, "[w]hen someone asks, 'Do you use a cane?,' he is not inquiring whether you have your grandfather's silver-handled walking stick on display in the hall; he wants to know whether you *walk* with a cane."[84] In Justice Scalia's view, the words "as a weapon" were "reasonably implicit" from the context of the statute.[85]

In a follow-up case to *Smith*, the court held in *Watson v. United States*[86] that a person who trades drugs for a gun does not "use" a firearm within the meaning of the statute.[87] According to the court, "the meaning of the verb 'uses' has to turn on the language as we normally speak it."[88] In the court's view, the proper interpretation must "appeal to the ordinary" because "there is no other source of a reasonable inference about what Congress understood when writing or what its words will bring to the mind of a careful reader."[89] Based on its own understanding of common usage, the Court reasoned as follows:

> [t]he Government may say that a person "uses" a firearm simply by receiving it in a barter transaction, but no one else would. A boy who trades an apple to get

a granola bar is sensibly said to use the apple, but one would never guess which way this commerce actually flowed from hearing that the boy used the granola.[90]

Significantly, the Court implicitly changed its interpretive methodology from the *Smith* case to the *Watson* case. In *Smith* the Court emphasized the dictionary meaning of "any" and discounted Justice Scalia's examples that were designed to distinguish between ordinary meaning and dictionary meaning. In contrast, in *Watson* the Court emphasized the language "as we normally speak it" and used the bartering hypothetical to emphasize what it viewed as the ordinary meaning of the provision. Also, although not connected to ordinary meaning, the Court's reliance in *Smith* on the provision's purpose of combating gun violence was notably missing from its decision in *Watson*. If the purpose of the provision is invoked when a court is justifying a broad interpretation, it should similarly be considered when the court is explaining a narrow interpretation.

5.9.2: Linguistic and Cognitive Science Insights Relevant to the Interpretation of 18 U.S.C. § 924(c)(1)(A)

As its interpretations of § 924(c)(1)(A) indicate, the Court purports to give textual language its ordinary meaning, but its methodology in the cases described above was flawed. Geis (1995, 1134) suggests that the majority in Smith was referring to the conventional or ordinary meaning of the language and the dissent the "contextual significance" of it. Such a distinction, though, should not be made as ordinary meaning must take account of some contextual evidence.[91] Both the majority and the dissent purported to focus on the ordinary meaning of the language, but the majority misconceived how the ordinary meaning should be determined. First, by relying so heavily on the dictionary definition of "use" in *Smith*, the Court failed to appreciate the characteristics of the verb, causing it to express the erroneous assumption that Congress would have used the phrase "as a weapon" if it had wanted the statute limited in that way. The verb "use," though, is designated as a "light verb" and a "weak verb" (Pustejovsky 1995, 87; Ritter and Rosen 1996, 29). The "light" and "weak verb" categorizations are meant to indicate the underspecified nature of "use."[92] Weak verbs "combine with their objects to form a complex semantic structure," but by themselves the verbs "would not have sufficient semantic resources to create" a complex semantic structure (Abdulkhaliq 2001, 68). Verbs such as "use" thus have great utility because they can occur with a variety of different objects and permit an economy of expression that allows fundamental information to be ellipsed, such as the nature of the particular activity that is denoted by the verb (Pustejovsky 1998b, 303).

In a broader sense, the Court failed to understand the nature of ellipsis and semantic composition. An important, and empirically based, principle of grammars is that speakers produce the minimum linguistic information sufficient to achieve the speaker's communicational needs (Hawkins 2004, 38). In its interpretations of § 924(c)(1)(A), the Court failed to appreciate this insight and thus failed to recognize the increased difficulty of lexical semantics when faced with legislative ellipsis of important sentential content. A linguistic ellipsis is a "truncated or partial linguistic form" "in which constituents normally occurring in a sentence are superficially absent, licensed by structurally present prior antecedents" (May 2002, 1094). It is a ubiquitous and natural way to avoid periphrastic constructions. For example, a case of verb-phrase ellipsis occurs in the following sentence:

(4)   Max went to the store, and Oscar did, too. (May 2002)

The sentence without ellipsis would read:

(5)   Max went to the store, and Oscar went to the store, too.

Psychologist Matthew Traxler and colleagues indicate that expressions with fully specified event structures are rare (i.e., are ellipsed) when the event is commonly associated with the noun (Traxler et al. 2005, 1–2). According to Traxler et al. (2005), in normal usage, a fully specified event structure is used less than 5 percent of the time. Full-event structures tend to occur only with less predictable activities.

On the basis of studies examining the processing of expressions argued to require enriched semantic composition, Traxler et al. (2005, 1–2) explain that a challenge for interpreters is that noun phrases denoting entities are difficult to process when they follow verbs that require event complements. The verbs "begin," "finish," and "enjoy," for example, require postverbal arguments that semantically represent events. Consider the sentence,

(6)   The boy began the book.

The sentence is difficult to process because it contains a noun phrase denoting an entity (namely, "book") that follows a verb requiring an event complement (namely, "began"). The increased processing difficulty is a result of related issues. First, the ellipsis of a fully specified event structure requires complex mental operations to construct a suitable event sense. Comprehenders construct an event sense of the complement by implicitly generating an activity that is commonly associated with the complement noun and compatible with the agent of the clause. For example, (6) could be interpreted as "The boy began reading the book."[93] Second, the ellipsis of a fully specified event structure may engender competition between alternative interpretations. Thus, (6) could either be interpreted as "The boy began writing the book" or, as indicated above, "The boy began reading the book." As Traxler et al. (2005) indicate, though, if the sentence were intended to be interpreted as "The boy began to translate the book," the full event structure would most likely have been specified. The reason is that "[f]ull event structures tend to occur only with less predictable activities like *translate the book*" (2).

According to Traxler et al. (2005, 5), the findings described above "provide behavioral evidence for the psychological reality of an enriched form of composition."[94] In short, a subordinate context may lead to selection of subordinate meanings, but "dominant meanings are understood more readily than are subordinate meanings in a wide range of tasks" (Klepousniotou, Titone, and Romero 2008, 1534). These kinds of cognitive science findings should have implications for ordinary meaning. If nothing else, they should convince courts that acontextual consideration of dictionary definitions, as occurred in the *Smith* case, will not result in interpretations that represent the ordinary meanings of the relevant provisions.

5.9.3: Debating the Proper Approach to Interpreting 18 U.S.C. § 924(c)(1)(A)

Even for a Supreme Court case, the *Smith* decision [and to a lesser degree the Court's other cases involving the interpretation of § 924(c)(1) (A)] has achieved a sort of notoriety among commentators on legal interpretation that far outstrips its importance as a legal precedent. Perhaps this is a result of the easily understandable facts and legal background. The case requires little legal knowledge to understand the reasoning used in the opinions, and the opinions focused primarily on linguistic issues rather than legal ones. In short, the case provides a perfect vehicle even among nonlawyers for debating the proper approach to ordinary meaning and legal interpretation. It is not necessary to rehearse all the various scholarly analyses that have been made of the Court's interpretations of § 924(c)(1)(A). Rather, a few different approaches that have been taken will very briefly be described. One objective of the discussion is to illustrate that the ordinary meaning of a statutory provision should be competently analyzed *before* general inferences and arguments about interpretation are made on the basis of the particular provision. A related and more important point is that while linguistic analysis is useful, when possible it should be done in light of some theory of meaning and interpretation that focuses on systematicities of language.

5.9.4: 18 U.S.C. § 924(c)(1)(A) and General Claims about Interpretation

A number of scholars have used the Court's interpretations of § 924(c) (1)(A) as an opportunity to derive general inferences about interpretation from the nature of the language in the provision. For instance, some have used *Smith* as a vehicle to argue against textualism. González (2011, 624), for instance, argues that § 924(c)(1)(A) is "ambiguous" and that the evidence of legislative intent regarding the meaning of the provision was both "sparse" and "inconclusive." In González's view, the majority and dissenting opinions miss the "pivotal question" of "[w]hat factors referee between two plausible but divergent understandings of ordinary meaning" (624). González reasons that

> Nothing in the law of interpretation can locate a single ordinary meaning for the word "uses" in the sentencing statute. In *Smith*, the underlying statutory text was fraught with irreducible ambiguity. Indeed, *Smith* seemed to be a case in which the precise outer contours of the word "uses"—specifically, as to whether that word included or excluded bartering drugs for a gun—took no discernible shape until after the Court had interpreted the statute. (624)

González concludes that "[t]o select between two plausible understandings of the word "uses," a court necessarily must exercise legally unconstrained judicial discretion and must resort to considerations outside the law of interpretation" (624).

Sosa (1998, 926) similarly argues that § 924(c)(1)(A) is indeterminate and that Scalia's dissenting opinion

> appears not to appreciate the degree to which language is often simply underdefined. In deciding whether the circumstances in *Smith* constituted a use, the Court could find no guidance in the statute. The language of the statute leaves the matter undetermined.

Sosa argues that the underdefined nature of the provision indicates that consideration of "legislative intent" is necessary. In his view (927), "[c]onsideration of the legislature's intent may take up the slack involved in the crucial term's meaning. Meaning cannot ultimately be independent of intention. To think otherwise is to commit what might be called: The Unintentional Fallacy."

In contrast to González and Sosa, other commentators have used the Court's interpretations of § 924(c)(1)(A) as vehicles to argue in favor of some objective theory of interpretation (such as textualism). Rickless (2005, 519), for example, argues that "[a]lmost every interesting dispute that arises under the law is the product of disagreement among reasonable and competent speakers of the language of the relevant provision." In his view (528), "use a firearm" is vague and in those situations what matters is not the intent of the legislature but rather "what a competent and reasonably well-informed reader of the relevant provision would consider to be part of the word's extension." One reason for choosing hearer meaning over speaker meaning is to satisfy the notice requirement of a criminal statute. Rickless reasons that, "[a]lthough citizens can be expected to determine the semantic intentions of their legislators . . . , they simply cannot be expected to determine their legislators' referential intentions" (528). In addition, he argues that selecting the hearer's interpretation respects legislative compromise, as contrasted with an intentionalist approach that may favor one legislator's intent over another legislator's intent.

5.9.5: Application of Generative Lexicon Theory to 18 U.S.C. § 924(c)(1)(A)

The above accounts of *Smith* might have valid points about such metainterpretive disputes as textualism and intentionalism, but invoking *Smith* and the language of § 924(c)(1)(A) in such discussions is unpersuasive and renders the argument incomplete, if the account glosses over the specifics of ordinary meaning. Consideration of ordinary meaning in a linguistically valid manner should be a prerequisite to broader arguments about interpretation, and there are a variety of ways in which one might approach the ordinary meaning question. An approach may focus on the intuition or "common sense" of the ordinary meaning interpretation or, conversely, may offer a systematic account of word meaning and its relation to sentential context. While systematic accounts and interpreter intuition are not mutually exclusive, and discretion cannot in any case be eliminated, systematic accounts, if available, should be preferred to intuition-based accounts. Most importantly, a systematic account may offer a methodology that is empirically valid and that can be applied in the same way to various interpretive disputes.

Consider a systematic account like Generative Lexicon Theory ("GL"). Slocum (2012) criticizes the Court's decision in *Smith* and argues that the application of GL to provisions like § 924(c)(1)(A) would result in accurate ordinary meaning determinations. A key aspect of GL is that it attempts to systematically describe the compositionality of meaning. As Jackendoff (2010, 2) explains, "the learnability of an unlimited variety of word meanings argues that word meanings are composite, built up in terms of a generative system from a finite stock of primitives and principles of combination." Consistent with this composite view of word meanings, GL views the lexicon as the key source for explaining the creative use of language. GL presents a framework that accounts for the disambiguation process involved in the determination of meaning. The function of GL is the production of a lexicon consisting of complex lexical entries over which a set of generative operations may apply in order to yield compositional interpretations (Pustejovsky 2006, 7).

The findings produced by GL are consistent with those of Traxler et al. (2005), explained above, and indicate that the Supreme Court's failure to recognize the underspecified nature of "use" when interpreting § 924(c)(1)(A) is tied to its failure to recognize the existence of ellipsis and its significance. Crucially, the Court failed to recognize that the ellipsed information in the relevant sentence is supplied by the complement (i.e., the word, phrase or clause that is necessary to complete the meaning of a given expression). In its combination with the object of the sentence, "use" forms a meaning that is more specific than either itself or the object (Abdulkhaliq 2001, 68). Consider the following examples from Pustejovsky (1995, 87):

(7)   (a) John *used* the new knife on the turkey.
      (b) Mary has *used* soft contact lenses since college.
      (c) My wife *uses* the subway every day.

According to Pustejovsky (1995), in (7)(a) our knowledge of knives as tools that can cut permits an economy of expression, whereby mention of the particular activity of cutting may be ellipsed. Similarly, in (7)(b), "contact lenses are visual aids, and the use of them refers to the act of wearing them" (87). In the same way, we should interpret (7)(c) as being a "near paraphrase" of "My wife travels on the subway every day" (87). It is possible of course to wonder what the speaker's wife likes to use the subway for, but it is not doubtful that the *expected* meaning is she "rides" the subway.

The above interpretation is consistent with the telicity (i.e., the purpose and function of the object) attributable to "subway." If one cannot predict that the ellipsed information explaining Sarah's use of the subway involves her riding it and one must assume instead that an idiosyncratic use is just as likely, it would seem that the notion of expected meaning does not exist. This would not, however, be a persuasive assumption. This is especially true considering that the subway is used every day. A common attack on GL by scholars is to posit unusual interpretations as a way of undermining the default interpretations generated by GL. Thus, Jayez (1999, 143) argues that "I am waiting for the bus" could mean "I am waiting for the bus to take a picture of it." These criticisms miss the point of GL and of ordinary meaning.

By relying on its attribute structures and generative mechanisms, GL is able to give a formal means of understanding how ordinary meaning interpretations of sentences can be generated. As applied to "use" and "firearm," GL would provide that

(8) Finn *used* the firearm

does not mean that "Finn used the firearm as a monetary device." Thus, contrary to the Supreme Court's interpretation of 18 U.S.C. § 924(c)(1)(A), the ordinary meaning of (8) is not synonymous with the ordinary meaning of

(9) Finn *used* money.

Instead, the default interpretation of (8) must be that "Finn used the firearm as a weapon."

The application of GL to § 924(c)(1)(A) underscores Justice Scalia's argument in *Smith* that the Court relied on a dubious presumption when it stated that Congress *could have* included the words "as a weapon" in the statute if it had intended that the firearm must have been used as a weapon. The foundation of the Court's error was its reliance on the multiple dictionary definitions of "use" to create an overly broad interpretation of the statute and its corresponding failure to recognize event ellipsis. Instead, the Court should have recognized that "use" has little semantic content of its own and yields divergent interpretations through its attachment to direct objects. Further undermining the Court's ordinary meaning methodology of relying on a dictionary definition for *use* in *Smith* was its unconvincing reasoning in *Watson v. United States*,[95] that a person who trades drugs for a gun does not "use" a firearm "during and in relation to . . . [a] drug trafficking crime."[96] The Court failed to recognize that, unlike the verbs "sell" or "give," "use" is not unidirectional. As the Court noted in its earlier decision in *Bailey v. United States*,[97] one of the dictionary definitions of "use" is "[t]o convert to one's service," and another was "to avail oneself of."[98] Certainly, the receipt of a firearm as one's possession means that the item has been "convert[ed] to one's service." Of course, the Court in *Watson* emphasized that it was determining the meaning of the statutory words in context (and not focusing on "use" in isolation), but its approach to ordinary meaning stands in contrast to that in *Smith*.

As established above, the Court's methodology of choosing broad dictionary interpretations and deciding on an ad hoc, and often linguistically suspect, basis whether the broad interpretation should be narrowed is unpredictable and unconstrained. By understanding ellipsis and sentential context, the Court would have flipped its erroneous presumption that Congress was required to add the phrase "as a weapon." The Court would have first generated an ordinary meaning for "uses a firearm" and then analyzed whether there was any clear evidence that Congress intended to adopt a broader, and highly anomalous, interpretation that would cancel the default interpretation and license the interpretation "use the firearm as currency." Certainly, idiosyncratic or anomalous uses of objects can be imagined (e.g., using a briefcase as a shield), but it is erroneous to assume in the absence of evidence to the contrary, when the ordinary meaning of the statute is being sought, that an unconventional meaning was intended.

5.9.6: Other Ordinary Meaning Accounts of 18 U.S.C. § 924(c)(1)(A)

In addition to Slocum (2012), others have offered accounts that have focused on how the Supreme Court should have approached the determination of ordinary meaning in its interpretations of § 924(c)(1)(A). One type of analysis focuses on lexical semantics and definitional issues, without addressing the systematicities of sentential context. Solan (2010), for instance, views the majority opinion in *Smith* as an instance of the court giving textual language its "definitional" meaning as opposed to its ordinary meaning. Solan (1995, 1076) reasons that "swapping a machinegun for drugs really is a 'use' of a machinegun, but it is a very peculiar one, in all likelihood remote from the core concept that motivated Congress to enact the statute and the President to sign it." In Solan's opinion, the flaw in the Court's approach was to privilege a wooden application of dictionary definitions at the expense of a more sophisticated consideration of whether a certain meaning is the ordinary meaning of the word or phrase at issue. With a definitional meaning approach, a court may choose an interpretation that falls within the range of a provision's possible meaning, but it may not capture the ordinary meaning of the provision. Solan (1995) observes that often the definitional approach will tend to lead to a broad interpretation and the ordinary meaning approach ("prototypical approach") will lead to a narrower interpretation.

Hobbs (2011) similarly criticizes the Court's semantic approach, arguing that the Court focused narrowly on the meaning of "to use" instead of the phrase "uses a firearm." In Hobbs's view, this focus was problematic because it is "highly unlikely that the average person would interpret phrases such as 'He used a gun to obtain drugs' or 'He obtained drugs by use of a gun' as referring to anything other than the use of a gun as a weapon" (333). The Court's analysis therefore shifted the "focus of the inquiry from the ordinary meaning of 'uses a weapon' to the *possible* meanings of the term" (334). Since the "ordinary meaning of 'used his MAC-10' would connote its use as a weapon, the fact that he used it 'as an item of barter' must be made explicit" (334).

Another approach is to illustrate how a linguist might address the interpretation of § 924(c)(1)(A). Cunningham and Fillmore (1995, 1178) provide such an analysis, noting that the "dictionary definitions of 'use' are particularly unhelpful," and the Court's attempts at defining "use" in *Smith* were circular. Instead of reliance on dictionary definitions, Cunningham and Fillmore (1173) demonstrate how the "methods of linguistics" could be used to analyze the meaning of a statutory provision. They described their methodology as follows:

> The methods we employ are those of standard linguistic analysis. These include, in part, an examination of the occurrence of particular linguistic forms (in our case the word "use") in different contexts, by, for example, exploring electronic

data bases containing a large number of texts, sorting the examples according to features of context, and considering native speaker judgments on the interpretation of those instances; performing changes in expressions using the word and seeking native speaker judgments on the results of those changes; and (in the case of so-called "negative evidence") seeking native-speaker agreement on the unacceptability of invented uses of the word. (1174)

In contrast to the above critiques, other approaches have, similar to Slocum (2012), argued that certain general theories of meaning could be used to guide the interpretation of § 924(c)(1)(A). Neale (2007), for example, argues that one approach to the statute involves *underarticulation*, which will not be described here in detail. Consider, though, how it might be used to analyze the *Smith* decision. The proposition (taken from Neale) expressed in connection with *Smith* and § 924(c)(1) is the following:

(10) Smith used a gun.

Under the underarticulation thesis, Neale (2007, 252) makes the following analysis:

> It can't just rain . . . ; raining has to take place *somewhere, somewhen*. Similarly, you can't just *use* something; and you can't just use that something to do *something,* or just use it as *something;* you have to use it to do *something in particular,* or use as it as *something in particular.* The proposition we express by stating a regulation governing the use of firearms contains an unarticulated constituent.

Neale (259) compares (10) to the following example:

(11) Through the inspired use of his new nine iron, Moravcsik triumphed over Hampshire on the 18th.

In Neale's (259) view, consistent with the underarticulation thesis,

> It makes a difference whether Moravcsik holed out with an extraordinary nine iron shot, smashed his nine iron shot straight into Hampshire, or whacked Hampshire on the shin with the aforementioned implement during a heated debate in the heavy rough, forcing Hampshire to retire and concede the match.

Some particular use, or particular range of uses, is understood when the verb "use" or the noun "use" or the adjective "useful" is *used* (even in utterances of "this has many uses" or "you can use this to do all sorts of things").

Thus, like GL described above, the underarticulation analysis underscores that a proper understanding of how language is used must account for the underdetermined nature of "use."

Undoubtedly, various other general theories in addition to those described above could be applied to 924(c)(1)(A). For example, a simple way to see the *Smith* case would be in terms of Inferential Role Semantics, where, as described by (Wilks 2001), the following rule would apply: X uses $Y \to X$ uses Y to do whatever is normally done with Y. Similarly, Levinson's (2000) heuristic 2 (described in chap. 4) provides that what is simply described is stereotypically exemplified. Certainly, that heuristic is relevant to ordinary meaning determinations and would be applicable to situations, like § 924(c)(1)(A), involving event ellipsis where phrases like "uses a firearm" can be seen as being simply described.

5.9.7: The Importance of Systematic Theories of Meaning

The *Smith* decision has been widely analyzed by commentators, but not all the critiques have approached its interpretive questions correctly. Contrary to the claims of some commentators, the interpretive process exemplified in the case includes an ineliminable degree of discretion, but the process should not be viewed as being entirely discretionary. Rather, there are accurate and inaccurate ways of thinking about the ordinary meaning of language and how that meaning is determined. As stated above, regardless of the structure of analysis chosen, whether it is GL, the underarticulation thesis, or some other theory, it is important that *some* adequate theory of language relevant to ordinary meaning be considered before general inferences about interpretation are made based on the interpretation of one provision. Antecedent reference to a theory of meaning helps make general conclusions about legal interpretation more precise and accurate.

For instance, González (2011) is correct, of course, that interpretation involves discretion and that legal considerations are not extrinsic to the interpretation of legal texts. He overstates matters, though, when he claims that, in reference to the *Smith* case, "[t]o select between two plausible understandings of the word "uses," a court necessarily must exercise legally unconstrained judicial discretion." Note the statement that the majority and dissent in *Smith* offered plausible (or equally plausible?) interpretations. Such a conclusion should be based on some theory of language that guides ordinary meaning interpretations and not on the fact that opinions were divided on the interpretive question (or that the case reached the Supreme Court), even if the determinations of meaning were made by competent users of language. The final interpretation chosen (as opposed to the default ordinary meaning) may, or may not in some cases such as *Smith* (which involved one clearly superior possible meaning), require a largely discretionary choice between at least two possible meanings. Notwithstanding the element of discretion, there are accurate and inaccurate ways of thinking about the ordinary meaning of language, and how that ordinary meaning is selected. A theory of meaning should help to guide and constrain interpretive discretion and allow the interpreter to make a judgment about whether a given interpretation is in fact persuasive in light of the nature of language. Only then should conclusions be made regarding the degree of interpretive discretion involved in the specific case, and more generally.

Likewise, while the linguistic methods demonstrated by Cunningham and Fillmore (1995) are useful to consider and illustrate how some linguists research word usage, the use of linguistic methods should, if possible, be in service of some general theory of ordinary meaning or communicative meaning. While Cunningham and Fillmore (1161) invoke the "'common sense' that judges share with all native speakers about everyday language," a reference to "common sense" is not a sufficient theory of meaning. Despite his insightful and influential work and use of lexical semantics, Solan (2010, 74–75) similarly argues that "simple introspection is generally an adequate way to discover" the ordinary sense of words.[99] Certainly, "introspection and intuition" are included within the traditional tools of the linguist (Katsos and Cummins 2010, 287). Like appeals to "common sense," "introspection" by the legal interpreter is inevitable and not intrinsically invalid. It is not, though, a *sufficient* theory of meaning, especially for those who must carefully justify their interpretations. Indeed, "common sense" is a rather unfortunate term to use in reference to legal interpretation. Judges often justify their interpretations by reference to "common sense," but the reference is often more accurately viewed as a reflection of the judge's personal opinion, formed without consideration of external sources and often unexplained.

A prototype analysis, as was suggested by Solan (1995), is certainly superior to "simple introspection," but as explained above in critiquing Judge Posner's decision in *Fitzgerald v. Chrysler Corp.*, simply identifying the stereotypical instance of a concept is not synonymous with identifying a criterion for class membership. Perhaps "uses a firearm" can be distinguished from a phrase like "pattern of racketeering activity," also discussed earlier in the chapter, because firearm is not intangible and has a common usage outside the law. Nevertheless, a prototype analysis will always be somewhat speculative and should be supplemented if possible by other linguistic evidence. For example, the theories described above that make sense of grammatical efficiency and ellipsis can provide a framework for analysis that goes beyond the generalities of prototype theory. Ordinary meaning should thus, to the extent possible, be determined on the basis of some external evidence or theory and, ideally, the most directly insightful theory. Instead of appeals to "common sense," a better approach would involve an empirically valid, explanatory, and general theory of meaning that is based on systematicities of language. Legal interpreters, like linguists, benefit from theoretical accounts of interpretation and experimental and other empirical evidence supporting those theories. One benefit of a theory is that, like a dictionary definition, the linguistic work has been at least partially performed by an expert with a greater understanding of language. Another benefit is that a theory has general application rather than being confined to the particular dispute before the interpreter. Finally, a theory can help focus a search for external evidence and guide the interpreter in evaluating any evidence discovered.

5.10: Conclusion

Previous chapters have explained how interpreters should consider various aspects of language when making ordinary meaning determinations, including how context restricts the domains of quantifiers, temporal preposition phrases, and catchall phrases (through the *ejusdem generis* canon). This chapter has offered an additional way in which context contributes to ordinary meaning. Too often courts approach lexical meaning in an ad hoc manner, relying heavily on acontextual dictionary definitions but not systematically considering sentential context. That judges often approach interpretation in such a manner is not surprising. It is a relatively straightforward process to define a meaning for each token in an alphabet, but considering the combinatorial aspects of language can make interpretation more nuanced and difficult. Such consideration is necessary, though, because sentential context can indicate that the ordinary meaning of a provision is narrower than what the acontextual dictionary definition would indicate. One example of this narrowing involves the ellipsis of fully specified event structures when the event is commonly associated with the noun. In situations involving an agent "using" something, linguistic evidence indicates that the invited inference is something like the following: if X uses Y, where Y is something that has a conventional/typical use, X uses Y for which Y is used. Instead of the invited reference, the Supreme Court in the *Smith* case chose a broad, acontextual dictionary definition, thereby extending the relevant provision beyond its ordinary meaning.

It is possible, of course, for an interpreter to consider sentential evidence and reach the correct interpretation without relying on any particular theory of meaning. Justice Scalia's dissenting opinion in *Smith*, for example, insightfully identified the crucial flaw in the court's interpretation of § 924(c)(1)(A). His opinion did not, however, offer any particular general understanding of language that could be applied to future ordinary meaning determinations (or that might have convinced the majority of the correctness of his interpretation). In fact, Justice Scalia himself tends to rely too heavily on dictionaries and uses the ordinary meaning doctrine selectively (Aprill 1998; McGowan 2008). An interpreter could have reached the same conclusion as Justice Scalia but with reasoning based on a consistent, systematic, and replicable theory of language. Application of some linguistic theory of meaning would provide a coherent and plausible basis for courts to change their practice of allowing pragmatic evidence to sometimes cancel a *broad* definition chosen on (typically faulty) semantic grounds to allowing pragmatic evidence to sometimes cancel a *narrow* definition chosen on semantic grounds.[100] Such an approach is also more congruent with many of the judiciary's interpretive principles than is the acontextual approach. As Shapiro (1992) has argued, many interpretive tools reflect a preference for continuity over change by narrowing the scope of legal provisions form their literal meanings. A preference for continuity over change is also advanced by choosing an ordinary meaning over a possible meaning. In contrast, a "possible meaning" approach is troubling considering that the creative nature of natural languages means that senses and possibilities might exist or can be expected to develop, resulting in surprising possibilities that the drafter may not have intended. A methodology that favors prototypical rather than unusual meanings therefore better fits the historical desire of courts to adopt broad interpretations cautiously.

Notwithstanding the various ways in which linguistic phenomena use context to restrict the literal meaning of a provision, determinations of category membership may be required in situations that do not involve some systematic aspect of context. Certainly, interpretation is a contextual matter. Yet, often the extension of a category must in general be determined, and if an interpreter is working from a flawed definition, the resulting interpretation may well be unpersuasive. Unfortunately, courts often choose to proceed by assuming that categories inherently possess necessary and sufficient membership criteria. Such an assumption, though, is inconsistent with research from linguists and psychologists on the prototypical structure of categories. Instead of clear criteria for membership, many categories are instead characterized by having no explicit definition, at least in terms of necessary and sufficient conditions. Similarity of features plays a significant role in category membership, with certain features being generally true of category members but not uniformly so. Many categories will thus have a graded structure in which some items are more clearly and uncontroversially members of the category than are others. The graded membership structure means that features do not involve simple binary truth values (i.e., membership vs. nonmembership). Instead, some items are members of a category to a greater extent than are other items.

As this chapter has argued, prototype theory can be accommodated to the need of the legal system for bivalent determinations and the reduced capacity for empirical research. Even with these limitations, prototype methodology is preferable to the classical model of viewing meaning in terms of necessary and sufficient membership criteria. Nevertheless, legal texts often reference intangible categories that either do not exist outside of the law (e.g., "pattern of racketeering activity") or exist only at high levels of generality compared to the needs of the legal system (e.g., "enterprise" and "pattern"). In such situations the ordinary meaning of the relevant term either does not exist or is not specific enough to decide many cases. Instead of relying on the ordinary meaning doctrine, the interpreter should decide the case on other grounds and be explicit about doing so. As this chapter explained with the RICO statute as an example, courts do not consistently recognize the underdetermined nature of a provision's key terms and instead portray the interpretive dispute as though it involves nothing more than straightforwardly determining the ordinary meaning of the terms. Although RICO has been the subject of sustained criticism from commentators, the amount of criticism it has received exaggerates its exceptional nature (and may be connected more to the importance of the statute). The use of terms unique to the law or with very general meanings is prevalent in legal provisions, and the problems illustrated by the Supreme Court's interpretations of RICO are endemic to the law.

CHAPTER SIX

Conclusion

6.1: What This Book Has Established

The first sentence in this book asked the following question: By what standard should legal texts be interpreted? As the various chapters of this book have acknowledged or demonstrated, the answer is that legal texts have a content that is not reducible to one standard of meaning. Rather, various categories of concerns contribute in different ways to the meaning of a legal text. These categories of concerns are necessarily based on objective views of meaning, as opposed to subjective theories of actual authorial intent. For principles of interpretation based on legal concerns, this is obviously true. Various interests relevant only to the law and not to linguistic communication more generally often contribute significantly to the meaning of a legal text. For instance, pursuant to the presumption against retroactivity, a clear textual statement is required in order for a statute to have retroactive application.[1] Similarly, pursuant to the presumption against extraterritoriality, a clear textual statement is required in order for a statute to have extraterritorial application.[2] These substantive canons of statutory construction cannot be said to contribute to the ordinary linguistic meaning of a legal text because they are judge-created principles that have no application to nonlegal texts.

Although concerns relevant only to the law undoubtedly often contribute to the meaning of a legal text, interpretive principles derived from these concerns are not the sole determinants of the meaning of such texts. Rather, courts typically focus on the communicative meaning of a text. Consideration of objective determinants of intent, though, is also necessary when focusing on communicative meaning. Interpreters of texts do not have direct access to the author's actual intentions. Further, with legal texts it is unclear that there is such a thing as actual intentions. With regard to legislation, some theory must be offered as to how a collective body of individuals, who may not have ever discussed the text with each other, or read it themselves, can nonetheless possess an intent regarding the meaning of the language in the text. Relatedly, those advocating in favor of actual intent are obligated to offer some theory of the level of generality at which intent should be measured. Thus, a choice must be made between defining intent at a high level of generality with a focus on the purpose of the provision or at a lower level of generality with a focus on the specific intent of the authors regarding the relevant interpretive dispute. Even if intent in a legal context can be adequately defined, the epistemic uncertainties inherent in its identification necessitate reliance, at least in part, on objective features of the context of interpretation. Perhaps the most important of these features are conventions of meaning. Thus, courts invariably claim that the language in legal provisions is to be interpreted in accordance with its ordinary meaning.

The judicial unanimity regarding the salience of the ordinary meaning doctrine should not be surprising as no other competing standard is coherent or persuasive. Primarily, the ordinary meaning doctrine is uncontroversial because it is intuitively the correct standard for determining textual meaning. The doctrine can be viewed in another light, though. Perhaps it is uncontroversial among the judiciary because it has not been well developed and thus can be easily manipulated by courts to justify a desired interpretation. Courts have given only very general answers to the constituent question of what makes some meaning the ordinary meaning and the evidential question of what are the determinants of ordinary meaning. Further, the process used by courts for determining the ordinary meaning of texts, such as significant reliance on dictionaries, often does not result in interpretations that reflect the ordinary meaning of the texts that are being interpreted, or only coincidentally does so. For textualists, the commitment to ordinary meaning is clear and, in their view, fits with Scalia and Garner's (2012, 69) argument that "most interpretive questions have a right answer," and "[v]ariability in interpretation is a distemper." Even if ignoring the significant discretion inherent in considering evidence from the "wide context," though, Scalia and Garner's argument is questionable. A proper conception of the ordinary meaning doctrine offers reasons to dismiss Scalia and Garner's claim that most interpretive questions have a right answer (at least those questions that are litigated) and to doubt that interpreters will agree on many interpretive questions, even if they all apply the same methodology.

The main reason for doubt about a causal connection between a commitment to ordinary meaning and interpreter unanimity concerns the tension between the inherent requirement of ordinary meaning that it be generalizable across contexts and the reality that meaning is inherently contextual. A significant aspect of framing the ordinary meaning inquiry, and considering textualist arguments about it, therefore involves considering the contribution that context makes to meaning. Any plausible conceptualization of ordinary meaning requires that context be accounted for explicitly. Contrary to Recanati's (2004) analysis, though, contextual consideration does not require that meaning be characterized as being primarily pragmatically derived. Instead, one way to capture generalizable meanings and maintain the gap between ordinary meaning and communicative meaning is to conceive of ordinary meaning as being primarily based on semantic meaning (or at least systematic accounts of meaning that blur the line between semantics and pragmatics). Also, as discussed throughout this book, a distinction between "narrow context" and "wide context" can be made, with ordinary meaning being determined on the basis of consideration of facts from narrow context. This way of framing ordinary meaning does not, however, eliminate interpretive discretion. When context is considered, the assignment of meaning invariably has an ineliminable element of interpreter discretion.

Properly considering how context contributes to meaning is a difficult matter, and courts have not been careful when making such considerations. For instance, courts often fail to properly consider the complexities that context can add to interpretations of indexicals and tend to rely instead on dictionary definitions. Even under a proper understanding of indexicals, though, an interpreter has significant discretion in determining their conventional meanings. In fact, with respect to indexicals in legal texts, it is questionable whether there is likely to be a difference between ordinary meaning and the meaning a court would choose if it explicitly focused on desirable legal outcomes. A proper consideration of indexicals would thus underscore the ineliminable discretion involved in determining their references in many cases, as well as refute the textualist notion that variability in interpretation is a sign of incorrect methodology.

Like the assignment of references to indexicals, the assignment of domains to quantifiers falls under the scope of "what is said" and therefore ordinary meaning. The assignment of a limited domain to a quantifier is intuitively connected to the ordinary meaning of an expression. Similar to indexicals, however, courts have not properly considered quantifier domain restriction when determining the ordinary meaning of textual language. Even so, and notwithstanding a viable semantic theory of quantifier domain restriction, the assignment of a domain to a quantifier is necessarily a discretionary determination. Furthermore, there are no reasons to believe that "common sense" or alignment of background assumptions and knowledge, even if possible, would be sufficient to create interpretive consensus.

Despite their often discretionary nature, one marked feature of the interpretive principles identified in this book is that they serve to restrict the domains of legal texts, thereby creating a gap between literal meaning and ordinary/communicative meaning. This feature of ordinary meaning has never before been systematically described. Not all the interpretive principles that serve to restrict the meaning of a text from its literal meaning, however, are relevant to ordinary linguistic meaning. At most, they are determinates of ordinary legal meaning. As indicated above, substantive canons contribute to the legal meaning of a text, but not to its ordinary linguistic meaning. In contrast, some textual canons can be considered to be determinants of ordinary linguistic meaning. They are determinants of ordinary meaning even though they may be classified as conversational implicatures and therefore fall under "what is communicated." The *ejusdem generis* canon is one such interpretive principle. Like the other determinants of ordinary meaning, a systematic account of the *ejusdem generis* canon cannot eliminate the discretionary nature of its application. Rather, the discretionary nature of interpretation holds regardless of whether a particular linguistic phenomenon is considered to be within "what is said" or "what is communicated."

Finally, any conceptualization of ordinary meaning should consider certain aspects of lexical semantics, including the contribution of sentential context to ordinary meaning. Notwithstanding the complexity of interpretation, and the inherent discretion involved in determining meaning, identifying systematicities of language should be viewed as a valuable contribution to legal interpretation. A significant flaw in the judiciary's current approach to ordinary meaning is that the dictionary definitions relied on often favor inappropriately broad meanings because they capture "possible" rather than "ordinary" meanings. Considering a theory of lexical semantics that accounts for sentential context would thus improve ordinary meaning interpretations. Specifically, such an account should produce default meanings via narrow context that can serve as the presumptive ordinary meanings of the relevant legal texts, subject of course to cancellation by interpreters after consideration of wide context.

Still, it is often important that the general extension of a word (also known as a "category" or "concept") be considered, without regard to any specific contributions from context. In such situations, courts must understand the inaccuracy of the classical theory of meaning that posits clear and unambiguous necessary and sufficient conditions for category membership determinations. Instead, legal interpreters should consider how categories are prototypically prototype concepts. Like the other linguistic phenomena considered in this book, such an understanding of meaning reveals the ineliminable discretion inherent in ordinary meaning. Explicitly contemplating the discretion inherent in ordinary meaning, however, is far superior to the classical approach, which disingenuously denies it. Further, even if judicial implementation of prototype theory is likely to be intuition based, judicial intuitions can be supplemented with empirical evidence. Nevertheless, judicial discretion is particularly great with respect to intangible categories that either do not exist outside of the law or exist only at high levels of generality compared to the needs of the legal system. Unlike many of the other linguistic phenomena, though, determining meaning via prototype theory does not create a gap between literal meaning and ordinary meaning. Instead, the two are synonymous.

6.2: Further Research Issues

Certainly, future research on ordinary meaning can focus on linguistic phenomena other than those addressed in this book and consider whether they should be determinants of ordinary meaning. For instance, the conclusion to chapter 4 outlined some preliminary thoughts on the ordinary meaning status of some of the textual canons of construction not considered in detail in the chapter. If a textual canon cannot properly be viewed as a determinant of ordinary meaning, responsible judges (and legislatures) might consider whether the canon should be retained. Similarly, researchers and courts can further develop the various ways in which empirical evidence from corpora and other resources can help inform ordinary meaning determinations. Conceivably, information from these sources can to some degree replace judicial reliance on "common sense" and other highly personal and nonverifiable conclusions about meaning.

Another area that should be explored is the contribution that syntax makes to ordinary meaning. Some of the textual canons address matters of syntax, such as the rule of the last antecedent, which concerns clause and comma placement. Often, though, judges draw other conclusions about meaning based on the broader structure of the relevant provision. For instance, one issue that has troubled courts has involved the issue of scienter in criminal cases. In *United States v. X-Citement Video, Inc.*,[3] the Supreme Court held that a federal child pornography statute, 18 U.S.C. § 2252, includes a scienter requirement regarding the age of the performer in a visual depiction. Section 2252 provides, in relevant part:

> (a) Any person who—
>> (1) knowingly transports or ships in interstate or foreign commerce by any means including by computer or mails, any visual depiction, if—
>>> (A) the producing of such visual depiction involves the use of a minor engaging in sexually explicit conduct; and
>>> (B) such visual depiction is of such conduct;
>
> ...
>
> shall be punished as provided in subsection (b) of this section.

The Court found that the "most natural grammatical reading" is that the term "knowingly"

> modifies only the surrounding verbs: transports, ships, receives, distributes, or reproduces. Under this construction, the word "knowingly" would not modify the elements of the minority of the performers, or the sexually explicit nature of the material, because they are set forth in independent clauses separated by interruptive punctuation.[4]

The Court declined, however, to adopt the "most grammatical reading," for reasons involving legal concerns, including constitutional ones.

Two linguists, Kaplan and Green (1995), have criticized the Court's linguistic reasoning in *X-Citement Video*. Interpreting § 2252 from a purely linguistic standpoint is, on the surface, fairly straightforward. A modifier, such as *knowingly*, within a verb phrase combines with other expressions within the verb phrase to form a larger expression of that same type. Expressions outside the verb phrase, though, would not be modified by the adverb. Section 2252 contains an *if* clause, which is not part of the verb phrase that contains "knowingly," or the noun phrase, "Any person who knowingly distributes a depiction." Semantically, the *if* clause can be said to function as a parenthetical. Thus, an initial linguistic analysis indicates that the Supreme Court's interpretation of § 2252 was erroneous.

A further problem is that the Court's decision in *X-Citement Video* has not provided a general framework for resolving the scienter issue. In 2009, in *Flores-Figueroa v. United States*,[5] the Supreme Court decided whether a federal criminal statute forbidding "[a]ggravated identity theft" requires the government to show that the defendant knew that the "means of iden-tification" he or she unlawfully transferred, possessed, or used, in fact, be-longed to "another person." The relevant part of the statute applies to one who "knowingly transfers, possesses, or uses, without lawful authority, a means of identification of another person."[6] Although the Court noted that "[a]s a matter of ordinary English grammar, it seems natural to read the statute's word 'knowingly' as applying to all the subsequently listed elements of the crime," it was unclear as to the circumstances in which this would be true.[7] Some state courts have disagreed with *Flores-Figueroa*, indicating that it is inconsistent with their interpretive practices.[8] Cer-tainly, then, there is a need for a theory of how these sorts of issues should be approached from an ordinary meaning perspective.

6.3: The Future of Ordinary Meaning

A remaining concern about ordinary meaning is the extent to which courts are willing to consider it to be a fundamental aspect of an ex-plicitly delineated, sequential process of reasoning. Chapter 3 offered rea-sons why ordinary meaning is useful as a separate level of meaning, as opposed to simply being conflated with communicative meaning. As this book has demonstrated, it is possible to conceptualize ordinary meaning in such a way that maintains a gap between ordinary meaning and com-municative meaning. Nevertheless, although courts do not express dissat-isfaction with the ordinary meaning doctrine, they have not in general sought to carefully distinguish ordinary meaning determinations from communicative meaning or legal meaning determinations. In theory, one could design a study that would place all of the determinants of mean-ing into either the narrow or wide context categories and discern when a court is determining ordinary meaning and when a court is focusing on other considerations. In reality, though, such an exercise is imprecise be-cause courts are generally not explicit regarding when they have finished an ordinary meaning determination and have moved on to other consid-erations, such as legal concerns or broader communicative meaning. The *Carcieri v. Salazar* case discussed in chapter 3 is an example where the Supreme Court was not inclined to carefully distinguish between ordinary meaning and communicative meaning. The case is exemplative of Supreme Court decisions. For instance, the Court will frequently examine its precedents throughout an opinion without clarifying for what purpose (i.e., ordinary meaning or communicative meaning) the examination is relevant. A similar phenomenon is true for legislative history, as well as other determinants of meaning.

There are no reasons to doubt as a general matter that courts believe that they are determining ordinary meaning. The doctrine cannot simply be dismissed on the basis that it serves merely as a pretense for decisions made on other grounds, or that it is a synonym for communicative meaning. Rather, courts justify their interpretations on various grounds, which often include ordinary meaning, and these rationales should be evaluated independently of a judge's possible motivations. Further, it is undeniable that the communicative meaning of a text might differ from its ordinary meaning and that sometimes the drafter intends the text to carry some unordinary meaning. Nevertheless, as this book has demonstrated, courts often do not properly analyze the determinants of ordinary meaning. Equally so, they are not careful in distinguishing between ordinary meaning and communicative or legal meaning. Judicial decisions would be much improved, as would confidence in judicial honesty, if these defects were remedied.

This book has disclaimed any desire to advocate in favor of any particular methodology of interpretation. Rather, this book's conceptualization of ordinary meaning positions it as a default interpretation that is consistent with the various interpretive methodologies that purport to give at least some weight to the meaning of the relevant text. Nevertheless, this book does make a normative claim. Like the "linguistic turn" that marked the development of philosophy in the last century, certain aspects of legal interpretation should be viewed as intrinsically linguistic phenomena subject to linguistic insights, operations, and advances. Galdia (2009, 51–52) remarks that the linguistic turn "did not take place in the legal science." While statutory interpretation theory and methodology is a growing area of scholarly inquiry, the concept of ordinary meaning (like other linguistic phenomena) receives comparably little attention from legal scholars, who primarily focus instead on doctrines and issues that are ideological or constitutional in nature. It is fair to wonder whether judges are capable of using linguistics and philosophy in neutral ways, rather than as devices for justifying results reached on other grounds. Solan (1993, 62) remarks that "judges do not make good linguists because they are using linguistic principles to accomplish an agenda distinct from the principles about which they write." As this book has detailed, it is of course true that all stages of interpretation, including ordinary meaning determinations, are inherently discretionary and hence subject to the policy and ideologically based pre-dilections of judges. Nevertheless, judges purport to take textual language seriously, perhaps more than ever before, and scholars should focus on providing theories of how they might better do so.

Synonyms for Ordinary Meaning

Term	Case citation
Regular usage	Lopez v. Gonzales, 549 U.S. 47, 53, 56 (2006)
Common usage	National Cable & Telecommunications Association v. Brand X Internet Services, 545 U.S. 967, 970, 990 (2005)
Ordinary usage	Boyle v. United States, 556 U.S. 938, 946 (2009) United States v. Santos, 553 U.S. 507, 512 (2008) National Cable & Telecommunications Association v. Brand X Internet Services, 545 U.S. 967, 970, 989 (2005)
Ordinary definitions	United States v. Santos, 553 U.S. 507, 513 (2008)
Ordinary or natural meaning	Warren v. Main Board of Environmental Protection, 547 U.S. 370, 376 (2006)
Ordinary and popular sense	Bedroc Limited, LLC v. United States, 541 U.S. 176, 184 (2004)
Ordinary, contemporary, and common meaning	Walters v. Metropolitan Educational Enterprises, Inc. and Equal Employment Commission v. Metropolitan Educational Enterprises, 519 U.S. 202, 207 (1997)
Primary meaning	United States v. Santos, 553 U.S. 507, 511 (2008)
Usual meaning	Gonzales v. Carhart, 550 U.S. 124, 152 (2007)
Common meaning	Warren v. Main Board of Environmental Protection, 547 U.S. 370, 382 (2006)
Natural meaning	Watson v. United States, 552 U.S. 74, 76 (2007)
Everyday understanding	Lopez v. Gonzales, 549 U.S. 47, 53 (2006)
Common understanding	Rousey v. Jacoway, 544 U.S. 320, 326 (2005)
Dictionary understanding	Rousey v. Jacoway, 544 U.S. 320, 320 (2005)

Term	Case citation
Ordinary sense	Warren v. Main Board of Environmental Protection, 547 U.S. 370, 376 (2006)
Everyday sense	Warren v. Main Board of Environmental Protection, 547 U.S. 370, 378 (2006)
Plain term	National Cable & Telecommunications Association v. Brand X Internet Services, 545 U.S. 967, 970, 986, 989 (2005)
Plain text	Leocal v. Ashcroft, 543 U.S. 1, 8 (2004)

Supreme Court Cases Using Ordinary Meaning

Year	Ordinary meaning	Ordinary understanding	Literal meaning	Ordinary and accepted meaning
2010–14	36	5	0	
2000–2009	62	4	5	
1990–99	65	7	8	
1980–89	64	4	16	
1970–79	24	3	11	
1960–69	14	3	14	
1950–59	15	0	6	
1940–49	16	2	7	1
1930–39	16	0	12	2
1920–29	22	0	10	
1910–19	12	0	12	
1900–1909	15		10	
1890–99	25	2	6	
1880–89	6	1	7	
1870–79	7	3	4	
1860–69	2	1	2	
1850–59	4	1	6	
1840–49	4		5	
1830–39	4		6	
1820–29	4		9	
1810–19	1		4	
1800–1810			2	
1790–99			0	
1780–89			2	
Total	418	36	164	3

Cases since 1986 Where the Supreme Court Used "Literal Meaning" as a Synonym for Ordinary Meaning

Case name	Subject matter	Key phrase
Hamdan v. Rumsfeld, 548 U.S. 557, 631 (2006)	Geneva Convention (Article 3)	"not of an international character"
Federal Communications Commission v. Nextwave Personal Communications Inc., 537 U.S. 293, 304 (2003)	Bankruptcy	"solely because," "debtor"
Lewis v. United States (1998) 523 U.S. 155, 160–62 (1998)	Assimilative Crimes Act (ACA)	"any enactment"
Concrete Pipe and Products of California v. Construction Laborers Pension Trust for Southern California, 508 U.S. 602, 652 (1993)	Multiemployer Pension Plan Amendments Act of 1980 (MPPAA)	"clearly erroneous"
Maryland v. Craig, 497 U.S. 836, 844 (1990)	Sixth Amendment Confrontation Clause	
Hallstrom v. Tillamook County, 493 U.S. 20, 29 (1989)	Resource Conservation and Recovery Act of 1976 (RCRA)	"[a]ctions prohibited"
Coy v. Iowa, 487 U.S. 1012, 1021 (1988)	Sixth Amendment Confrontation Clause	
Schiavone v. Fortune (1986) 477 U.S. 21, 31; and 106 S. Ct. 2379, 2385	Federal Rule of Civil Procedure 15(c)	"relates back"

Case name	Subject matter	Key phrase
Brock v. Pierce (1986) 476 U.S. 253	Comprehensive Employment and Training Act (CETA)	"shall"

Recent Supreme Court Cases Regarding Ordinary Meaning with Dissenting Opinions

Case name	Does the case involve dissenting justices on interpretative grounds?	Circuit split?	Majority	Dissent
Sebelius v. Cloer, 133 S. Ct. 1886 (2013)	No		All (Scalia and Thomas do not join as to part II-B–discussing purpose)	
Levin v. U.S., 133 S. Ct. 1224 (2013)	No		All (Scalia did not join footnotes 6 and 7; discusses purpose and legislative history)	
Marx v. General Revenue Corp., 133 S. Ct. 1166 (2013)	Yes	Yes	Thomas, Roberts, Scalia, Kennedy, Ginsburg, Breyer, and Alito	Sotomayor and Kagan (discuss "ordinary meaning")
National Federation of Independent Business v. Sebelius, 132 S. Ct. 2566 (2012)	Yes		Roberts, Ginsburg, Breyer, Sotomayor, and Kagan (parts I, II, and II-C)	Dissent 1: Ginsburg, Sotomayor, Breyer (partial), and Kagan (partial); Dissent 2: Scalia, Kennedy, Thomas, and Alito; Dissent 3: Thomas

Case name	Does the case involve dissenting justices on interpretative grounds?	Circuit split?	Majority	Dissent
Arizona v. U.S., 132 S. Ct. 2492 (2012)	Yes		Kennedy, Roberts, Ginsburg, Breyer, and Sotomayor	Thomas (discussing ordinary meaning in regards to preemption)
Christopher v. SmithKline Beecham Corp., 132 S. Ct. 2156 (2012)	Yes	Yes	Alito, Roberts, Scalia, Kennedy, and Thomas	Breyer, Ginsburg, Sotomayor, and Kagan
Salazar v. Ramah Navajo Chapter, 132 S. Ct. 2181 (2012)	Yes			Roberts, Ginsburg, Breyer, and Alito
Match-E-Be-Nash-She-Wish Band of Pottawatomi Indians v. Patchak, 132 S. Ct. 2199 (2012)	Yes		Sotomayor, Scalia, Kennedy, Thomas, and Kagan	Roberts, Ginsburg, Breyer, and Alito
Taniguchi v. Kan Pacific Saipan, Ltd., 132 S. Ct. 1997 (2012)	Yes	Yes		Ginsburg, Breyer, and Sotomayor
Hall v. U.S., 132 S. Ct. 1882 (2012)	Yes	Yes		Breyer, Kennedy, Ginsburg, and Kagan
Mohamad v. Palestinian Authority, 132 S. Ct. 1702 (2012)	No			
Federal Aviation Administration v. Cooper, 132 S. Ct. 1441 (2012)	Yes			Sotomayor, Ginsburg, and Breyer
Roberts v. Sea-Land Services Inc., 132 S. Ct. 1350 (2012) 2012 WL 912953	Yes			Ginsburg
Pliva v. Mensing LLC, 131 S. Ct. 2567 (2011)	Yes			Sotomayor, Ginsburg, Breyer, and Kagan

Case name	Does the case involve dissenting justices on interpretative grounds?	Circuit split?	Majority	Dissent
Microsoft Corp v. i4i Limited Partnership, 131 S. Ct. 2238 (2011)	No			
Schindler Elevator Corporation v. United States, 131 S. Ct. 1885 (2011)	Yes			Ginsburg, Breyer, and Sotomayor
Milner v. Department of the Navy, 562 U.S. 562 (2011)	Yes			Breyer (said that the Court should have gone with the previous interpretation)
Wall v. Kholi, 562 U.S. 545 (2011)	No			
Federal Communications Commission v. AT&T Inc., 562 U.S. 397 (2011)	No			
CSX Transportation Inc. v. Alabama Department of Revenue, 562 U.S. 277 (2011)	Yes			Thomas and Ginsburg
Ransom v. FIA Card Services, 562 U.S. 61 (2011)	Yes			Scalia
Bilski v. Kappos, 561 U.S. 593 (2010)	No			
Holder v. Humanitarian Law Project, 561 U.S. 1 (2010)	Yes			Breyer, Ginsburg, and Sotomayor
Hamilton v. Lanning, 560 U.S. 505 (2010)	Yes			Scalia
Alabama v. North Carolina, 559 U.S. 460 (2010)	Yes			Breyer and Roberts

Case name	Does the case involve dissenting justices on interpretative grounds?	Circuit split?	Majority	Dissent
United States v. Stevens, 559 U.S. 460 (2010)	Yes			Alito
Mac's Shell Service Inc. v. Shell Oil Products Co., 559 U.S. 175 (2010)	No			
Hardt v. Reliance Standard Life Insurance, 560 U.S. 242 (2010)	No			
Johnson v. U.S., 559 U.S. 133 (2010)	Yes			Alito and Thomas
Forest Grove School District v. T.A., 557 U.S. 230 (2009)	Yes-			Souter, Scalia, and Thomas
Gross v. FBL Financial Services, Inc., 557 U.S. 167 (2009)	Yes			Stevens, Souter, Ginsburg, and Breyer
Boyle v. United States, 556 U.S. 938 (2009)	Yes			Stevens and Breyer
Burlington Northern and Santa Fe Railway Company v. U.S., 556 U.S. 599 (2009)	Yes			Ginsburg
Flores-Figueroa v. United States, 556 U.S. 646 (2009)	No			
Ministry of Defense and Support for the Armed Forces of the Islamic Republic of Iran v. Elahi, 556 U.S. 366 (2009)	Yes			Kennedy, Souter, and Ginsburg
Carcieri v. Salazar, 555 U.S. 379 (2009)	Y			Souter, Ginsburg, and Stevens (with a separate dissent)

Case name	Does the case involve dissenting justices on interpretative grounds?	Circuit split?	Majority	Dissent
Crawford v. Metropolitan Government of Nashville and Davidson County, Tennessee, 555 U.S. 271 (2009)	No			
United States v. Santos, 553 U.S. 507 (2008)	Yes			Dissent 1: Breyer; Dissent 2: Alito, Roberts, Kennedy, and Breyer
Watson v. United States, 552 U.S. 74 (2007)	No			
Logan v. United States, 552 U.S. 23 (2007)	No			
National Association of Home Builders v. Defenders of Wildlife, 551 U.S. 644 (2007)	Yes			Stevens, Souter, Ginsburg, and Breyer (Breyer also filed own)
James v. United States, 550 U.S. 192 (2007)	Yes			Dissent 1: Scalia, Stevens, and Ginsburg; Dissent 2: Thomas
Gonzales v. Carhart, 550 U.S. 124 (2007)	No			
BP America Production Co. v. Burton, 549 U.S. 84 (2006)	No			
Lopez v. Gonzales, 549 U.S. 47 (2006)	Yes	Yes		Thomas
Sanchez-Llamas v. Oregon, 548 U.S. 331 (2006)	Yes			Breyer, Stevens, Souter, and Ginsburg

Case name	Does the case involve dissenting justices on interpretative grounds?	Circuit split?	Majority	Dissent
Arlington Central School District Board of Education v. Murphy, 548 U.S. 291 (2006)	Yes			Souter, Breyer, and Stevens
S.D. Warren Co. v. Maine Board of Environmental Protection 126 S. Ct. 1843	No			
Dolan v. United States Postal Service, 546 U.S. 481 (2006)	Yes			Thomas
National Cable & Telecommunications Association v. Brand X Internet Services, 545 U.S. 967 (2005)	Yes			Scalia and Souter
Rousey v. Jacoway, 544 U.S. 320 (2005)	No			
Leocal v. Ashcroft, 543 U.S. 1 (2004)	No			
Engine Manufacturers Association v. South Coast Air Quality Management District, 541 U.S. 246 (2004)	Yes			Souter
Bedroc Limited, LLC v. United States, 541 U.S. 176 (2004)	Yes			Stevens and Ginsburg
General Dynamics Land Systems, Inc. v Cline, 540 U.S. 581 (2004)	Yes			Dissent 1: Scalia; Dissent 2: Thomas and Kennedy

Notes

Chapter One

1. 18 U.S.C. § 924(c)(1)(A). This provision and the multiple Supreme Court cases interpreting it are discussed in chap. 5.

2. 25 U.S.C. § 479. This provision and the Supreme Court case interpreting it are discussed in chap. 3.

3. 28 U.S.C. § 1346(b)(1). This provision and the Supreme Court case interpreting it are discussed in chap. 4.

4. Tariff Act of 1883, 22 Stat. 504, 519. This provision and the Supreme Court case interpreting it are discussed in chap. 5.

5. This contractual provision and the case interpreting it, White City Shopping Center v. PR Restaurants, 21 Mass.L.Rptr. 565, 2006 WL 3292641 (Mass. Super. Ct. 2006), are discussed in chap. 5.

6. District of Columbia v. Heller, 554 U.S. 570, 576–77 (2008).

7. Id. (quoting United States v. Sprague, 282 U.S. 716, 731 (1931)).

8. 132 S. Ct. 1997 (2012).

9. See id. at 2000 (interpreting 28 U.S.C. § 1920(6)).

10. Id. at 2002.

11. Id. at 2003.

12. Johnson v. United States, 529 U.S. 694, 718 (2000) (Scalia, J., dissenting).

13. Id. at 706n9.

14. Yates v. United States, 135 S. Ct. 1074, 1089 (2015) (Alito, J., concurring in the judgment).

15. Throughout this book there will be references to "objective" theories and methodologies of interpretation. The term should not be taken as an assertion that these theories and methodologies are scientific in nature. In fact, a major theme of this book is that many proponents of objective theories of interpretation underappreciate the significant degree of judicial discretion involved in interpreting legal texts. Instead, the term is used in contrast with "subjective" theories and method-

ologies, which posit the ascertainment of authorial intent as the goal of interpretation.

16. One of the most notable commentators on the law, James Kent, stated in 1826 (432) that "[t]he words of a statute are to be taken in their natural and ordinary signification and import; and if technical words are used, they are to be taken in a technical sense."

17. See, e.g., Estelle v. McGuire, 502 U.S. 62, 72 (1991) (explaining that jury instructions are to be interpreted according to their "common and ordinary meaning."); Sanchez-Llamas v. Oregon 548 U.S. 331, 346 (2006) (indicating that "international agreements" are to be interpreted in accordance with their ordinary meaning); Baze v. Rees 553 U.S. 35, 97 (2008) (Thomas, J., concurring) (referring to the "ordinary meaning of the word 'cruel'" in connection with the Eighth Amendment); Ruby v. Ruby 973 N.E.2d 361, 366–367 (Ill. App. 2012) (stating that "[w]hen interpreting a trust, a court's goal is to ascertain the settlor's intent using the same principles as those used to interpret a will, namely, by examining the plain and ordinary meaning of the words used in the instrument within the context of the entire document"); and Solan (2007) (explaining the presumption that the ordinary meaning of a contract's terms was the meaning intended by the parties).

18. Redco Const. v. Profile Properties, LLC 2012 WL 579415, 7 (Wyo. 2012). See also CSX Transp., Inc. v. Alabama Dept. of Revenue, 131 S. Ct. 1101, 1107 (2011) ("We begin, as in any case of statutory interpretation, with the language of the statute").

19. Id.

20. Zuni Pub. Sch. Dist. No. 89 v. Dep't of Educ., 550 U.S. 81, 90 (2007).

21. The notion of communicative meaning is developed and clarified in chap. 2.

22. The communicative meaning of the text could be based on context (such as the legislative history of a statute) that is not considered in determining the ordinary meaning of the text, as chap. 3 explains. Thus, it could be that the ordinary meaning would be decisive if accepted, but the communicative meaning, which differs because the consideration of additional contextual evidence undermines the ordinary meaning, is not decisive. Nevertheless, such a complication is unnecessary to consider when discussing the ways in which the legal meaning of a text may not correspond with its communicative meaning (or its ordinary meaning).

23. Flanagan (2010, 257) describes an utterance's literal meaning as the "proposition you would attribute to it if you referred to just the symbols in question and the appropriate community's conventions on linguistic meaning, i.e. to the appropriate set of rules for the meanings of words and sentence construction." Although I distinguish ordinary meaning from literal meaning later in this chapter, and in following chapters demonstrate the frequent gaps between the two concepts, Flanagan's definition of literal meaning makes it indistinguishable from ordinary meaning for the purposes of his point.

24. Hardt v. Reliance Standard Life Ins. Co., 560 U.S. 242, 251 (2010).

25. See Manning (2003) for a discussion of the absurdity doctrine.

26. The Supreme Court's decision in Church of Holy Trinity v. United States, 143 U.S. 457, 459 (1892), is a famous case in part due to the Court's view that "[i]t is a familiar rule, that a thing may be within the letter of the statute and yet not within the statute, because not within its spirit, nor within the intention of its makers." In Zuni Public School Dist. No. 89 v. Department of Educ., 550 U.S. 81 (2007), Justices Stevens and Scalia debated the continuing vitality of *Holy Trinity*'s proposition that textual meaning should yield to legislative purpose.

27. Spector v. Norwegian Cruise Line Ltd., 545 U.S. 119, 139 (2005).

28. Marx v. General Revenue Corp., 133 S. Ct. 1166, 1172 (2013). Some judges, including Justice Scalia, allow that the text may express legislative purpose but reject the concept that extratextual evidence of legislative intent or purpose is relevant. In particular, Scalia and Garner (Scalia and Garner 2012, 397) disagree that the language of a statute is only evidence of the legislative intent and maintain that the "enacted text is itself the law."

29. Some scholars, such as Solan (2005a), have made arguments in favor of recognizing a kind of collective legislative intent. Such arguments are considered in chap. 2.

30. See United States v. Locke, 471 U.S. 84 (1985). Dickerson (1975) suggests that the concept might, in fact, be a constitutionally required mode of interpretation, at least in some circumstances.

31. Although the rule of lenity is a long-standing principle of interpretation, some scholars have accused courts of inconsistently applying it. See Jeffries (1985) for a discussion.

32. It should be noted that some, including Manning (2013), doubt whether legal process devotees considered themselves bound by the meaning of the textual language. Manning argues that they considered themselves free to interpret the relevant provision more narrowly or more broadly than the language would warrant.

33. See Watson v. United States, 552 U.S. 74 (2007) and Smith v. United States, 508 U.S. 223 (1993). These cases will be discussed in chap. 5 as examples where the Supreme Court failed to properly analyze how sentential context influences the ordinary meaning of words.

34. See Nix v. Hedden, 149 U.S. 304 (1893). The case is discussed in chap. 5.

35. See General Dynamics Land Systems, Inc. v. Cline, 540 U.S. 581, 586–98 (2004).

36. See McBoyle v. United States, 283 U.S. 25 (1931).

37. See Carcieri v. Salazar, 555 U.S. 379 (2009). The case is examined in chap. 3.

38. Unless otherwise specified explicitly or implicitly by context, for purposes of this book the term "utterance" should be taken as including both oral and written communications and "utterer" as someone who makes both.

39. This hypothetical resembles McBoyle v. United States, 283 U.S. 25 (1931), where the Court held that an airplane is not a "vehicle." The Court noted, though, that airplanes were well known in 1919 when the statute was passed.

40. These issues must be addressed even under the ordinary meaning doctrine. The court must decide whether to take an originalist position and determine the ordinary meaning of the language at the time of the statute's enactment or determine it at the time of judicial decision (or some other date).

41. Some of the interpretations may be said to more accurately focus on the "significance" of a text, where a critic explores some broader or psychologically deeper context than that defined by conscious intention, rather than on the verbal meaning of the text (Hirsch 1967).

42. A judicial methodology based on broad purposivist reasoning can be said to narrow the situations where indeterminacy is recognized, although in such situations the judge is, of course, abstracting away from identifying the communicative content of the text.

43. This principle will also be (very briefly) discussed in chap. 3 when distinguishing between the ordinary meaning doctrine and communicative meaning.

44. This reason and others for the ordinary meaning doctrine are discussed at the beginning of chap. 3.

45. Hotchkiss v. National City Bank. 200 F. 287, 293 (S.D.N.Y. 1911).

46. Id.

47. Judges are particularly likely to adopt such interpretations when the dispute involves a standardized form contract that does not allow for a consumer to negotiate or where there is a power imbalance between the parties that results in unfair terms.

48. The canon of constitutional avoidance allows a court to choose a less persuasive, but plausible, interpretation in order to avoid serious constitutional issues (Slocum 2007). This principle of interpretation, along with other substantive canons, is discussed in chap. 4.

49. Appendix B also lists results for the terms often used as synonyms for "ordinary meaning."

50. Although scholars often identify three separate theories of interpretation, intentionalism and purposivism exist on a continuum. That is, no judge considers herself a purposivist in the sense that the language of a statute, whatever the words might mean, must always yield to some judicially identified overall legislative purpose. Rather, an interpretation that is based on the perceived specific intent of the legislature may be characterized as "intentionalist," while an interpretation that is based not on specific intent but on a more general sense of legislative purpose may be characterized as "purposivist." Thus, a term such as "intentionalist," which can refer to different levels of generality of intent, is typically sufficient as a category for both intentionalist and purposivist decisions.

51. Chap. 3 describes justifications for the ordinary meaning doctrine as a com-

ponent of judicial interpretations. One justification is that it provides "notice" to individuals of the requirements of the law. This justification is particularly persuasive in certain contexts, such as the interpretation of criminal provisions. Such a justification is consistent with textualist views of the judicial role in interpretation. Nevertheless, the ordinary meaning doctrine does not depend on the notice justification and would exist independently of it.

52. More accurately, it might be said that the plain language rule reflects at some intuitive level a high degree of confidence in people's potential to communicate *easily*, based on a very limited consideration of context.

53. This characterization of literal meaning is taken from Recanati (2004). The characterization makes literal meaning equivalent to 'sentence meaning' plus the assignment of references to explicitly context-dependent elements, such as indexicals. These terms are explained in chap. 3.

54. Murphy and Koskela (2010, 131) define a "proposition," in part, as "the meaning of a sentence that makes a statement about some state of affairs. As such, a proposition has a truth value: it can be either true or false."

55. 555 U.S. 379 (2009).

56. Id. at 388.

57. 552 U.S. 214 (2008).

58. 508 U.S. 223 (1993).

Chapter Two

1. Although some intentionalists like Knapp and Michaels (1982, 1987, 2005) embrace the meaning and interpretation theses but disclaim any position on the particulars of the interpretation thesis, the interpretation thesis includes for some intentionalists the question of what evidence can be legitimately employed in order to determine the speaker or author's intended meaning (Neale 2011).

2. Chapter 4 examines conversational implicatures as being determinates of ordinary meaning, even though they have traditionally been viewed as being pragmatic in nature. Recent scholars have emphasized the systematicity of some implicatures, suggesting that they could rightly be viewed as semantic. Regardless of the outcome of this debate, it will be demonstrated in later chapters that context and nonliteral interpretations are both aspects of ordinary meaning.

3. They also use examples involving texts where the author and interpreter are intimately acquainted. Campos (1996), e.g., uses an example of a note given by a wife to her husband. Such examples are as inapposite to the interpretation of legal texts as is using examples from ordinary conversations.

4. If, in contrast, Fish takes the position that the literal meaning concept he argues against cannot take account of context, he would be arguing against a view of meaning in which few (if any) subscribe.

5. Of course, not all written language involves a context of interpretation that is far removed from the context of utterance. For example, a note passed in class would involve a context of interpretation that is very similar to the context of utterance.

6. Although legal texts themselves are unsponsored, McCubbins and Rodriguez (2011, 988) have argued that the "congressional process is, in essence, a running conversation in which some members—specifically those to whom the majority party has delegated authority to set the agenda and write statutes—use the tools required by their principals (e.g., committee reports, statements by the bill manager, communications by the party whips, etc.) to signal the meaning of their actions (i.e., the statutes they have written) to the remaining members of the majority party."

7. The prominent judge and legal scholar Richard Posner (1988a, 849) has made a similar observation.

8. There are, of course, some legal texts that have a single author. Wills are one example. Even these texts, though, are dissimilar to ordinary conversations in the largely the same ways as are multiauthored legal texts.

9. If the speaker uses "dried," as in (1b), the speaker will have said nothing about how the drying came about, though the use of a tea towel, and "wiping" is one possibility.

10. Vagueness could still exist, however, because it is tied more to the nature of language and less to authorial intent. For example, a term is vague if it presents borderline difficulties (Sorensen 1989). Wasow, Perfors, and Beaver (2005, 2) note that "[m]ost expressions in natural languages are vague–that is, the denotations of most expressions are fuzzy around the edges." When, e.g., is something green instead of brown or blue? The answer to the question, whatever it may be, is orthogonal to any concept of ambiguity. The concept of vagueness is further examined in chap. 5.

11. For a somewhat similar response to this claim and others by Alexander and Prakash, see Sinnott-Armstrong (2005).

12. A distinction between categorical and semantic intentions is irrelevant to most legal texts because there is no doubt as to their proper categorization as legal texts.

13. This example references 18 U.S.C. § 924(c)(1)(A), which provides for enhanced punishment if the defendant "uses" a firearm "during and in relation to . . . [a] drug trafficking crime." The interpretive difficulties raised by the provision are examined in chap. 5.

14. Recall that most, but not all, legal texts either have multiple authors or are agreements among multiple people.

15. Note that in contract law two main situations exist in which there is a choice between a subjective or objective view of each party's intent. One involves contract formation, where the court must decide whether the party intended to enter

into a contract. The other involves the interpretation of the contract that was formed. While a rule that focuses on the subjective intent of each party is possible for the formation issue, and in fact has in the past been used by some courts, it is much less persuasive for contractual interpretation. Of course, both parties can agree that the words should have some unordinary meaning.

16. See Solan (2005a) for an excellent examination of such a theory. Raz (1996) makes a similar claim.

17. Speech act theory attempts to explain how speakers use language to accomplish intended actions and how hearers infer intended meaning from what is said.

18. Indexicals are further examined in chap. 3.

19. Quantifiers are further examined in chap. 4.

20. Such a mistake is not limited to communications via language. Trivedi (2001) points to an example where a sculptor intended a sculpture to be curvaceous but it instead looks angular.

21. Hancher (1981) asserts that the concept of sharability or communicability enters into Donnellan's account of linguistic intention only in a narrow, speaker-relative way, as the speaker's assumption regarding what meaning can be shared or communicated by uttering the words in question. Hirsch (1967), by contrast, repeatedly speaks of sharability or communicability, or the lack thereof, as absolute aspects of an author's willed meaning, without special attention to the author's (perhaps eccentric) sense of what is sharable or communicable. For the reasons explained below, Hirsch's version of sharability, with a focus on absolute aspects of an author's meaning, is superior to the speaker-relative version. As explained below, though, hypothetical intentionalism is superior to any version of moderate intentionalism.

22. Note that Levinson's "pragmatic model" describes the communicative meaning of a text. Chapter 3 describes the differences between the communicative meaning and the ordinary meaning of a text, which is not built on a pragmatic model of meaning.

23. Fish (2008, 1131) seems, in fact, to discount the idea of actual authorial intent, stating that you do not interpret legislation through the "lens of what you may happen to know about [the judges'] psychological and neurological profiles." Despite the importance of authorial intent to his description of interpretation, Fish (2005, 634) describes intent from an interpreter's perspective as the "interpreter's confidence in an interpretation."

24. Theory, referred to by Hogan (2008) as "*Theory* (capital 't')," can also refer to a specific theoretical discourse that focuses on the intrinsically political nature of criticism and theory and the political progress value of exploring such instability and relativity. I share Hogan's view that programs of research do not need to be legitimated by their contribution to social change or empowerment, and I refer to theory in a narrow way as standing for the proposition that interpretation is not entirely an empirical exercise.

25. Fish (1985) is correct that it is difficult to make a distinction between text and context considering the contextual knowledge that interpreters inevitably bring to any interpretation. Such an observation, while undermining the claims of textualism to some degree, does not, however, establish the persuasiveness of actual intentionalism.

26. For example, courts will apply a presumption that Congress does not intent for its laws to apply extraterritorially unless it has given explicit indications of such intent. The explicitness required is a matter of debate, as it is for other interpretive presumptions. These issues are discussed in chap. 4.

27. Courts have long considered the legislative history of a provision when interpreting it (Vermeule 1998). The Supreme Court's decision in Church of Holy Trinity v. United States, 143 U.S. 457 (1892), is generally recognized as the first case to sanction the use of legislative history. Many, including (Vermeule 1998), however, have argued against the use of legislative history by courts on the grounds that it does not help determine legislative intent.

28. See Olson v. Haley, 549 U.S. 225, 263 (2007). It may be, as Gluck and Bressman (2013) reveal, that congressional drafters purport not to consider interpretive principles like the *in pari materia* canon. It is not clear, though, that such a finding undermines the interpretive principle. In any case, whether the *in pari materia* canon is a legitimate interpretive principle is not material to the arguments made in this chapter.

29. Of course, as Wilson (1992) asserts, the intentionalist meaning and interpretation theses are themselves theories, making the intentionalist failure to understand that interpretation is a theoretical exercise somewhat peculiar.

30. What came to be known as the *Chevron* doctrine was announced by the in Chevron U.S.A. Inc. v. Natural Resources Defense Council, Inc., 467 U.S. 837 (1984).

31. Davis (2006) questions whether hypothetical intentionalism can draw a principled and coherent distinction between admissible and inadmissible types of evidence. Such concerns are typically exaggerated, although the epistemic issue of the proper determinants of meaning does not need to be resolved in this chapter. Rather, the focus is on conventions of meaning as the foundation of the ordinary meaning concept. Nevertheless, like other aspects of interpretation, it is unsurprising that there are suggestions regarding allowable determinants of meaning that rely on generalized assumptions regarding intent. Nathan (2005), for instance, suggests that authors of public documents, such as artistic works and legal statutes, have the second-order intention that extratextual sources of their first-order intentions regarding what their documents mean should not be sought or needed. Certainly, such a presumption, if adopted, would sometimes be applied even in situations where it did not coincide with authorial intent.

Chapter Three

1. 555 U.S. 379 (2009).

2. Id. at 388 (quoting *Webster's New International Dictionary* 1671 (2d ed. 1934)).

3. 132 S. Ct. 1997 (2012).

4. Id. at 2004. For similar cases see FCC v. AT&T Inc. 131 S. Ct. 1177, 1179 (2011) (indicating that "AT&T has provided no sound reason in the statutory text or context to disregard the ordinary meaning of the [statutory] phrase"); and Holder v. Humanitarian Law Project 130 S. Ct. 2705, 2721–2722 (2010) (relying on dictionary definitions for the ordinary meaning of "service" and indicating that "[c]ontext confirms that ordinary meaning here").

5. 529 U.S. 694 (2000).

6. Id. at 706n9. In a dissenting opinion, Justice Scalia exhibited confusion regarding the concept of conventional meaning. Justice Scalia argued that "when the Court admits that it is giving the word 'revoke' an 'unconventional' meaning, it says that it is choosing to ignore the word 'revoke.'" Id. at 717n1. It is not true, though, that giving a word an unordinary meaning indicates that the word is being eliminated or ignored. Otherwise, the concept of ordinary meaning would be incoherent. Instead, choosing an unordinary meaning is an indication, based on a broad consideration of contextual clues, that the author intended some unusual or idiosyncratic meaning. Considering the polysemous and dynamic nature of language, such a result is a perfectly valid way of determining meaning (and one that fits well with the concept of ordinary meaning).

7. McBoyle v. United States, 283 U.S. 25, 27 (1931).

8. Id.

9. Chapter 1 described Solan's argument when illustrating the differences between oral and textual communications.

10. Justice Scalia would respond, of course, that the actual intentions of the legislature are irrelevant. While such sentiments are widely shared, many others continue to maintain that a legislature's intent should inform, if not control, the judicial interpretation.

11. Of course, the ordinary meaning may not be definite, which is undoubtedly common, and precisification will result in a meaning that differs from the ordinary meaning of the language.

12. For example, the hugely important *Chevron* doctrine, derived from the Supreme Court's decision in Chevron, U.S.A., Inc. v. Natural Resources Defense Council, Inc., 467 U.S. 837 (1984), which requires courts to defer to reasonable agency interpretations of ambiguous statutes, is often ignored by courts even when it is clearly relevant (Kerr 1998).

13. Johnson v. United States, 529 U.S. 694, 718 (2000) (Scalia, J., dissenting).

14. Ogden v. Saunders, 25 U.S. 213, 332 (1827).

15. See, e.g., United States v. Costello, 666 F.3d 1040, 1043–44 (7th Cir. 2012) (citations omitted) (stating that "[i]f multiple definitions are available, which one best fits the way an ordinary person would interpret the term?").

16. Seeck v. Geico General Ins. Co., 212 S.W.3d 129, 132 (Mo. banc 2007).

17. These interpretive principles, and other similar ones, are discussed in more detail in chap. 4.

18. Scalia and Garner (Scalia and Garner 2012, 16) also indicate that "[i]n their full context, words mean what they conveyed to reasonable people at the time they were written."

19. 135 S. Ct. 1074 (2015).

20. Id. at 1079.

21. Id. at 1091 (Kagan, J., dissenting).

22. Recall that actual intentionalists claim that there is no such thing as the ordinary meaning of language but only the actual meaning intended by the speaker or author. These arguments were rejected in chap. 2.

23. Karl Llewellyn wrote a famous critique of interpretive canons in 1950, which argued that for every canon there is another canon pointing to the opposite interpretation. Although Llewellyn's arguments are overstated, it is indisputable that interpretive principles often conflict.

24. Others, including Solan (2011), have made similar observations.

25. Waisman (1951) refers to "ordinary content," which is synonymous with ordinary meaning.

26. See, e.g., Kariuki v. Tarango, 709 F.3d 495, 502 (5th Cir. 2013) (stating that "[i]n determining what Congress meant by its use of the word 'hearing' . . . we must consider the context in which the word is used and give to the term its ordinary meaning within that context") (citation omitted).

27. Molot (2006, 34–35) concurs that "[m]odern textualists have rejected the old 'plain meaning' version of textualism that served as a foil for purposivism in prior decades." Recall that chap. 1 also distinguished between the ordinary meaning doctrine and the plain meaning rule.

28. Graham Cnty. Soil & Water Conservation Dist. v. United States ex rel. Wilson, 545 U.S. 409, 415 (2005) (Thomas, J.); see also Jones v. United States, 527 U.S. 373, 389 (1999) (Thomas, J.) ("Statutory language must be read in context and a phrase 'gathers meaning from the words around it'") (quoting Jarecki v. G.D. Searle & Co., 367 U.S. 303, 307 (1961)).

29. Chapter 1 describes the distinction between ordinary meaning and literal meaning. For the purposes of this discussion, the two can be seen as synonymous.

30. One exception is Green's (2009) examination of indexicals in the federal constitution.

31. Demonstratives, such as "this" and "that" are very similar to indexicals in that they are expressions whose reference depends on the context of use. Some

distinguish between "pure indexicals," such as "I," that can be determined on the basis of the general context and demonstratives, which require the speaker to direct the hearer's attention in order to establish the reference (Murphy and Koskela, 2010).

32. 555 U.S. 379 (2009).

33. Id. at 383.

34. Id. at 384.

35. 25 U.S.C. §§ 1701–16 (2006).

36. *Carcieri*, 555 U.S. at 384.

37. Id.

38. 25 CFR § 83.2 (2008) (providing that federal recognition is needed before an Indian tribe may seek "the protection, services, and benefits of the Federal government").

39. 25 U.S.C. § 465 (2006).

40. *Carcieri*, 555 U.S. at 385.

41. Id. at 382.

42. 25 U.S.C. § 465.

43. 555 U.S. at 388 (quoting *Webster's New International Dictionary* 1671 (2d ed. 1934)).

44. Id. (quoting *Black's Law Dictionary* 1262 (3d ed. 1933) (defining "now" to mean "[a]t this time, or at the present moment")).

45. Id. at 388–89. The Court cited to Franklin v. United States, 216 U.S. 559, 568–69 (1910) (interpreting a federal criminal statute to have "adopted such punishment as the laws of the State in which such place is situated now provide for the like offense") (emphasis added) and Montana v. Kennedy, 366 U.S. 308, 310–11 (1961) (interpreting a statute granting citizenship to foreign-born "children of persons who *now* are, or have been citizens of the United States") (emphasis added).

46. The provision stated "[t]hat no part of such funds shall be used to acquire additional land outside of the exterior boundaries of [the] Navajo Indian Reservation . . . in the event that the proposed Navajo boundary extension measures now pending in Congress . . . become law." IRA, § 5, 48 Stat. 985.

47. The Court gave the examples of 25 U.S.C. § 468 (referring to "the geographic boundaries of any Indian reservation now existing or established hereafter") and § 472 (referring to "Indians who may be appointed . . . to the various positions maintained, now or hereafter, by the Indian Office").

48. *Carcieri*, 555 U.S. at 389.

49. Id. at 390.

50. Id. at 391 (quoting Deal v. United States, 508 U.S. 129, 131–32 (1993)).

51. Id. at 392.

52. Id. at 396.

53. Justice Breyer cited to Montana v. Kennedy, 366 U.S. 308, 311–312 (1961) ("now" refers to time of statutory enactment); Difford v. Secretary of HHS, 910

F.2d 1316, 1320 (C.A.6 1990) ("now" refers to time of exercise of delegated authority); and In re Lusk's Estate, 336 Pa. 465, 467–68 (1939) (property "now" owned refers to property owned when a will becomes operative).

54. Justice Breyer (id. at 398) pointed out that following the Indian Reorganization Act's enactment, the department compiled a list of 258 tribes covered by the act but wrongly left off the list. The department later recognized some of those tribes on grounds that showed that it should have recognized them in 1934 even though it did not. See id. Justice Breyer also stated that the department has sometimes acknowledged that a tribe was "under Federal Jurisdiction" in 1934 even though the department did not know it at the time. See id. at 398–99.

55. Carcieri v. Norton, 290 F. Supp. 2d 167, 179 (D.R.I. 2003), aff'd sub nom. Carcieri v. Kempthorne, 497 F.3d 15 (1st Cir. 2007) (en banc), rev'd sub nom. Carcieri v. Salazar, 129 S. Ct. 1058 (2009).

56. Id. The tribe easily satisfied the first requirement because "[t]he Narragansett community and its predecessors have existed autonomously since first contact, despite undergoing many modifications." Id. at 180 (quoting Final Determination for Federal Acknowledgement of Narragansett Indian Tribe of Rhode Island, 48 Fed. Reg. 6177, 6178 (Feb. 10, 1983)) (internal quotation marks omitted). The second requirement, too, was easily satisfied as the tribe had attained federal recognition in 1983. Id. at 181.

57. Id.

58. *Carcieri*, 290 F. Supp. 2d at 179 (quoting Rhode Island v. Narragansett Indian Tribe, 19 F.3d 685, 694 (1st Cir. 1994)) (internal quotation marks omitted).

59. *Carcieri*, 497 F.3d at 22.

60. Id. at 26 (citations omitted).

61. Kaplan (1989, 491n12) did recognize the existence of situations where (6) might be true, including in cases in which "there is a significant lag between our production of speech and its audition, for instance in cases of messages recorded for later broadcast."

62. This example was modified from one offered by Romdenh-Romluc (2008, 147).

63. Stevens (2009) defends the Kaplan account on the basis that (11) is not communicated by an assertion and therefore involves an improper context. As such, it falls outside the scope of formal semantics. Stevens focuses on the distinction between a sentence being true or false with respect to a context (at a world) and of a sentence being asserted in a context. An assertion is an illocutionary act, but if no assertion has taken place, as is the case with (11), there is little interest, from a certain formal semantics perspective, in evaluating (11) with respect to it. Stevens' theory thus assumes that any indexical sentence is false with respect to all improper indexes and views answerphone message occurrences as simply recordings of false utterances. The utterance of (11) can therefore be seen, in the spatio-temporal location, as just a recording of the utterance. Because the deci-

sion has been made to base the semantic system on sentences under interpretations rather than mere utterances, it is irrelevant whether (11) is false with respect to the context in which it is uttered. That they can be used to communicate truths has no impact on their truth conditions. Under Stevens's theory, then, the focus is solely on the evaluation of sentences with respect to proper indexes. Notwithstanding its contributions in other areas, a theory that is cashed out in terms of truth conditions cannot offer a complete explanation of mismatched communications. Furthermore, a theory, such as Stevens's, that focuses on assertions rather than utterances offers an account of (as least some) mismatched communications, but not one that should be thought to operate to the exclusion of other (more explanatory) types of theories.

64. This example was taken from Corazza (2004, 290).

65. This example was taken from Corazza (2004, 291).

66. Gauker (2008) distinguishes between a stronger and weaker intentionalist claim. The stronger claim is that intentions are the sole and ultimate determinants of the content of indexicals. The weaker claim is that intentions play a role in determining the content. The weaker claim is consistent with the position that external factors play a role in determining the content, whereas the stronger claim is consistent with the position that the speaker's intentions determine the context.

67. As Gorvett (2005, 295) notes, the debate over intentionalism with respect to indexicals is similar to the debate over intentionalism with respect to definite descriptions (which was discussed in chap. 2).

68. Ac is the relevant audience (and is assumed to be linguistically competent and attentive) based on a conclusion that it is reasonable to take the speaker to be addressing Ac. The relevant audience, however, but might not be the person U intends to address.

69. In a sense, all the relevant facts are found outside the text considering that it is the interpreter who decides what words mean, whether this knowledge comes from personal experience or some other source such as a dictionary definition.

70. Of course, even the most determinate rules raise serious interpretive problems. For example, with (14) the meaning of "home" and "minors" might be subject to dispute, as well as what it means to "be home." What if the minor is staying with a relative? What if the minor is just pulling into the driveway at 10 p.m.? Also, as Lasersohn (1999) has described, "pragmatic slack" allows people to speak with varying degrees of precision and sometimes quite loosely. Thus, is it a violation of the convention in (14) if the minor arrives home at one second after 10 p.m.?

71. Traditionally, at common law, courts decided the issue by analyzing whether the bequest at issue involved a class devise. A class is an entity (a set) whose members are the beneficiaries living from time to time. A class gift is a devise to a class. If the bequest in (16) is seen as a class gift, which is likely, the temporal reference for *children* is determined by a majority of courts to be the time of the testator's death. Also, the referents must be those designees who are capable of taking the

property, that is, those who satisfy the description (those who are living) at the testator's death. Under the common law, this default rule would be chosen instead of a distribution of Madre's share under the will's residuary clause or according to intestate succession rules.

72. Even though it is phrased in the present tense, the testator's commissive act is, obviously, not intended to be carried out until the testator's death.

73. Wills are said to be "ambulatory," that is, inoperative until the testator's death.

74. Id. at 388 (quoting *Webster's New International Dictionary* 1671 [2d ed. 1934]).

75. Id. at 391 (quoting Deal v. United States, 508 U.S. 129, 131–32 [1993]).

76. Id. at 392 (quoting Connecticut Nat. Bank v. Germain, 503 U.S. 249, 253–54 [1992]).

Chapter Four

1. Recall that speech act theory attempts to explain how speakers use language to accomplish intended actions and how hearers infer intended meaning form what is said. In contrast, according to Murphy and Koskela (2010, 70), a "formal semantic theory is one that uses a formal metalanguage—i.e., a logic or similar mathematical language—in order to represent natural language meanings. Such approaches are valued for their precision. Since the metalanguage has very clear rules and its elements have very specific meanings, formal representations avoid the problem of ambiguity and are very testable."

2. Whether listeners can systematically distinguish between "what is said" and "what is implicated" is the subject of considerable debate and empirical inquiry (Doran et al. 2012). For purposes of this project of conceptualizing ordinary meaning, it is not essential that it be shown that listeners can systematically distinguish between the two concepts. Rather, it is clear that all the linguistic phenomena examined in this book are accessible to legal interpreters and are thus capable of being considered accurately.

3. 520 U.S. 1 (1997).

4. Id. at 5

5. Id. at 6.

6. 544 U.S. 385 (2005).

7. Id. at 388–89.

8. 541 U.S. 125 (2004).

9. Id. at 140–41. See also (Scalia, J., concurring) (pointing to the interpretive principle as requiring the result reaching by the Court).

10. 528 U.S. 250 (2000).

11. Id. at 743–44.

12. 552 U.S. 214 (2008).

13. Id. at 216.

14. Id.

15. Id.

16. Id. at 216–17.

17. See 28 U.S.C. § 1346(b)(1).

18. Id.

19. Id. at 217.

20. F.Supp.2d, 2006 WL 4560162 (N.D.Ga. 2006).

21. 204 Fed.Appx. 778, 2006 WL 2990216 (11th Cir. 2006).

22. See Bramwell v. Bureau of Prisons, 348 F.3d 804 (9th Cir. 2003); Chapa v. Dept. of Justice, 339 F.3d 388 (5th Cir. 2003); Hatten v. White, 275 F.3d 1208 (10th Cir. 2002); Cheney v. United States, 972 F.2d 247(8th Cir. 1992); Ysasi v. Rivkind, 856 F.2d 1520 (Fed. Cir. 1988).

23. See ABC v. DEF, 500 F.3d 103 (2d Cir. 2007); Dahler v. United States, 473 F.3d 769 (7th Cir. 2007); Andrews v. United States, 441 F.3d 220 (4th Cir. 2006); Bazuaye v. United States, 83 F.3d 482 (D.C. Cir. 1996); and Kurinsky v. United States, 33 F.3d 594 (6th Cir. 1994).

24. 552 U.S. 214, at 219 (quoting United States v. Gonzales, 520 U.S. 1, 5 (1997) (quoting *Webster's Third New International Dictionary* 97 (1976)).

25. Id. at 219–20.

26. Id. at 220.

27. Id. at 221–22.

28. According to Recanati (2004), normal interpreters (i.e., not linguists) are aware only of the output of the primary processes involved in contextual adjustment.

29. Recall that an unarticulated constituent is part of the intuitive meaning of the utterance yet does not correspond to anything in the sentence itself.

30. Nevertheless, this project will continue to refer to quantifier domain restriction since it appears to be the more common term.

31. Of course, the wide context might also be consulted in order to disambiguate or to precisify vague language.

32. Id. at 220.

33. Id. at 223.

34. All of the justices would agree to this restriction of the literal meaning even if there is general disagreement amongst the justices about whether universal quantifiers include foreign events, as the Court's decision in Small v. United States, 544 U.S. 385 (2005), illustrates.

35. Id. at 227.

36. Recall from chap. 3 that in *Carcieri v. Salazar*, 555 U.S. 379 (2009), the Supreme Court made a similar mistake when confusing ambiguity with determining the correct reference of indexicals.

37. *Ali,* 552 U.S. at 219–20 (discussing United States v. Gonzales, 520 U.S. 1 (1997) and Harrison v. PPG Industries, Inc., 446 U.S. 578 (1980)).

38. Id.

39. Id. at 232.

40. 528 U.S. 250 (2000).

41. United States v. Palmer, 3 Wheat. 610, 631 (1818).

42. 544 U.S. 385 (2005).

43. Id. at 388.

44. 552 U.S. at 243–44 (Breyer, J., dissenting).

45. Id. at 243.

46. 544 U.S. at 395 (Thomas, J., dissenting).

47. 533 U.S. 678 (2001).

48. See id. at 684–85.

49. See id.

50. See id. at 684–86.

51. See id. at 684, 686.

52. 8 U.S.C. § 1231(a)(6) (1994 ed., Supp. V).

53. Kim Ho Ma v. Reno, 208 F.3d 815 (9th Cir. 2000).

54. Zadvydas v. Underdown, 185 F.3d 279 (5th Cir. 1999).

55. Duy Dac Ho. V. Greene, 204 F.3d 1045 (10th Cir. 2000).

56. 8 U.S.C. § 1226(c).

57. Zadvydas, 533 U.S. at 689.

58. Id. at 697.

59. INS v. St. Cyr, 533 U.S. 289, 299–300 (2001).

60. 533 U.S. at 689.

61. See id. at 701.

62. Id. at 707.

63. Clark v. Martinez, 543 U.S. 371, 400 (2005) (Thomas, J., dissenting).

64. 533 U.S. at 689.

65. See id. at 701.

66. Id.

67. The necessity defense has long been recognized in the common law, and eventually in statues, and is applicable in situations where a technical breach of the law is more advantageous to society than the consequences of strict adherence to the law. Typically, the following elements must be proved: (1) the defendant acted to avoid a significant risk of harm; (2) no adequate lawful means could have been used to escape the harm; and (3) the harm avoided was greater than that caused by breaking the law.

68. The relationship between canon creation and the proper judicial role has been extensively debated. For one contribution see Barrett (2010).

69. McNary v. Haitian Refugee Center, Inc., 498 U.S. 479, 496 (1991).

70. See Schacter (1995) for a description of how courts use rules of interpretation to pursue various visions of democracy.

71. Currently, courts do not consider the inherent temporal issue that is present whenever the constitutional rule that could potentially invalidate all or part of the statute in question was established after the enactment of the statute (Scheef 2003).

72. See St. Cyr, 533 U.S. at 327 (Scalia, J., dissenting) (arguing that the Court's opinion established "a superclear statement, 'magic words' requirement for the congressional expression of" an intent to preclude habeas review).

73. St. Cyr, 533 U.S. at 299–300.

74. Spector v. Norwegian Cruise Line Ltd., 545 U.S. 119, 141 (2005).

75. Zadvydas v. Davis, 533 U.S. 678, 689 (2001).

76. Boston Sand & Gravel Co. v. United States, 278 U.S. 41, 48 (1928).

77. See Patrie v. Area Coop. Educ. Serv., 37 Conn. L. Rptr. 470 (Conn. Super. Ct. 2004) (finding that it should carry its ordinary linguistic meaning).

78. See INS v. St. Cyr, 533 U.S. 289, 327 (2001) (Scalia, J., dissenting) (arguing that the Court's opinion established "a superclear statement, 'magic words' requirement for the congressional expression of" an intent to preclude habeas review).

79. Although the proviso canon is listed under the "sound principles of interpretation" heading, the authors (154) indicate that "[b]ecause of regular abuse of provisos . . . the rule that a proviso introduces a condition has become a feeble presumption."

80. Yates v. United States, 135 S. Ct. 1074, 1097 (2015).

81. See Sierra Club v. Kenney, 88Ill.2d. 110, 127 (Ill. 1981).

82. Id.

83. Id.

84. Id. at 127–28.

85. 532 U.S. 105, 109, 115 (2001).

86. Id. at 119.

87. Id. at 118.

88. United States v. Vulcan Society, Inc., 897 F.Supp.2d 30, 37 (E.D.N.Y. 2012).

89. An accurate scale might be more complex than what is depicted in the text. As indicated below, a general term followed by a list of specific items does not trigger the *ejusdem generis* canon, at least according to some courts. Similarly, it is not applicable when a single specific term is followed by a general term. The scale might more accurately be depicted as follows: {specific list, list + "other" clause, general term, specific term + general term, general term + specific list}. The additional detail does not change the analysis in the text, though, and adds complication that might distract from the basic point that scales can help explain the role of the *ejusdem generis* canon.

90. In a dissenting opinion, Justice Kennedy argued that the *ejusdem generis* canon's application "is not limited to those statutes that include a laundry list of items." 552 U.S. 214, 231 (Kennedy, J., dissenting). Whether Justice Kennedy is correct is relevant to the convention of language associated with the *ejusdem generis*

canon, but the precise contours of the canon are irrelevant to the issue of whether the canon in general is a proper aspect of an ordinary meaning determination.

91. In a later publication, Marmor (2014) clarifies his position, stating that "I am not denying the possibility that some implicatures in law would work," although he does not offer any examples.

92. Asgeirsson (2012) disagrees with some of Marmor's analysis, particularly his claim that a speaker succeeds in asserting something other than what she literally says only if it is obvious that she cannot be intending to assert the literal content of her remark. However, he agrees with Poggi that the legislative context is typically equivocal and rarely supports the application of conversational implicatures.

93. 552 U.S. 214 (2008).

94. Sarangi and Slembrouck (1992) address the applicability of the cooperativeness principle to institutional discourse.

95. Rector, Holy Trinity Church v. U.S., 143 U.S. 457 (1892).

96. For example, recall the example (1) gin, bourbon, vodka, rum and other beverages. As (2) illustrates, "(2) gin, bourbon, vodka, run and other beverages. Thus, all beverages fall under the prohibition," in contrast to the situation with a conventional implicature, the addition of a second sentence can negate the implicature without a perceived contradiction.

Chapter Five

1. 552 U.S. 214 (2008). The case is discussed in chap. 4.

2. Indexicals were examined in chap. 3 and temporal preposition phrases and substantive canons in chap. 4.

3. 508 U.S. 223 (1993).

4. The statute also applies to anyone who "carries" or, since an amendment to the statute in 1998, "possesses" a firearm "during and in relation to . . . [a] drug trafficking crime." 18 U.S.C. § 924(c)(1)(A). In the cases described in this section, the defendants were all charged with "use" of the firearm.

5. 21 Mass.L.Rptr. 565, 2006 WL 3292641 (Mass. Super. Ct. 2006).

6. Id. at *3 (citing Ober v. National Casualty Co., 318 Mass. 27, 39 (1945)).

7. Id.

8. The court noted in a footnote that the "parties have submitted numerous dictionary definitions for the term 'sandwich,' as well as expert affidavits" but did not explain whether the expert affidavits influenced the court's interpretation. Id. at *3n3.

9. Id.

10. Id.

11. 149 U.S. 304 (1894).

12. Id. at 306.

13. Id.

14. Id.

15. Id. (quoting Robertson v. Salomon, 130 U.S. 412, 414 (1889)).

16. Id. at 307.

17. *United States Department of Agriculture* (2005).

18. Id.

19. Id.

20. A concept is a subpropositional mental representation rather than something that expresses a whole proposition (Margolis and Laurence 1999). Thus, a word or phrase can be a concept but, generally, not a sentence.

21. Charnock (2013, 130) remarks that it would "require some generosity" to designate Hart's famous remark regarding open texture as a theory of semantics, "especially as Hart makes little further use of ordinary language analysis."

22. Chap. 3 introduced the distinction between "narrow context" and "wide context." For the ordinary meaning concept to be meaningful there must be some gap, at least in some cases, between ordinary meaning and communicative meaning. This requires some division of context into that relevant for ordinary meaning determinations and that relevant for communicative meaning determinations. In short, narrow context concerns, amongst other things, information specifically relevant to determining the semantic values of context-sensitive expressions such as indexicals.

23. As Geeraerts (2010) and others have explained, even a category like "even number," which has necessary and sufficient conditions of membership, has prototypical members.

24. The sorites paradox typically proceeds in some variation of the following:

> The subject first agrees that a certain amount of beans is a "heap" and then agrees that the difference of one bean should not prevent it from being considered a "heap." A second bean is (rhetorically) removed, and the victim must again agree that the removal of the bean should not prevent the beans from constituting a "heap." And so on.

The paradox only works if the subject believes, at the outset, that the 'heap' is capable of precise definition but, realizing in each instance that the removal of one of many beans should not matter, is unable to quantify its limits. If the victim that the outset believed that terms such as 'heap' are general concepts with blurred lines not subject to precise limitation, arguably the sorites paradox would lose its power.

25. See Slocum (2000) for a discussion of the void-for-vagueness doctrine.

26. Indeed, there are various advanced statistical theories of how items may be clustered based on partially correlated dimensions (Hampton et al. 1993).

27. 461 F.2d 651 (5th Cir. 1972).

28. 434 F.2d 1284 (6th Cir. 1970).

29. See chap. 2 for a description of the differences between ordinary conversations and interpretation of legal texts.

30. Under such a methodology the interpreter would not have to be particularly concerned with constructing a prototype and a criterion of similarity.

31. In McBoyle v. United States, 283 U.S. 25 (1931), the Supreme Court held that an airplane was not a vehicle for purposes of a statute that criminalizes the interstate transportation of stolen vehicles.

32. 21 Mass.L.Rptr. 565, 2006 WL 3292641 *3.

33. Of course, one would also want to know whether these menus list burritos under the category of sandwiches.

34. Posner states that the slices of bread do not have to be thin, but it is not entirely clear what the adjective "thin" means in the context of a sandwich. Its meaning is entirely dependent on the context and basis of comparison (i.e., thin vs. fat), but according to what basis of comparison could slices of bread or a filing not be "thin"?

35. The Wikipedia entry can be found at http://en.wikipedia.org/wiki/Sandwich wrap (accessed February 21, 2014).

36. Id.

37. Like with other categories there might situations where the object is neither clearly an artifact nor clearly a natural kind.

38. Courts have discretion even when the legislature does provide a definition because the definition, being the product of natural language, is unlikely to clearly resolve every interpretive dispute that may arise.

39. RICO was enacted as Title IX of the Organized Crime Control Act of 1970. 18 U.S.C.A. §§ 1961–68.

40. Standen (1998, 289), e.g., argues that RICO's definitions are tautological and "accomplish little more than to grant authority to prosecutors and judges to shape the contours of the law." See Cunningham et al. (1994) for a discussion of RICO and concepts with fuzzy boundaries.

41. 18 U.S.C. § 1962(a).

42. 18 U.S.C. § 1962(b).

43. 18 U.S.C. § 1962(c).

44. 18 U.S.C. § 1961(1).

45. 18 U.S.C. § 1961(5).

46. See Slocum (2000) for a description of the other ways in which the Supreme Court was forced to precisify the terms of RICO, at the expense of invalidating the criminal provisions for being overly vague.

47. 473 U.S. 479 (1985).

48. 492 U.S. 229 (1989).

49. Id. at 238.

50. Id. (quoting 11 *Oxford English Dictionary* 357 (2d ed. 1989)).

51. Id. at 238.

52. Id. at 237, 238.

53. Id. at 240 (quotations and citation omitted).

54. Id. at 241.

55. Id. at 242.

56. Justice Scalia argued, "A gang of hoodlums that commits one act of extortion on Monday in New York, a second in Chicago on Tuesday, a third in San Francisco on Wednesday, and so on through an entire week, and then finally and completely disbands, cannot be reached under RICO [under the decision]. I am sure that is not what the statute intends, but I cannot imagine what else the Court's murky discussion can possibly mean." See id. at 252 (Scalia, J., dissenting).

57. 452 U.S. 576 (1981).

58. 510 U.S. 249 (1994).

59. Note that I am not arguing that the interpretations were incorrect. Cunningham et al. (1994), e.g., demonstrate through linguistic research that "enterprise" is not synonymous with "business" and that a profit motive is not generally deemed to be a necessary component.

60. 533 U.S. 158 (2001).

61. Id. at 163.

62. Id.

63. 116 F.3d 225, 226 (7th Cir. 1997).

64. Id. at 226.

65. Id.

66. Id. at 227.

67. Id.

68. Id.

69. Id.

70. 508 U.S. 223 (1993).

71. The statute also applies to anyone who "carries" or, since an amendment to the statute in 1998, "possesses" a firearm "during and in relation to . . . [a] drug trafficking crime." 18 U.S.C. § 924(c)(1)(A). In the cases described in this section, the defendants were all charged with "use" of the firearm.

72. Id. at 228. Because the defendant traded a "machinegun," the sentence was thirty years. See id. at 226.

73. Id.

74. Id. at 229.

75. See id.

76. Id. at 230.

77. Id.

78. Id. at 229.

79. Id. at 230.

80. Id. at 229.

81. Id. at 241–42 [quoting the Court's decision in Deal v. United States, 508 U.S. 129, 132 (1993), that the "meaning of a word cannot be determined in isolation"].

82. Id. at 242.

83. Id.

84. Id.

85. Id. at 244.

86. 552 U.S. 74 (2007).

87. Id. at 79.

88. Id.

89. Id.

90. Id.

91. This should not be taken as a criticism of Geis's (1995) conclusions about *Smith*. He correctly argues that the linguistic context provided in 18 U.S.C. § 924(c)(1)(A) provides support for the position that "use a firearm" means "use a firearm as a weapon." This meaning is not, however, merely the "contextual meaning" but, rather, the ordinary meaning of the provision.

92. In his dissent in Smith v. United States, 508 U.S. 223 (1993), Justice Scalia also recognized the unspecified nature of "use." See id. at 242.

93. In contrast, "The author began the book" is typically interpreted as "The author began writing the book."

94. Frisson and McElree (2008) confirm, through another study, the hypothesis that the increased processing cost reflects the on-line construction of an event sense for the complement. Similarly, McElree et al. (2006) have found that enriched composition requires the online deployment of complex compositional operations.

95. 552 U.S. 74 (2007).

96. Id. at 79.

97. 516 U.S. 137 (1995).

98. Id. at 145.

99. As his distinction between ordinary meaning and definitional meaning illustrates, as well as his voluminous work on language and law, Solan does not argue that "simple introspection" constitutes sufficient knowledge of how language works. Using one of his quotes to make a point about the necessity of theories of language should not be taken as a criticism of his excellent and rightly influential work.

100. Conceivably, the opposite is also possible.

Chapter Six

1. See Landgraf v. USI Film Products, 511 U.S. 244, 272–73 (1994) (stating that there is "a presumption against retroactivity [unless] Congress itself has affirmatively considered the potential unfairness of retroactive application and determined that it is an acceptable price to pay for the countervailing benefits").

2. See EEOC v. Arabian American Oil Co., 499 U.S. 244, 248 (1991) (stating

that it is a "longstanding principle of American law that legislation of Congress, unless a contrary intent appears, is meant to apply only within the territorial jurisdiction of the United States").

3. 513 U.S. 64 (1994).

4. Id. at 68.

5. 556 U.S. 646 (2009).

6. 18 U.S.C. § 1028A(a)(1).

7. Id. at 650.

8. See, e.g., State v. Hunter, 2011 WL 5825358 (Wash. App. Div. 2011).

References

Abdulkhaliq, M. 2001. "English Noun Classes and Generative Lexical Mechanisms." PhD dissertation, Stanford University.

Aitchison, J. 2012. *Words in the Mind: An Introduction to the Mental Lexicon*. West Sussex: Wiley-Blackwell Publishing.

Akerman, J. 2009. "A Plea for Pragmatics." *Synthese* 170 (1): 155–67.

Akinnaso, F. Niyi. 1982. "On the Differences between Spoken and Written Language." *Language and Speech* 25 (2): 97–125.

Alexander, L. 1995. "All or Nothing At All? The Intentions, Authorities and the Authority of Intentions." In *Law and Interpretation: Essays in Legal Philosophy*, edited by Andre Marmor, 357–95. Oxford: Oxford University Press.

———. 2010. "Telepathic Law." *Constitutional Commentary* 27:139–50.

Alexander, L., and S. Prakash. 2003. "Mother May I? Imposing Mandatory Prospective Rules of Statutory Interpretation." *Constitutional Commentary* 20: 97–109.

———. 2004. "'Is That English You're Speaking?' Why Intention Free Interpretation is an Impossibility." *San Diego Law Review* 41:967–94.

Anderson, S. 2010. *Legal Contextualism: Law's "Open Texture" as Contextual Vagueness*. Saarbrucken: VDM Verlag Dr. Muller.

Aprill, E. 1998. "The Law of the Word: Dictionary Shopping in the Supreme Court." *Arizona State Law Journal* 30:275–320.

Ariel, M. 2010. *Defining Pragmatics*. Cambridge: Cambridge University Press.

Armstrong, P. 1990. *Conflicting Readings: Variety and Validity in Interpretation*. Chapel Hill: University of North Carolina Press.

Asgeirsson, H. 2012. "On the Possibility of Non-Literal Legislative Speech." Unpublished manuscript. Social Science Research Network. Consulted August 1, 2014. Pdf. file.

Azar, M. 2007. "Transforming Ambiguity into Vagueness in Legal Interpretation." In *Interpretation, Law and the Construction of Meaning*, edited by A. Wagner, W. Werner, and D. Cao, 121–37. New York: Springer.

Azuelos-Atias, S. 2011. "On the Incoherence of Legal Language to the General Public." *International Journal for the Semiotics of Law* 24 (1): 41–59.

Azzouni, J. 2013. *Semantic Perception: How the Illusion of a Common Language Arises and Persists.* Oxford: Oxford University Press.

Bach, K. 2002. "Semantic, Pragmatic." In *Meaning and Truth*, edited by J. Campbell, M. O'Rourke, and D. Shier, 284–92. New York: Seven Bridges Press.

———. 2005. "Context ex machine." In *Semantics Versus Pragmatics*, edited by Z. Szabo, 15–44. Oxford: Oxford University Press.

———. 2007. "Regressions in Pragmatics (and Semantics)." In *Advances in Pragmatics*, edited by N. Burton-Roberts. England: Palgrave Macmillan.

Barrett, A. 2010. "Substantive Canons and Faithful Agency." *Boston University Law Review* 90:109–82.

Beardsley, M. 1992. "The Authority of the Text." In *Intention and Interpretation*, edited by G. Iseminger, 24–40. Philadelphia: Temple University Press.

Benson, R. 2008. *The Interpretation Game: How Judges and Lawyers Make the Law.* Durham: Carolina Academic Press.

Bianchi, C. 2006. "'Nobody Loves Me': Quantification and Context." *Philosophical Studies* 130 (2): 377–97.

Biber, D. 1986. "Spoken and Written Textual Dimensions in English: Revolving the Contradictory Findings." *Language* 62 (2): 384–414.

———. 1988. *Variation Across Speech and Writing.* Cambridge: Cambridge University Press.

Biber, D., and B. Gray. 2010. "Challenging Stereotypes about Academic Writing: Complexity, Elaboration, Explicitness." *Journal of English for Academic Purposes* 9 (1): 2–20.

Blatt, W. 2001. "Interpretive Communities: The Missing Element in Statutory Interpretation." *Northwestern University Law Review* 95 (2): 629–89.

Blome-Tillmann, M. 2013. "Conversational Implicatures (and How to Spot Them)." *Philosophy Compass* 8 (2): 170–85.

Borg, E. 2007. *Minimal Semantics.* Oxford: Oxford University Press.

———. 2012. *Pursuing Meaning.* Oxford: Oxford University Press.

Botne, R. 2001. "To Die Across Languages: Towards a Typology of Achievement Verbs." *Linguistic Typology* 7 (2): 233–78.

Boudreau, C., McCubbins, M., and Rodriguez, D. 2005. "Statutory Interpretation and the Intentionalist Stance." *Loyola of Los Angeles Law Review* 38:2131–46.

Bradley, C. 1998. "The Charming Betsy Canon and Separation of Powers: Rethinking the Interpretive Role of International Law." *Georgetown Law Journal* 86:507–37.

Bressman, L., and Gluck, A. 2014. "Statutory Interpretation from the Inside—An Empirical Study of Congressional Drafting, Delegation, and the Canons: Part II." *Stanford Law Review* 66:725–801.

Brudney, J. 2013. "Faithful Agency Versus Ordinary Meaning Advocacy." *Saint Louis University Law Journal* 57:975–96.

Brudney, J., and Baum, L. 2013. "Oasis or Mirage: The Supreme Court's Thirst for Dictionaries in the Rehnquist and Roberts Eras." *William and Mary Law Review* 55: 483–579.

Campos, P. 1996. "A Text Is Just a Text." *Harvard Journal of Law and Public Policy* 19:327–33.

Canale, D. 2007. "On Legal Inferentialism: Toward a Pragmatics of Semantic Content in Legal Interpretation?" *Ratio Juris* 20 (1): 32–44.

Cann, R., Kempson, R., and Gregoromichelaki, E. 2009. *Semantics: An Introduction to Meaning in Language.* Cambridge: Cambridge University Press.

Capone, A. 2001. "The Semantics/Pragmatics Interface from Different Points of View." *Journal of Linguistics* 37 (2): 445–50.

Cappelen, H. 2007. "Semantics and Pragmatics: Some Central Issues." In *Context-Sensitivity and Semantic Minimalism*, edited by G. Preyer and G. Peter, 3–22. Oxford: Clarendon Press.

Cappelen, H., and Lepore, E. 2005. *Insensitive Semantics: A Defense of Semantic Minimalism and Speech Act Pluralism.* West Sussex: Wiley-Blackwell Publishing.

Carroll, L. (1865) 1971. *Alice's Adventures in Wonder-land and Through the Looking-Glass and What Alice Found There.* Edited by R. Green. Oxford: Oxford University Press.

Carroll, N. 1992. "Art, Intention and Conversation." In *Intention and Interpretation*, edited by G. Iseminger, 117–18. Philadelphia: Temple University Press.

———. 2000. "Interpretation and Intention: The Debate Between Hypothetical and Actual Intentionalism." *Metaphilosophy* 1/2:75–95.

———. 2007. "Art, Mind, and Intention." *Philosophy and Literature* 31 (2): 394–404.

———. 2011. "Art Interpretation: The 2010 Richard Wollheim Memorial Lecture." *British Journal of Aesthetics* 51 (2): 117–35.

Carston, R. 2013. "Legal Texts and Canons of Construction: A View From Current Pragmatic Theory." In *Current Legal Issues: Law and Language*, edited by M. Freeman and F. Smith, 8–33. Oxford: Oxford University Press.

Chafe, W., and D. Tannen. 1987. "The Relation between Written and Spoken Language." *Annual Review of Anthropology* 16:383–407.

Chaigneau, S. E., L. W. Barsalou, and S. A. Sloman. 2004. "Assessing the Causal Structure of Function." *Journal of Experimental Psychology: General* 133 (4): 601–25.

Charnock, R. 2006. "Clear Ambiguity: The Interpretation of Plain Language in English Legal Judgments." In *Legal Language and the Search for Clarity*, edited by S. Cacciaguidi-Fahy and A. Wagner, 65–103. Bern: Peter Lang.

———. 2013. "Hart as Contextualist? Theories of Interpretation in Language and the Law." In *Current Legal Issues: Law and Language*, edited by M. Freeman and F. Smith, 128–50. Oxford: Oxford University Press.

Chierchia, G., D. Fox, and B. Spector. 2012. "Scalar Implicature as a Grammatical Phenomenon." In *Semantics: An International Handbook of Natural Language*

Meaning, Volume 3, edited by C. Maienborn, K. von Heusinger, and P. Portner, 2297–31. Berlin: Mouton-De Gruyter.

Cohen, J. 2013. "Indexicality and the Answering Machine." *Journal of Philosophy* 110 (1): 5–32.

Cohen, J., and E. Michaelson. 2013. "Indexicality and the Answering Machine Paradox." *Philosophy Compass* 8 (6): 580–92.

Comrie, B. 1985. *Tense*. Cambridge: Cambridge University Press.

Connolly, A., Fodor, J., Gleitman, and H. Gleitman. 2007. "Why Stereotypes Don't Even Make Good Defaults." *Cognition* 103 (1): 1–22.

Cooren, F., and R. Sanders. 2002. "Implicatures: A Schematic Approach." *Journal of Pragmatics* 34 (8): 1045–67.

Corazza, E. 2004. " On the Alleged Ambiguity of 'Now' and 'Here.'" *Synthese* 138 (2): 289–313.

Corazza, E., W. Fish, and J. Gorvett, J. 2002. "Who is I?" *Philosophical Studies* 107 (1): 1–21.

Cruse, D. A. 1983. *Lexical Semantics*. Cambridge: Cambridge University Press.

Cunningham, C., and C. Fillmore. 1995. "Using Common Sense: A Linguistic Perspective on Judicial Interpretations of 'Use a Firearm.'" *Washington University Law Quarterly* 73:1159–214.

Cunningham, C., J. Levi, G. Green, and J. Kaplan. 1994. "Plain Meaning and Hard Cases." *Yale Law Journal* 103:1561–625.

Currie, G. 2005. *Arts and Minds*. Oxford: Oxford University Press.

Davidson, D. 1967. "Truth and Meaning." *Synthese* 17 (1): 304–23.

———. 1984. *Inquiries into Truth and Interpretation*. Oxford: Oxford University Press.

———. 1986. "A Nice Derangement of Epitaphs." In *Truth and Interpretation: Perspectives on the Philosophy on Donald Davidson*, edited by E. Lepore, 433–46. Oxford: Basil Blackwell.

Davies, S. 2006. "Authors' Intentions, Literary Interpretation, and Literary Value." *British Journal of Aesthetics* 46 (3): 223–47.

Davis, W. A. 1998. *Implicature: Intention, Convention, and the Principle in the Failure of Gricean Theory*. Cambridge: Cambridge University Press.

———. 2007. "How Normative Is Implicature." *Journal of Pragmatics* 39 (10): 1655–72.

De Man, P. 1982. "The Resistance to Theory." *Yale French Studies* 63:3–20.

Dickerson, R. 1975. *The Interpretation and Application of Statutes*. Boston: Little, Brown and Company.

Dickie, G., and W. Wilson. 1995. "The Intentional Fallacy: Defending Beardsley." *Journal of Aesthetics and Art Criticism* 53 (3): 233–50.

Donnellan, K. 1968. "Putting Humpty Dumpty Together Again." *Philosophical Review* 77 (2): 203–15.

Doran, R., G. Ward, M. Larson, Y. McNabb, and R. Baker. 2012. "A Novel Experimental Paradigm for Distinguishing between What Is Said and What Is Implicated." *Language* 88 (1): 124–54.

Duarte, D. 2011. "Linguistic Objectivity in Norm Sentences: Alternatives in Literal Meaning." *Ratio Juris* 24 (2): 112–39.

Dummett, M. 1986. "A Nice Derangement of Epitaphs: Some Comments on Davidson and Hacking." In *Truth and Interpretation: Perspectives on the Philosophy on Donald Davidson*, edited by E. Lepore, 459–76. Oxford: Basil Blackwell.

Dupuy, J. P. 2000. *The Mechanization of the Mind: On the Origins of Cognitive Science.* Princeton: Princeton University Press.

Elhauge, E. 2002. "Preference-Eliciting Statutory Default Rules." *Columbia Law Review* 102:2162–286.

Endicott, T. 1994. "Putting Interpretation in Its Place." *Law and Philosophy* 13 (4): 451–79.

———. 2000. *Vagueness in Law.* Oxford: Oxford University Press.

———. 2001. "Law is Necessarily Vague." *Legal Theory* 7 (4): 379–85.

Engberg, J., and D. Heller. 2008. "Vagueness and Indeterminacy in Law." In *Legal Discourse across Cultures and Systems*, edited by V. Bhatia, C. Candlin, and J. Engberg, 145–68. Hong Kong: Hong Kong University Press.

Eskridge, W., and P. Frickey. 1995. *Cases and Materials on Legislation: Statutes and the Creation of Public Policy.* St. Paul: Thomson West.

Esquibel, A. 1989. "Protecting Competition: The Role of Compensation and Deterrence for Improved Antitrust Enforcement." *Florida Law Review* 41: 153–77.

Fabb, N. 2010. "Is Literary Language a Development of Ordinary Language?" *Lingua* 120 (5): 1219–32.

Farnsworth, W., D. Guzior, and A. Mulani. 2010. "Ambiguity about Ambiguity: An Empirical Inquiry into Legal Interpretation." *Journal of Legal Analysis* 2 (1): 257–300.

Fish, S. 1980. *Is There a Text in This Class?* Cambridge: Harvard University Press.

———. 1985. "Consequences." In *Against Theory: Literary Studies and the New Pragmatism*, edited by W. J. T. Mitchell, 106–31. Chicago: University of Chicago Press.

———. 1989. *Doing What Comes Naturally: Change, Rhetoric, and the Practice of Theory in Literary and Legal Studies.* Durham: Duke University Press.

———. 1999. "Response: Interpretation Is Not a Theoretical Issue." *Yale Journal of Law and the Humanities* 11:509–15.

———. 2005. "There Is No Textualist Position." *San Diego Law Review* 42:629–50.

———. 2008. "Intention Is All There Is: A Critical Analysis of Aharon Barak's Purposive Interpretation in Law." *Cardozo Law Review* 29:1109–46.

Flanagan, B. 2010. "Revisiting the Contribution of Literal Meaning to Legal Meaning." *Oxford Journal of Legal Studies* 30(2): 255–71.

Frankfurter, F. 1947. "Some Reflections on the Reading of Statutes." *Columbia Law Review* 47: 527–44.

Frederking, R. 1996. "Grice's Maxims: 'Do the Right Thing.'" In Proceedings of the Computational Implicature Workshop at the AAAI-96 Spring Symposium Series, Stanford, March 25–27, 1996. http://www.aaai.org/Library/Symposia /symposia-library.php.

Frege, G. (1903) 1997. *Grundgesetze der Arithmetik*. Volume II. In *The Frege Reader*, edited by M. Beaney and translated by P. Geach, 258–89. Oxford: Blackwell Publishing Ltd.

———. 1980. *Philosophical and Mathematical Correspondence*. Translated by G. Gabriel, H. Hermes, F. Kambartel, C. Thiel, and A. Veraart. Chicago: University of Chicago Press.

Friggieri, J. 2009. "Interpretations: Conflicting, Competing, Complementary." *Philosophical Inquiry* 31 (3–4): 27–38.

Frisson, S., and B. McElree. 2008. "Complement Coercion Is Not Modulated by Competition: Evidence from Eye Movements." *Journal of Experimental Psychology: Learning, Memory and Cognition* 34 (1):1–11.

Fuller, L. 1949. "The Case of the Speluncean Explorers." *Harvard Law Review* 62:616–45.

———. 1958. "Positivism and Fidelity to Law—A Response to Professor Hart." *Harvard Law Review* 71 (4): 630–72.

Gabora, L., E. Rosch, D. Aerts. 2008. "Toward an Ecological Theory of Concepts." *Ecological Psychology* 20 (1): 84–116.

Gadamer, H. 2004. *Truth and Method*. New York: Continuum International Publishing Group.

Galdia, M. 2009. *Legal Linguistics*. Bern: Peter Lang.

Gärdenfors, P. 2000. *Conceptual Spaces — The Geometry of Thought*. Cambridge: Bradford Books.

Gauker, C. 2008. "Zero Tolerance for Pragmatics." *Synthese* 165 (3): 359–71.

Geeraerts, D. 2010. *Theories of Lexical Semantics*. Oxford: Oxford University Press.

Geis, M. 1995. "The Meaning of Meaning in the Law." *Washington University Law Quarterly* 73:1125–44.

Gelman, S. A. 2003. *The Essential Child*. New York: Oxford University Press.

Geurts, B., and N. Pouscoulous. 2009. "Embedded Implicatures?!?" *Semantics and Pragmatics* 2 (4): 1–34.

Gibbs, R. 2002. "A New Look at Literal Meaning in Understanding What Is Said and Implicated." *Journal of Pragmatics* 34 (4): 457–86.

Gluck, A., and L. Bressman. 2013. "Statutory Interpretation from the Inside—An Empirical Study of Congressional Drafting, Delegation, and the Canons: Part I." *Stanford Law Review* 65:901–1025.

Goldsmith, A. 2003. "The Void-for-Vagueness Doctrine in the Supreme Court, Revisited." *American Journal of Criminal Law* 30:279–313.

Goldsworthy, J. 1995. "Marmor on Meaning, Interpretation, and Legislative Intention." *Legal Theory* 1 (4): 439–64.

———. 2005. "Moderate Versus Strong Intentionalism: Knapp and Michaels Revisited." *San Diego Law Review* 42:669–82.

González, C. 2011. "Turning Unambiguous Statutory Material into Ambiguous Statutes: Ordering Principles, Avoidance, and Transparent Justification in Cases of Interpretive Choice." *Duke Law Journal* 61:583–647.

Goodrich, P. 1987. *Legal Discourse: Studies in Linguistics, Rhetoric and Legal Analysis.* London: St. Martin's Press.

Gorvett, J. 2005. "Back Through the Looking Glass: On the Relationship between Intentions and Indexicals." *Philosophical Studies* 124 (3): 295–312.

Green, C. 2009. "'This Constitution': Constitutional Indexicals as a Basis for Textualist Semi-Originalism." *Notre Dame Law Review* 84:1607–74.

Green, G. 1996. *Pragmatics and Natural Language Understanding.* 2nd edition. London: Routledge.

Greenawalt, K. 2000. "Are Mental States Relevant for Statutory and Constitutional Interpretation?" *Cornell Law Review* 85:1609–72.

———. 2010. *Legal Interpretation.* Oxford: Oxford University Press.

———. 2013. *Statutory and Common Law Interpretation.* Oxford: Oxford University Press.

Greenberg, M. 2010. "The Communication Theory of Legal Interpretation and Objective Notions of Communicative Intent." Unpublished manuscript. Accessed December 18, 2010. http://papers.ssrn.com/s013/papers.cfm?abstract_id =1726524.

———2011. "Legislation as Communication? Legal Interpretation and the Study of Linguistic Communication." In *Philosophical Foundations of Language in the Law*, edited by A. Marmor and S. Soames, 217–64. Oxford: Oxford University Press.

Greene, A. 2006. "The Jurisprudence of Justice Stevens Panel III: The Missing Step of Textualism." *Fordham Law Review* 74:1913–36.

Grice, H. P. 1957. "Meaning." *Philosophical Review* 66 (3): 377–88.

———. 1969. "Utterer's Meaning and Intention." *Philosophical Review* 78 (2): 147–77.

———. 1989. *Studies in the Way of Words.* Cambridge: Harvard University Press.

Halliday, M. A. K., and C. Yallop. 2007. *Lexicology.* New York: Continuum International Publishing Group.

Halpin, A. 2013. "Language, Truth, and Law." In *Current Legal Issues: Law and Language*, edited by M. Freeman and F. Smith, 62–78. Oxford: Oxford University Press.

Hampton, J. A. 1979. "Polymorphous Concepts in Semantic Memory." *Journal of Verbal Learning and Verbal Behavior* 18 (4): 441–61.

———. 1981. "An Investigation of the Nature of Abstract Concepts." *Memory and Cognition* 9 (2): 149–56.

————. 1995. "Similarity-Based Categorization: The Development of Prototype Theory." *Psychologica Belgica* 35:103–25.

————. 1998. "Similarity-Based Categorization and Fuzziness of Natural Categories." *Cognition* 65 (2): 137–65.

————. 2007. "Typicality, Graded Membership, and Vagueness." *Cognitive Science* 31 (3): 355–84.

Hampton, J. A., D. Dubois, and W. Yeh. 2006. "Effects of Classification Context on Categorization in Natural Categories." *Memory and Cognition* 34 (7): 1431–43.

Hampton, J. A., Z. Estes, and S. Simmons. 2007. "Metamorphosis: Essence, Appearance, and Behavior in the Categorization of Natural Kinds." *Memory and Cognition* 35 (7): 1785–800.

Hampton, J. A., and M. Jönsson. 2012. "Typicality and Compositionality: The Logic of Combining Vague Concepts." In *The Oxford Handbook of Compositionality*, edited by M. Werning, W. Hinzen, and E. Machery, 385–402. Oxford: Oxford University Press.

Hampton, J. A., M. L. Jönsson, and A. Passanisi. 2009a. "The Modifier Effect: Default Inheritance in Complex Noun Phrases." In Proceedings of the 31st Annual Conference of the Cognitive Science Society, 303–8.

Hampton, J. A., R. Michalski, P. Theuns, and I. Van Mechelen. 1993. *Categories and Concepts: Theoretical Views and Inductive Data Analysis*. New York: Academic Press, Inc.

Hampton, J. A., G. Storms, C. L. Simmons, and D. Heussen, D. 2009b. "Feature Integration in Natural Language Concepts." *Memory and Cognition* 37 (8): 1150–63.

Hancher, M. 1981. "Humpty Dumpty and Verbal Meaning." *Journal of Aesthetics and Art Criticism* 40 (1): 49–58.

Hanks, P. 2013. *Lexical Analysis: Norms and Exploitations*. Cambridge: MIT Press.

Harris, R. 1989. "How Does Writing Restructure Thought?" *Language and Communication* 9 (2/3): 99–106.

————. 2001. *Rethinking Writing*. New York: Continuum International Publishing Group.

Harris, R., and C. Hutton. 2007. *Definition in Theory and Practice*. New York: Continuum International Publishing Group.

Hart, H., and A. Sacks. 1994. *The Legal Process: Basic Problems in the Making and Application of Law*, edited by W. Eskridge and P. Frickey. New York: Foundation Press.

Hart, H. L. A. 1958. "Positivism and the Separation of Law and Morals." *Harvard Law Review* 71:593–629.

————. 1961. *The Concept of Law*. Oxford: Oxford University Press.

Hawkins, J. 2004. *Efficiency and Complexity in Grammars*. Oxford: Oxford University Press.

Hays, P., and R. Rust. 1979. "'Something Healing': Fathers and Sons in *Billy Budd*." *Nineteenth-Century Fiction* 34 (3): 326–36.

Henket, M. 1989. "Contracts, Promises and Meaning: The Question of Intent." *International Journal for the Semiotics of Law* 2 (2): 129–48.

Hirsch, E. D. 1967. *Validity in Interpretation*. New Haven: Yale University Press.

Hobbs, Pamela. 2011. "Defining the Law: (Mis)using the Dictionary to Decide Cases." *Discourse Studies* 13 (3): 327–47.

Hogan, P. 1996. *On Interpretation: Meaning and Inference in Law, Psychoanalysis, and Literature*. Athens: University of Georgia Press.

Holmes, O. 1899. "The Theory of Legal Interpretation." *Harvard Law Review* 12:417–20.

Horn, L. R. 1972. *On the Semantic Properties of Logical Operators in English*. PhD dissertation. Mimeo, Indiana University Linguistics Club.

———. 1989. *A Natural History of Negation*. Chicago: University of Chicago Press.

Hoy, D. 1992. "Intentions and the Law: Defending Hermeneutics." In *Legal Hermeneutics: History, Theory, and Practice*, edited by G. Leyh, 173–86. Berkeley: University of California Press.

Hutton, C. 2009. *Language, Meaning and the Law*. Edinburgh: Edinburgh University Press.

Irwin, W. 1999. *Intentionalist Interpretation: A Philosophical Explanation and Defense*. Westport: Greenwood Press.

Iseminger, G. 1992. "An Intentional Demonstration?" In *Intention and Interpretation*, edited by G. Iseminger, 76–96. Philadelphia: Temple University Press.

———. 1996. "Actual Intentionalism vs. Hypothetical Intentionalism." *Journal of Aesthetics and Art Criticism* 54 (4): 319–26.

———. 1998. "Interpretive Relevance, Contradiction, and Compatibility with the Text: A Rejoinder to Knight." *Journal of Aesthetics and Art Criticism* 56 (1): 58–61.

Ivanic, R. 1994. "Characterizations of Context for Describing Spoken and Written Discourse." In *Writing Vs. Speaking: Language, Text, Discourse Communication: Proceedings of the Conference Held at the Czech Language Institute of the Academy of Sciences of the Czech Republic, Prague, October, 14–16, 1992*, edited by S. Cmejrkova, F. Danes, and E. Havlova, 180–86. Tübingen: Narr Francke Attempto Verlag GmbH & Co. KG.

Jackendoff, R. 2010. *Meaning and the Lexicon: The Parallel Architecture 1975–2010*. Oxford: Oxford University Press.

Jackson, B. 1995. *Making Sense in Law: Linguistic, Psychological and Semiotic Perspectives*. Liverpool: Deborah Charles Publications.

Jaszczolt, K. M. 2005. *Default Semantics: Foundations of a Compositional Theory of Acts of Communication*. Oxford: Oxford University Press.

Jayez, J. 1999. "Underspecification, Context Selection, and Generativity." In *The Language of Word Meaning*, edited by P. Bouillon and F. Busa, 124–47. Cambridge: Cambridge University Press.

Jeffries, J. 1985. "Legality, Vagueness, and the Construction of Penal Statutes." *Virginia Law Review* 71:189–245.

Jönsson, M. L., and J. A. Hampton. 2008. "On Prototypes as Defaults (comment on Connolly, Fodor, Gleitman, and Gleitman 2007)." *Cognition* 106 (2): 913–23.

Jónsson, O. 2009. "Vagueness, Interpretation, and the Law." *Legal Theory* 15 (3): 193–214.

Jori, M. 1993. "Legal Semiotics." In *The Encyclopedia of Language and Linguistic*, edited by R. Asher, 2113–22. Oxford: Pergamon Press.

Kaplan, D. 1989. *"Demonstratives."* In *Themes from Kaplan*, edited by J. Almog, J. Perry, and H. Wettstein, 481–563. Oxford: Oxford University Press.

Kaplan, J., and G. Green. 1995. "Grammar and Inferences of Rationality in Interpreting the Child Pornography Statute." *Washington University Law Quarterly* 73:1223–51.

Katsos, N., and C. Cummins. 2010. "Pragmatics: From Theory to Experiment and Back Again." *Language and Linguistics Compass* 4 (5): 282–95.

Kay, P. 1977. "Language Evolution and Speech Style." In *Sociocultural Dimensions of Language Change*, edited by B. Blount and M. Sanches, 21–33. Waltham: Academic Press Inc.

———. 1987. "Three Properties of the Ideal Reader." In *Cognitive and Linguistic: Analyses of Test Performance*, edited by R. Freedle and R. Duran, 208–24. Norwood: Ablex.

Keefe, R. 2000. *Theories of Vagueness*. Cambridge: Cambridge University Press.

Keil, F. C. 1986. "The Acquisition of Natural Kind and Artifact Terms." In *Language Learning and Concept Acquisition: Foundational Issues*, edited by W. Demopoulos and A. Marras, 133–53. Norwood: Ablex.

———. 1989. *Concepts, Kinds, and Cognitive Development*. Cambridge: MIT Press.

———. 2006. "Explanation and Understanding." *Annual Review of Psychology* 57:227–54.

Kent, J. 1826. *Commentaries on American Law, Volume 1*. New York: O. Halsted.

Kerr, O. 1998. "Shedding Light on *Chevron*: An Empirical Study of the *Chevron* Doctrine in the U.S. Courts of Appeals." *Yale Journal on Regulation* 15:1–60.

Keysar, B. 2007. "Communication and Miscommunication: The Role of Egocentric Processes." *Intercultural Pragmatics* 4 (1): 71–84.

Keysar, B., and A. Henly. 2002. "Speakers' Overestimation of Their Effectiveness." *Psychological Science* 13 (3): 207–12.

Kiefer, A. 2005. "The Intentional Model of Interpretation." *Journal of Aesthetics and Art Criticism* 63 (3): 271–81.

Kilgarriff, A. 1999. "Generative Lexicon Meets Corpus Data: The Case of Non-Standard Word Uses. In *The Language of Word Meaning*, edited by P. Bouillon and F. Busa, 312–28. Cambridge: Cambridge University Press.

Klepousniotou, E., D. Titone, and C. Romero. 2008. "Making Sense of Word Senses: The Comprehension of Polysemy Depends on Sense Overlap." *Journal of Experimental Psychology: Learning, Memory, and Cognition* 34 (6): 1534–43.

Knapp, S., and W. Michaels. 1982. "Against Theory." *Critical Inquiry* 8 (4): 723–42.

———. 1983. "A Reply to Our Critics." *Critical Inquiry* 9 (4): 790–800.

———. 1987. "Against Theory 2: Hermeneutics and Deconstruction." *Critical Inquiry* 14 (1): 49–68.

———. 1992. "Reply to George Wilson." *Critical Inquiry* 19 (1): 186–93.

———. 1994. "Reply to John Searle." *New Literary History* 25 (3): 669–75.

———. 2005. "Not a Matter of Interpretation." *San Diego Law Review* 42:651–68.

Knapp, V. 1991. "Some Problems of Legal Language." *Ratio Juris* 4 (1): 1–17.

Kowalski, R. 1992. "Legislation as Logic Programs." *Logic Programming in Action, Lecture Notes in Computer Science* 630:203–30.

Kress, G. 1989. *Linguistic Processes in Sociocultural Practice.* Oxford: Oxford University Press.

Kripke, S. A. 1972. "Naming and Necessity." In *Semantics of Natural Language*, edited by D. Davidson and G. Harman, 253–355. Dordrecht: Reidel.

Labov, W. 1973. "The Boundaries of Words and Their Meanings." In *New Ways of Analyzing Variation in English*, edited by C. Bailey and R. Shuy, 340–71. Washington, DC: Georgetown University Press.

Lasersohn, P. 1999. "Pragmatic Halos." *Language* 75 (3): 522–51.

Levin, B., and M. Rappaport Hovav. 1995. *Unaccusativity.* Cambridge: MIT Press.

Levinson, J. 1992. "Intention and Interpretation: A Last Look." In *Intention and Interpretation*, edited by G. Iseminger, 221–56. Philadelphia: Temple University Press.

———. 1996. "Intention and Interpretation in Literature." In *The Pleasures of Aesthetics*, edited by J. Levinson, 175–213. Ithaca: Cornell University Press.

———. 2002. "Hypothetical Intentionalism: Statement, Objections, and Replies." In *Is There a Single Right Interpretation?*, edited by M. Krausz, 309–18. University Park: Pennsylvania State University Press.

———. 2010. "Defending Hypothetical Intentionalism." *British Journal of Aesthetics* 50 (2): 139–50.

Levinson, S. C. 1983. *Pragmatics.* Cambridge: Cambridge University Press.

———. 1995. "Three Levels of Meaning." In *Grammar and Meaning: Essays in Honour of Sir John Lyons*, 90–115. Cambridge: Cambridge University Press.

———. 2000. *Presumptive Meanings: The Theory of Generalized Conversational Implicature.* Cambridge: MIT Press.

Livingston, P. 1998. "Intentionalism in Aesthetics." *New Literary History* 29 (4): 831–46.

———. 2005. *Art and Intention: A Philosophical Study.* Oxford: Oxford University Press.

Llewellyn, K. 1950. "Remarks on the Theory of Appellate Decision and the Rules or Canons About How Statutes Are To Be Construed." *Vanderbilt Law Review* 3:395–420.

Ludlow, P. 2014. *Living Words: Meaning Underdetermination and the Dynamic Lexicon.* Oxford: Oxford University Press.

Lumsden, D. 2008. "Kinds of Conversational Cooperation." *Journal of Pragmatics* 40 (11): 1896–908.

Macey, J., and G. Miller. 1992. "The Canons of Statutory Construction and Judicial Preferences." *Vanderbilt Law Review* 45:647–72.

Malt, B. C., S. P. Gennari, M. Imai, E. Ameel, N. Tsuda, and A. Majid. 2008. "Talking about Walking: Biomechanics and the Language of Locomotion." *Psychological Science* 19 (3): 232–40.

Malt, B. C., and S. A. Sloman. 2007. "Artifact Categorization: The Good, the Bad, and the Ugly." In *Creations of the Mind: Theories of Artifacts and Their Representation*, edited by E. Margolis and S. Laurence, 85–123. Oxford: Oxford University Press.

Manning, J. 1999. "Constitutional Structure and Statutory Formalism." *University of Chicago Law Review* 66:685–97.

———. 2001. "Textualism and the Equity of the Statute." *Columbia Law Review* 101:1–126.

———. 2003. "The Absurdity Doctrine." *Harvard Law Review* 116:2387–486.

———. 2005. "Textualism and Legislative Intent." *Virginia Law Review* 91:419–450.

———. 2006. "What Divides Textualists From Purposivists." *Columbia Law Review* 106:70–111.

———. 2010. "Second-Generation Textualism." *California Law Review* 98:1287–318.

———. 2011. "Separation of Powers as Ordinary Interpretation." *Harvard Law Review* 124:1939–2040.

———. 2013. "Justice Ginsburg and the New Legal Process." *Harvard Law Review* 127:455–60.

Margolis, E. 1994. "A Reassessment of the Shift from the Classical Theory of Concepts to Prototype Theory." *Cognition* 51 (1): 73–89.

Margolis, E., and S. Laurence, eds. 1999. *Concepts: Core Readings.* Cambridge: MIT Press.

Margolis, J. 1976. "Robust Relativism." *Journal of Aesthetics and Art Criticism* 35 (1): 37–46.

Marmor, A. 2005. *Interpretation and Legal Theory.* Oxford: Hart Publishing.

———. 2008a. "Is Literal Meaning Conventional." *Topoi* 27 (1–2): 101–13.

———. 2008b. "The Pragmatics of Legal Language." *Ratio Juris* 21 (4): 423–52.

———. 2014. *The Language of Law.* Oxford: Oxford University Press.

Marx, L. 1953. "Melville's Parable of the Walls." *Sewanee Review* 61 (4): 602–27.

Mattila, H. 2002. *Comparative Legal Linguistics.* Translated by C. Goddard. Burlington: Asgate Publishing Co.

May, R. 2002. "Ellipsis." In *Macmillan Encyclopedia of Cognitive Science*, edited by L. Nadel, 1094–102. London: Nature Publishing Group.

McCloskey, M. E., and S. Glucksberg. 1978. "Natural Categories: Well Defined or Fuzzy Sets?" *Memory and Cognition* 6 (4): 462–72.

McCubbins, M., and D. Rodriguez. 2011. "Deriving Interpretive Principles from a Theory of Communication and Lawmaking." *Brooklyn Law Review* 76: 979–95.

McElree, B., L. Pylkkanen, M. Pickering, and M. Traxler. 2006. "A Time Course Analysis of Enriched Composition." *Psychonomic Bulletin and Review* 13 (1): 53–59.

McGowan, M. 2008. "Do as I Do, Not as I Say: An Empirical Investigation of Justice Scalia's Ordinary Meaning Method of Statutory Interpretation." *Mississippi Law Journal* 78:129–50.

McGreal, P. 2004. "Slighting Context: On the Illogic of Ordinary Speech in Statutory Interpretation." *University of Kansas Law Review* 52:325–83.

Mellinkoff, D. 1963. *Language of the Law.* Boston: Little Brown.

Melville, H. 2004. "Bartleby, the Scrivener: A Story of Wall-Street." In *Great Short Works of Herman Melville,* 39–74. New York: Harper Perennial Modern Classics.

———. 2004. "Billy Budd, Sailor." In *Great Short Works of Herman Melville,* 429–505. New York: Harper Perennial Modern Classics.

Michaels, W. 1979. "Against Formalism: The Autonomous Text in Legal and Literary Interpretation." *Poetics Today* 1 (1–2): 23–34.

Michaelson, E. 2014. "Shifty Characters." *Philosophical Studies* 167 (3): 519–40.

Miller, G. 1990. "Pragmatics and the Maxims of Interpretation." *Wisconsin Law Review 1990:* 1179–225.

Molot, J. 2006. "The Rise and Fall of Textualism." *Columbia Law Review* 106:1–69.

Moran, M. 2010. "The Reasonable Person: A Conceptual Biography in Comparative Perspective." *Lewis and Clark Law Review* 14:1233–83.

Moravcsik, E. 2006. *An Introduction to Syntactic Theory.* New York: Continuum International Publishing Group.

Moravcsik, J. M. 1975. "Aitia as a Generative Factor in Aristotle's Philosophy." *Dialogue* 14 (4): 622–36.

Mount, A. 2008. "The Impurity of 'Pure' Indexicals." *Philosophical Studies* 138 (2): 193–209.

Medin, D. L., W. D. Wattenmaker, and S. E. Hampson, S. E. 1987. "Family Resemblance, Conceptual Cohesiveness, and Category Construction." *Cognitive Psychology* 19 (2): 242–79.

Murphy, G. L., and D. L. Medin. 1985. "The Role of Theories in Conceptual Coherence." *Psychological Review* 92 (3): 289–316.

Murphy, L. 2010. *Lexical Meaning.* Cambridge: Cambridge University Press.

Murphy, L., and A. Koskela. 2010. *Key Terms in Semantics.* New York: Continuum International Publishing Group.

Nathan, D. 2005. "A Paradox in Intentionalism." *British Journal of Aesthetics* 45 (1): 32–48.

Neale, S. 2007. "On Location." In *Situating Semantics: Essays on the Philosophy of*

John Perry, edited by M. O'Rourke and C. Washington, 251–393. Cambridge: MIT Press.

———. 2008. "Textualism With Intent." Manuscript. Discussion at the Law Faculty, University of Oxford. Microsoft Word file.

———. In press. "Implicit Meaning." In *Meaning and Other Things: Essays on Stephen Schiffer*, edited by G. Ostertag. Oxford: Oxford University Press.

Nehamas, A. 1981. "The Postulated Author: Critical Monism as a Regulative Ideal." *Critical Inquiry* 8 (1): 122–49.

———. 1986. "What an Author Is." *Journal of Philosophy* 83 (11): 685–91.

Nelson, C. 2005. "What is Textualism?" *Virginia Law Review* 91:347–418.

Nourse, V. 2011. "Two Kinds of Plain Meaning." *Brooklyn Law Review* 76:997–1005.

Nourse, V., and J. Schacter. 2002. "The Politics of Legislative Drafting: A Congressional Case Study." *New York University Law Review* 77:575–624.

Nunberg, G. 1993. "Indexicality and Deixis." *Linguistics and Philosophy* 16 (1): 1–42.

Olsen, S. 1987. *The End of Literary Theory*. Cambridge: Cambridge University Press.

Olson, D. 1977. "From Utterance to Text: The Bias of Language in Speech and Writing." *Harvard Educational Review* 47 (3): 257–81.

Ong, W. 2002. *Orality and Literacy*. London: Routledge.

Paradix, M. 2007. "Just Reasonable, Can Linguistic Analysis Help Us Know What It Is To Be Reasonable?" *Jurimetrics Journal* 47 (2): 169–91.

Pavlidou, T. 1991. "Cooperation and the Choice of Linguistic Means: Some Evidence from the Use of the Subjunctive in Modern Greek." *Journal of Pragmatics* 15 (1): 11–42.

Perry, J. 1979. "The Problem of the Essential Indexical." *Nous* 13 (1): 3–20.

Phillips, A. 2003. *Lawyers' Language: How and Why Legal Language is Different*. London: Routledge.

Plato. 360 B.C.E.. *Phaedrus*. Translated by B. Jowett. http://classics.mit.edu/Plato/phaedrus.html.

Poggi, F. 2008. "Semantics, Pragmatics, and Interpretation: A Critical Reading of Some of Marmor's Theses." In *Analisi e diritto*, edited by P. Comanducci and R. Guastini, 159–78. Torino: Giappichelli.

———. 2011. "Law and Conversational Implicatures." *International Journal for the Semiotics of Law* 24 (1): 21–40.

Popkin, W. 1999. *Statutes in Court: The History and Theory of Statutory Interpretation*. Durham: Duke University Press.

———. 2007. *A Dictionary of Statutory Interpretation*. Durham: Carolina Academic Press.

Posner, M. 1986. "Empirical Studies of Prototypes." In *Noun Classes and Categorization*, edited by C. Craig, 53–61. Amsterdam: Benjamins.

Posner, R. 1986. "Legal Formalism, Legal Realism, and the Interpretation of Statutes and the Constitution." *Case Western Reserve Law Review* 37:179–217.

———. 1988a. "The Jurisprudence of Skepticism." *Michigan Law Review* 86:827–91.

———. 1988b. *Law and Literature: A Misunderstood Relation.* Cambridge: Harvard University Press.

———. 2012. "The Incoherence of Antonin Scalia." *New Republic*, September 13. http://www.newrepublic.com/article/magazine/books-and-arts/106441/scalia-garner-reading-the-law-textual-originalism.

Potts, C. 2005. *The Logic of Conventional Implicatures.* Oxford: Oxford University Press.

Pratt, I., and N. Francez. 2001. "Temporal Prepositions and Temporal Generalized Quantifiers." *Linguistics and Philosophy* 24 (2): 187–222.

Predelli, S. 1998. "I Am Not Here Now." *Analysis* 58 (2): 107–15.

———. 2002. "Intentions, Indexicals, and Communication." *Analysis* 62 (276): 310–16.

———. 2006. "The Automatic and the Incomplete. Remarks on Recanati's Literal Meaning." *Critica, Revista Hispanoamericana de Filosofia* 38 (112): 21–33.

———. 2010. "Malapropisms and the Simple Picture of Communication." *Mind and Language* 25 (3): 329–45.

———. 2011. "I Am Still Not Here Now." *Erkenn* 74 (3): 289–303.

Price, Z. 2004. "The Rule of Lenity as a Rule of Structure." *Fordham Law Review* 72:885–941.

Pustejovsky, J. 1992. "The Syntax of Event Structure." In *Lexical and Conceptual Semantics*, edited by B. Levin and S. Pinker, 47–81. Oxford: Blackwell Publishing.

———. 1995. *The Generative Lexicon.* Cambridge: MIT Press.

———. 1998a. "Generativity and Explanation in Semantics: A Reply to Fodor and Lepore." *Linguistic Inquiry* 29 (2): 289–311.

———. 1998b. "The Semantics of Lexical Underspecification." *Folia Linguistica* 32 (3–4): 323–47.

———. 2000. "Syntagmatic Processes." In *Handbook of Lexicology and Lexicography*, edited by V. Herausgegeban, A. Cruse, F. Hundsnurscher, M. Job, and P. Lutzeier, 1–9. Berlin: De Gruyter.

———. 2006. "Introduction to Generative Lexicon." Unpublished manuscript. Microsoft Word file.

Putnam, H. 1970. "Is Semantics Possible." *Meaphilosophy* 1 (3): 187–201.

———. 1975. *Mind, Language, and Reality: Philosophical Papers, Volume 2.* Cambridge: Cambridge University Press.

Ramscar, M., and U. Hahn, eds. 2001. *Similarity and Categorization.* Oxford: Oxford University Press.

Rappaport Hovav, M., and B. Levin. 2010. "Reflections on Manner/Result Complementarity." In *Syntax, Lexical Semantics, and Event Structure*, edited by

E. Doron, M. Hovav Rappaport, and I. Sichel, 21–38. Oxford: Oxford University Press.

Raz, J. 1996. "Intention in Interpretation." In *The Autonomy of Law: Essays on Legal Positivism*, edited by R. George, 249–86. Oxford: Oxford University Press.

Recanati, F. 2002. "Does Linguistic Communication Rest on Inference?" *Mind and Language* 17 (1–2): 105–26.

———. 2004. *Literal Meaning*. Cambridge: Cambridge University Press.

———. 2006a. "Predelli and Garcia-Carpintero on 'Literal Meaning.'" *Critica, Revista Hispanoamericana de Filosofia* 38 (112): 69–79.

———. 2006b. "Crazy Minimalism." *Mind and Language* 21 (1): 21–30.

———. 2010. *Truth-Conditional Pragmatics*. Oxford: Oxford University Press.

———. 2012. *Mental Files*. Oxford: Oxford University Press.

Rehder, B. 2003. "A Causal-Model Theory of Conceptual Representation and Categorization." *Journal of Experimental Psychology: Learning, Memory, and Cognition* 29 (6): 1141–59.

Rey, G. 1994. "Concepts and Conceptions: A Reply to Smith, Medin, and Rips." *Cognition* 15:297–303.

Rickless, S. 2005. "A Synthetic Approach to Legal Adjudication." *San Diego Law Review* 42:519–32.

Ritter, E., and S. Rosen. 1996. "Strong and Weak Predicates: Reducing the Lexical Burden." *Linguistic Analysis* 26 (1–2): 29–62.

Robertson, M. 2009. "The Impossibility of Textualism and the Pervasiveness of Rewriting in Law." *Canadian Journal of Law and Jurisprudence* 22 (2): 381–406.

Rodriguez, D., and B. Weingast. 2007. "The Paradox of Expansionist Statutory Interpretations." *Northwestern University Law Review* 101:1207–65.

Romdenh-Romluc, K. 2002. "Now the French Are Invading England!" *Analysis* 62 (1): 34–41.

———. 2006. "I." *Philosophical Studies* 128 (2): 257–83.

———. 2008. "First-Person Thought and the Use of 'I.'" *Synthese* 163 (2): 145–56.

Rorty, R. 1985. "Philosophy without Principles." *Critical Inquiry* 11 (3): 459–65.

Rosch, E. 1973a. "Natural Categories." *Cognitive Psychology* 4 (3): 328–50.

———. 1973b. "On the Internal Structure of Perceptual and Semantic Categories." In *Cognitive Development and the Acquisition of Language*, edited by T. Moore, 111–44. New York: Academic Press, Inc.

———. 1975. "Cognitive Representations of Semantic Categories." *Journal of Experimental Psychology* 104 (3): 192–233.

———. 1978. "Principles of Categorization." In *Cognition and Categorization*, edited by E. Rosch and B. Lloyd, 27–48. Hillsdale: Erlbaum.

Rosch, E., and C. B. Mervis. 1975. "Family Resemblances: Studies in the Internal Structure of Categories." *Cognitive Psychology* 7 (4): 573–605.

Rosenkranz, N. 2002. "Federal Rules of Statutory Interpretation." *Harvard Law Review* 115:2085–157.

Rozenblit, L., and F. Keil. 2002. "The Misunderstood Limits of Folk Science: An Illusion of Explanatory Depth." *Cognitive Science* 26 (5): 521–62.

Sarangi, S. K., and S. Slembrouck. 1992. "Non-Cooperation in Communication: A Reassessment of Gricean Pragmatics." *Journal of Pragmatics* 17 (2): 117–54.

Sauerland, U. 2012. "The Computation of Scalar Implicatures: Pragmatic, Lexical or Grammatical?" *Language and Linguistics Compass* 6 (1): 36–49.

Saussure, F. de. 2011. *Course in General Linguistics*. Edited by P. Meisel and H. Saussy. Translated by W. Baskin. New York: Columbia University Press.

Scalia, A. 1997. *A Matter of Interpretation: Federal Courts and the Law*. Princeton: Princeton University Press.

Scalia, A., and B. Garner. 2012. *Reading Law: The Interpretation of Legal Texts*. St. Paul: Thomson/West.

Scalia, A., and J. Manning. 2012. "A Dialogue on Statutory and Constitutional Interpretation." *George Washington Law Review* 80:1610–19.

Schacter, J. 1995. "Metademocracy: The Changing Structure of Legitimacy in Statutory Interpretation." *Harvard Law Review* 108:613–46.

Schauer, F. 1990. "Statutory Construction and the Coordinating Function of Plain Meaning." *Supreme Court Review* 1990:231–56.

———. 2008. "A Critical Guide to Vehicles in the Park." *New York University Law Review* 83:1109–34.

Scheef, R. 2003. "Temporal Dynamics in Statutory Interpretation: Courts, Congress, and the Canon of Constitutional Avoidance." *University of Pittsburgh Law Review* 64:529–87.

Schiffer, S. 2003. *The Things We Mean*. Oxford: Oxford University Press.

Schroth, P. 1998. "Language and Law." *American Journal of Comparative Law* 18:17–39.

Searle, J. 1978. "Literal Meaning." *Erkenntnis* 13 (1): 207–24.

———. 1979. *Expression and Meaning*. Cambridge: Cambridge University Press.

———. 1980. "The Background of Meaning." In *Semantic Act Theory and Pragmatics*, edited by J. Searle, F. Kiefer, and M. Bierwisch. Dordrecht: Reidel.

———. 1990. "Collective Intentions and Actions." In *Intentions in Communication*, edited by P. R. Cohen, J. Morgan, and M. A. Pollack, 403–16. Cambridge: MIT Press.

Seidman, L. 1988. "Ambivalence and Accountability." *Southern California Law Review* 61:1571–600.

Shane, S. 2006. *Language and the Law*. New York: Continuum International Publishing Group.

Shapiro, D. 1992. "Continuity and Change in Statutory Interpretation." *New York University Law Review* 67:921–48.

Shapiro, S. 2006. *Vagueness in Context*. Oxford: Oxford University Press.

Sidelle, A. 1991. "The Answering-Machine Paradox." *Canadian Journal of Philosophy* 21 (4): 525–39.

Silcox, M. 2005. "Semantic Holism vs. Semantic Atomism." *Language and Communication* 25 (4): 335–49.

Sinclair, M. 1985. "Law and Language: The Role of Pragmatics in Statutory Interpretation." *University of Pittsburgh Law Review* 46:373–420.

———. 2005–6. "'Only a Sith Thinks Like That'": Llewellyn's 'Dueling Canons,' Pairs One to Seven." *New York Law School Law Review* 50:919–92.

———. 2006–7. "'Only a Sith Thinks Like That': Llewellyn's 'Dueling Canons,' Pairs Eight to Twelve." *New York Law School Law Review* 51:1003–54.

———. 2008–9. "'Only a Sith Thinks Like That'": Llewellyn's 'Dueling Canons,' Pairs Thirteen to Sixteen." *New York Law School Law Review* 53:953–93.

Singer, N. 2000. *Sutherland on Statutes and Statutory Construction*. 6th edition. Eagan: West Group.

Sinnott-Armstrong, W. 2005. "Word Meaning in Legal Interpretation." *San Diego Law Review* 42:465–92.

Slocum, B. 2000. "RICO and the Legislative Supremacy Approach to Federal Criminal Lawmaking." *Loyola University Chicago Law Journal* 31 (4): 639–92.

———. 2003. "The Immigration Rule of Lenity and Chevron Deference." *Georgetown Immigration Law Journal* 17 (4): 515–82.

———. 2007. "Canons, the Plenary Power Doctrine, and Immigration Law." *Florida State University Law Review* 34 (2): 394–97.

———. 2008. "Overlooked Temporal Issues in Statutory Interpretation." *Temple Law Review* 81 (3): 635–87.

———. 2010. "The Importance of Being Ambiguous: Substantive Canons, Stare Decisis and the Central Role of Ambiguity Determinations in the Administrative State." *Maryland Law Review* 69 (4): 791–848.

———. 2012. "Linguistics and 'Ordinary Meaning' Determinations." *Statute Law Review* 33 (1): 39–83.

Sloutsky, V. M. 2003. "The Role of Similarity in the Development of Categorization." *Trends in Cognitive Sciences* 7 (6): 246–51.

Smits, T., G. Storms, Y. Rosseel, and P. De Boeck. 2002. "Fruits and Vegetables Categorized: An Application of the Generalized Context Model." *Psychonomic Bulletin and Review* 9 (4): 836–44.

Soames, S. 2008a. "The Gap between Meaning and Assertion: Why What We Literally Say Often Differs from What Our Words Literally Mean." *Philosophical Essays* 1:278–97.

———. 2008b. "Interpreting Legal Texts: What Is, and What Is Not, Special about the Law." In *Philosophical Essays: Natural Language What It Means and How We Use It*, edited by S. Soames, 403–24. Princeton: Princeton University Press.

———. 2010. "What Vagueness and Inconsistency Tell Us About Interpretation." In *Philosophical Foundations of Language in the Law*, edited by A. Marmor and S. Soames, 31–57. Oxford: Oxford University Press.

———. 2011. "Toward a Theory of Legal Interpretation." *NYU Law School Journal of Law and Liberty* 6:231–59.

Solan, L. 1993. *The Language of Judges.* Chicago: University of Chicago Press.

———. 1995. "Judicial Decisions and Linguistic Analysis: Is There a Linguist in the Court?" *Washington University Law Quarterly* 73:1069–80.

———. 2004. "Pernicious Ambiguity in Contracts and Statutes." *Chicago-Kent Law Review* 79:859–88.

———. 2005a. "Private Language, Public Laws: The Central Role of Legislative Intent in Statutory Interpretation." *Georgetown Law Journal* 93:427–86.

———. 2005b. "The New Textualists' New Text." *Loyola of Los Angeles Law Review* 38:2027–62.

———. 2007. "Contract as Agreement." *Notre Dame Law Review* 83:353–408.

———. 2010. *The Language of Statutes: Laws and Their Interpretation.* Chicago: University of Chicago Press.

———. 2011. "Statutory Interpretation, Morality, and the Text." *Brooklyn Law Review* 76: 1033–48.

———. 2013. "Judging Language Plain." In *Ens Queda la Paraula: Estudis de Lingüística Aplicada en Honor a M. Teresa Turel*, edited by R. Casenoves, M. Forcadell, and N. Gavaldà. http://papers.ssrn.com/sol3/papers.cfm?abstract_id=2342350.

Solan, L., T. Rosenblatt, and D. Osherson. 2008. "False Consensus Bias in Contract Interpretation." *Columbia Law Review* 108 (5): 1268–300.

Solum, L. 2013. Legal Theory Lexicon 071: The New Originalism." *Legal Theory Lexicon.* http://lsolum.typepad.com/legal_theory_lexicon/.

Sorensen, R. 1989. "The Ambiguity of Vagueness and Precision." *Pacific Philosophical Quarterly* 70 (2): 174–83.

Sosa, D. 1998. "The Unintentional Fallacy." *California Law Review* 86:919–38.

Spaak, T. 2008. "Relativism in Legal Thinking: Stanley Fish and the Concept of an Interpretive Community." *Ratio Juris* 21 (1): 157–71.

Standen, J. 1998. "An Economic Perspective on Federal Criminal Law Reform." *Buffalo Criminal Law Review* 2:249–95.

Stanley, J. 2000. "Context and Logical Form." *Linguistics and Philosophy* 23 (4): 391–434.

———. 2007. *Language in Context: Selected Essays.* Oxford: Oxford University Press.

Stanley, J. and Z. Szabo. 2000. "On Quantifier Domain Restriction." *Mind and Language* 15 (2–3): 219–61.

Stecker, R. 2003. *Interpretation and Construction: Art, Speech, and the Law.* Oxford: Blackwell Publishing.

———. 2006. "Moderate Actual Intentionalism Defended." *Journal of Aesthetics and Art Criticism* 64 (4): 429–38.

Stecker, R., and S. Davies. 2010. "The Hypothetical Intentionalist's Dilemma: A Reply to Levinson." *British Journal of Aesthetics* 50 (3): 307–12.

Stevens, G. 2009. "Utterance at a Distance." *Philos Stud* 143 (2):213–21.

Stojanovic, I. 2008. "The Scope and Subtleties of the Contextualism-Literalism-Relativism Debate." *Language and Linguistics Compass* 2 (6): 1171–88.

———. 2012. "Domain-Sensitivity." *Synthese* 184 (2): 137–55.

Stokke, A. 2010. "Intention-Sensitive Semantics." *Synthese* 175 (3): 383–404.

Storms, G., P. De Boeck, and W. Ruts. 2001. "Categorization of Novel Stimuli in Well-Known Natural Concepts: A Case Study." *Psychonomic Bulletin and Review* 8 (2): 377–84.

Strauss, D. 1997. "Why Plain Meaning?" *Notre Dame Law Review* 72:1565–82.

Tabossie, P., and F. Zardon. 1993. "Processing Ambiguous Words in Context." *Journal of Memory and Language* 32 (3): 359–79.

Talmage, C. 1994. "Conventional Meaning and First Meaning." *Erkenntnis* 40 (2): 213–25.

———. 1996. "Davidson and Humpty Dumpty." *Nous* 30 (4): 537–44.

Taylor, J. 2003. *Linguistic Categorization.* Oxford: Oxford University Press.

Thumma, S., and J. Kirchmeier. 1999. "The Lexicon Has Become a Fortress: The United States Supreme Court's Use of Dictionaries." *Buffalo Law Review* 47:227–60.

Tiersma, P. 1993. "The Judge as Linguist." *Loyola of Los Angeles Law Review* 27:269–83.

———. 1995. "The Ambiguity of Interpretation: Distinguishing Interpretation From Construction." *Washington University Law Review* 73:1095–101.

———. 1999. *Legal Language.* Chicago: University of Chicago Press.

———. 2001. "A Message in a Bottle: Text, Autonomy, and Statutory Interpretation." *Tulane Law Review* 76:431–82.

———. 2005a. "Some Myths About Legal Language." *Law, Culture and Humanities* 2 (1): 29–50.

———. 2005b. "Writing, Text, and the Law." In *Handbook of Research on Writing: History, Society, School, Individual, Text*, edited by C. Bazerman, 156–71. New York: Taylor and Francis Group.

———. 2005c. "Categorical Lists in the Law." In *Legal Discourse across Cultures and Systems*, edited by V. Bhatia, C. Candlin, and J. Engberg, 109–30. Hong Kong: Hong Kong University Press.

———. 2012. "A History of the Languages of Law." In *The Oxford Handbook of Language and Law*, edited by L. Solan and P. Tiersma, 13–26. Oxford: Oxford University Press.

Tolhurst, W. 1979. "On What a Text Is and How It Means." *British Journal of Aesthetics* 19 (1): 3–14.

Traxler, M., B. McElree, R. Williams, and M. Pickering. 2005. "Context Effects in Coercion: Evidence from Eye Movements." *Journal of Memory and Language* 53 (1): 1–25.

Trivedi, S. 2001. "An Epistemic Dilemma for Actual Intentionalism." *British Journal of Aesthetics* 41 (2): 192–206.

United States Department of Agriculture. 2005. "Food Standards and Labeling Policy Book." Washington, DC: US Government Printing Office. Accessed

March 17, 2015. http://www.fsis.usda.gov/OPPDE/larc/Policies/Labeling_Policy
_Book_082005.pdf.

Van Berkum, J. 2008. "Understanding Sentences in Context: What Brain Waves
Can Tell Us." *Current Directions in Psychological Science* 17 (6): 376–80.

Van Berkum, J., D. van den Brink, C. Tesink, M. Kos, and P. Hagoort. 2008. "The
Neural Integration of Speaker and Message." *Journal of Cognitive Neuro-
science* 20 (4): 580–91.

Van Schooten, H. 2007. "Law as Fact, Law as Fiction: A Tripartite Model of Legal
Communication." In *Interpretation, Law and the Construction of Meaning*, edited by A. Wagner, W. Werner, and D. Cao, 3–20. AA Dordrecht: Springer.

Vermeule, A. 1998. "Legislative History and the Limits of Judicial Competence:
The Untold Story of Holy Trinity Church." *Stanford Law Review* 50:1833–96.

———. 2006. *Judging Under Uncertainty: An Institutional Theory of Legal Interpretation.* Cambridge: Harvard University Press.

Vogel, C. 2009. "Law Matters, Syntax Matters and Semantics Matters." In *Formal
Linguistics and Law*, edited by G. Grewendorf and M. Rathert, 25–54. Berlin:
Mouton de Gruyter.

von Savigny, E. 1985. "An Emergence View of Linguistic Meaning." *American
Philosophical Quarterly* 22 (3): 211–20.

Voorspoels, W., W. Vanpaemel, and G. Storms. 2008. "Exemplars and Prototypes
in Natural Language Concepts: A Typicality-Based Evaluation." *Psychonomic
Bulletin and Review* 15 (3): 630–37.

———. 2011. "A Formal Ideal-Based Account of Typicality." *Psychonomic Bulletin
and Review* 18 (5): 1006–14.

Waismann, F. 1951. "Analytic-Synthetic IV." *Analysis* 11 (6): 115–24.

Wasow, T., A. Perfors, and D. Beaver. 2005. "The Puzzle of Ambiguity." In *Morphology and the Web of Grammar: Essays in Memory of Steven G. Lapointe*, edited by O. Orgun, and P. Sells, 1–17. Stanford: CSLI Publications.

Wattenmaker, W. D. 1995. "Knowledge Structures and Linear Separability: Inte-
grating Information in Object and Social Categorization." *Cognitive Psychology* 28 (3): 274–328.

Weberman, D. A. 1999. "Reconciling Gadamer's Non-Intentionalism With Standard Conversational Goals." *Philosophical Forum* XXX (4): 317–28.

Weiskopf, D. A. 2009. "The Plurality of Concepts." *Synthese* 169 (1): 145–73.

———. 2011. "The Theory-Theory of Concepts." In *An Internet Encyclopedia of
Philosophy.* http://www.iep.utm.edu/th-th-co/.

Wierzbicka, A. 1988. "Oats and Wheat: Mass Nouns, Iconicity, and Human Categorization." In *The Semantics of Grammar*, edited by A. Wierzbicka, 499–560.
Amsterdam: John Benjamins Publishing.

Wilensky, R. 1989. "Primal Content and Actual Content: An Antidote to Literal
Meaning." *Journal of Pragmatics* 13 (2): 163–86.

Wilks, Y. 2001. "The 'Fodor'-FODOR Fallacy Bites Back." In *The Language of*

Word Meaning, edited by P. Bouillon and F. Busa, 75–85. Cambridge: Cambridge University Press.

Willems, K. 2006. "Logical Polysemy and Variable Verb Valency." *Language Sciences* 28 (6): 580–603.

Williamson, T. 1996. *Vagueness*. London: Routledge.

Wilson, G. 1992. "Again, Theory: On Speaker's Meaning, Linguistic Meaning, and the Meaning of a Text." *Critical Inquiry* 19 (1): 164–85.

Wimsatt, W. K., and Beardsley, M. C. 1946. "The Intentional Fallacy." *Sewanee Review* 54 (3): 468–88.

Winkler, K. 2009. "Signification, Intention, Projection." *Philosophia* 37 (3): 477–501.

Winter, S. L. 2013. "Frame Semantics and the 'Internal Point of View.'" In *Current Legal Issues: Law and Language*, edited by M. Freeman and F. Smith, 115–27. Oxford: Oxford University Press.

Wittgenstein, L. 1953. *Philosophical Investigations*. New York: Macmillan.

Wroblewski, J. 1985. "Legal Language and Legal Interpretation." *Law and Philosophy* 4 (2): 239–55.

Zegarac, V. 2006. "Believing In: A Pragmatic Account." *Lingua* 116 (10): 1703–21.

Zwicky, A., and J. Sadock. 1975. "Ambiguity Tests and How to Fail Them." *Syntax and Semantics* 4 (1): 1–36.

Index